Kaplan Publishing are constantly finding new ways to make a difference to your studies and our exciting online resources really do offer something different to students looking for exam success.

This book comes with free MyKaplan online resources so that you can study anytime, anywhere. This free online resource is not sold separately and is included in the price of the book.

Having purchased this book, you have access to the following online study materials:

CONTENT	ACCA (including FFA,FAB,FMA)		FIA (excluding FFA,FAB,FMA)	
	Text	Kit	Text	Kit
Eletronic version of the book	✓	✓	✓	✓
Check Your Understanding Test with instant answers	✓			
Material updates	✓	✓	✓	✓
Latest official ACCA exam questions*		✓		
Extra question assistance using the signpost icon**		✓		
Question debriefs using clock icon***		✓		
Consolidation Test including questions and answers	✓			

* Excludes AB, MA, FA, LW, FAB, FMA and FFA; for all other subjects includes a selection of questions, as released by ACCA

** For ACCA SBR, AFM, APM, AAA only

*** Excludes AB, MA, FA, LW, FAB, FMA and FFA

How to access your online resources

Kaplan Financial students will already have a MyKaplan account and these extra resources will be available to you online. You do not need to register again, as this process was completed when you enrolled. If you are having problems accessing online materials, please ask your course administrator.

If you are not studying with Kaplan and did not purchase your book via a Kaplan website, to unlock your extra online resources please go to www.mykaplan.co.uk/addabook (even if you have set up an account and registered books previously). You will then need to enter the ISBN number (on the title page and back cover) and the unique pass key number contained in the scratch panel below to gain access.

You will also be required to enter additional information during this process to set up or confirm your account details.

If you purchased through Kaplan Flexible Learning or via the Kaplan Publishing website you will automatically receive an e-mail invitation to MyKaplan. Please register your details using this email to gain access to your content. If you do not receive the e-mail or book content, please contact Kaplan Publishing.

Your Code and Information

This code can only be used once for the registration of one book online. This registration and your online content will expire when the final sittings for the examinations covered by this book have taken place. Please allow one hour from the time you submit your book details for us to process your request.

Please scratch the film to access your MyKaplan c

D1344807

Please be aware that this code is case-sensitive and you will need to include the dashes within the passcode, but not when entering the ISBN. For further technical support, please visit www.MyKaplan.co.uk

KAPLAN PUBLISHING

ACCA

Strategic
Professional – Option

Advanced Performance Management (APM)

Study Text

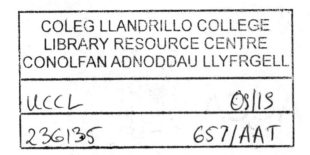
British library cataloguing-in-publication data

A catalogue record for this book is available from the British Library.

Published by:

Kaplan Publishing UK
Unit 2 The Business Centre
Molly Millars Lane
Wokingham
Berkshire
RG41 2QZ

ISBN 978-1-78740-092-4

© Kaplan Financial Limited, 2018

Acknowledgements

These materials are reviewed by the ACCA examining team. The objective of the review is to ensure that the material properly covers the syllabus and study guide outcomes, used by the examining team in setting the exams, in the appropriate breadth and depth. The review does not ensure that every eventuality, combination or application of examinable topics is addressed by the ACCA Approved Content. Nor does the review comprise a detailed technical check of the content as the Approved Content Provider has its own quality assurance processes in place in this respect.

We are grateful to the Association of Chartered Certified Accountants and the Chartered Institute of Management Accountants for permission to reproduce past examination questions. The answers have been prepared by Kaplan Publishing.

Contents

Introduction

How to Use the Materials

These Kaplan Publishing learning materials have been carefully designed to make your learning experience as easy as possible and to give you the best chances of success in your examinations.

The product range contains a number of features to help you in the study process. They include:

1   Detailed study guide and syllabus objectives

2   Description of the examination

3   Study skills and revision guidance

4   Study text

5   Question practice

The sections on the study guide, the syllabus objectives, the examination and study skills should all be read before you commence your studies. They are designed to familiarise you with the nature and content of the examination and give you tips on how to best to approach your learning.

The **Study Text** comprises the main learning materials and gives guidance as to the importance of topics and where other related resources can be found. Each chapter includes:

- The **learning objectives** contained in each chapter, which have been carefully mapped to the examining body's own syllabus learning objectives or outcomes. You should use these to check you have a clear understanding of all the topics on which you might be assessed in the examination.

- The **chapter diagram** provides a visual reference for the content in the chapter, giving an overview of the topics and how they link together.

- The **content** for each topic area commences with a brief explanation or definition to put the topic into context before covering the topic in detail. You should follow your studying of the content with a review of the illustration/s. These are worked examples which will help you to understand better how to apply the content for the topic.

- **Test your understanding** sections provide an opportunity to assess your understanding of the key topics by applying what you have learned to short questions. Answers can be found at the back of each chapter.

- **Summary diagrams** complete each chapter to show the important links between topics and the overall content of the syllabus. These diagrams should be used to check that you have covered and understood the core topics before moving on.

KAPLAN PUBLISHING

Quality and accuracy are of the utmost importance to us so if you spot an error in any of our products, please send an email to mykaplanreporting@kaplan.com with full details, or follow the link to the feedback form in MyKaplan.

Our Quality Co-ordinator will work with our technical team to verify the error and take action to ensure it is corrected in future editions.

Icon Explanations

 Definition – Key definitions that you will need to learn from the core content.

 Supplementary reading – These sections will help to provide a deeper understanding of core areas. The supplementary reading is **NOT** optional reading. It is vital to provide you with the breadth of knowledge you will need to address the wide range of topics within your syllabus that could feature in an exam question. **Reference to this text is vital when self studying**

 Test your understanding – Exercises for you to complete to ensure that you have understood the topics just learned.

Some of the test your understandings in this material are shorter or more straightforward than questions in the Advanced Performance Management (APM) exam. They are contained in the material for learning purposes and will help you to build your knowledge and confidence so that you are ready to tackle past exam questions during the revision phase.

 Illustration – Worked examples help you understand the core content better.

On-line subscribers

Our on-line resources are designed to increase the flexibility of your learning materials and provide you with immediate feedback on how your studies are progressing.

If you are subscribed to our on-line resources you will find:

1   On-line reference ware: reproduces your Study Text on-line, giving you anytime, anywhere access.

2   On-line testing: provides you with additional on-line objective testing so you can practice what you have learned further.

3   On-line performance management: immediate access to your on-line testing results. Review your performance by key topics and chart your achievement through the course relative to your peer group.

Syllabus introduction

Syllabus background

The aim of ACCA **Advanced Performance Management (APM)** is to apply relevant knowledge and skills and to exercise professional judgement in selecting and applying strategic management accounting techniques in different business contexts, and to contribute to the evaluation of the performance of an organisation and its strategic development.

Objectives of the syllabus

- Use strategic planning and control models to plan and monitor organisational performance.

- Assess and identify key external influences on organisational performance.

- Identify and evaluate the design features of effective performance management information and monitoring systems.

- Apply appropriate strategic performance measurement techniques in evaluating and improving organisational performance.

- Advise clients and senior management on strategic business performance evaluation and on recognising vulnerability to corporate failure.

Core areas of the syllabus

- Strategic planning and control (A).

- Impact of risk and uncertainty on organisational performance (B).

- Performance measurement systems and design (C).

- Strategic performance measurement (D).

- Performance evaluation and corporate failure (E).

Syllabus objectives

We have reproduced the ACCA's syllabus below, showing where the objectives are explored within this book. Within the chapters, we have broken down the extensive information found in the syllabus into easily digestible and relevant sections, called Content Objectives. These correspond to the objectives at the beginning of each chapter.

Syllabus learning objective	Chapter reference
A STRATEGIC PLANNING AND CONTROL	
1 Strategic management accounting	
(a) Explain the role of strategic performance management in strategic planning and control.[2]	1
(b) Discuss the role of performance measurement in checking progress towards the corporate objectives. [2]	1
(c) Compare planning and control between the strategic and operational levels within a business entity. [2]	1
(d) Discuss the scope for potential conflict between strategic business plans and short-term localised decisions. [2]	1
(e) Evaluate how models such as SWOT analysis, Boston Consulting Group, balanced scorecard, Porter's generic strategies and 5 Forces may assist in the performance management process.[3]	1, 2 & 11
(f) Apply and evaluate the methods of benchmarking performance.[3]	1
(g) Assess the changing role of the management accountant in today's business environment as outlined by Burns and Scapens.[3]	1
2 Impact of external factors on performance management	
(a) Discuss the need to consider the environment in which an organisation is operating when assessing its performance using models such as PEST and Porter's 5 forces, including such areas as: [2]	2
(i) Political climate	
(ii) Market conditions	
3 Performance hierarchy	
(a) Discuss how the purpose, structure and content of a mission statement impacts on performance measurement and management.[2]	1

(b) Discuss how strategic objectives are cascaded down the organisation via the formulation of subsidiary performance objectives.[2] 1

(c) Apply critical success factor analysis in developing performance metrics from business objectives.[3] 1

(d) Identify and discuss the characteristics of operational performance.[2] 1

(e) Discuss the relative significance of planning as against controlling activities at different levels in the performance hierarchy.[3] 1

4 Performance management and control of the organisation

(a) Evaluate the strengths and weaknesses of alternative budgeting models and compare such techniques as fixed and flexible, rolling, activity based, zero based and incremental.[3] 3

(b) Evaluate different types of budget variances and how these relate to issues in planning and controlling organisations.[3] 3

5 Changes in business structure and management accounting

(a) Identify and discuss the particular information needs of organisations adopting a functional, divisional or network form and the implications for performance management.[2] 4

(b) Assess the changes to management accounting systems to reflect the needs of modern service orientated businesses compared with the needs of a traditional manufacturing industry.[3] 4

(c) Assess the influence of Business Process Re-engineering on systems development and improvements in organisational performance.[3] 4

(d) Analyse the role that performance management systems play in business integration using models such as the value chain and McKinsey's 7Ss.[3] 4

(e) Discuss how changing an organisation's structure, culture and strategy will influence the adoption of new performance measurement methods and techniques.[3] 4

(f) Assess the need for businesses to continually refine and develop their management accounting and information systems if they are to maintain or improve their performance in an increasingly competitive and global market. [3] 5

6   Other environmental and ethical issues

(a)   Discuss the ways in which stakeholder groups operate and how they influence an organisation, and its performance measurement and performance management systems (e.g. using Mendelow's matrix).[2]   2

(b)   Discuss the social and ethical issues that may impact on strategy formulation and, consequently, business performance.[3]   2

(c)   Discuss, evaluate and apply environmental management accounting using for example lifecycle costing and activity-based costing.[3]   14

B   IMPACT OF RISK AND UNCERTAINTY ON PERFORMANCE MANAGEMENT

1   Impact of risk and uncertainty on performance management

(a)   Assess the impact of different risk appetites of stakeholders on performance management.[3]   2

(b)   Evaluate how risk and uncertainty play an important role in long term strategic planning and decision-making that relies upon forecast and exogenous variables.[3]   2

(c)   Apply different risk analysis techniques in assessing business performance such as maximin, maximax, minimax regret and expected values.[3]   2

C   PERFORMANCE MEASUREMENT SYSTEMS AND DESIGN

1   Performance management information systems

(a)   Discuss, with reference to performance management, ways in which the information requirements of a management structure are affected by the features of the structure.[2]   4

(b)   Evaluate the compatibility of management accounting objectives and management accounting information systems.[3]   5

(c)   Discuss the integration of management accounting information within an overall information system, for example the use of enterprise resource planning systems.[2]   5

(d)   Evaluate whether the management information systems are lean and the value of the information that they provide (e.g. using the 5 S's).[3]   13

(e)   Evaluate the external and internal factors (e.g. anticipated human behaviour) which will influence the design and use of a management accounting system.[3]   4 & 5

2   Sources of management information

(a) Discuss the principal internal and external sources of management accounting information, their costs and limitations.[2]   5

(b) Demonstrate how the information might be used in planning and controlling activities, e.g. benchmarking against similar activities.[2]   5

(c) Discuss the development of Big Data and its impact on performance measurement and management, including the risks and challenges it presents.[3]   5

3   Recording and processing methods

(a) Demonstrate how the type of business entity will influence the recording and processing methods.[2]   4

(b) Discuss how IT developments, e.g. unified corporate databases, RFIDs and network technology, may influence management accounting systems.[2]   5

(c) Explain how information systems provide instant access to previously unavailable data that can be used for benchmarking and control purposes and help improve business performance (for example, through the use of enterprise resource planning systems and data warehouses).[2]   5

(d) Discuss the difficulties associated with recording and processing data of a qualitative nature.[2]   6

4   Management reports

(a) Evaluate the output reports of an information system in the light of [3]   6

    (i)   best practice in presentation

    (ii)   the objectives of the report/organisation

    (iii) the needs of the readers of the report; and

    (iv)   avoiding the problem of information overload.

(b) Advise on common mistakes and misconceptions in the use of numerical data used for performance measurement. [3]   6

(c) Explore the role of the management accountant in providing key performance information for integrated reporting to stakeholders. [2]   1

D STRATEGIC PERFORMANCE MEASUREMENT

1 Strategic performance measures in private sector

(a)	Demonstrate why the primary objective of financial performance should be primarily concerned with the benefits to shareholders.[2]	8
(b)	Discuss the appropriateness of, and apply different measures of performance, including: [3]	8 & 9

    (i)   Gross profit and operating profit

    (ii)   Return on Capital Employed (ROCE)

    (iii) Return on Investment (ROI)

    (iv) Earnings Per Share (EPS)

    (v)   Earnings Before Interest, Tax and Depreciation Adjustment (EBITDA)

    (vi   Residual Income (RI)

    (vii) Net Present Value (NPV)

    (viii) Internal Rate of Return and modified internal rate of return (IRR, MIRR)

    (ix) Economic Value Added (EVA^{TM}).

(c)	Discuss why indicators of liquidity and gearing need to considered in conjunction with profitability.[3]	8
(d)	Compare and contrast short and long run financial performance and the resulting management issues.[3]	8
(e)	Assess the appropriate benchmarks to use in assessing performance.[3]	1 & 8

2 Divisional performance and transfer pricing issues

(a)	Describe, compute and evaluate performance measures relevant in a divisionalised organisation structure including ROI, RI and Economic Value Added (EVA).[3]	9
(b)	Discuss the need for separate measures in respect of managerial and divisional performance.[2]	9
(c)	Discuss the circumstances in which a transfer pricing policy may be needed and discuss the necessary criteria for its design.[2]	9
(d)	Demonstrate and evaluate the use of alternative bases for transfer pricing.[3]	9
(e)	Explain and demonstrate issues that require consideration when setting transfer prices in multinational companies.[2]	9

3   Strategic performance measures in not-for-profit organisations

(a)	Highlight and discuss the potential for diversity in objectives depending on organisation type.[3]	10
(b)	Discuss the difficulties in measuring outputs when performance is not judged in terms of money or an easily quantifiable objective.[2]	10
(c)	Discuss the use of benchmarking in public sector performance (league tables) and its effects on operational and strategic management and client behaviour.[3]	10
(d)	Discuss how the combination of politics and the desire to measure public sector performance may result in undesirable service outcomes e.g. the use of targets.[3]	10
(e)	Assess 'value for money' service provision as a measure of performance in not-for-profit organisations and the public sector.[3]	10

4   Non-financial performance indicators

(a)	Discuss the interaction of non-financial performance indicators with financial performance indicators.[2]	11
(b)	Identify and discuss the significance of non-financial performance indicators in relation to product/service quality e.g. customer satisfaction reports, repeat business ratings, customer loyalty, access and availability.[3]	11
(c)	Discuss the issues in interpreting data on qualitative issues.[2]	11
(d)	Discuss the significance of brand awareness and company profile and their potential impact on business performance.[3]	11

5   The role of quality in management information and performance measurement systems

(a)	Discuss and evaluate the application of Japanese management practices and management accounting techniques, including:	13

(i)   Kaizen costing,

(ii)   Target costing,

(iii)   Just-in-time, and

(iv)   Total Quality Management. [3]

	(c)	Apply and evaluate the work of Fitzgerald and Moon that considers performance measurement in business services using building blocks for dimensions, standards and rewards.[3]	11
	(d)	Discuss and evaluate the application of activity-based management.[3]	3
	(e)	Evaluate and apply the value-based management approaches to performance management.[3]	9

2   Strategic performance issues in complex business structures

| | (a) | Discuss the problems encountered in planning, controlling and measuring performance levels, e.g. productivity, profitability, quality and service levels, in complex business structures.[3] | 4 & 9 |
| | (b) | Discuss the impact on performance management of the use of business models involving strategic alliances, joint ventures and complex supply chain structures.[3] | 4 |

3   Predicting and preventing corporate failure

	(a)	Discuss how long-term survival necessitates consideration of life-cycle issues.[3]	12
	(b)	Assess the potential likelihood for/of corporate failure utilising quantitative and qualitative performance measures and models (such as Z-scores and Argenti).[3]	12
	(c)	Assess and critique quantitative and qualitative corporate failure prediction models.[3]	12
	(d)	Identify and discuss performance improvement strategies that may be adopted in order to prevent corporate failure.[3]	12
	(e)	Identify and discuss operational changes to performance management systems required to implement the performance improvement strategies.[3]	12

The superscript numbers in square brackets indicate the intellectual depth at which the subject area could be assessed within the examination. Level 1 (knowledge and comprehension) broadly equates with the Knowledge module, Level 2 (application and analysis) with the Skills module and Level 3 (synthesis and evaluation) to the Strategic Professional level. However, lower level skills can continue to be assessed as you progress through each module and level.

The Examination

Examination format

- The examination is three hours 15 minutes duration.

- The examination is in two sections:

	Number of marks
Section A One compulsory question	50
Section B Two compulsory questions each worth 25 marks	50
Total	**100**

- Syllabus sections A, C and D are examinable in Section A.

- Section B will contain one question mainly from syllabus section E. The other question will be from any other syllabus sections.

- There will be four professional marks available in Section A.

- The pass mark is 50%.

- Candidates will receive a present value table and an annuity table.

Examination tips

Spend approximately the first 15 minutes reading the questions and start planning your answers. You are allowed to annotate the question paper, so make use of this – e.g. highlighting key issues in the questions, planning calculations, brainstorming requirements – ensure that you understand the question

For the remaining three hours, **divide the time** you spend on questions in proportion to the marks on offer. One suggestion **for this examination** is to allocate 1 and 4/5ths minutes to each mark available, so a 10-mark requirement should be completed in approximately 18 minutes. A danger in Advanced Performance Management (APM) is that you spend too long on the calculation aspects and neglect the written elements, so allocate your time within questions as well as between them.

Stick to the question and **tailor your answer** to what you are asked. Pay particular attention to the verbs in the question.

Spend the last five minutes reading through your answers and making any additions or corrections.

If you **get completely stuck** with a question, leave space in your answer book and **return to it later**.

If you do not understand what a question is asking, state your assumptions. Even if you do not answer in precisely the way the examiner hoped, you should be given some credit, if your assumptions are reasonable.

You should do everything you can to make things easy for the marker. The marker will find it easier to identify the points you have made if your answers are legible.

Computations: It is essential to include all your workings in your answers. Many computational questions require the use of a standard format. Be sure you know these formats thoroughly before the exam and use the layouts that you see in the answers given in this book and in model answers.

Scenario-based questions: Most questions will contain a hypothetical scenario. To write a good case answer, first identify the area in which there is a problem, outline the main principles/theories you are going to use to answer the question, and then apply the principles/theories to the case. It is vital that you relate your answer to the specific circumstances given.

Reports, memos and other documents: some questions ask you to present your answer in the form of a report or a memo or other document. So use the correct format – there could be easy marks to gain here.

Study skills and revision guidance

This section aims to give guidance on how to study for your ACCA exams and to give ideas on how to improve your existing study techniques.

Preparing to study

Set your objectives

Before starting to study decide what you want to achieve – the type of pass you wish to obtain. This will decide the level of commitment and time you need to dedicate to your studies.

Devise a study plan

Determine which times of the week you will study.

Split these times into sessions of at least one hour for study of new material. Any shorter periods could be used for revision or practice.

Put the times you plan to study onto a study plan for the weeks from now until the exam and set yourself targets for each period of study – in your sessions make sure you cover the course, course assignments and revision.

If you are studying for more than one paper at a time, try to vary your subjects as this can help you to keep interested and see subjects as part of wider knowledge.

When working through your course, compare your progress with your plan and, if necessary, re-plan your work (perhaps including extra sessions) or, if you are ahead, do some extra revision/practice questions.

KAPLAN PUBLISHING

Effective studying

Active reading

You are not expected to learn the text by rote, rather, you must understand what you are reading and be able to use it to pass the exam and develop good practice. A good technique to use is SQ3Rs – Survey, Question, Read, Recall, Review:

1   **Survey the chapter** – look at the headings and read the introduction, summary and objectives, so as to get an overview of what the chapter deals with.

2   **Question** – whilst undertaking the survey, ask yourself the questions that you hope the chapter will answer for you.

3   **Read** through the chapter thoroughly, answering the questions and making sure you can meet the objectives. Attempt the exercises and activities in the text, and work through all the examples.

4   **Recall** – at the end of each section and at the end of the chapter, try to recall the main ideas of the section/chapter without referring to the text. This is best done after a short break of a couple of minutes after the reading stage.

5   **Review** – check that your recall notes are correct.

You may also find it helpful to re-read the chapter to try to see the topic(s) it deals with as a whole.

Note-taking

Taking notes is a useful way of learning, but do not simply copy out the text. The notes must:

- be in your own words
- be concise
- cover the key points
- be well-organised
- be modified as you study further chapters in this text or in related ones.

Trying to summarise a chapter without referring to the text can be a useful way of determining which areas you know and which you don't.

Three ways of taking notes:

Summarise the key points of a chapter.

Make linear notes – a list of headings, divided up with subheadings listing the key points. If you use linear notes, you can use different colours to highlight key points and keep topic areas together. Use plenty of space to make your notes easy to use.

Try a diagrammatic form – the most common of which is a mind-map. To make a mind-map, put the main heading in the centre of the paper and put a circle around it. Then draw short lines radiating from this to the main sub-headings, which again have circles around them. Then continue the process from the sub-headings to sub-sub-headings, advantages, disadvantages, etc.

Highlighting and underlining

You may find it useful to underline or highlight key points in your study text – but do be selective. You may also wish to make notes in the margins.

Revision

The best approach to revision is to revise the course as you work through it. Also try to leave four to six weeks before the exam for final revision. Make sure you cover the whole syllabus and pay special attention to those areas where your knowledge is weak. Here are some recommendations:

Read through the text and your notes again and condense your notes into key phrases. It may help to put key revision points onto index cards to look at when you have a few minutes to spare.

Review any assignments you have completed and look at where you lost marks – put more work into those areas where you were weak.

Practise exam standard questions under timed conditions. If you are short of time, list the points that you would cover in your answer and then read the model answer, but do try to complete at least a few questions under exam conditions.

Also practise producing answer plans and comparing them to the model answer.

If you are stuck on a topic find somebody (e.g. your tutor or, where appropriate, a member of Kaplan's Academic Support team) to explain it to you.

Read good newspapers and professional journals, especially ACCA's Student Accountant – this can give you an advantage in the exam.

Ensure you **know the structure of the exam** – how many questions and of what type you will be expected to answer. During your revision attempt all the different styles of questions you may be asked.

KAPLAN PUBLISHING

Further reading

You can find further reading and technical articles under the student section of ACCA's website.

The following publication may also support your studies for this, and other, ACCA examinations:

A Student's Guide to Writing Business Reports by Zoe Robinson and Stuart Pedley-Smith.

Technical update

This text has been updated to reflect Examinable Documents September 2018 to June 2019 issued by ACCA.

Present value table

Present value of 1, i.e. $(1 + r)^{-n}$

Where r = discount rate

                 n = number of periods until payment

Periods (n)	Discount rate (r)									
	1%	2%	3%	4%	5%	6%	7%	8%	9%	10%
1	0.990	0.980	0.971	0.962	0.952	0.943	0.935	0.926	0.917	0.909
2	0.980	0.961	0.943	0.925	0.907	0.890	0.873	0.857	0.842	0.826
3	0.971	0.942	0.915	0.889	0.864	0.840	0.816	0.794	0.772	0.751
4	0.961	0.924	0.888	0.855	0.823	0.792	0.763	0.735	0.708	0.683
5	0.951	0.906	0.863	0.822	0.784	0.747	0.713	0.681	0.650	0.621
6	0.942	0.888	0.837	0.790	0.746	0.705	0.666	0.630	0.596	0.564
7	0.933	0.871	0.813	0.760	0.711	0.665	0.623	0.583	0.547	0.513
8	0.923	0.853	0.789	0.731	0.677	0.627	0.582	0.540	0.502	0.467
9	0.914	0.837	0.766	0.703	0.645	0.592	0.544	0.500	0.460	0.424
10	0.905	0.820	0.744	0.676	0.614	0.558	0.508	0.463	0.422	0.386
11	0.896	0.804	0.722	0.650	0.585	0.527	0.475	0.429	0.388	0.350
12	0.887	0.788	0.701	0.625	0.557	0.497	0.444	0.397	0.356	0.319
13	0.879	0.773	0.681	0.601	0.530	0.469	0.415	0.368	0.326	0.290
14	0.870	0.758	0.661	0.577	0.505	0.442	0.388	0.340	0.299	0.263
15	0.861	0.743	0.642	0.555	0.481	0.417	0.362	0.315	0.275	0.239

Periods (n)	Discount rate (r)									
	11%	12%	13%	14%	15%	16%	17%	18%	19%	20%
1	0.901	0.893	0.885	0.877	0.870	0.862	0.855	0.847	0.840	0.833
2	0.812	0.797	0.783	0.769	0.756	0.743	0.731	0.718	0.706	0.694
3	0.731	0.712	0.693	0.675	0.658	0.641	0.624	0.609	0.593	0.579
4	0.659	0.636	0.613	0.592	0.572	0.552	0.534	0.516	0.499	0.482
5	0.593	0.567	0.543	0.519	0.497	0.476	0.456	0.437	0.419	0.402
6	0.535	0.507	0.480	0.456	0.432	0.410	0.390	0.370	0.352	0.335
7	0.482	0.452	0.425	0.400	0.376	0.354	0.333	0.314	0.296	0.279
8	0.434	0.404	0.376	0.351	0.327	0.305	0.285	0.266	0.249	0.233
9	0.391	0.361	0.333	0.308	0.284	0.263	0.243	0.225	0.209	0.194
10	0.352	0.322	0.295	0.270	0.247	0.227	0.208	0.191	0.176	0.162
11	0.317	0.287	0.261	0.237	0.215	0.195	0.178	0.162	0.148	0.135
12	0.286	0.257	0.231	0.208	0.187	0.168	0.152	0.137	0.124	0.112
13	0.258	0.229	0.204	0.182	0.163	0.145	0.130	0.116	0.104	0.093
14	0.232	0.205	0.181	0.160	0.141	0.125	0.111	0.099	0.088	0.078
15	0.209	0.183	0.160	0.140	0.123	0.108	0.095	0.084	0.074	0.065

Annuity table

Present value of an annuity of 1, i.e. $\dfrac{1-(1+r)^{-n}}{r}$

Where   r = discount rate

n = number of periods

Periods (n)	Discount rate (r)									
	1%	2%	3%	4%	5%	6%	7%	8%	9%	10%
1	0.990	0.980	0.971	0.962	0.952	0.943	0.935	0.926	0.917	0.909
2	1.970	1.942	1.913	1.886	1.859	1.833	1.808	1.783	1.759	1.736
3	2.941	2.884	2.829	2.775	2.723	2.673	2.624	2.577	2.531	2.487
4	3.902	3.808	3.717	3.630	3.546	3.465	3.387	3.312	3.240	3.170
5	4.853	4.713	4.580	4.452	4.329	4.212	4.100	3.993	3.890	3.791
6	5.795	5.601	5.417	5.242	5.076	4.917	4.767	4.623	4.486	4.355
7	6.728	6.472	6.230	6.002	5.786	5.582	5.389	5.206	5.033	4.868
8	7.652	7.325	7.020	6.733	6.463	6.210	5.971	5.747	5.535	5.335
9	8.566	8.162	7.786	7.435	7.108	6.802	6.515	6.247	5.995	5.759
10	9.471	8.983	8.530	8.111	7.722	7.360	7.024	6.710	6.418	6.145
11	10.368	9.787	9.253	8.760	8.306	7.887	7.499	7.139	6.805	8.495
12	11.255	10.575	9.954	9.385	8.863	8.384	7.943	7.536	7.161	6.814
13	12.134	11.348	10.635	9.986	9.394	8.853	8.358	7.904	7.487	7.103
14	13.004	12.106	11.296	10.563	9.899	9.295	8.745	8.244	7.786	7.367
15	13.865	12.849	11.938	11.118	10.380	9.712	9.108	8.559	8.061	7.606

Periods (n)	Discount rate (r)									
	11%	12%	13%	14%	15%	16%	17%	18%	19%	20%
1	0.901	0.893	0.885	0.877	0.870	0.862	0.855	0.847	0.840	0.833
2	1.713	1.690	1.668	1.647	1.626	1.605	1.585	1.566	1.547	1.528
3	2.444	2.402	2.361	2.322	2.283	2.246	2.210	2.174	2.140	2.106
4	3.102	3.037	2.974	2.914	2.855	2.798	2.743	2.690	2.639	2.589
5	3.696	3.605	3.517	3.433	3.352	3.274	3.199	3.127	3.058	2.991
6	4.231	4.111	3.998	3.889	3.784	3.685	3.589	3.498	3.410	3.326
7	4.712	4.564	4.423	4.288	4.160	4.039	3.922	3.812	3.706	3.605
8	5.146	4.968	4.799	4.639	4.487	4.344	4.207	4.078	3.954	3.837
9	5.537	5.328	5.132	4.946	4.772	4.607	4.451	4.303	4.163	4.031
10	5.889	5.650	5.426	5.216	5.019	4.833	4.659	4.494	4.339	4.192
11	6.207	5.938	5.687	5.453	5.234	5.029	4.836	4.656	4.486	4.327
12	6.492	6.194	5.918	5.660	5.421	5.197	4.968	4.793	4.611	4.439
13	6.750	6.424	6.122	5.842	5.583	5.342	5.118	4.910	4.715	4.533
14	6.982	6.628	6.302	6.002	5.724	5.468	5.229	5.008	4.802	4.611
15	7.191	6.811	6.462	6.142	5.847	5.575	5.324	5.092	4.876	4.675

Introduction to strategic management accounting

Chapter learning objectives

Upon completion of this chapter you will be able to:

- explain the role of strategic performance management in strategic planning and control

- assess the changing role of the management accountant in today's business environment as outlined by Burns and Scapens

- explore the role of the management accountant in providing key performance information for integrated reporting to stakeholders

- discuss the role of performance measurement in checking progress towards the corporate objectives

- compare planning and control between the strategic and operational levels within a business entity

- discuss the scope for potential conflict between strategic business plans and short-term localised decisions

- apply and evaluate the methods of benchmarking performance

- assess the appropriate benchmarks to use in assessing performance

- discuss how the purpose, structure and content of a mission statement impacts on performance measurement and management

- discuss how strategic objectives are cascaded down the organisation via the formulation of subsidiary performance objectives

- apply critical success factor analysis in developing performance metrics from business objectives

- identify and discuss the characteristics of operational performance

- discuss the relative significance of planning against controlling activities at different levels of the performance hierarchy

- evaluate how models such as SWOT analysis, Boston Consulting Group, balanced scorecard, Porter's generic strategies and 5 Forces may assist with the performance management process

- assess the statement 'what gets measured gets done'.

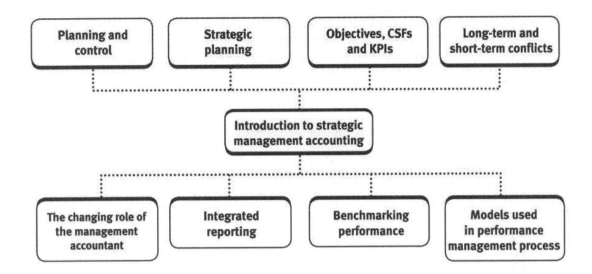

1 Introduction to Advanced Performance Management (APM)

APM will require you to assess different approaches to performance management from a variety of perspectives. This will require you to know what the approaches are and, more importantly, you should be able to compare one with another.

This exam will focus on performance management systems. These are the systems within the organisation by which the performance of the organisation is measured, controlled and improved.

2 Common knowledge

APM builds on knowledge gained in Performance Management (PM). It also includes knowledge contained in the Strategic Business Leader (SBL) exam but it is not a problem if you are yet to study for this exam.

PM tested your knowledge and application of core management accounting techniques. APM develops key aspects introduced at PM level with a greater focus on linking the syllabus topics together and evaluation of the key topics and techniques. Therefore, you should not expect to be retested in a PM style but need to be aware that all PM knowledge is assumed to be known.

In the same way, APM contains knowledge included in the SBL exam but it is important to draw a distinction between the two exams. You need to approach the common topics from an APM perspective, i.e. how do they influence performance management and measurement.

For example, in terms of strategy planning and choice, a SBL question might look at evaluating a strategic decision. However,

- The focus in APM would look at whether the company has a suitable mission and some key strategic objectives, then at what the critical success factors (CSFs) are for these objectives and then at what key performance indicators (KPIs) are being used.

- APM very much focuses on that hierarchy and questions revolve around whether the CSFs/KPIs are appropriate for the objectives and why. If they aren't, then why not and what could the organisation do better.

- APM thus looks more at what performance management systems are needed and what performance measures are most appropriate.

Chapter 1 includes the following topics from SBL:

- Strategy and strategic planning

- CSFs and KPIs

- Benchmarking

- SWOT

- BCG matrix

- Porter's generic strategies.

3 Introduction to Chapter 1

This chapter sets the scene to Part A of the syllabus, **'strategic planning and control'**. It introduces the process of strategic planning and control and evaluates how models such as SWOT, Boston Consulting Group and Porter's generic strategies may assist in the performance management process and reviews the methods for benchmarking performance.

It also explores the changing role of the management accountant and explores the role of the management accountant in integrated reporting (syllabus section C).

4 Introduction to planning and control

4.1 Definitions

Planning and control are fundamental aspects of performance management.

Strategic planning is concerned with:

- where an organisation wants to be (usually expressed in terms of its objectives) and

- how it will get there (strategies).

 Control is concerned with monitoring the achievement of objectives and suggesting corrective action.

4.2 Planning and control at different levels within an organisation

Planning and control takes place at different levels within an organisation. The performance hierarchy operates in the following order:

(1)   Mission

(2)   Strategic (corporate) plans and objectives

(3)   Tactical plans and objectives

(4)   Operational plans and targets.

4.3 Mission

A **mission statement** outlines the broad direction that an organisation will follow and summarises the reasons and values that underlie that organisation.

A mission should be:

- succinct

- memorable

- enduring, i.e. the statement should not change unless the entity's mission changes

- a guide for employees to work towards the accomplishment of the mission

- addressed to a number of stakeholder groups, for example shareholders, employees and customers.

Illustration 1 – Mission statement examples

American Express – famous for their great customer service. They believe that customers will never love a company until the employees love it first. Their mission reads:

'At American Express we have a mission to be the world's most

respected service brand. To do this, we have to establish a culture that supports our team members, so they can provide exceptional service to our company.'

IKEA – their mission could have been a promise for beautiful, affordable furniture. Instead IKEA dream big with their mission:

'To create a better everyday life for the many people. Our business ideas support this by offering a wide range of well-designed, functional home furnishing products at prices so low that as many people as possible will be able to afford them.'

Nike – view each customer as an athlete. Their mission is:

'To bring inspiration and innovation to every athlete in the world. If you have a body, you are an athlete.'

> **The Motor Neurone Disease Association (MNDA)** – mission is just as applicable for not-for-profit organisations. This charity's mission is:
>
> 'We improve care and support for people with MND, their families and carers. We fund and promote research that leads to new understanding and treatments, and brings us closer to a cure for MND. We campaign and raise awareness so the needs of people with MND and everyone who cares for them are recognised and addressed by wider society.'

The mission forms a key part of the planning process and should enhance organisational performance:

- It acts as a source of inspiration and ideas for the organisation's detailed plans and objectives.

- It can be used to assess the suitability of any proposed plans in terms of their fit with the organisation's mission.

- It can impact the day to day workings of an organisation, guiding the organisational culture and business practices used.

Drucker

Drucker concluded that a mission statement should address four fundamental questions.

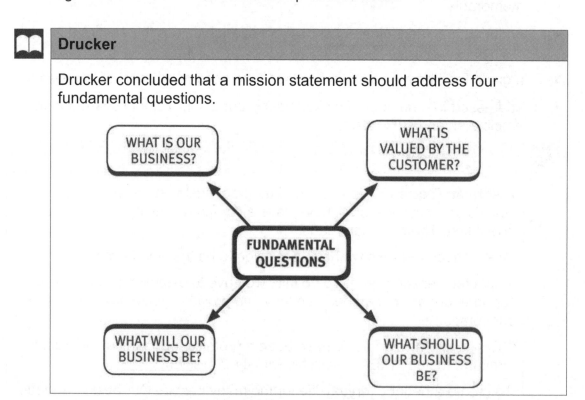

Test your understanding 1

Required:

What are the potential benefits to an organisation of setting a mission statement and what are the potential drawbacks or failings of a mission statement?

The lifespan of a mission

There are no set rules on how long a mission statement will be appropriate for an organisation. It should be reviewed periodically to ensure it still reflects the organisation's environment.

If the market or key stakeholders have changed since the mission statement was written, then it may no longer be appropriate.

A change in the mission statement may result in **new performance measures** being established to monitor the achievement (or otherwise) of the new mission.

4.4 Strategic, tactical and operational plans

To enable an organisation to fulfil its mission, the mission must be translated into strategic, tactical and operational plans.

Each level should be consistent with the one above.

This process will involve moving from general broad aims to more specific objectives and ultimately to detailed targets.

In this chapter we will focus on strategic and operational plans.

Comparing planning and control between strategic and operational levels

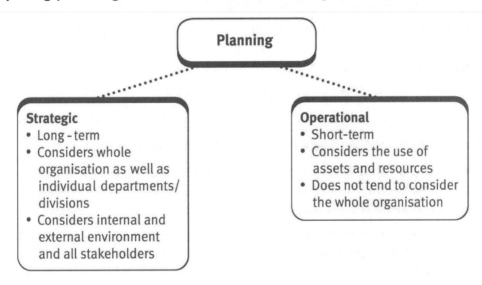

 Illustration 2 – Strategic planning

Strategic planning is usually, but not always, concerned with the long-term. It raises the question of **which business shall we be in**? For example, a company specialising in production and sale of tobacco products may forecast a declining market for these products and may therefore decide to change its objectives to allow a progressive move into the leisure industry, which it considers to be expanding.

Strategic and operational planning

Planning

Strategic planning is characterised by the following:

- long-term

- considers the whole organisation as well as individual SBUs

- matches the activities of an organisation to its external environment

- matches the activities of an organisation to its resource capability and specifies future resource requirements

- will be affected by the expectations and values of all stakeholders, not just shareholders

- its complexity distinguishes strategic management from other aspects of management in an organisation. There are several reasons for this including:

    - it involves a high degree of uncertainty

    - it is likely to require an integrated approach to management— it may involve major change in the organisation.

Quite apart from strategic planning, the management of an organisation has to undertake a regular series of decisions on matters that are purely **operational** and short-term in character. Such decisions:

- are usually based on a given set of assets and resources

- do not usually involve the scope of an organisation's activities

- rarely involve major change in the organisation

- are unlikely to involve major elements of uncertainty and the techniques used to help make such decisions often seek to minimise the impact of any uncertainty

- use standard management accounting techniques such as cost-volume-profit analysis, limiting factor analysis and linear programming.

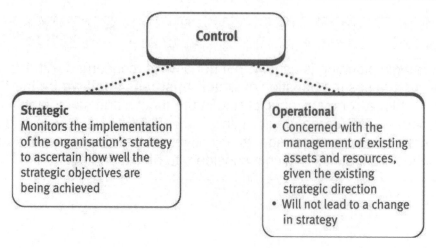

Control

Strategic
Monitors the implementation of the organisation's strategy to ascertain how well the strategic objectives are being achieved

Operational
- Concerned with the management of existing assets and resources, given the existing strategic direction
- Will not lead to a change in strategy

KAPLAN PUBLISHING

Test your understanding 2

Required:

Is the activity of setting a profit-maximising selling price for a product a strategic or operational decision?

Give reasons for your answer.

The role of performance management in planning and control

Performance management is any activity that is designed to improve the organisation's performance and ensure that its goals are met.

- Planning will take place first to establish an appropriate **mission** and **objectives**. These should be aligned with the organisation's critical success factors (see Section 6).

- SMART objectives (targets) (see Section 5.3) should be set and appropriate **performance indicators** (performance measures) for each target established.

- Performance management techniques will then be used to put the most appropriate **strategies** in place in order to achieve the organisation's mission and objectives.

- Finally, performance management techniques will aim to measure the achievement of the targets set and hence the mission and objectives and to recommend any improvement strategies required.

Performance management aims to direct and support the performance of all employees and departments so that the organisation's goals are achieved. Therefore, any performance management system should be linked to performance measures at different levels of the hierarchy. One model of performance management that helps to link the different levels of the hierarchy is the performance pyramid.

The **performance pyramid** derives from the idea that an organisation operates at different levels, each of which has a different focus. However, it is vital that these levels support each other. It translates objectives from the top down and measures from the bottom up, the aim being that these are co-ordinated and support each other (this will be explored in more detail in Chapter 11).

5 Strategic (corporate) planning

We are now going to explore in more detail the role of strategic planning in performance management.

5.1 What is strategy?

The core of a company's strategy is about choosing:

- **where** to compete and

- **how** to compete.

It is a means to achieve **sustainable competitive advantage**.

In terms of performance management, the test of a good strategy is whether it enables an organisation to use its resources and competencies advantageously in the context of an ever changing environment.

 Strategic (or corporate) planning involves formulating, evaluating and selecting strategies to enable the preparation of a long-term plan of action and to attain objectives.

5.2 Strategic analysis, choice and implementation (rational model)

This three stage model of strategic planning is a useful framework for seeing the 'bigger picture' of performance management (and should be very familiar to you).

Strategic analysis

- External analysis to identify opportunities and threats
- Internal analysis to identify strengths and weaknesses
- Stakeholder analysis to identify key objectives and to assess power and interest of different groups
- Gap analysis to identify the difference between desired and expected performance.

↓

Strategic choice

- Strategies are required to 'close the gap'
- Competitive strategy – for each business unit
- Directions for growth – which markets/products should be invested in
- Whether expansion should be achieved by organic growth, acquisition or some form of joint arrangement.

↓

Strategic implementation

- Formulation of detailed plans and budgets
- Target setting for KPIs
- Monitoring and control.

Each of these areas will be explored in greater detail throughout the course. However, it is worth noting that although strategy is still included in this exam, the main thrust in APM will be looking at where objectives come from, identifying critical success factors, choosing metrics and how to implement strategy. Theory will be secondary.

5.3 Clarifying corporate objectives

 Corporate objectives concern the business as a whole and focus on the desired performance and results that a business intends to achieve.

Put more simply, objectives are the targets that an organisation sets out to achieve.

The first stage of the strategic planning process, strategic analysis, will generate a range of objectives, typically relating to:

- maximisation of shareholder wealth
- maximisation of sales
- growth
- survival
- research and development
- leadership
- quality of service
- contented workforce
- respect for the environment.

These need to be clarified in two respects:

- **conflicts need to be resolved**, e.g. profit versus environmental concerns
- to facilitate implementation and control, objectives need to be translated into **SMART** (specific, measurable, achievable, relevant and time bound) targets.

 Illustration 3 – SMART objectives

A statement such as 'maximise profits' would be of little use in corporate planning terms. The following would be far more helpful:

- achieve a growth in earnings per share (EPS) of 5% pa over the coming ten-year period
- obtain a turnover of $10 million within six years
- launch at least two new products per year.

5.4 Role of performance measurement in making strategic choices

The viability of a strategic choice should be assessed using three criteria:

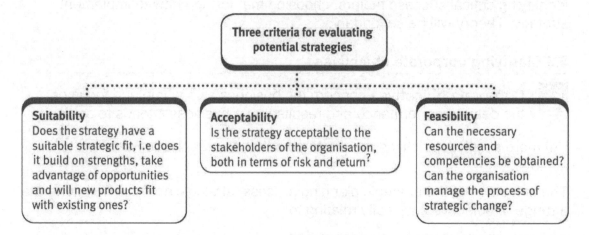

Three criteria for evaluating potential strategies

Suitability
Does the strategy have a suitable strategic fit, i.e does it build on strengths, take advantage of opportunities and will new products fit with existing ones?

Acceptability
Is the strategy acceptable to the stakeholders of the organisation, both in terms of risk and return?

Feasibility
Can the necessary resources and competencies be obtained? Can the organisation manage the process of strategic change?

5.5 The role of performance measurement in checking towards the objectives set

It is not enough merely to make plans and implement them.

- The results of the plans have to be measured and compared against stated objectives to assess the firm's performance.

- Action can then be taken to remedy any shortfalls in performance.

Performance measurement is an ongoing process, which must react quickly to the changing circumstances of the firm and of the environment.

Diagram of performance measurement activities

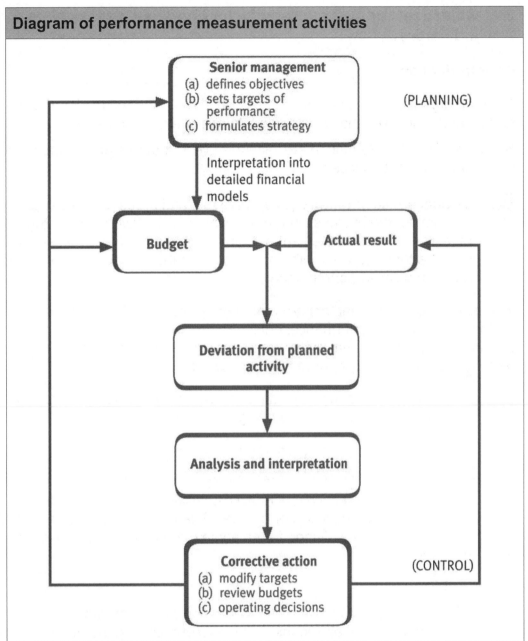

Senior management
(a) defines objectives
(b) sets targets of performance
(c) formulates strategy

(PLANNING)

Interpretation into detailed financial models

Budget

Actual result

Deviation from planned activity

Analysis and interpretation

Corrective action
(a) modify targets
(b) review budgets
(c) operating decisions

(CONTROL)

 Test your understanding 3

Required:

Why do you think managers need to understand performance measurement?

6 Objectives, critical success factors and key performance indicators

6.1 Introduction

Once an organisation has established its objectives, it needs to identify the key factors and processes that will enable it to achieve those objectives.

Some aspects of performance are 'nice to have' but others are critical to the organisation if it is to succeed.

 Critical success factors (CSFs) are the vital areas 'where things must go right' for the business in order for them to achieve their strategic objectives. The achievement of CSFs should allow the organisation to cope better than rivals with any changes in the competitive environment and to maximise performance.

Just as critical success factors are more important than other aspects of performance, not all performance indicators are created equal. The performance indicators that measure the most important aspects of performance are the key performance indicators.

 Key performance indicators (KPIs) are the measures which indicate whether or not the CSFs are being achieved.

 Illustration 4 – CSFs and KPIs

A parcel delivery service, such as DHL, may have an objective to increase revenue by 4% year on year. The business will establish CSFs and KPIs which are aligned to the achievement of this objective, for example:

CSF	KPI
Speedy collection from customers after their request for a parcel to be delivered.	Collection from customers within 3 hours of receiving the orders, in any part of the country, for orders received before 2.30pm on a working day.
Rapid and reliable delivery.	Next day delivery for destinations within the UK or delivery within 2 days for destinations in Europe.

6.2 CSFs

The organisation will need to have in place the **core competencies** that are required to achieve the CSFs, i.e. something that they are able to do that is difficult for competitors to follow.

There are **five prime sources** of CSFs:

(1) **The structure of the industry** – CSFs will be determined by the characteristics of the industry itself, e.g. in the car industry 'efficient dealer network organisation' will be important where as in the food processing industry 'new product development' will be important.

(2) **Competitive strategy, industry position and geographic location**

- Competitive strategies such as differentiation or cost leadership will impact CSFs.

- Industry position, e.g. a small company's CSFs may be driven by a major competitor's strategy.

- Geographical location will impact factors such as distribution costs and hence CSFs.

(3) **Environmental factors** – factors such as increasing fuel costs can have an impact on the choice of CSFs.

(4) **Temporary factors** – temporary internal factors may drive CSFs, e.g. a supermarket may have been forced to recall certain products due to contamination fears and may therefore generate a short term CSF of ensuring that such contamination does not happen again in the future.

(5) **Functional managerial position** – the function will affect the CSFs, e.g. production managers will be concerned with product quality and cost control.

6.3 Classifying CSFs

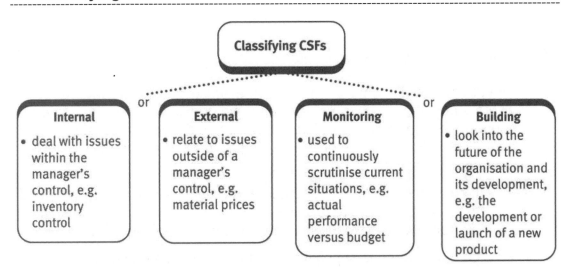

Classifying CSFs

or   or

Internal
- deal with issues within the manager's control, e.g. inventory control

External
- relate to issues outside of a manager's control, e.g. material prices

Monitoring
- used to continuously scrutinise current situations, e.g. actual performance versus budget

Building
- look into the future of the organisation and its development, e.g. the development or launch of a new product

Further detail on classifying CSFs

Internal versus external sources of CSFs

Every manager will have internal CSFs relating to the department and the people they manage. These CSFs can range across such diverse interests as human resource development or inventory control. The primary characteristic of such internal CSFs is that they deal with issues that are entirely within the manager's sphere of influence and control.

External CSFs relate to issues that are generally less under the manager's direct control such as the availability or price of a particular critical raw material or source of energy.

Monitoring versus building/adapting CSFs

Managers who are geared to producing short-term operating results invest considerable effort in tracking and guiding their organisation's performance, and therefore employ monitoring CSFs to continuously scrutinise existing situations.

Almost all managers have some monitoring CSFs, which often include financially-oriented CSFs such as actual performance versus budget or the current status of product or service transaction cost. Another monitoring CSF might be personnel turnover rates.

Managers who are either in reasonable control of day-to-day operations, or who are insulated from such concerns, spend more time in a building or adapting mode. These people can be classified as future-oriented planners whose primary purpose is to implement major change programmes aimed at adapting the organisation to the perceived emerging environment.

Typical CSFs in this area might include the successful implementation of major recruitment and training efforts, or new product or service development programmes.

Test your understanding 4

The directors of Dream Ice Cream (DI), a successful ice cream producer, with a reputation as a quality supplier, have decided to enter the frozen yogurt market in its country of operation. It has set up a separate operation under the name of Dream Yogurt (DY). The following information is available:

- DY has recruited a management team but production staff will need to be recruited. There is some concern that there will not be staff available with the required knowledge of food production.

- DY has agreed to supply yogurts to Jacksons, a chain of supermarkets based in the home country. They have stipulated that delivery must take place within 24 hours of an order being sent.

- DY hopes to become a major national producer of frozen yogurts.

- DY produces four varieties of frozen yogurt at present; Mango Tango, Very Berry, Orange Burst and French Vanilla.

Required:

Explain five CSFs on which the directors must focus if DY is to achieve success in the marketplace.

(10 marks)

Student accountant article: visit the ACCA website, www.accaglobal.com, to review the article on 'defining managers' information requirements'.

6.4 KPIs

KPIs are essential to the achievement of strategy since:

'what gets measured gets done'

i.e. things that are measured get done more often than things that are not measured.

Features of good performance measures

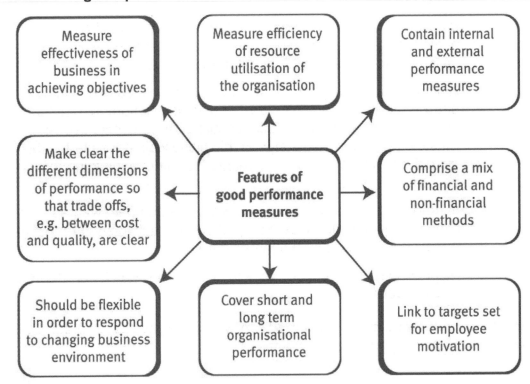

In addition, KPIs should be SMART (**s**pecific, **m**easurable, **a**ttainable, **r**elevant and **t**ime-bound).

Care must be taken when choosing what to measure and report. An unbalanced set of indicators may be valid for fulfilling the short-term needs of the organisation but will not necessarily result in long-term success. The **balanced scorecard** approach will seek to address this and is discussed in Chapter 11.

What gets measured gets done

In the previous section the quote "what gets measured gets done" was referred to. In some respects the statement seems obvious – measuring something gives you the information you need in order to make sure you actually achieve what you set out to do. Without a standard, there is no logical basis for making a decision or taking action.

However, there can be some problems with this approach:

- It assumes that staff have some motivation to deliver what is measured, whether due to the potential of positive feedback and/or rewards or the consequences of failure. The statement could thus be modified to say "What gets measured and fed back gets done well. What gets rewarded gets repeated."

- It assumes that staff have been informed up front that the particular issue would be measured and have thus been able to change their behaviour.

- It assumes that the factor being measured can be directly influenced by staff. In many situations factors have elements that are not controllable – for example, sales volume is partly due to the state of the economy.

- It assumes that expectations and targets are seen to be fair and achievable – failure on either of these counts could result in staff giving up and not trying to meet targets.

- A significant potential problem is that a firm will focus on what is easy to measure, such as cost, but ultimately ignore factors that are more difficult to measure, such as customer perception. Albert Einstein reportedly had a sign on his office wall that stated: "Not everything that counts can be counted, and not everything that can be counted counts."

- It implies that "what gets done" is what management wanted - for example, a focus on measuring profit may result in short termism at the expense of long term shareholder value.

- Measurement may foster unhealthy rivalry whereas before there was cooperation.

Student accountant article: visit the ACCA website, www.accaglobal.com, to review the article on 'performance indicators'.

6.5 Past exam question

Some of the test your understandings in this material are shorter or more straightforward than questions in the APM exam. They are contained in the material for learning purposes and will help you to build your knowledge and confidence so that you are ready to tackle past exam questions during the revision phase.

However, it is useful to look at some past exam/exam standard questions right from the beginning of this course in order to understand how the areas covered may be tested in the real exam. You need to understand how to interpret the requirements read and understand the scenario and plan and structure your answer. You may not be able to tackle the entire question at this point but you should read and learn from the answer.

Note: requirement (d) has been included for completeness but the areas tested have not been covered in the material as yet.

> ### Test your understanding 5
>
> Film Productions Co (FP) is a small international company producing films for cinema release and also for sale on DVD or to television companies. FP deals with all areas of the production from casting, directing and managing the artists to negotiating distribution deals with cinema chains and TV channels. The industry is driven by the tastes of its films' audience, which when accurately predicted can lead to high levels of profitability on a successful film.
>
> The company's stated mission is to 'produce fantastic films that have mass appeal'. The company makes around $200 million of sales each year equally split between a share of cinema takings, DVD sales and TV rights. FP has released 32 films in the past five years. Each film costs an average of $18 million and takes 12 months to produce from initial commissioning through to the final version. Production control is important in order to hit certain key holiday periods for releasing films at the cinema or on DVD.
>
> The company's films have been moderately successful in winning industry awards although FP has never won any major award. Its aims have been primarily commercial with artistic considerations secondary.
>
> The company uses a top-down approach to strategy development with objectives leading to critical success factors (CSFs) which must then be measured using performance indicators. Currently, the company has identified a number of critical success factors. The two most important of these are viewed as:
>
> (i)   improve audience satisfaction
>
> (ii) strengthen profitability in operations.

At the request of the board, the chief executive officer (CEO) has been reviewing this system in particular the role of CSFs. Generally, the CEO is worried that the ones chosen so far fail to capture all the factors affecting the business and wants to understand all possible sources for CSFs and what it means to categorise them into monitoring and building factors.

These CSFs will need to be measured and there must be systems in place to perform that role. The existing information system of the company is based on a fairly basic accounting package. However, the CEO has been considering greater investment in these systems and making more use of the company's website in both driving forward the business' links to its audience and in collecting data on them.

The CEO is planning a report to the board of Film Productions and has asked you to help by drafting certain sections of this report.

Required:

You are required to draft the sections of the CEO's report answering the following questions:

(a)   Explain the difference between the following two types of CSF: monitoring and building, using examples appropriate to FP.

(4 marks)

(b)   Identify information that FP could use to set its CSFs and explain how it could be used giving two examples that would be appropriate to FP.

(6 marks)

(c)   For each of the two critical success factors given in the question, identify two performance indicators (PIs) that could support measurement of their achievement and explain why each PI is relevant to the CSF.

(10 marks)

(d)   Discuss the implications of your chosen PIs for the design and use of the company's website, its management information system and its executive information system.

(9 marks)

2 professional marks will be awarded for appropriateness of style and structure of the answer.

(Total: 31 marks)

7 Long-term and short-term conflicts

Strategic planning is a long-term, top-down process. The decisions made can conflict with the short-term localised decisions:

- Divisional managers tend to be rewarded on the short-term results they achieve. Therefore, it will be difficult to motivate managers to achieve long-term strategic objectives.

- Divisional managers need to be able to take advantage of short-term unforeseen opportunities or avoid serious short-term crisis. Strict adherence to a strategy could limit their ability to do this.

Long-term and short-term conflicts

The whole concept of strategic planning explored earlier in this chapter implies a certain top-down approach. Even in the era of divisional autonomy and employee empowerment it is difficult to imagine that a rigorous strategic planning regime could be associated with a bottom-up management culture. There is a potential for conflict here.

- The idea of divisional autonomy is that individual managers operate their business units as if they were independent businesses – seeking and exploiting local opportunities as they arise.

- Managers are rewarded in a manner which reflects the results they achieve.

- The pressures on management are for short-term results and ostensibly strategy is concerned with the long-term. Often it is difficult to motivate managers by setting long-term expectations.

- Long-term plans have to be set out in detail long before the period to which they apply. The rigidity of the long-term plan, particularly in regard to the rationing and scheduling of resources, may place the company in a position where it is unable to react to short-term unforeseen opportunities, or serious short-term crisis.

- Strict adherence to a strategy can limit flair and creativity. Operational managers may need to respond to local situations, avert trouble or improve a situation by quick action outside the strategy. If they then have to defend their actions against criticisms of acting 'outside the plan', irrespective of the resultant benefits, they are likely to become apathetic and indifferent.

- The adoption of corporate strategy requires a tacit acceptance by everyone that the interests of departments, activities and individuals are subordinate to the corporate interests. Department managers are required to consider the contribution to corporate profits or the reduction in corporate costs of any decision. They should not allow their decisions to be limited by short-term departmental parameters.

- It is only natural that local managers should seek personal advancement. A problem of strategic planning is identifying those areas where there may be a clash of interests and loyalties, and in assessing where an individual has allowed vested interests to dominate decisions.

Test your understanding 6

Required:

How might an organisation take steps to avoid conflict between strategic business plans and short-term localised decisions?

8 The changing role of the management accountant

8.1 What is strategic management accounting?

Strategic management accounting is a form of management accounting which aims to provide information that is relevant to the process of strategic planning and control. The focus is on both **external** and **internal** information and **non-financial** as well as **financial** factors.

```
                    ┌─────────────────────┐
                    │ Role of management  │
                    │     accountant      │
                    └─────────────────────┘
                     /                   \
        ┌────────────────────┐   ┌────────────────────┐
        │    Historically    │   │       Today        │
        │ • Role limited to  │   │ • Strategic role   │
        │   implementation   │   │   providing        │
        │   stage,           │   │   information on   │
        │   e.g. responsible │   │   financial        │
        │   for operational  │   │   aspects of       │
        │   budgeting and    │   │   strategic        │
        │   control.         │   │   planning e.g.    │
        │ • Focus is on      │   │   competitors'     │
        │   internal factors │   │   costs.           │
        │   and financial    │   │ • Uses internal    │
        │   information.     │   │   and external     │
        │ • Focus is on the  │   │   information      │
        │   past             │   │ • Monitors         │
        │                    │   │   performance in   │
        │                    │   │   financial and    │
        │                    │   │   non-financial    │
        │                    │   │   terms.           │
        │                    │   │ • Focus is on the  │
        │                    │   │   future.          │
        └────────────────────┘   └────────────────────┘
```

The strategic management accountant plays a **key role in performance management** helping to determine the financial implications of an organisation's activities and decisions and in ensuring that these activities are focused on shareholders' needs for profit.

Test your understanding 7

A company selling wooden garden furniture in northern Europe is facing a number of problems:

- demand is seasonal

- it is sometimes difficult to forecast demand as it varies with the weather – more is sold in hot summers than when it is cooler or wetter

- the market is becoming more fashion-conscious with shorter product life cycles

- there is a growth in the use of non-traditional materials such as plastics.

As a result the company finds itself with high inventory levels of some items of furniture which are not selling, and is unable to meet demand for others. A decision is needed on the future strategic direction and possible options which have been identified are to:

- use largely temporary staff to manufacture products on a seasonal basis in response to fluctuations in demand – however it has been identified that this could result in quality problems

- automate production to enable seasonal production with minimum labour-related problems

- concentrate on producing premium products which are smaller volume but high-priced and less dependent on fashion.

Required:

How could strategic management accounting help with the decision making?

8.2 Changes in the role of the management accountant

The role of the management accountant has changed as a result of environmental pressures. **Burns and Scapens** studied how the role has changed in recent years.

- The role has changed focus from financial control to **business support** making the management accountant more of a generalist.

  Management accountants may now spend much of their time as internal consultants and although they still produce standardised reports, more time is spent analysing and interpreting information rather than preparing reports.

- This new role has been called a **hybrid accountant** since the management accountant has a valuable combination of both accounting and operational/commercial knowledge.

- Traditionally, it was thought that accountants needed to be independent from operational managers in order to allow them to objectively judge and report their accounting information to senior managers. However, today accountants do **not necessarily work in a separate accounting department** but may be fully integrated into other departments, thus playing a key part in the operations and decision making process of the department.

Role of a management accountant

A scan of current job advertisements for management accountants would show that they are frequently being asked to:

- inform strategic decisions and formulate business strategies

- lead the organisation's business risk management

- ensure the efficient use of financial and other resources

- advise on ways of improving business performance

- liaise with other managers to put the finance view in context

- train functional and business managers in budget management

- identify the implications of product and service changes

- work in cross-functional teams involved in strategic planning or new product development.

8.3 Driving forces for change

Driving force	Explanation
Management structure	• Head office has delegated much responsibility to the strategic business units thus reducing the involvement of management accountants in areas such as detailed budgeting. • The management accountant may now provide a link between the operational reports, the financial consequences and the strategic outcomes desired by the board.
Technology	• Management Information Systems (MIS) allow access for users across the organisation to input data and run reports giving the type of analysis once only provided by the management accountant.
Competition	• The competitive environment has driven organisations to take a more strategic focus. • Management accountants no longer focus their efforts on the final profit figure (this is seen as short-termism) but focus on a number of measures which try to capture long-term performance.

8.4 Benefits of the changes for performance management

- From an organisation's perspective, the accountant will be a guide to the strategic business unit manager to ensure that strategic goals are reflected in performance management.

- The management accountant will take a supporting role in assisting strategic business unit managers in getting the most from their management information system. This will entail the accountant understanding the needs of the particular manager and then working with them to extract valuable reports from the management information system.

- The management accountant can develop a range of performance measures to capture the different factors that will drive its success.

8.5 Role of the management accountant in providing information to stakeholders

Introduction

The demands placed on management accountants have grown in recognition of significant **sustainability** challenges.

> **Illustration 5 – Ben and Jerry's**
>
> Let's revisit mission. The ice-cream manufacturer, Ben and Jerry's operate a three part mission that aims to create linked prosperity for everyone that's connected to the business: suppliers, employees, farmers, franchisees, customers and neighbours alike.
>
> 'Our Product Mission drives us to make fantastic ice-cream – for its own sake.'
>
> 'Our Economic Mission asks us to manage our Company for sustainable financial growth.'
>
> 'Our Social Mission compels us to use our Company in innovative ways to make the world a better place.'
>
> These demands require a rich supply of information, capable of informing stakeholders of the financial and non-financial impact of the company's decisions.
>
> Conventional management accounting systems often failed to provide this information.

The triple bottom line

Whilst all businesses are used to monitoring their profit figures, there are also environmental and social aspects to consider in the longer term.

The triple bottom line focuses on economic, environmental and social areas of concern.

Area of concern	Explanation
Economic performance	• The management accountant must monitor the financial performance of the organisation to ensure its continued prosperity and fulfilment of shareholders' needs.
Environmental performance	• Improved environmental practices may include taking steps to reduce waste, increase recycling and use energy efficient equipment. • The management accountant must monitor the costs and benefits of such actions to ensure that the needs of stakeholders are being met.
Social performance	• Many examples exist such as a contribution by a company to community projects. • Perhaps harder to measure than the economic and environmental aspects. • Many activities don't have to cost the organisation much (for example, giving staff time off every year to volunteer for charitable causes) but can have far reaching social benefits. • The management accountant must monitor the costs and benefits (as above).

The management accountant has an important role in preparing sustainability reports and capturing non-financial information.

There is a growing trend for companies to issue sustainability reports, sometimes as part of traditional financial reports. The problem with this type of 'add-on' to the annual financial report is that it is very selective and may communicate only the good news for readers, ignoring or obscuring the bad.

Illustration 6 – Enron

US energy giant Enron was well known for its social and environmental work and published reports on all the good work they did in this area.

However, at the same time it was misleading its stakeholders about its profits. When the truth emerged, it led to the company's collapse in 2001 and top executives were jailed for conspiracy and fraud.

All of its community and environmental work was undermined by the fact that it was carried out by a company with dishonest business practices.

KAPLAN PUBLISHING

9 Integrated Reporting

9.1 Introduction

To tackle the problem discussed above, a new approach is being recommended called integrated reporting (IR).

With IR, instead of having environmental and social issues reported in a separate section of the annual report, or a standalone 'sustainability' report, the idea is that one report should capture the strategic and operational actions of management in its holistic approach to business and stakeholder 'wellbeing'.

9.2 The management accountant's role in providing key performance information for IR

The management accountant must now be able to collaborate with top management in the integration of financial wellbeing with community and stakeholder wellbeing. This is a more strategic view considering factors that drive long-term performance.

IR will bring statutory reporting closer to the management accountant and will make management accountants even more important in bridging the gap between stakeholders and the company's reports.

The management accountant will be expected to produce information that:

- is a balance between quantitative and qualitative information. The information system must be able to capture both financial and non-financial measures

- links past, present and future performance. The forward looking nature will require more forecasted information

- considers the regulatory impacts on performance

- provides an analysis of opportunities and risks that could impact in the future

- considers how resources should be best allocated

- is tailored to the specific business situation but remains concise.

There is clearly a need for the profession to accept the challenge for being the mechanism for a new type of transparency and accountability; one that incorporates social and environmental impacts as well as economic ones.

The role of the management accountant in sustainability is as yet not well established. However, it is anticipated that over time, IR will become the corporate reporting norm. This will offer a productive and rewarding future, not only for the management accountant but for society as a whole.

9.3 The International Integrated Reporting Council (IIRC)

The IIRC was formed in August 2010 and aims to create a globally accepted framework for a process that results in communication by an organisation about value creation over time.

The IIRC seeks to secure the adoption of an Integrated Reporting Framework (an alternative to the recommendations by the GRI) by report preparers. The Framework sets out several **guiding principles** and **content elements** that have to be considered when preparing an integrated report.

Illustration 7 – Guiding principles

There are **seven** guiding principles, as follows:

Strategic focus and future orientation – the report should provide and insight into the organisation's strategy and how it relates to the organisation's ability to create value in the short, medium and long term.

Connectivity of information – the report should show a holistic picture of the combination, inter-relatedness and dependencies between the factors that affect the organisation's ability to create value over time.

Stakeholder relationships – the report should provide an insight into the nature and quality of the organisation's relationships with its stakeholders.

Materiality – the report should disclose information about matters that substantively affect the organisation's ability to create value.

Conciseness – the report should be concise and include relevant information only.

Reliability and completeness – the report should include all material matters, both positive and negative, in a balanced way and without material error.

Consistency and comparability – the report should be consistent and comparable over time.

Illustration 8 – Content elements

There are **eight** content elements. The first six are particularly relevant to APM.

Organisational overview and external environment – what does the organisation do and what are the circumstances under which it operates? The organisation's mission and objectives, stakeholder analysis and PEST analysis would be relevant in this section.

Risks and opportunities – what are the risks and opportunities, both internal and external, that affect the organisation's ability to create value over the short, medium and long term and how is the organisation dealing with them?

Strategy and resource allocation – where does the organisation want to go and how does it intend to get there? This section may make use of Porter's 5 Forces, the BCG matrix and the value chain.

Business model – what is the organisation's business model, i.e. what activities will it carry out to create value? Many of the performance management models (such as the value chain) and methods (such as BPR, VBM and ABM) are relevant here.

Future outlook – what challenges and uncertainties is the organisation likely to encounter in pursuing its strategy and what are the implications for future performance? PEST and Porter's 5 Forces are likely to be particularly relevant here.

Performance – to what extent has the organisation achieved its strategic objectives for the period? The most appropriate performance indicators should be chosen here.

Governance – how does the organisation's governance structure support its ability to create value in the short, medium and long term?

Basis of preparation and presentation – how does the organisation determine what matters to include in the integrated report and are such matters quantified or evaluated?

The models and methods above will be discussed later on in the text.

Student accountant article: visit the ACCA website, www.accaglobal.com, to review the article on 'integrated reporting'.

9.4 IR and capital

The IR Framework recognises the importance of looking at financial and sustainability performance in an integrated way – one that emphasises the relationships between what it identifies as the "six capitals":

- Financial capital

  This is what we traditionally think of as 'capital' – e.g. shares, bonds or banknotes. It enables the other types of Capital described below to be owned and traded.

- Manufactured capital

  This form of capital can be described as comprising of material goods, or fixed assets which contribute to the production process rather than being the output itself – e.g. tools, machines and buildings.

- Intellectual capital

  This form of capital can be described as the value of a company or organisation's employee knowledge, business training and any proprietary information that may provide the company with a competitive advantage.

- Human capital

  This can be described as consisting of people's health, knowledge, skills and motivation. All these things are needed for productive work.

- Social and relationship capital

  This can be described as being concerned with the institutions that help maintain and develop human capital in partnership with others; e.g. Families, communities, businesses, trade unions, schools, and voluntary organisations.

- Natural capital

  This can be described as any stock or flow of energy and material within the environment that produces goods and services. It includes resources of a renewable and non-renewable materials e.g. land, water, energy and those factors that absorb, neutralise or recycle wastes and processes – e.g. climate regulation, climate change, CO_2 emissions.

The fundamental assumption of the IR Framework is that each of these types of capital – whether internal or external to the business, tangible or intangible – represents a potential source of value that must be managed for the long run in order to deliver sustainable value creation.

As well as external reporting to a range of stakeholders, the principles of IR can be extended to performance management systems. This is sometimes referred to as 'internal IR'.

An emphasis on these types of capital could result in more focussed performance management in the following ways:

- KPIs can be set up for each of the six capitals, ensuring that each of the drivers of sustainable value creation are monitored, controlled and developed.

- These can be developed further to show how the KPIs connect with different capitals, interact with, and impact each other.

- The interaction and inter-connectedness of these indicators should then be reflected in greater integration and cooperation between different functions and operations within the firm.

- This should result in greater transparency of internal communications allowing departments to appreciate better the wider implications of their activities.

- Together this should result in better decision making and value creation over the longer term.

Test your understanding 8

For each of the six capitals outlined in the Integrated Reporting Framework, suggest appropriate KPIs.

9.5 The Global Reporting Initiative (GRI)

The most accepted framework for reporting sustainability is the GRI's Sustainability Reporting Guidelines, the latest of which 'G4' – the fourth of the guidelines – was issued in May 2013. The G4 Guidelines consist of principles and disclosure items.

- The principles help to define report content, quality of the report and give guidance on how to set the report boundary.

- The disclosure items include disclosures on management of issues as well as performance indicators themselves.

Reporting principles and disclosures

Reporting principles

Reporting principles are essentially the required characteristics of the Report Content and the Report Quality. The Principles for Defining Report Content are given as:

- Stakeholder Inclusiveness

- Sustainability Context

- Materiality

- Completeness.

The Principles for Defining Report Quality are given as:

- Balance

- Comparability

- Accuracy

- Timeliness

- Clarity

- Reliability.

Standard disclosures

Two types of disclosure are required: General standard disclosures:

- Strategy and Analysis

- Organisational Profile

- Identified Material Aspects and Boundaries

- Stakeholder Engagement
- Report profile
- Governance
- Ethics and Integrity.

Specific Standard Disclosures

- Disclosures on Management's Approach
- Indicators.

The G4 guidelines encourage disclosure of various 'aspects' in the three categories: Economic, Environmental and Social.

Illustration 9 – Categories and aspects in the G4 guidelines

Examples of the aspects grouped by category are:

Economic

- Economic Performance
- Market Presence

Environmental

- Materials, energy and water
- Biodiversity
- Emissions
- Effluents and Waste

Social – this category is split into four sub-categories, each with several aspects associated with it as follows:

Labour Practices and Decent Work

- Labour/Management Relations
- Occupational Health and Safety
- Training and Education
- Diversity and Equal Opportunity

Human rights

- Non-discrimination

- Child Labour

- Human Rights Grievance Mechanisms.

Society

- Local Communities

- Anti-corruption

Product responsibility

- Customer Health and Safety

- Product and Service Labelling

10 Benchmarking performance

10.1 What is benchmarking?

 Benchmarking is the process of identifying **best practice** in relation to the products (or services) and the processes by which those products (or services) are created and delivered. The objective of benchmarking is to understand and evaluate the current position of a business or organisation in relation to best practice and to identify areas and means of performance improvement.

10.2 Types of benchmarks

There are three basic types:

- **Internal:** this is where another function or department of the organisation is used as a benchmark.

  Can be straightforward but may lack innovative solutions due to there being no external focus.

  Furthermore it is difficult to use such benchmarks to understand if the company as a whole has a competitive advantage.

- **Competitor:** uses a direct competitor in the same industry with the same or similar processes as the benchmark.

  The biggest problem will be obtaining information from the competitor.

  However, such benchmarks will be much more useful for indicating relative competitive advantage or the lack of it.

- **Process or activity:** focuses on a similar process in another company which is not a direct competitor.

  Can prove easier to obtain information from a non-competitor and can still find innovative solutions.

Illustration 10 – Process benchmarking at Xerox

Among the pioneers in the benchmarking 'movement' were Xerox, Motorola, IBM and AT&T. The best known is the Xerox Corporation.

Some years ago, Xerox confronted its own unsatisfactory performance in product warehousing and distribution. It did so by identifying the organisation it considered to be the very best at warehousing and distribution, in the hope that 'best practices' could be adapted from this model. The business judged to provide a model of best practice in this area was L L Bean, a catalogue merchant (i.e. it existed in an unrelated sector). Xerox approached Bean with a request that the two engage in a co-operative benchmarking project. The request was granted and the project yielded major insights in inventory arrangement and order processing, resulting in major gains for Xerox when these insights were adapted to its own operations.

Strategic, functional and operational benchmarks

Benchmarks could include the following:

Strategic benchmarks

- market share

- return on assets

- gross profit margin on sales.

Functional benchmarks

- % deliveries on time

- order costs per order

- order turnaround time

- average stockholding per order.

Operational benchmarks

These are at a level below functional benchmarks. They yield the reasons for a functional performance gap. An organisation has to understand the benchmarks at the operational level in order to identify the corrective actions needed to close the performance gap.

10.3 The benchmarking process

Step 1: Set objectives and determine which areas or functions to benchmark.

↓

Step 2: Identify key performance indicators and drivers that will be measured during benchmarking.

↓

Step 3: Select organisations/partners for benchmarking comparison.

↓

Step 4: Measure performance of all organisations/partners involved in benchmarking using measures identified in step 2.

↓

Step 5: Measure own performance and compare it to the benchmark. Identify gaps in performance.

↓

Step 6: Specify actions required to close the gap.

↓

Step 7: Implement and monitor actions.

10.4 Benchmarking and the strategic planning process

Benchmarking can be used in all three areas of the strategic planning process:

- **Strategic analysis** – a company's mission may be to be 'the premium provider of its products' but without comparison through benchmarking how will they know if they are delivering premium products? In addition, a company's position can be summarised in a SWOT analysis. Each of these factors can be identified through benchmarking and any gaps identified.

- **Strategic choice** – benchmarking can help in assessing generic strategy. For example, an organisation may compare its costs to the leading competitor. If the organisation cannot better or equal those results then cost leadership is an inappropriate strategy to pursue.

- **Strategic implementation** – for example, budgetary targets should be benchmarked against other organisations to ensure that they are both challenging and attainable.

10.5 Benchmarking metrics

Once an organisation has decided which aspects of its performance should be benchmarked, it must then establish metrics for these, i.e. how can performance be measured? Some areas will be easy to measure (such as material used) where as others will be more difficult (such as customer service).

 Illustration 11 – Benchmarking success at Kelloggs

Kelloggs' factories all use the same monitoring techniques, so it is possible to compare performance between sites, although there are always some things that are done differently.

They can interrogate this information to improve performance across every site. As things have improved, Kelloggs have also had to reassess their baseline figures and develop more sophisticated tools to monitor performance to ensure they continue to make progress.

They have seen a 20% increase in productivity in a six year period using this system.

10.6 Benchmarking evaluation

Benefits	Drawbacks
• Identifies gaps in performance and sets targets which are challenging but achievable. • Can help in assessing its current strategic position (more on SWOT analysis in section 11.1).	• Best practice companies may be unwilling to share data. • Lack of commitment by management and staff. Staff need to be reassured that their status, remuneration and working conditions will not suffer.

• A method for learning and applying best practices. • Encourages continuous improvement. • A method of learning from the success of others. • Can help to assess generic strategy. • Minimises complacency and self-satisfaction with your own performance and can provide an early warning of competitive disadvantage.	• Identifying best practice is difficult. • Costly in terms of time and money. • What is best today may not be so tomorrow. • Differences, for example in accounting treatment, may make comparisons meaningless. • Too much attention is paid to the aspects of performance that are measured as a result of the benchmarking exercise, to the detriment of the organisation's overall performance.

Performance comparison with the competition

Comparative analysis can be usefully applied to any value activity which underpins the competitive strategy of an organisation, an industry or a nation.

To find out the level of investment in fixed assets of competitors, the business can use physical observation, information from trade press or trade association announcements, supplier press releases as well as their externally published financial statements, to build a clear picture of the relative scale, capacity, age and cost for each competitor.

The method of operating these assets, in terms of hours and shift patterns, can be established by observation, discussions with suppliers and customers or by asking existing or ex-employees of the particular competitor. If the method of operating can be ascertained it should enable a combination of internal personnel management and industrial engineering managers to work out the likely relative differences in labour costs. The rates of pay and conditions can generally be found with reference to nationally negotiated agreements, local and national press advertising for employees, trade and employment associations and recruitment consultants. When this cost is used alongside an intelligent assessment of how many employees would be needed by the competitor in each area, given their equipment and other resources, a good idea of the labour costs can be obtained.

Another difference which should be noted is the nature of the competitors' costs as well as their relative levels. Where a competitor has a lower level of committed fixed costs, such as lower fixed labour costs due to a larger proportion of temporary workers, it may be able to respond more quickly to a downturn in demand by rapidly laying off the temporary staff. Equally, in a tight labour market and with rising sales, it may have to increase its pay levels to attract new workers.

In some industries, one part of the competitor analysis is surprisingly direct. Each new competitive product is purchased on a regular basis and then systematically taken apart, so that each component can be identified as well as the processes used to put the parts together. The respective areas of the business will then assess the costs associated with each element so that a complete product cost can be found for the competitive product.

A comparison of similar value activities between organisations is useful when the strategic context is taken into consideration. For example, a straight comparison of resource deployment between two competitive organisations may reveal quite different situations in the labour cost as a percentage of the total cost. The conclusions drawn from this, however, depend upon circumstances. If the firms are competing largely on the basis of price, then differentials in these costs could be crucial. In contrast, the additional use of labour by one organisation may be an essential support for the special services provided which differentiate that organisation from its competitors.

One danger of inter-firm analysis is that the company may overlook the fact that the whole industry is performing badly, and is losing out competitively to other countries with better resources or even other industries which can satisfy customers' needs in different ways. Therefore, if an industry comparison is performed it should make some assessment of how the resource utilisation compares with other countries and industries. This can be done by obtaining a measurement of stock turnover or yield from raw materials.

Benchmarking against competitors involves the gathering of a range of information about them. For quoted companies financial information will generally be reasonably easy to obtain, from published accounts and the financial press. Some product information may be obtained by acquiring their products and examining them in detail to ascertain the components used and their construction ('reverse engineering'). Literature will also be available, for example in the form of brochures and trade journals.

However, most non-financial information, concerning areas such as competitors' processes, customer and supplier relationships and customer satisfaction will not be so readily available. To overcome this problem, benchmarking exercises are generally carried out with organisations taken from within the same group of companies (intragroup benchmarking) or from similar but non-competing industries (inter-industry benchmarking).

Question practice

The following question is an exam standard and style question on benchmarking. Make sure that you take the time to attempt this question and to review the recommended answer.

Test your understanding 9

AV is a charitable organisation, the primary objective of which is to meet the accommodation needs of persons within its locality.

In an attempt to improve its performance, AV's directors have started to carry out a benchmarking exercise. They have identified a company called BW which is a profit seeking private provider of rented accommodation.

BW has provided some operational and financial data which is summarised below along with the most recent results for AV for the year ended 31 May 20X4.

Income and expenditure accounts for the year ended 31 May 20X4 were as follows:

	AV ($)	BW ($)
Rents received	2,386,852	2,500,000
Less:		
Staff and management costs	450,000	620,000
Major repairs and planned maintenance	682,400	202,200
Day-to-day repairs	478,320	127,600
Sundry operating costs	305,500	235,000
Net interest payable and other similar charges	526,222	750,000
Total costs	2,442,442	1,934,800
Operating (deficit/surplus)	(55,590)	565,200

Operating information in respect of the year ended 31 May 20X4 was as follows:

1   **Property and rental information:**

AV – size of property	AV – number of properties	AV – rent payable per week ($)	BW – number of properties
1 bedroom	80	40	40
2 bedrooms	160	45	80
3 bedrooms	500	50	280
4 bedrooms	160	70	nil

AV had certain properties that were unoccupied during part of the year. The rents lost as a consequence of unoccupied properties amounted to $36,348. BW did not have any unoccupied properties at any point during the year.

2 Staff salaries were payable as follows:

AV – number of staff	AV – salary per staff member per year	BW – number of staff	BW – salary per staff member per year
	$	$	$
2	35,000	3	50,000
2	25,000	2	35,000
3	20,000	20	20,000
18	15,000	–	–

3 Planned maintenance and major repairs undertaken

Nature of work	AV – number of properties	AV – cost per property ($)	BW – number of properties	BW – cost per property ($)
Miscellaneous construction work	20	1,250	–	–
Fitted kitchen replacements (all are the same size)	90	2,610	10	5,220
Heating upgrades/ replacements	15	1,500	–	–
Replacement sets of windows and doors for 3 bedroomed properties	100	4,000	25	6,000

All expenditure on planned maintenance and major repairs may be regarded as revenue expenditure.

4 Day-to-day repairs information:

Classification of repair	AV – number of repairs undertaken	AV – total cost	BW – number of repairs undertaken
		$	
Emergency	960	134,400	320
Urgent	1,880	225,600	752
Non-urgent	1,020	118,320	204

Each repair undertaken by BW costs the same irrespective of classification of repair.

Required:

(a) Assess the progress of the benchmarking exercise to date, explaining the actions that have been undertaken and those that are still required.

(8 marks)

> (b) Evaluate, as far as possible, AV's benchmarked position.
>
> **(9 marks)**
>
> (c) Evaluate the benchmarking technique being used and discuss whether BW is a suitable benchmarking partner for AV to use.
>
> **(8 marks)**

Student accountant article: visit the ACCA website, www.accaglobal.com to review the article on 'benchmarking'.

11 Models used in the performance management process

A number of models can assist in the performance management process. These include:

- SWOT analysis

- Boston Consulting Group

- Porter's generic strategies

- Porter's 5 Forces and

- the balanced scorecard.

The first three of these are discussed below. Porter's 5 Forces is covered in Chapter 2 and the balanced scorecard is discussed in Chapter 11.

11.1 SWOT analysis

 The purpose of **SWOT analysis** (corporate appraisal) is to provide a summarised analysis of the company's present situation in the market place. It can also be used to identify CSFs and KPIs.

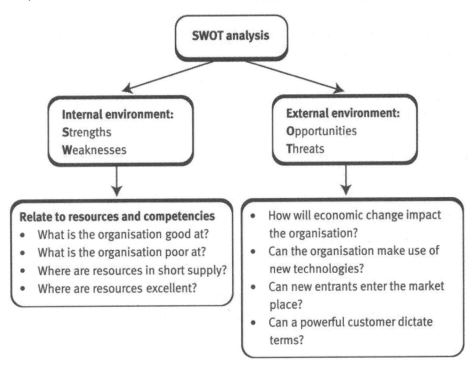

Using a SWOT analysis

Once a SWOT analysis has been carried out strategies can be developed that:

- neutralise weaknesses or convert them into strengths.

- convert threats into opportunities.

- match strengths with opportunities – a strength is of little use without an opportunity.

Test your understanding 10

Required:

What types of strengths, weaknesses, opportunities and threats would a 'no frills' airline have?

SWOT analysis and the performance management process

SWOT analysis helps an organisation to understand its environment and its internal capacities and hence to evaluate the potential strategic options it could pursue in its quest to improve organisational performance and to close any performance gaps that exist.

It can also help an organisation to identify key aspects of performance (CSFs) that need measuring (through the establishment of KPIs).

Finally, it can help in determining the information needs of the business in relation to measuring and reporting on the KPIs set.

Test your understanding 11

Envie Co owns a chain of retail clothing stores specialising in ladies' designer fashion and accessories. Jane Smith, the original founder, has been pleasantly surprised by the continuing growth in the fashion industry during the last decade.

The company was established 12 years ago, originally with one store in the capital city. Jane's design skills and entrepreneurial skills have been the driving force behind the expansion. Due to unique designs and good quality control, the business now has ten stores in various cities.

Each store has a shop manger that is completely responsible for managing the staff and stock levels within each store. They produce monthly reports on sales. Some stores are continually late in supplying their monthly figures.

Envie runs several analysis programmes to enable management information to be collated. The information typically provides statistical data on sales trends between categories of items and stores. The analysis and preparation of these reports are conducted in the marketing department. In some cases the information is out of date in terms of trends and variations.

As the business has developed Jane has used the service of a local IT company to implement and develop their systems. She now wants to invest in website development with the view of reaching global markets.

Required:

(a) Construct a SWOT analysis with reference to the proposal of website development.

(b) Explain how the use of SWOT analysis may be of assistance to Envie Co's performance management and measurement process.

11.2 Boston Consulting Group (BCG)

The BCG matrix **shows whether the firm has a balanced portfolio** in terms of the products it offers and the market sectors it operates in. The matrix is constructed using the following steps:

1   Divide the business into divisions/strategic business units or products

2   Allocate each of these to the matrix.

3   Assess the prospects of each division or product.

4   Develop strategies and targets for each division or product.

	Star	Problem child
High	• Large share of high-growth market. • High reinvestment rate required to hold/build position. • Moderate cash flow.	• Small share of high-growth market. • Large investment required to grow (so cash user). • **Or** divest.
Market growth **Low**	**Cash cow** • Large share of low-growth market. • Cash generator. • Strategy is minimal investment to keep the product going.	**Dog** • Small share of low-growth market. • Moderate or negative cash flow. • Divest.

High	**Relative market share**	**Low**

If the relevant information is available, market growth and relative market share should be calculated as follows:

- **Market growth** = the % increase/decrease in annual market revenue

  Note: if market revenue is given for a number of successive years the average % increase/decrease in annual market revenue can be calculated as follows:

  $1 + g = \sqrt[n]{}$ most recent market revenue ÷ earliest market revenue

  where g = the increase/decrease in annual market revenue as a decimal and

  n = the number of periods of growth

  As a guide, 10% is often used as the dividing line between high and low growth. However, this is a general guide only – do refer to and use the information given in the scenario.

- **Relative market share** = division's market share ÷ largest competitor's market share

  where divisional market share = divisional revenue ÷ market revenue

  A relative market share greater than 1 indicates that the division or product is the market leader. 1 can be used as the dividing line between high and low market share. However, this is a general guide only – do refer to and use the information given in the scenario.

Factors to consider for performance management

When conducting a BCG assessment an organisation should consider:

- how to manage the different categories in order to optimise the performance of the organisation.

- what performance indicators are required for each category.

- the alignment of the performance indicators with the objectives of the organisation and the individuals within it.

- how to measure market growth and relative market share and the reliability of these measurements.

BCG evaluation

Benefits	Drawbacks
• Ensures that a balanced portfolio of products or divisions exists, i.e. are there enough cash cows to support our question marks and stars? Are there a minimum number of dogs?	• Too simplistic, i.e. market growth is just one indicator of industry attractiveness and market share is just one indicator of competitive advantage. Other factors will also be determinants of profit.
• Can use to manage divisions in different ways, e.g. divisions in a mature market should focus on cost control and cash generation.	• Designed as a tool for product portfolio analysis rather than performance measurement.

- Metrics used by the division can be in line with the analysis, e.g. metrics for high growth prospects may be based on profit and ROI and metrics for lower growth prospects will focus on margin and cash generation.

- Looks at the portfolio of divisions or products as a whole rather than assessing the performance of each one separately.

- Can be used to assess performance, e.g. if an organisation consists mainly of cash cows we would expect to see static or low growth in revenue.

- Downgrades traditional measures such as profit and so may not be aligned with shareholder's objectives.

- Determining what 'high' and 'low' growth and share mean in different situations is difficult.

- Does not consider links between business units, e.g. a dog may be required to complete a product range.

Test your understanding 12

Food For Thought (FFT) has been established for over 20 years and has a wide range of food products. The company's objective is the maximisation of shareholder wealth.

The organisation has four divisions:

1   Premier

2   Organic

3   Baby

4   Convenience.

The Premier division manufactures a range of very high quality food products, which are sold to a leading supermarket, with stores in every major city in the country. Due to the specialist nature of the ingredients these products have a very short life cycle.

The Organic division manufactures a narrow range of food products for a well-established Organic brand label.

The Baby division manufactures specialist foods for infants, which are sold to the largest UK Baby retail store.

The Convenience division manufactures low fat ready-made meals for the local council.

FFT's board have decided to perform a Boston Consulting Group (BCG) analysis to understand whether they have right mix of businesses.

The following revenue data has been gathered:

Year ending 31st March:

		$m				
		20X3	**20X4**	**20X5**	**20X6**	**20X7**
Premier	Market size	180	210	260	275	310
	Sales revenue	10	12	18	25	30
Organic	Market size	18.9	19.3	19.6	19.8	20.4
	Sales revenue	13.5	14	14.5	15	16
Baby	Market size	65	69	78	92	96
	Sales revenue	2.5	2.7	2.8	2.9	3
Convenience	Market size	26	27.2	27.6	28	29
	Sales revenue	0.9	0.9	0.92	0.94	0.9

The management accountant has also collected the following information for 20X7 for comparison purposes.

Largest competitor	% share
Premier	17%
Organic	20%
Baby	25%
Convenience	31%

Each of division's performance is measured using EVA. The divisional manager's remuneration package contains a bonus element which is based on the achievement of the division's cost budget (this is set at board level).

Required:

Using the BCG matrix assess the competitive position of Food For Thought. Evaluate the divisional manager's remuneration package in light of the divisional performance system and your BCG analysis.

Measurement problems using the BCG matric

There are a number of measurement problems regarding the BCG growth share matrix.

Measurement problems inherent in the model

The BCG matrix is a model and the weakness of any model is inherent in its assumptions. For example many strategists are of the opinion that the axes of the model are much too simplistic when trying to measure market attractiveness and competitive strength.

The model implies that competitive strength is indicated by relative market share. This would imply that economies of scale and/or the experience curve are usually dominating factors in markets and that market share is achieved through cost leadership. However other factors such as strength of brands, perceived product/service quality and costs structures also contribute to competitive strength.

Likewise the model implies that the attractiveness of the marketplace is indicated by the growth rate of the market. This is not necessarily the case as organisations that lack the necessary capital resources may find low-growth markets an attractive proposition especially as they tend to have a lower risk profile than hi-growth markets.

Measurement issues when applying the model

The main measurement problem when trying to apply the model lies in defining the market. The model requires management to define the market place within which a business is trading in order that its rate of growth and relative market share can be calculated.

Even having defined the appropriate market segment, ideally growth needs to be an estimate of future growth. This could involve a range of approaches, including analysing historic growth, time series analysis and looking at underlying drivers using a PEST analysis. Alternatively it could also include evaluating budgets and forecasts in terms of increasing potential customers, new customers and so on.

Similarly there may be issues in identifying the lead competitor within that market to enable a calculation of relative market share to be made. This can prove problematic in comparing competitors since if they supply different products and services then the absence of a consistent basis for comparison impairs the usefulness of the model.

The application of the BCG matrix may thus prove costly and time-consuming since it necessitates the collection of a large amount of data.

Further detail on applying the BCG matric

Star	Problem Child

• Is the high investment being spent effectively?
 	
• Is market share being gained, held or eroded?
 	
• Is customer perception (e.g. brand, quality) improving?
 	
• Are customer CSFs changing as the market grows?
 	
• What is the net cash flow?
 	
• Is the star becoming a cash cow?
	1 **Assuming the strategy is to invest**
	
	   – Is market share being gained?
	
	   – Effectiveness of advertising spend.
	
	2 **Assuming the strategy is to divest**
	
	   – Monitor contribution to see whether to exit quickly or divest slowly.

Cash Cow	**Dog**
• What is the net cash flow? • Is market share being eroded – could the cash cow be moving towards becoming a dog?	• Monitor contribution to see whether to exit quickly or divest slowly. • Monitor market growth as an increase in the growth rate could justify retaining the product.

The logical thrust here is that, if you enjoy a high market share, then you will probably have a strong position because of low unit production cost and a high market profile. A product that has a high growth potential offers obvious advantages but it is typically associated with high development costs because of the need to develop the product itself and/or maintain the high market share.

The nature of the four classifications shown above is self-explanatory. An understanding of where given products stand in relation to this matrix can be another essential element in strategic planning. For example, if a product is a cash cow, then it may be very useful, but it should be appreciated that it may be at an advanced stage in its life cycle and the cash it generates should be invested in potential stars.

However, it is not always easy to distinguish between a star and a dog. Many businesses have poured money into the development of products that they believed were potential stars only to find that those products turned into dogs. The Sinclair C5 (a small, battery-powered car) is often quoted as an example of this phenomenon. The promoters of this product in the 1980s proceeded on the basis that there was a market for such a car as a means of urban transport and that the C5 would enjoy a high share of this market. In fact, the only niche it found was as a children's toy and it achieved only a low market share with little growth potential as such.

The general point this model makes is that current period cash flow is not an unambiguous statement on the performance of a product or business sector. To appreciate fully the performance of a product, one has to appreciate where the product stands in terms of the above matrix. A poor current cash flow may be acceptable from a product or service considered to be a 'Star'.

Other application issues

Following the advice of the model may lead to unfortunate consequences, such as

- Moving into areas where there is little experience

- Over-milking of cash cows

- Abandonment of potentially healthy businesses labelled as problem children

- Neglect of interrelationships among businesses, and

- Too many problem children within the business portfolio largely as a consequence of incorrect focus of management attention.

Student accountant article: visit the ACCA website, www.accaglobal.com to review the article on 'performance management models'.

11.3 Porter's generic strategies

An important part of strategic choice is deciding on what basis to compete. Porter identified three generic strategies through which an organisation could achieve competitive advantage and optimise performance.

	Lower cost	Higher cost
Broad target	Cost leadership	Differentiation
Narrow target	Focus	
	Cost focus	Differentiation focus

Cost leadership

 The organisation sets out to be the lowest cost producer in the industry.

Performance should improve due to:

- the ability to earn the highest unit profits

- lower costs acting as a barrier to entry and reducing competition.

However:

- There is no fall back if the leadership position is lost, for example strengthening of the currency may make imports of substitute goods cheaper.

- The organisation must continually adapt to ensure unit prices are kept low and consumer needs are met.

Requirements include:

- Mass production facilitating the achievement of economies of scale.

- Investment in the latest technology reducing labour costs.

- Improving productivity, for example through the use of value chain analysis (Chapter 4) or zero based budgeting (Chapter 3).

- Use of bargaining power to lower the cost of supplies and overheads.

 Differentiation

The organisation offers a product that can't be matched by rivals and charges a premium for this 'difference'.

Methods of differentiation include:

- quality differentiation, e.g. better reliability, durability or performance

- image and branding

- design

- support, for example offering 0% finance or next day delivery.

Performance should improve due to:

- higher margins

- loyalty increases with repeat custom

- reduction in the power of customers.

However:

- there is a need to continually innovate to defend the position

- smaller volumes

- associated costs, such as marketing, are higher

- performance in a recession may be poor.

Focus

Position the business in one particular niche in the market. Competition may be on the basis of costs or differentiation.

Performance should improve due to:

- little competition often exists in the identified niche

- the development of brand loyalty.

However:

- if successful it may attract other cost leaders/ differentiators due to potential low barriers to entry

- low volumes may be sold.

12 Exam focus

Exam sitting	Area examined	Question number	Number of marks
Sept/ Dec 2017	Role of management accountant in IR	1(ii)	6
Sept/ Dec 2017	Benchmarking	2(b)	9
March/Jun 2017	KPIs and mission	1(i)(ii)	20
Sept/Dec 2016	CSFs and KPIs	4(a)	8
Sept/Dec 2015	CSFs	1(ii)(iii)	21
June 2015	BCG	4(c)	10
June 2015	Choice of metrics, SWOT	1(i)(iv)	26
December 2014	Benchmarking	1(iii)	16
June 2014	Mission	1 (v)	6
December 2013	KPIs and CSFs	1(i)(iii)(iv)(v)	35
December 2012	Changing role of management accountant	5(a)	12
June 2012	Benchmarking	4	17
June 2012	KPIs	2(a)	12
December 2011	KPIs	2(a)	7
June 2011	BCG	4	20
December 2010	CSFs and KPIs	1 (a)–(c)	20
December 2010	KPIs	4(a)	4

Chapter summary

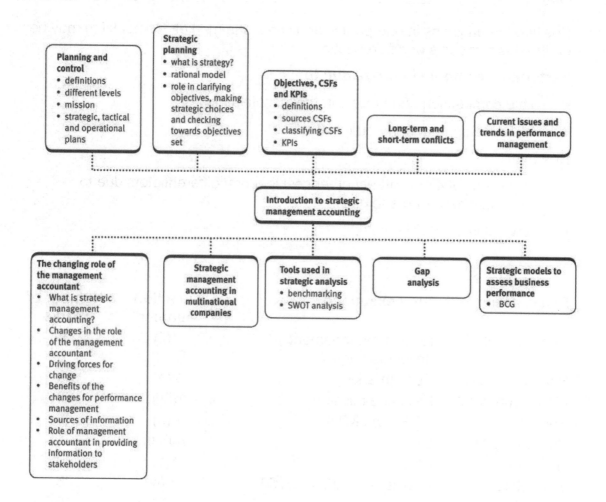

Test your understanding answers

Test your understanding 1

Benefits	Drawbacks
• Provides strategic direction thereby assisting in the formation of acceptable strategies. • Assists in resolving conflict between stakeholder groups. • Provides a framework within which managerial decisions can be made. • Assists in communicating key cultural values to employees and other stakeholders. • Helps to prevent potential misinterpretations of the organisation's reason for being.	• They may be unclear or vague. • They may be unrealistic. • There may be inconsistencies between the different elements of the mission statement. • They may be inconsistent with management action. • They may lack sufficient external focus. • It may be difficult to measure the achievement of the mission statement or appropriate performance measures may not be established to begin with.

Test your understanding 2

This is an **operational** decision. Setting a profit-maximising selling price is an exercise based on forecast demand and marginal costs over a coming period such as a year. It does not involve asking whether a product should be sold at all, whether its design should be modified or how its selling price should be influenced by the position of the product in its life cycle or the product matrix of the business.

Test your understanding 3

- An understanding of corporate planning is essential for all management because lower-level objectives are inexorably linked to higher-level strategies. An appreciation of these strategies and how they are formulated can be an effective guide to action and improving performance.

- Moreover, whatever the level at which a manager operates within an organisation, he or she can have some influence over that organisation's strategic (corporate) strategy.

Test your understanding 4

Critical success factors (CSFs) are as follows:

Product quality – the fact that production staff may have no previous experience in a food production environment is likely to prove problematic. It is vital that a comprehensive training programme is put in place at the earliest opportunity. DY need to reach and maintain the highest level of quality as soon as possible.

Supply quality – the quality and timeliness of delivery into Jacksons supermarkets assumes critical significance. Hence supply chain management must be extremely robust as there is little scope for error.

Technical quality – compliance with existing regulators regarding food production including all relevant factory health and safety requirements is vital in order to establish and maintain the reputation of DY as a supplier of quality products. The ability to store products at the correct temperature is critical because yogurts are produced for human consumption and in extreme circumstances could cause fatalities.

External credibility – accreditation by relevant trade associations/ regulators will be essential if nationwide acceptance of DY as a major producer of frozen yogurts is to be established.

New product development – while DY have produced a range of frozen yogurts it must be recognised that consumer tastes change and that in the face of competition there will always be a need for a continuous focus on new product development.

Margin – while DY need to recognise all other CSFs they should always be mindful that the need to obtain desired levels of gross and net margin remain of the utmost importance.

Note: only five CSFs were required. Alternative relevant discussion and examples would be appropriate.

Test your understanding 5

(a) Building and Monitoring critical success factors

Critical success factors (CSFs) are those areas of business performance where the company must succeed in order to achieve its overall strategic objectives. Monitoring CSFs are those that are used to keep abreast of ongoing operations, for example, comparison of actual results to budgets or industry averages. Building CSFs are those which look to the future of the organisation and its development, for example, the launch of niche products such as music concert films or the use of new distribution methods such as downloadable films.

(b) Information for establishing CSFs

The company can use information about the internal and external environment to set its CSFs. Relevant external information would include the structure of the industry and the strategy of FP's competitors. The geographical location of production and the main sales markets may also be relevant. Film is a hit driven industry where word of mouth can lead to success, therefore, recognition of the product and the brand ('Film Productions') by the public would lead to success. For example, the Walt Disney Company has achieved a high level of brand recognition that has enabled it to expand into other entertainment areas using characters from its films.

Relevant internal information would include measures of seasonality on sales which will dictate the timing of film releases and effectiveness of marketing campaigns. By forecasting the size of the market along with likely levels of competition, profit can be optimised. However, these forecasts will be subject to uncertainty and so the information systems will need to be flexible and allow probabilistic analysis. A CSF based on the quality of these forecasts would therefore be appropriate. Other internal sources could include measures of the cost per film and the time taken to produce a film.

Other possible information could include contingent factors (those that depend on specific threats or opportunities facing FP).

(c) Performance indicators linked to the CSFs

Audience satisfaction – performance indicators are:

- Sales per film – currently the company releases an average of 6.4 films per year and makes about $31.25 million on each one. These figures should be compared to industry averages. Trends on sales per film should be monitored for indications of changes in consumer taste.

- Brand recognition – consumers should be surveyed to identify if the FP name is known and used as an indicator of quality when selecting films. If FP regularly uses certain artists (directors or film stars) then positive consumer recognition of these names will indicate satisfaction.

- Repeat viewings – with TV showings, it will be possible to measure viewers for each showing of the film and monitor the decline in viewing over repetitions. The level of DVD purchases following a cinema release will also indicate customer satisfaction with customers actively wanting to own their own copy of a favourite film.

- Awards won – number of awards won will indicate success. However, the level of recognition of any award must be brought into account as major ones such as those voted on by the public or those whose ceremonies are widely reported have the greatest impact.

- Response of the media – scores by film critics often appear in the media and these give a measure of satisfaction although this category must be treated carefully as critics often look for artistic merit while FP is seeking commercial success and broad audience acceptance.

Profitability in operations – performance indicators are:

- Industry average margin – collect data on competitor companies to set an appropriate benchmark. This will require care to ensure that appropriate comparator companies are chosen, for example, those with a production budget similar to FP's of $18 million per film.

- Time in production – the cost of a film will depend on the length of time it takes to produce. If the film is intended to meet a current customer demand it may require to be produced quickly, in order to meet revenue targets. Therefore, the time in production will affect both sales and cost levels so altering the gross margin. Again, it would be helpful to identify if films meet their production schedule and if these schedules compare favourably to those of other film companies.

- Costs – the costs should be broken down into categories such as those for artists, production technicians and marketing. The cost structure for each film should be compared internally, to others that FP produces and also externally, to available figures for the industry.

(d)   Impact on FP's information systems

The company website can collect audience survey results and comments posted on the site. Consumers can be drawn to the site with clips and trailers from current films and those in production. The site can log the frequency with which films are viewed and if audience members create accounts then further detail on the age, gender and location of the audience can be collected. This will allow a more detailed profile of the customer base for FP to be created and will be used to help in decisions about what films to commission in the future. The account members can be given the opportunity to score each film providing further information about satisfaction.

The company could also consider scanning the websites of its competitors to identify their performance – especially their published results which will provide benchmark information on gross margin levels.

A management information system (MIS) will collate the information from individual transactions recorded in the accounting system to allow middle level management to control the business. This system will allow customer purchases to be summarised into reports to identify both products that sell well and the customers (such as cinema chains and TV networks) who provide the main sources of revenue (indicators of satisfaction). The level of repeat business on a customer account will give an indication of the satisfaction with FP's output. The system will also produce management accounts from which gross margins will be drawn and it should be capable of breaking this down by film and by customer to aid decision-making by targeting FP's output to the most profitable areas. This will aid decision-making about the performance of the production team on a film and can be used to set rewards for each team.

An executive information system (EIS) is one that will supply information to the senior management of the organisation allowing them to drill down into the more detailed transaction reports where necessary. The EIS will provide summarised information, focused on the key performance indicators in order to allow the directors to quickly judge whether the company is meeting its CSFs. It will draw on internal sources such as the MIS and also external sources such as market data on revenues that different films are earning at the box office.

Test your understanding 6

Possible steps include:

- involving local managers in strategy formulation

- agreeing strategies with business units within certain boundaries

- ensuring performance management reflects a combination of short- and long-term issues

- permitting flexibility within the strategic planning process to allow for changes due to local circumstances

- a combination of strategic planning and freewheeling opportunism (no strategic plans). For example, strategic planning may be used for activities such as identifying the organisation's resource capability and its resources. Freewheeling opportunism may be used to exploit an organisation's competences, e.g. the skills of particular individuals or groups.

Test your understanding 7

Strategic management accounting may assist the decision making process as follows:

- analysis of the market for different types of product:

    - review of competitors' products

    - likely size and value of different market sectors

    - price comparison of different products

- forecasts of costs of manufacturing new products, comparing different levels of automation/ use of temporary staff

- forecasts of profitability of different products

- investigation of capital costs of different options and investment appraisal of possible options

- analysis of the cost of holding inventory under different options.

Test your understanding 8

Obviously (!) KPIs need to be matched to CSFs, which will depend on the precise circumstances of an organisation and the environment within which it operates. However, some generic KPIs could include the following:

Financial capital

- Conventional performance measures may be relevant here including revenue growth, margins, ROCE, interest cover, key costs as a % of revenue, etc.

- EVA^{TM}.

Manufactured capital

- Inventory days, inventory turnover, size of forward order book compared to annual production, etc.

- Investment in different classes of NCAs. These could also include intangible assets, such as measuring annual investment in R+D as a % of revenue.

Intellectual capital

- Staff turnover of skilled staff

- Utilisation of skilled staff

- Percentage of patented products

- A measurement of brand strength such as elasticity of demand (i.e. the change in demand as a result of a change in price)

- R+D expenditure.

Human capital

- Number of staff, staff turnover

- Productivity/efficiency measures such as sales per employee for a sales team

- Sickness rates.

Social and relationship capital

- Staff satisfaction surveys, looking in particular at staff confidence in leadership, opinions about growth and wellbeing.

Natural capital

- Any environmental KPIs could be used here such as energy consumption and efficiency, output of greenhouse gasses and carbon footprint, water usage, % of waste recycled verses landfill, % of products produced that can be recycled, etc.

Test your understanding 9

(a) The benchmarking process can be described using seven steps. These are outlined below, together with AV's current progress against these stages.

1   **Set objectives and decide areas to benchmark**

It is not clear exactly what AV's objectives are here, as "improve performance" is too generic. AV must carefully identify what specific areas it is looking to improve upon – for example, reduced repair costs, improved staff productivity, better rental collections.

2   **Identify key performance drivers and indicators**

To some extent these can be identified by looking at the expense headings in the Income statement. AV will improve performance by operating more efficiently across its major cost headings. It should be noted here that as a not for profit organisation performance will be measured in a different way from BW. For example, AV will not wish to increase rentals charged in order to report a surplus, so measures of efficiency become much more important so that it can provide good quality accommodation within the cost constraints imposed by the rents received.

3   **Select organisations for benchmarking comparison**

AV has selected a profit motivated company, BW, for benchmarking against, so this step has been carried out. However, it is not clear how this partner has been selected. Whilst there may be some examples of best practice to be learned from, it should again be noted that BW is profit motivated and so will have fundamentally different objectives from AV.

4   **Measure performance of all organisations involved**

Some basic data has been gathered here.

5   **Compare performance**

This is the stage that AV has now reached, as there is as yet no comparison of, or commentary on, the relative performance of the two organisations. Part (b) addresses this area.

6   **Specify areas for improvement**

Once the comparisons above are made this should identify areas for improvement. Care should be taken that processes identified at BW can be transferred across to AV. Again, given their widely different objectives, this may not be possible. AV may also need to retrain some staff (or even recruit others) to ensure the requisite skills are in place.

7 Implement and monitor improvements

Management must continuously monitor the impact of any changes implemented to make sure that the intended benefits are realised. Without this monitoring, any changes may be short lived because staff may soon revert back to their familiar way of doing things.

So, in conclusion, AV has identified a benchmarking partner (albeit one that may not be wholly suitable), and has collected some basic operational and financial data for comparison. It needs to more clearly define its objectives before it can proceed to specify actions for improvement.

(b) As discussed in part (c) below, it is not surprising that we see some major differences between the two organisations as they have very different objectives.

1 Rental income

AV has average rental income per property of $52 per week compared to $120 per week for BW. This is not surprising, given that AV wants to make cheap housing available to as many people as possible, and BW seeks to charge higher rates for premium properties to tenants who can afford to pay. This should not be seen as an indicator that AV should increase its rents.

It should also be noted that the mix of properties is different. AV has a larger proportion of 3 and 4 bedroomed properties (presumably to cope with large families), whereas BW has no four bedroomed property. Taking this into account, the rentals on a "per room" basis are even higher for BW.

2 Staff salaries

The average annual salary per employee in AV is $18000, whereas it is $24800 for BW. Again, this can largely be explained by the differing objectives that will encourage AV to keep costs to a minimum. It should be noted, however, that there may be a trade – off here between cost and productivity. If AV paid higher salaries would it be able to recruit better quality staff who are more productive? Staff numbers (25 in total) are the same for both companies, even though AV has 900 properties compared to only 400 for BW. This may lead to a reduced level of service for AV, which in turn could lead to a delay in dealing with problems such as repairs or collecting overdue rent.

3 **Planned maintenance and repairs**

The major repair and maintenance cost for AV totalled $682,400, which is over three times as much as BW. There are two likely reasons for this. Firstly AV has more than twice as many properties (900 compared to 400), and secondly it may well be that their housing stock is in poorer condition and therefore needs more maintenance. It should also be noted that the repair costs are higher per property for BW (replacement kitchens cost twice as much as for BW for example), which will again reflect their different objectives and the needs of their clients. This should not be interpreted to mean that AV is "more efficient" as it is almost certainly not a like for like comparison. Hence, as noted in part (c) below, benchmarking against other not-for-profits may yield more meaningful comparisons.

One point that should be noted – there is always a possible trade-off between cost and quality. If AV paid more per repair, would the quality be better and therefore the repairs last longer before further expenditure is needed?

4 **Day-to-day repairs**

AV has undertaken a total of 3,860 repairs in the year at an average cost of $124 per repair. BW has carried out 1,276 repairs at a cost of $100 per repair. Whilst there is not a massive difference per repair, a saving of $24 per repair would result in overall cost savings of 3860 × $24 = $92,640.

AV should carry out further research as to how BW has obtained a fixed fee per repair, and see if it can obtain a similar contract as this could produce significant savings.

5 **Sundry operating costs**

Whilst these are 30% higher for AV ($305,500 compared to $235,000), we have no breakdown of the figures and so cannot really comment further. It seems reasonable that, since AV has more than twice as many properties and tenants, it will incur a higher level of costs here.

6 **Net interest and other charges**

Again no analysis is given, so no further comment is possible.

KAPLAN PUBLISHING

Conclusion

AV clearly operates at the "lower end" of the rental market compared with BW. It has more properties and charges lower rents per property. It is likely that the housing stock is in poorer condition, and so necessitates more ongoing repairs and maintenance. Attention should be given to getting the best possible deals from suppliers on repair work, perhaps negotiating a "fixed fee" in the same way as BW has done. It is surprising that staffing levels are the same for both companies as AW has more than twice as many properties.

Overall though, it should be noted that the two organisations have totally different objectives that may well go some way towards explaining these differences.

(c)   AV has chosen to benchmark itself against BW, a profit seeking company operating in the same sector. There are a number of **advantages** to this chosen method of benchmarking. Firstly, it is method of **learning from the success of BW and for learning and applying best practices**. Secondly, it will help AV in **assessing its current positioning and identifying any gaps in performance**.

However, there are a number of **drawbacks**. Firstly, this benchmarking exercise will be **costly in terms of time and money**. Before investing any more funds in the exercise, it is important that AV's directors determine if the cost of the exercise is less than the benefit. Secondly, **BW may not be the best practice organisation**. How was this benchmarking partner chosen? Another drawback is that **too much attention may be paid to the aspects of performance that are measured as a result of the benchmarking exercise**, to the detriment of the organisation's overall performance.

Finally and most importantly, as mentioned previously, **the two organisations differ fundamentally because of their objectives**. The objectives of not-for-profit organisations like AV can vary significantly. AV's primary objective is to "meet the accommodation needs of persons in its locality". So, it is likely to want to keep as many people as possible in accommodation regardless of cost. How can it measure whether or not it has met this non quantitative objective? Could it in fact have provided more properties if it had adopted different policies relating to staff or repairs?

BW has a primary objective of maximising profit. This is a clear and measureable objective that will probably lead BW to provide high quality accommodation in desirable areas that will generate high revenues and profits. This will support high rents (the average property rental for BW is $120 per week compared to $52 per week for AV) and will necessitate quality repairs and maintenance and customer service levels. Whilst efficiency will still be important for BW, to some extent it can pass on higher costs to its tenants by increasing rents.

AV on the other hand will seek to maintain low rents, and to provide as much housing as possible within its budgetary constraints. This will necessitate a very high level of efficiency as it will not seek to pass on high costs to its tenants. So, like any not-for-profit the critical measures of economy, efficiency and effectiveness must be considered.

Because of these fundamental differences AV would be better advised to consider benchmarking against other similar charities. This would give it much more meaningful comparisons as the objectives of the organisations would be more closely aligned. In addition, charitable organisations are generally more willing to share information to their mutual benefit, so such benchmarking partners may be readily found.

The use of a benchmarking partner that shares similar objectives would allow AV to obtain a much more objective comparison for its own performance.

Test your understanding 10

Strengths:	Weaknesses:
• Airports used are better than those used by competitors	• Airports used are worse than those used by the big carriers
• Management skills	• Punctuality
• Lower costs than established airlines	• Cash flows
• Ease of booking flights	• No established safety record
• Recognised logo	• Poorer than average customer service.
• IT facilities	
• Good employee relations.	

Opportunities:	Threats:
• Strong business demand for cheap air fares • Strong leisure demand for cheap air fares • Full exploitation of the Internet • Many secondary airports underused.	• Higher airport charges • Stringent security checks • Entry of subsidiaries of big carriers.

Test your understanding 11

(a) **Strengths:**
- Successful company
- Steady increase in market share
- Experience in the market
- Founder's entrepreneurial skills
- Good designs
- Good quality control
- Keen to exploit to technology
- Strong IT

Weakness:
- Management of information is often out of date – No in-house IT expertise
- No web experience
- Not sure if the new system will generate new sales – Lack of control over store managers
- Out of date reporting from some stores
- Over reliance on IT provider

Opportunities:

- E-trading can provide a new sales channel and revenue stream

- Identification and recording of customer details to enhance customer relationships

- Extension of customer base

- Global market potential

- Cut costs in many areas

- Create a vision of a modern company

- Develop product range further

- Look at employing an IT specialist

Threats:

- Customer resistance to on-line shopping

- Loss of unique identity; may become just another website trader

- Resistance within the company

- Effects on existing personnel and working conditions

- Costs of developing the website may outweigh the benefits

- Security issues

- Loss of competitive edge

Note: marks would be awarded for other relevant points.

(b) It is important to consider how these factors link to performance measurement in Envie Co:

- **Identifying weaknesses:** SWOT analysis has identified that Envie's lack of web experience is a weakness and therefore Envie needs to try to address this weakness and turn it into a strength by developing a website to reach global markets. It will be important for Envie Co to measure revenue and revenue growth for its website in order to assess how well it is performing. The use of SWOT analysis will focus management attention on current strengths and weaknesses of the organisation which will be of assistance in formulating the business strategy. It will also enable management to monitor trends and developments in the changing business environment. Each trend or development may be classified as an opportunity or a threat that will provide a stimulus for an appropriate management response. Management can make an assessment of the feasibility of required actions in order that the company may capitalise upon opportunities whilst considering how best to negate or minimise the effect of any threats.

- **Identifying CSFs:** SWOT analysis has identified unique designs and good quality control as key to the expansion of Envie Co. This therefore suggests that it will be important to have performance measures which look at the effectiveness of the design team and the quality of the products produced.

- **Setting targets:** one of the opportunities identified is 'the extension of the customer base'. This could be linked to financial objectives, such as revenue growth targets for new customers. Envie's managers will need to monitor the targets set to assess how well performance compares to them.

- **Information needs:** Envie Co will need to collect information in relation to measuring and reporting on the KPIs set.

Test your understanding 12

	Market growth (% change in annual market revenue)*	Division's market share (most recent divisional revenue/market revenue)	Relative market share (division's market share/largest competitor's market share)
Premier	14.6%	10%	0.58
Organic	1.9%	78%	3.90
Baby	10.2%	3%	0.12
Convenience	2.8%	3%	0.10

* This is the average growth over the four year period.

The management could use the BCG matrix in order to classify its subsidiaries in terms of their rate of market growth and relative market share.

The model has four categories. These are:

Stars

A star product has a relatively high market share in a growth market.

The **Premier** division is experiencing strong growth in a growing market.

It has a 10% market share and therefore it seems reasonable to categorise the Premier division as a star.

Problem child

They have a relatively low market share in a high growth market. The **Baby** division would appear to fall into this category. The market leader enjoys a 25% share whilst the Baby division appear to be struggling to achieve growth in turnover and hence profits.

Cash cow

A cash cow is characterised by a relatively high market share in a low growth market and should generate significant cash flows.

The **Organic** division appears to be a cash cow since it has a very high market share in what can be regarded as a low growth market.

Dog

A dog is characterised by a relatively low market share in a low growth market and might well be loss making. The **Convenience** division would appear to fall into this category since its market share is very low and it has low growth.

Food for thought has a dog and a problem child that both require immediate attention.

Competitors within the sector will resist any attempts to reduce their share of a low growth or declining market. As far as the problem child is concerned, the management need to devise appropriate strategies to convert them into stars.

Remuneration package

The existing remuneration policy links the divisional manager's bonus to the achievement of the cost budget set at board level. This may be seen as appropriate for the Organic and the Convenience divisions since they are both in low growth markets and therefore adherence to cost budgets should be possible. However, the Premier and Baby divisions are in high growth markets. Therefore, linking the manager's bonus to the achievement of the cost budget may discourage the manager from making the investment that is required to take advantage of the growth opportunity.

There also seems to be an inconsistency between the way the remuneration package is determined and the method used to evaluate divisional performance. Divisional performance is measured using EVA and this is broadly consistent with the company's objective of maximisation of shareholder wealth. However, by failing to link the remuneration policy to EVA and the company's objective, dysfunctional behaviour may occur.

Environmental influences

Chapter learning objectives

Upon completion of this chapter you will be able to:

- discuss the ways in which stakeholder groups operate and how they influence an organisation and its performance measurement and performance management systems (e.g. using Mendelow's matrix)

- discuss the social and ethical issues that may impact on strategy formulation, and consequently, business performance

- assess the impact of different risk appetites of stakeholders on performance management

- evaluate how risk and uncertainty play an important role in long term strategic planning and decision-making that relies upon forecasts and exogenous variables

- apply different risk analysis techniques in assessing business performance such as maximax, maximin, minimax regret and expected values

- discuss the need to consider the environment in which an organisation is operating when assessing its performance using models such as PEST and Porter's 5 forces, including areas:

  - political climate

  - market conditions

- evaluate how models such as SWOT analysis, Boston Consulting Group, Porter's generic strategies and Porter's 5 Forces may assist in the performance management process.

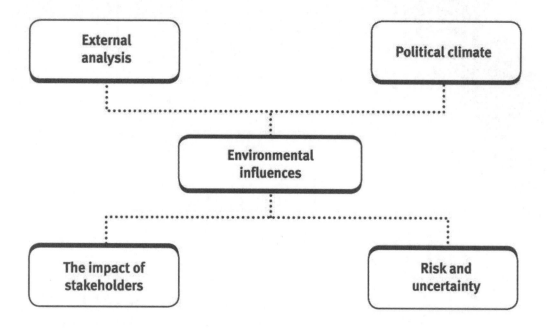

1 Assumed knowledge

Chapter 2 builds on the following knowledge from other exams:

PM

Risk and uncertainty including:

- expected values (EVs)

- maximax

- maximin

- minimax regret

SBL

- Stakeholders

- Porter's 5 forces and PEST

2 Introduction

This chapter focuses on Sections A and B of the syllabus. All organisations will be impacted by the environment in which they operate and it is imperative that they consider the effect that factors such as risk, government regulations and social/ethical issues will have on performance.

3 External analysis

3.1 Introduction

As mentioned above, it is important that an organisation considers the impact of external factors on its performance. The organisation can use two different models when considering this impact. Each model focuses on a different level in the external environment.

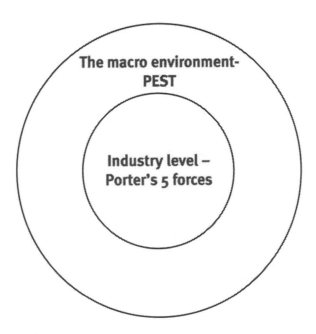

External analysis forms an important part of the 'strategic analysis' stage of the strategic planning process (as reviewed in Chapter 1).

3.2 PEST analysis

The PEST model looks at the macro-environment and its influence on organisational performance, using the following headings:

Heading	Examples
Political factors	• Taxation policy
	• Government stability
	• Foreign trade regulations
	• Taxation
	• Employment law
	• Monopoly legislation
	• Environmental protection legislation
Economic factors	• Interest rates
	• Inflation
	• Unemployment
	• Business cycles
Social factors	• Population demographics
	• Social mobility
	• Income distribution
	• Lifestyle changes

	• Attitudes to work and leisure
	• Levels of education and consumerism
	• How to produce goods with minimal environmental damage
Technological factors	• Speed of technological transfer
	• Rates of obsolescence

(**Note:** This model is sometimes referred to as PESTEL. The additional 'E' is for environmental factors (included as part of social factors in PEST) and the additional 'L' is for legal factors (included as part of political factors in PEST)).

The key issue in APM is to appreciate that, **as well as being used for strategic analysis, this model can be used to identify key performance management issues**. For example:

- PEST analysis can assist in the **identification of relevant CSFs and the development of KPIs** linked to these. For example, an organisation may decide to source supplies from politically stable countries or may adapt its product portfolio to reflect social factors such as a change in consumer tastes.

- Changes in the macro environment may result in the **revision of KPIs and the targets** based around these KPIs.

- **Risk and uncertainty** in the macro environment can be **identified** and **monitored** and **action** can be taken to manage it.

Illustration 1 – PEST and performance management

PEST can be used to identify key performance management issues:

Identifying CSFs and KPIs

Current trends have indicated that British consumers have moved towards 'one-stop' and 'bulk' shopping which is due to a variety of social changes. As a result, supermarkets such as Tesco have increased the amount of non-food items for sale. This may be seen as a CSF and necessary to meet the needs of the modern customer. Tesco may develop KPIs around this CSF, for example by measuring the number or proportion of non-food items for sale in each store.

Revising targets

Increasing public concern for the natural environment has resulted in many supermarkets setting targets for say, wastage, recycling and energy efficiency. These targets may need revising if the external environment changes. For example, in the UK it was recently reported that more than two thirds of the bagged salad sold by Tesco ends up being thrown away. As a result of this investigation, Tesco (and a number of other retailers) have put more stringent wastage targets in place, recognising that performance would deteriorate if no action was taken.

PEST analysis and performance measurement

Environmental legislation may have been identified as being particularly important to a chemicals producer, in which case it should set up a series of targets to measure compliance. For example:

- level of fines

- number of environmental prosecutions

- number of environmental enforcement actions

- number of 'notifiable' incidents (local legislation will define what is 'notifiable' and what is not)

- percentage of employees working within an ISO 14001 compliant Environmental Management System

- the firm's rating in independent benchmarking such as the 'Business in the Environment' Index.

3.3 Porter's 5 forces model

The level of competition in the industry can also affect an organisation's performance. All businesses in a particular industry are likely to be subject to similar pressures that determine how attractive the sector is. Industry attractiveness depends on five factors or forces:

The **stronger each of the five forces is, the lower the profitability of the industry.**

Porter's 5 forces

- **Competitive rivalry:** There will be a tough environment if there are many competitors but a much easier one if there is a monopoly.

- **Buyer's bargaining power:** A few, large customers can exert powerful bargaining power. Many, small customers find it harder to apply pressure.

- **Supplier's bargaining power:** A monopoly supplier of a vital component can apply great pressure. Any one of many suppliers of an ordinary component cannot.

- **Threat from potential entrants:** The key issue here is to assess barriers to entry. For example, high capital costs, know-how and regulation of all present barriers to entry which will help to reduce competition.

- **Threat from substitutes:** The level of the threat is determined by relative price/performance.

Porter's 5 forces and performance management

Porter's 5 forces model can be used for strategic analysis and can also be used to identify key performance management issues.

When conducting a 5 forces assessment an organisation should consider:

- how to measure the strength of the forces

- how reliable those measurements are

- how to manage the forces identified to optimise organisational performance. The organisation should:

  - avoid business sectors which are unattractive because of the 5 forces

  - try to mitigate the effects of the 5 forces. For example, supplier power is lessened if a long-term contract is negotiated or competition is reduced by taking over a rival.

- suitable performance indicators to monitor the forces.

It is important that an organisation considers its performance in the context of its industry. For example, rising supplier prices may initially be blamed on an inefficient purchasing function. However, on further investigation it may be found that the industry is supplied by a relatively small number of large suppliers who have the power to increase prices.

Illustration 2 – Supplier's bargaining power

In 2016, the supermarket giant, Tesco, and the UK's largest food manufacturer, Unilever, became locked in a battle over wholesale prices. A fall in the value of UK Sterling as a result of the UK's decision in 2016 to leave the European Union left suppliers such as Unilever with higher costs for imported goods.

As a result, Unilever had wanted to raise its prices by 10%. However, Tesco refused to pay the additional amount resulting in Unilever exercising their power and halting supply. Unilever, recognising the importance of its income stream from Tesco, did eventually compromise ensuring much loved brands such as Persil washing powder and Marmite spread were fully available on Tesco's shelves again.

As part of its strategic performance evaluation, a business could assess the strength of the forces it is facing using suitable metrics:

Threat	Possible metrics
Threat from potential entrants	• Brand value • Customer loyalty • % of revenue protected by patents
Competitive rivalry	• Market share • Market growth • Market capacity
Threat from substitutes	• Price of substitutes • Quality/performance of substitutes
Buyers' bargaining power	• Number of buyers • Size of buyers • Switching costs • Elasticity of demand
Suppliers' bargaining power	• Number of suppliers • Size of suppliers • Switching costs • Quality/price of suppliers used.

Test your understanding 1

PEST and Porter's 5 forces model

In the United Kingdom (UK), railways are facing major challenges. Customers are complaining about poor services. The government is reluctant to spend vast amounts of public money on developing the decaying infrastructure. The inflated costs of commuting by car, such as fuel and congestion charges, are increasing the number of people wanting to use the railways.

Required:

Use PEST and Porter's 5 forces to identify the issues in the external environment and discuss the impact of these factors on the performance of the railways in the UK.

4 The impact of stakeholders

4.1 Introduction

 A **stakeholder** of an organisation is anyone affected by the organisation.

The mission and objectives of an organisation need to be developed with the needs of the stakeholders in mind.

4.2 Stakeholders' influence on business performance

- The interest and power of different stakeholder groups can affect an organisation's performance. A stakeholder isn't simply any party that is affected by the organisation but **they can also have a huge influence on organisational performance**. This is explored in more detail in the discussion of 'stakeholder mapping' below.

- In addition, the **interests of different stakeholder groups might affect the areas of performance that are measured**.

Illustration 3 – Stakeholders' influence

The airline, Ryanair, has regular labour relations problems with pilots, cabin attendants and check-in staff. For example, in 2017 pilots at Ryanair threatened a mass strike (and possible desertion to a competitor airline) if there were not significant improvements in pay and conditions. Ryanair cannot operate without these staff so these employees have great power and have shown that they are happy to exercise that power.

 Illustration 4 – Strategic planning and stakeholder needs

When planning, management has to take into account stakeholder requirements, power and ambition. For example, there is no point devising changes to production methodologies if:

- employees will not be prepared to adapt to them

- customers do not like the quality of what is offered

- suppliers cannot supply parts at the required frequency.

4.3 Stakeholder mapping

Mendelow's matrix looks at the level of power and interest of different stakeholder groups.

Managers can make use of Mendelow's matrix to help manage stakeholders' conflicting demands and to establish its priorities in terms of managing stakeholders' expectations.

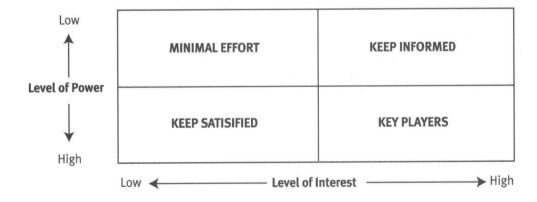

Mendelow's matrix

- **Key players:** These stakeholders are the major drivers of change and could stop management plans and hinder success if not satisfied. Their participation in the planning process is vital.

- **Keep satisfied:** These stakeholders have high power and need to be reassured of the outcome of the strategy well in advance to stop them from gaining interest and negatively impacting business performance.

- **Keep informed:** These stakeholders are interested in the strategy but lack power. Managers must justify their plans to these stakeholders. Otherwise they will gain power by joining forces with other stakeholders.

- **Minimal effort:** These stakeholders lack interest and power and are more likely than others to accept what they are told and follow instructions.

Test your understanding 2

Chatman Theatre is a charitable trust with the objective of making multicultural films and stage productions available to a regional audience. The organisation is not for profit. The aim is to bring diversity of films, plays and dance that would otherwise be inaccessible to a regional audience.

The theatre needs to have strict budget focus, since a charity can become bankrupt. In order to achieve the required income, relationships must be built with a range of stakeholders.

Required:

Identify a few key stakeholders and ideas that would assist in building relationships and hence improving performance.

4.4 Stakeholder conflict

Stakeholders' requirements and aspirations often conflict:

Shareholders want increased profit	←→	Employees want increased wages
Shareholders want increased profit	←→	Customers want lower prices and higher quality
Customers want 24/7 operations	←→	Employees want 9 – 5, 5 days/week
Suppliers want long-term orders	←→	Managers want to retain flexibility

Unless these conflicts are managed, performance will be affected.

Resolving conflicting objectives (Cyert and March)

Management can seek to manage conflicting objectives through the following:

- Prioritisation

- Negotiation and 'satisficing'

- Sequential attention

- Side payments

- Exercise of power.

Resolving conflicting (Cyert and March)

Prioritisation – this could follow from Mendelow's matrix above.

Negotiation and 'satisficing' – finding the minimum acceptable outcome for each group to achieve a compromise.

Sequential attention – each period a different stakeholder group is focused upon, e.g. the workers' canteen could be updated this year with the implication that employees should not expect any improvements in working conditions for the next few years.

Side payments – this can often involve benefiting a group without giving them what they actually want, e.g. the local community may be concerned with cuts in jobs and increased pollution but the firm seeks to placate them by building new sports facilities and sponsoring a local fete.

Exercise of power– when a deadlock is resolved by a senior figure forcing through a decision simply based on the power they possess.

Test your understanding 3

The trustees of a museum are faced with the following conflicting objectives:

- to educate the public

- to preserve antiquities for study and research.

Required:

Give two examples of policies that would be affected by the prioritisation of these objectives.

5   The impact of ethical issues

5.1 Ethics

- Ethics is a set of moral principles that guide behaviour, based on what is 'felt' to be right.

- Comprises principles and standards that govern business behaviour.

- Actions can be judged to be right or wrong, ethical or unethical by individuals inside or outside the organisation.

For example, is it ethical to:

- experiment on animals?

- drill for oil?

- build roads through the countryside?

- allow smoking in public areas?

- pay senior executives large increases in salary?

- train students to pass exams?

> **Illustration 5 – Nestle and Ethics**
>
> Nestle was criticised in the past for taking advantage of the poor and uneducated populations in developing countries in order to increase their own profits.
>
> The company gave gifts and incentives to local health officials, as encouragement in promoting their baby milk formula and therefore discouraging breast feeding. Nestle employees were heard telling midwives that 'all western women use formula to feed their babies, so that they grow up big and strong'.
>
> Nestle didn't educate mothers about sterilising bottles and therefore mothers mixed the formula with dirty water at the cost of many babies' health. The free samples provided to mothers in hospitals and clinics soon dried up and mothers then had to pay almost western prices for the baby milk formula, a price that most families could not afford.

Ethics and performance management

Apart from any moral duty to be ethical, the prime purpose of a business is to maximise shareholder wealth and the chance of this happening is increased by the adoption of ethical behaviour.

Test your understanding 4

Required:

How can the adoption of ethical behaviour by an organisation help to assist to maximise shareholder wealth?

5.2 Corporate social responsibility

Corporate social responsibility (CSR) refers to the idea that a company should be sensitive to the needs of all stakeholders in its business operations and not just shareholders. As such, ethics is just one dimension of corporate social responsibility.

CSR and performance management

By aligning the company's core values with the values of society, the company can improve its reputation and ensure it has a long term future.

Benefits of a CSR strategy

- Differentiation – the firm's CSR strategy can act as a method of differentiation.

- High calibre staff will be attracted and retained due to the firm's CSR policies.

- Brand strengthening – due to the firm's honest approach.

- Lower costs – can be achieved in a number of ways, e.g. due to the use of less packaging or energy.

- The identification of new market opportunities and of changing social expectations.

- An overall increase in profitability as a result of the above – project.

- NPVs will increase due to increased sales, lower costs, an extended project life and a lower level of risk.

Test your understanding 5

Required:

Many commentators believe that CSR is a morally correct pursuit, but there are powerful arguments against it. Identify and discuss these arguments.

CSR and metrics

It is really important for the organisation to have some clear goals in mind with regards to its CSR strategy.

Remember, **things that get measured get done** more often than things that are not measured. Therefore, the company should measure the result of any CSR programme using appropriate metrics.

Test your understanding 6

RFG has set up manufacturing plants in many developing countries, some of which have much lower legislation standards regarding health and safety than RFG's target markets. To improve its global reputation, the firm wishes to improve its performance for health and safety.

Required:

Suggest some metrics for measuring health and safety.

6 Political climate

6.1 Introduction

This area was introduced when we looked at PEST. However, it will now be explored in more detail.

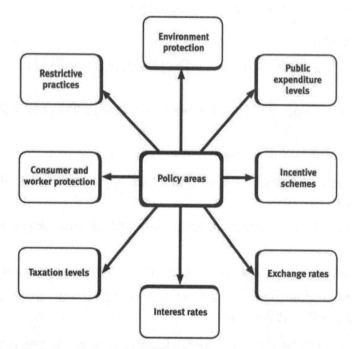

Test your understanding 7

Required:

Give some examples of areas of government policy that are likely to affect a multinational electronics company and how the impact will be felt?

Porter's view

The influence of government on an industry

Porter identifies seven ways in which a government can affect the structure of an industry.

- **Capacity expansion.** The government can take actions to encourage firms or an industry as a whole to increase or cut capacity. Examples include capital allowances to encourage investment in equipment; regional incentives to encourage firms to locate new capacity in a particular area, and incentives to attract investment from overseas firms. The government is also (directly or indirectly) a supplier of infrastructure such as roads and railways, and this may influence expansion in a particular area.

- **Demand.** The government is a major customer of business in all areas of life and can influence demand by buying more or less. It can also influence demand by legislative measures. The tax system for cars is a good example: a change in the tax relief available for different engine sizes has a direct effect on the car manufacturers' product and the relative numbers of each type produced. Regulations and controls in an industry will affect the growth and profits of the industry, for example minimum product quality standards.

- **Divestment and exit.** A firm may wish to sell off a business to a foreign competitor or close it down, but the government might prevent this action because it is not in the public interest (there could be examples in health, defence, transport, education, agriculture and so on).

- **Emerging industries may be controlled by the government.** For instance governments may control numbers of licences to create networks for next generation mobile phones.

- **Entry barriers.** Government policy may restrict investment or competition or make it harder by use of quotas and tariffs for overseas firms. This kind of protectionism is generally frowned upon by the World Trade Organisation, but there may be political and economic circumstances in which it becomes necessary.

- **Competition policy.** Governments might devise policies which are deliberately intended to keep an industry fragmented, preventing one or two producers from having too much market share.

- **New product adoption.** Governments regulate the adoption of new products (e.g. new drugs) in some industries. They may go so far as to ban the use of a new product if it is not considered safe (a new form of transport, say). Policies may influence the rate of adoption of new products, e.g. the UK government 'switch off' of the analogue television networks by 2012, effectively forcing users to buy digital cable or satellite services.

Legislation and regulation

Strategic planners cannot plan intelligently without a good working knowledge of the laws and regulations that affect their own companies and the businesses they operate in.

- There is an almost endless list of laws, or categories of legislation, that affect business enterprises in domestic, national or international dimensions. The main categories are listed below:
  - local by-laws (for example planning permission, construction of roads, licences)
  - labour legislation (such as safety at work, employee protection, redundancy payments)
  - trade union legislation
  - consumer protection legislation
  - company legislation
  - taxation legislation
  - anti-trust (monopolies) legislation and rulings
  - trade legislation (e.g. countries restricted for export) – business legislation (e.g. contract and agency law) – social legislation such as welfare benefits.
- At a more general level, laws are passed that enable government to levy taxes which will have an impact both on demand and the organisation's profits.
- There are special regulatory regimes for particular industries or sectors, such as nuclear energy, transport, broadcasting or food.
- Legislation is becoming more complex, particularly for those companies that trade internationally where the interface, indeed probable conflict, between domestic laws, the host country's laws, and probably also the laws of the trading block of nations the host country belongs to, provides an extremely complicated legal scenario.

Government and the public sector

In public sector organisations the government is the major stakeholder. This can have a number of particular impacts:

- the motivation to meet customer needs may be reduced
- the consequences of failure to provide an appropriate level of service for the organisation and the individual are reduced

KAPLAN PUBLISHING

- being dependent on government policy also means that objectives may change rapidly as policy changes and this political dimension reduces the scope of management options and increases the time for decisions to be taken

- when the public sector companies are privatised they may still remain subject to elaborate regulatory regimes. The performance of the operations involved is monitored and measured using various indicators, with the possibility of fines for poor performance or price restrictions imposed by regulators.

Planning for political change

The problem facing strategic planners is how to plan for changes in the political environment. It is necessary to consider what type of political change could affect the enterprise rather than trying to estimate all the political changes that might occur, by:

- examining changes in social behaviour and values, economic activity, and problems arising from the physical infrastructure or environment which can be related to the trend of political actions

- monitoring indicators of possible or intended future government actions and policy. These indicators are obtained from:

  - annual conferences of political parties

  - public utterances of party leaders and seniors – international events

  - directives from international trading groups – political commentators and analysts

  - international summit meetings

  - staged legislation

  - efforts of public pressure groups (particularly with regard to local government policy)

  - political manifestos.

6.2 The impact of fiscal policy and monetary policy

Fiscal and monetary policies are the tools used by governments to control their economies.

Fiscal policy

- Looks at the balance between government income (taxation + borrowing) and expenditure.

Monetary policy

- Is the process by which the government and central bank controls the supply, availability and cost of money.

Fiscal policy	Monetary policy
Government adjusts:	Government adjusts:
• taxation	• money supply
• public borrowing	• interest rates
• public spending.	• exchange rates
	• availability of credit.

Fiscal and monetary policy – more details

Fiscal policy

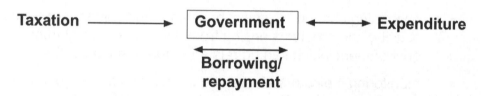

- To stimulate the economy, the government can spend more money. However, if the extra expenditure is met by raising taxes, the public will have less to spend and economic growth will be small. To really get things moving, the government needs to borrow and spend.

- The economy can also be stimulated by cutting tax and allowing individuals to spend more. If government expenditure is cut to match the tax cuts, there will be little stimulation, so government borrowing is needed to keep government spending high.

- Too much economic stimulation is likely to cause inflation as consumers compete for resources and services.

Monetary policy

Changes in monetary policy will influence the following factors:

- The availability and cost of finance. These in turn affect the level of investment and expenditure by firms.

- The level of consumer demand e.g. low interest rates will stimulate the economy as it is cheaper to borrow and savings do not earn a lot of interest. Similarly, the easy availability of credit also encourages borrowing and spending).

- The level of inflation.

- The level of exchange rates.

Impact of macroeconomics

In order for macroeconomic policy to work, its instruments must have an impact on economic activity. This means that it must affect the business sector. It does so in two broad forms.

Macroeconomic policy will influence the level of aggregate demand (AD) and thus activity in the economy as a whole. (AD is the total demand for goods and services in the economy.)	<ul><li>The level of AD is central to the determination of the level of unemployment and the rate of inflation.</li><li>If AD is too low, unemployment might result; if AD is too high, inflation induced by excess demand might result.</li><li>Changes in AD will affect all businesses to varying degrees. Thus effective business planning requires that businesses can:<ul><li>– predict the likely thrust of macroeconomic policy in the short to medium-term</li><li>– predict the consequences for sales growth of the overall stance of macroeconomic policy and any likely changes in it.</li></ul></li><li>The more stable government policy is, the easier it is for businesses to plan, especially in terms of investment, employment and future output capacity.</li></ul>
Macroeconomic policy may influence the costs of the business sector.	<ul><li>Macroeconomic policy may involve changes in **exchange rates**. This can have the effect of raising the domestic price of imported goods. Most businesses use some imported goods in the production process; hence this leads to a rise in production costs.</li><li>**Fiscal policy** involves the use of **taxation**: changes in tax rates or the structure of taxation will affect businesses. For example, a change in the employer's national insurance contribution will have a direct effect on labour costs for all businesses. Changes in indirect taxes (for example, a rise in sales tax or excise duties) will either have to be absorbed or the business will have to attempt to pass on the tax to its customers.</li></ul>

> - **Monetary policy** involves changes in **interest rates**; these changes will directly affect firms in two ways:
>   - costs of servicing debts will change especially for highly geared firms
>   - the viability of investment will be affected since all models of investment appraisal include the rate of interest as one, if not the main, variable.

Test your understanding 8

Required:

A carpet retailer imports carpets and sells them domestically. The domestic currency does not have a fixed exchange rate with any other currency. What are the likely effects on this business of a rise in domestic interest rates?

Test your understanding 9

Suppose the two main political parties in a hypothetical country have the following priorities:

	Party A (currently in government)	**Party B** (the opposition)
Priorities	• Low unemployment	• Low inflation
Policy choices	• Fiscal policy • Increase government spending to boost demand to create jobs • High government intervention in business	• Monetary policy • Increase interest rates to reduce inflation • Low taxes • Low levels of intervention

Recent polls suggest that Party B could win the next election.

Required:

Comment on the implications of this for a major construction company based in the country concerned.

6.3 Supply-side policies

- Supply-side economists take the view that **the supply of suitable, cost-effective and adequate materials, services and labour is vital to an economy**.

- If these resources are made available, then they will be used to produce goods and services.

- The amounts paid to suppliers and employees will create the extra income necessary to buy the extra outputs.

- For example, improving education would increase the supply of educated workers in the workforce.

Supply side policies examples

Supply-side policies are therefore largely anti-regulation and anti-government interference. For example, supply-side economists would claim that:

- wage regulation prevents the labour market from achieving full employment

- government grants encourage weak businesses

- employment legislation limits risk taking and can lead to over manning of industries

- high taxes act as a disincentive to work and enterprise and lead ultimately to lower output, employment and wealth.

6.4 Green policies/externalities

 A **negative externality** is the cost of production experienced by society but not by producers or consumers themselves, for example:

- production, e.g. river pollution from manufacturing

- consumption, e.g. car emissions causing air pollution.

As a result, the government may impose green policies, e.g. an increase in tax on fuel.

7   Risk and uncertainty

7.1 Introduction

Strategic planning deals with future events but these future events cannot always be accurately predicted. Planning must therefore take risk and uncertainty into account.

 Risk is the variability of possible returns. There are a number of possible outcomes and the probability of each outcome is known.

Uncertainty also means that there are a number of possible outcomes. However, the probability of each outcome is not known.

 Exogenous variables are variables that do not originate from within the organisation itself and are not controllable by management, e.g. government policy, weather conditions, state of the economy, competitors' actions etc. Their existence means that strategic planning will always be subject to some risk and uncertainty.

All businesses face risk/uncertainty. Risk management is the process of understanding and managing the risks that an organisation is inevitably subject to.

The impact of exogenous variables

A hospital has developed a new surgical technique as a more expensive alternative to existing treatments. It is considering whether to begin to provide the treatment to all its patients, which would mean building a new facility. In order to inform the decision, the hospital is considering the likely effect of a number of variables.

- The likelihood that another alternative cheaper treatment, either a surgical technique or a drug regime, will be discovered.

- The likelihood that other hospitals will begin to offer similar services which will limit demand.

- Government policy – changes in the way that treatment is funded and therefore whether the costs of the treatment will be paid for.

7.2 Dealing with risk/uncertainty

A number of tools can be used to incorporate the impact of risk/uncertainty.

Tool	Explanation
Scenario planning	Looks at a number of different but plausible future situations. For example, Shell was the only major oil company to have prepared for the shock of the 1970s oil crisis through scenario planning and was able to respond faster than its competitors.
Computer simulations	A modelling technique which shows the effect of more than one variable changing at a time and gives management a view of the likely range and level of outcomes so that a more informed decision can be taken.
Sensitivity analysis	Takes each uncertain factor in turn, and calculates the change that would be necessary in that factor before the original decision is reversed.

Expected values (EVs)	Shows the weighted average of all possible outcomes.
Maximax, maximin and minimax regret	Three different tools for incorporating risk/uncertainty. The attitude of management towards risk will determine which of the three tools is used.

EVs and maximin, maximax and minimax regret will be explored in more detail below:

7.3 Expected values (EVs)

The expected value is the average return that will be made if a decision is repeated again and again.

Each of the possible outcomes is weighted with their relative probability of occurring. It is the weighted arithmetic mean of the outcomes.

The formula for expected values is: **EV = $\sum$px**

where: x = the value of the possible outcome

p = the probability of the possible outcome.

Illustration 6 – Simple EV calculation

Returns from a new restaurant depend on whether a company decides to open in the same area. The following estimates are made:

Competitor opens up	Probability (p)	Project NPV (x)	px
Yes	0.30	($10,000)	($3,000)
No	0.70	$20,000	$14,000
			————
			$11,000

The EV = $\sum$px = $11,000. Since the expected value shows the long run average outcome of a decision which is repeated time and time again, it is a useful decision rule for a **risk neutral decision maker**. This is because a risk neutral decision maker neither seeks nor avoids risk; he is happy to accept the average outcome.

Pay-off (profit) tables

A pay-off (profit) table is useful for calculating EVs when there is a range of possible outcomes and a variety of possible responses.

Illustration 7 – Simple pay-off (profit) table

Geoffrey Ramsbottom runs a kitchen that provides food for various canteens throughout a large organisation. A particular salad generates a profit of $2 based on a selling price of $10 and a cost of $8. Daily demand is as follows:

Demand	Probability
40 salads	0.10
50 salads	0.20
60 salads	0.40
70 salads	0.30
	———
	1.00

Required:

The kitchen must prepare the salad in batches of 10. Its staff have asked you to help them decide how many salads it should supply per day.

Answer:

There are a range of possible outcomes (levels of demand) and a variety of possible responses (number of salads to supply) and therefore it is useful to construct a payoff table:

Daily demand	Prob (p)	Daily supply profit/(loss) outcome (x)			
		40 salads	50 salads	60 salads	70 salads
40 salads	0.10	$80 (W1)	$0	($80)	($160)
50 salads	0.20	$80	$100	$20	($60)
60 salads	0.40	$80	$100	$120	$40
70 salads	0.30	$80	$100	$120	$140
		———	———	———	———
	EV =	$80	$90	$80	$30 (W2)
		———	———	———	———

Workings:

W1 Profit is calculated as follows = 40 salads × $2 = **$80**

W2 EV is calculated as follows = (0.10 × –$160) + (0.20 × –$60) + (0.40 × $40) + (0.30 × $140) = **$30**

Conclusion:

Therefore, based on EVs, daily supply should be **50 salads** since this yields the highest expected value of $90.

In the illustration above, there was only one variable outcome, i.e. the level of demand. However, in some situations there may be more than one variable outcome, for example demand and inflation. In this case, a **two way data table** should be prepared before the EV is calculated.

Test your understanding 10

Confused Company is seeking to establish the likely profit to be generated for the forthcoming year. This is very much dependent upon the anticipated demand, and the impact of inflation upon the fixed costs of the business.

Probabilities have been estimated for both demand and inflation as shown below:

Demand	Probability	Inflation	Probability
Strong	0.20	None	0.30
Normal	0.50	2%	0.50
Weak	0.30	4%	0.20

A **two way data table** has been prepared which estimates the changes in net profit (in $) for a range of changes in demand and inflation:

		Inflation				
		None	1%	2%	3%	4%
Demand	Strong	95,000	85,000	75,000	65,000	55,000
	Normal	60,000	50,000	40,000	30,000	20,000
	Weak	25,000	15,000	5,000	(5,000)	(15,000)

Required:

Prepare a summary that shows:

- the range of possible net profit and loss outcomes

- the combined probability of each outcome

- the expected value of the profit for the year.

Management will be awarded a bonus if profit exceeds $50,000. What are the chances of this occurring?

Usefulness of EVs

Since the expected value shows the long-run average outcome of a decision which is repeated again and again, it is a useful decision tool for a **risk neutral** decision maker. This is because a risk neutral person neither seeks risk nor avoids it; they are happy to accept an average outcome. This technique would not be useful:

- for decisions which occur only once (the EV is the average and not an actual outcome)

- if the probabilities and/ or the values of the various outcomes are unknown or uncertain

- for a non-risk neutral decision maker.

7.4 Maximax, maximin and minimax regret

The **maximax rule** looks at the best possible outcome for each course of action and selects the alternative that maximises the maximum pay-off achievable.

The **maximin rule** looks at the worst possible outcome for each course of action and selects the alternative that maximises the minimum pay-off achievable.

The **minimax regret** looks at the maximum regret (opportunity cost) for each course of action and aims to choose the strategy that minimises the maximum regret.

Illustration 8 – Geoffrey Ramsbottom

Required:

Using the information from illustration 7 decide how many salads should be supplied per day using:

* the maximax rule

* the maximin rule

* the minimax regret rule.

Answer:

(a)   **Maximax**

Daily demand	Prob (p)	Daily supply profit/(loss) outcome (x)			
		40 salads	50 salads	60 salads	70 salads
40 salads	0.10	$80	$0	($80)	($160)
50 salads	0.20	$80	$100	$20	($60)
60 salads	0.40	$80	$100	$120	$40
70 salads	0.30	$80	$100	$120	$140
		——	——	——	——
Maximum profit =		$80	$100	$120	**$140**
		——	——	——	——

The maximax rule involves selecting the alternative that maximises the maximum pay-off achievable. Looking at the table above, the maximum profit achievable is $140. This will be achieved if **70 salads** are supplied.

(b)   Maximin

Daily demand	Prob (p)	Daily supply profit/(loss) outcome (x)			
		40 salads	50 salads	60 salads	70 salads
40 salads	0.10	$80	$0	($80)	($160)
50 salads	0.20	$80	$100	$20	($60)
60 salads	0.40	$80	$100	$120	$40
70 salads	0.30	$80	$100	$120	$140
		———	———	———	———
Minimum profit =		**$80**	**$0**	**($80)**	**($160)**
		———	———	———	———

The maximin rule involves selecting the alternative that maximises the minimum pay-off achievable. Looking at the table above, the maximum of the minimum profits is $80. This will be achieved if **40 salads** are supplied.

(c)   Minimax regret

The minimax regret strategy is the one that minimises the maximum regret (opportunity cost). A regret table should be used:

Daily demand	Daily supply regret (opportunity cost)			
	40 salads	50 salads	60 salads	70 salads
40 salads	Right decision	$80 (W1)	$160 (W1)	$240 (W1)
50 salads	$20	Right decision	$80	$160
60 salads	$40	$20	Right decision	$80
70 salads	$60	$40	$20	Right decision
	———	———	———	———
Maximum regret =	**$60**	$80	$160	$240
	———	———	———	———

Therefore, to minimise the maximum regret, 40 salads should be supplied.

(W1): If daily demand is 40 salads, it would be the right decision for the business to supply 40 salads since the profit of supplying **40 salads** is the highest, i.e. $80.

- If the business decided instead to supply 50 salads, the regret (opportunity cost) would be the $80 it could have made supplying 40 salads minus the $0 it did make supplying the 50 salads = $80.

> - If the business decided instead to supply 60 salads, the regret (opportunity cost) would be the $80 it could have made supplying 40 salads minus the $80 loss it did make supplying the 60 salads = $160.
>
> - If the business decided instead to supply 70 salads, the regret (opportunity cost) would be the $80 it could have made supplying 40 salads minus the $160 loss it did make supplying the 70 salads = $240.

Usefulness of maximin, maximax and minimax regret

With **maximin** the decision maker chooses the outcome which is guaranteed to minimise his losses. In the process, he loses out on the opportunity to make big profits. It is often seen as a pessimistic approach to decision making (assuming the worst outcome will occur) and is used by decision makers who are **risk averse**. It may be viewed as being an overly pessimistic approach.

With **maximax** the decision maker chooses the outcome which is guaranteed to maximise his profit. In this process he risks making a lower profit. It is often seen as an optimistic approach to decision making (assuming the best outcome will occur) and is used by decision makers who are **risk seeking**. It may be viewed as being an overly optimistic approach.

With **minimax regret** the decision maker chooses the outcome which minimises the maximum regret. In the process, he risks making a lower profit. It is often seen as a technique for a **'sore loser'** who does not want to make the wrong decision.

Each of the above techniques can be used for one-off or repeated decisions.

Question practice

It is useful to take the time to look at scenario-based questions that are in a similar style as the exam questions. Make sure that you attempt the question below and carry out a detailed review of the recommended answer.

Test your understanding 11

Cement Co is a listed company specialising in the manufacture of cement, a product used in the building industry. The company has been a major player in the construction sector of European country, Q, since its formation in 1987. It is passionate about customer care and proud of its active approach to safety and sustainability (recognising the need to minimise any adverse environmental impact of its operations).

The company operates in a very traditional industry but profits can be volatile. Q's economy has been in recession for the last three years and this has had a direct impact on Cement Co's profitability. Shareholders are concerned about this fall in profit and have expressed their desire for a secure return. Competitors, keen to find ways of increasing profit and market share, in these difficult economic circumstances, have started to increase the level of investment in research and development, ensuring their products anticipate and meet the needs of its customers.

When Q entered recession, many workers left the country in search of more lucrative and secure work. This has had a significant impact on Cement Co which is now facing labour shortages and increased labour costs. At the same time, suppliers have also increased their prices putting further pressure on Cement Co's margins.

The company has found that when weather conditions are good, the demand for cement increases since more building work is able to take place. Last year, the weather was so good, and the demand for cement was so great, that Cement Co was unable to meet demand. Cement Co is now trying to work out the level of cement production for the coming year in order to maximise profits. The company doesn't want to miss out on the opportunity to earn large profits by running out of cement again. However, it doesn't want to be left with large quantities of the product unsold at the end of the year, since it deteriorates quickly and then has to be disposed of. The company has received the following estimates about the probable weather conditions and corresponding demand levels for the coming year:

Weather	Probability	Demand
Good	25%	350,000 bags
Average	45%	280,000 bags
Poor	30%	200,000 bags

Each bag of cement sells for $9 and costs $4 to make. If cement is unsold at the end of the year, it has to be disposed of at a cost of $0.50 per bag.

Cement Co has decided to produce at one of the three levels of production to match forecast demand. It now has to decide which level of cement production to select.

As an incentive to increase profitability a new bonus scheme has just been introduced for a select group of Cement Co's directors. A bonus will be received by each of these directors if annual profit exceeds a challenging target.

Required:

(a) Identify the risks facing Cement Co and assess the impact of different risk appetites of managers and shareholders on their response to these risks.

(10 marks)

(b) Evaluate the proposed levels of cement production using methods for decision making under risk and uncertainty and assess the suitability of the different methods used.

(15 marks)

(Total: 25 marks)

7.5 Impact of risk appetite of stakeholders on performance management

As mentioned earlier in the chapter, a business must consider the needs of its stakeholders when making decisions. Different stakeholders will have different risk perspectives or different risk appetites. For example:

- **Shareholders** – may be prepared to take a risk (risk seeking) in order to maximise the possible return, especially since shareholders are able to spread their risk by holding a portfolio of investments. However, shareholders are not always classed as risk seeking. For example, the shareholders of a company that is in financial distress may prefer the business to take a more risk neutral or risk averse approach in order to secure the future of the business.

- **Employees and managers** – they should act in the best interests of the shareholders but this does not always happen since they may be:

  - **risk averse:** employees and managers may be reluctant to take risks, e.g. to invest in a new project, if an unsuccessful outcome would impact their performance evaluation or the survival of the company (and hence their job). Therefore, even though risk taking may be in the best interests of the company and its shareholders they tend to exercise caution and are unwilling to take risks.

  - **risk seeking:** employees and managers may be encouraged to take risks by the promise of huge rewards or bonuses.

Illustration 9 – Risk appetite of employees

The collapse of Lehman brothers, a sprawling global bank, in September 2005, almost brought down the world's financial system. The then governor of the bank of England, Mervyn King, criticised City banks who rewarded staff with huge sums for taking risks and concluded that the credit crisis was caused, in part, by bankers betting on high-risk complex financial products. A culture of risk taking had developed due to the huge potential bonuses and rewards offered to bankers.

Financiers – these include:

- **Venture capitalists** (VCs) – VCs are likely to be rational investors seeking the maximum return for minimum risk. They will invest in a number of companies and so are prepared for some of their investments to fail, provided that some of their investments perform well. Steps will be taken to reduce risks, for example performance will be monitored on a regular basis to ensure that any agreed exit strategy can be achieved. In addition, the VCs will also place employees on the management team so that they can influence decisions.

- **Banks** – traditionally, banks would have been considered to have a reasonably conservative approach to risk with a desire to secure their funds and guarantee returns.

Illustration 10 – Banks and risk taking

As mentioned above, banks are not normally considered to be risk seeking. However, the financial crisis which commenced in 2007 was triggered by US banks giving high risk loans (sub-prime mortgages) to people with poor credit histories. A sharp rise in US interest rates resulted in a huge number of American home owners defaulting on their mortgages. The impact of these defaults were felt across the financial system as many of the mortgages had been sold to big banks who turned them into supposedly low risk securities. However, this assumption proved wrong. In fact, huge uncalculated risks had been taken with the bankers being spurred on by the potential to earn huge bonuses.

Therefore, in order to effectively manage business performance, it will be necessary for the business to align its decisions with the stakeholder's risk appetite.

Student accountant articles: visit the ACCA website, accaglobal.com, to review two articles on 'the risks of uncertainty'.

8 Exam focus

Exam sitting	Area examined	Question number	Number of marks
Sept/ Dec 2017	PEST, Risk	4	25
June 2015	Expected values, decision making under uncertainty	1(iii), (iv)	16
December 2014	Stakeholders	1(ii)	14
June 2014	Risk	3(a)(b)	17
December 2013	PEST	1(ii)	11
June 2013	Porter's 5 forces and risk	3(a)(c)	21
December 2011	Risk	1	35
June 2011	Stakeholders	2(c)	6
December 2010	PEST	4(a)	4

Chapter summary

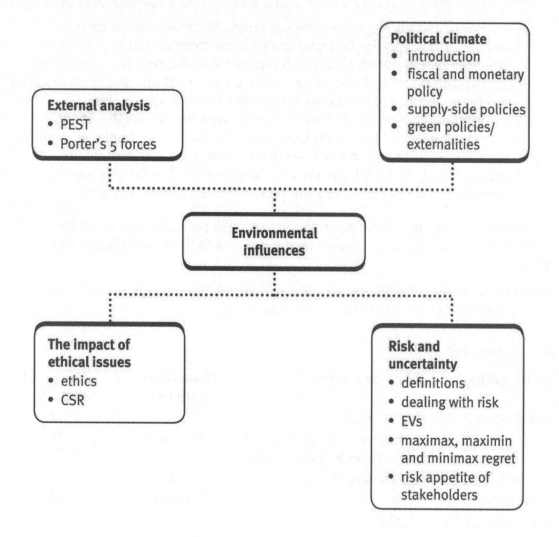

Test your understanding answers

Test your understanding 1

PEST analysis for UK railways

Political

The balance of public-private involvement in the running costs and capital investment for rail development is a major issue. Any changes in government policy could have dramatic consequences for companies operating in the rail industry.

Economic

The growth of commuter travel on the rail system means it is working at close to full capacity. This trend is likely to continue with the rising costs of fuel, making car travel expensive. This, however, can be seen as a positive for rail companies who can cease the opportunity to increase profits and improve performance.

However, there is a need for investment in infrastructure in areas such as longer platforms and new signal systems. Financing this investment may be difficult but the performance of railway companies will deteriorate in the long-term if the investment is not made.

Social

Increasing concerns about reliability, particularly in rural areas, could detract from profitability as passengers switch to more reliable forms of transport.

Concerns about the effect that railway construction and travel has on the environment could again detract from profitability since customers may be lost.

Safety issues on trains and at railway stations – train travel is comparatively very safe but it is still necessary for the railway companies to monitor safety and address any issues identified.

Technological

The development of new train technologies such as high speed railways could result in a long term boost in profit but will require significant investment.

Also following the trends set by air travel by introducing ways to improve the customer experience. For example, offering Internet access and on-train entertainment. Fulfilment of customers' needs could, once again, result in improved performance.

Porter's 5 forces model – UK railways

Competitive rivalry

In certain areas rail operators may be directly competing over the same routes. If the force is medium or high then performance will be negatively impacted.

Threats from substitutes

There are other forms of transport available such as travel by road (e.g. cars and buses) and travel by air. However, the rising cost of petrol and diesel and the inappropriateness of air travel for shorter journeys may make this force low and the performance of the railway companies should not suffer as a result.

Buyers' bargaining power

Severe competition over price with low-cost airlines on longer city routes (but again this would not be a suitable alternative for shorter routes).

Online price comparisons make it easy for customers to select lowest cost option but transparency of ticket prices and types in the UK is still poor.

Overall, this force may be classed as medium and the impact on performance will be limited.

Threat from potential entrants

New companies may enter the market when rail franchises become available for re-tender. For example, Virgin entered the UK market some years ago. Any threat should be investigated and acted on since the entry of any new players could seriously reduce market share and profitability.

Suppliers' bargaining power

With an increasing number of discrete rail and train operators, the allocation of capacity becomes an issue. This is similar to landing slots at airports. Close working relations with suppliers could help to understand this issue and to negotiate the level of service required. If these steps are taken, performance may not suffer.

Test your understanding 2

Loyal customers

Chatman Theatre, which is a charity, can make use of a database to profile their interests and wants. A tailored communication can then be sent.

Given the need to contain costs, this might be by getting customers to sign up to an e-list to get up-to-date news and information on future performances.

They could set up a website with booking facilities and send confirmation by email rather than post.

Develop a friend of the theatre group, giving discounts to regular loyal customers.

First time customers

The website could be linked to other relevant websites, such as local attractions and tourist boards, to attract new customers.

The theatre could produce an information pack to attract new mailing list subscribers. These could be made available in local churches and shops.

Local arts groups

A partnership agreement could be established with arts groups, to co-sponsor events of special interest to given groups of customers.

Local organisations

Try to obtain commercial sponsorship from local companies. Acknowledgement could be given in the monthly programme mailings and preferential facilities offered for corporate hospitality.

Media

Personal invitations could be issued to opening nights, to interview the performers and give an overview of the show.

Note: The above is just a selection of potential relationships with stakeholders.

Test your understanding 3

- **Whether or not the museum should charge an entry fee** – this would discourage some people from going to the museum (compromising the first objective) but would provide extra cash for funding research.

- **Which artefacts should be displayed** – education would require a wide range of exhibits with the most prestigious on display. An emphasis on preservation would prevent the most significant items from being displayed for fear of damage.

Test your understanding 4

- Ethical behaviour is likely to be favoured by: – customers: resulting in higher sales volumes and/or prices.

    - employees: resulting in the attraction/retention of the best employees and increased employee productivity.

    - business collaborators: resulting in increased opportunities for profitable projects.

- Ethical behaviour reduces risk and gives access to cheaper funds which in turn increase project NPVs.

- Unethical behaviour will, at some point be discovered resulting in a damage to reputation and potential legal charges.

Test your understanding 5

- The purpose of a business is to make profits. Profit is a good thing in its own right as it supports stable employment, innovation, allows higher taxes to be paid and makes economies richer. Companies have no need to feel guilty about making profits and buying off some of that guilt by embarking on good works.

- The prime stakeholders are the shareholders and directors should always attempt to maximise shareholder wealth. If directors embark on a CSR programme, have shareholders given permission? It is, after all, shareholders' money that is being used.

- CSR allows directors to feel generous and righteous – but with someone else's money. Better, perhaps, that directors and shareholders make private donations out of their remuneration and dividends.

- What is the democratic basis which companies use to choose between CSR projects? Simply choosing a project because the chief executive likes it does not mean the money is being well spent – the project could be already well-funded.

Test your understanding 6

Suitable metrics could include:

- number of fatalities
- number of permanently disabling injuries
- number of enforcement actions
- accident frequency rate (AFR) e.g. the number of reportable accidents per 100,000 hours worked
- lost time incident frequency rate (LTIFR)
- sickness absence rate
- health and safety training rate (days/employee)
- percentage of employees working within an ISO 18001 compliant Health and Safety Management System.

Test your understanding 7

Areas could include:

Interest rates

Changes in the interest rates for consumer debt may affect demand for luxury goods which may include high-value electronic products.

The company's cost of debt may change, affecting the cost of developing new facilities.

Exchange rates

Changes in interest rates may change the value of profits earned in different countries or the price to consumers of imported goods.

Taxation levels

The level of personal taxation will affect the demand for products. Changes in the company tax regime will affect the returns to shareholders.

Incentive schemes

The availability of incentive schemes may make expanding into certain countries more attractive.

Worker protection

Legislation in this area may have an impact on the requirements for facilities and their costs.

Restrictive practices

These may affect the company's ability to export to certain countries.

Environment protection

The company may need to develop new products which are more economical to run or which use materials which are less harmful to the environment when thrown away.

Test your understanding 8

(1) Customers' mortgages and loans will become more expensive, giving less net disposable income for major purchases, such as new carpets.

(2) Customers will be less motivated to borrow to finance carpet purchase.

(3) The cost of capital will rise so the retailer will be less prepared to undertake major projects.

(4) The domestic currency will strengthen, reducing the cost of imports.

Test your understanding 9

- Higher interest rates will increase the cost of borrowing and the gearing risk of the firm, making it less likely that long-term earnings targets will be met.

- A fall in government spending could see a downturn in orders, particularly if the firm currently is engaged in government contracts (e.g. building roads, hospitals). Future plans may have to be revised to reflect this and alternative strategies sought. Analysis of sales mix between public and private sector contracts will become more important.

- Potentially lower levels of taxation could increase profitability.

- Lower inflation will reduce business uncertainty, making planning easier. Plans may have to be revised to reflect lower inflation.

- Higher unemployment in the economy could allow the firm to reduce planned pay increases.

Test your understanding 10

Possible demand	Possible inflation	Net profit $ = x	Combined prob = p	px ($)	Bonus prob (profit > $50,000)
Strong (prob 0.20)	None (prob 0.30)	95,000	0.20 × 0.30 = 0.06	5,700	0.06
	2% (prob 0.50)	75,000	0.20 × 0.50 = 0.10	7,500	0.10
	4% (prob 0.20)	55,000	0.20 × 0.20 = 0.04	2,200	0.04
Normal (prob 0.50)	None (prob 0.30)	60,000	0.50 × 0.30 = 0.15	9,000	0.15
	2% (prob 0.50)	40,000	0.50 × 0.050 = 0.25	10,000	–
	4% (prob 0.20)	20,000	0.50 × 0.20 = 0.10	2,000	–
Weak (prob 0.30)	None (prob 0.30)	25,000	0.30 × 0.30 = 0.09	2,250	–
	2% (prob 0.50)	5,000	0.30 × 0.50 = 0.15	750	–
	4% (prob 0.20)	(15,000)	0.30 × 0.20 = 0.06	(900)	–
				_____	_____
			EV = ∑px	**38,500**	**0.35**
				_____	_____

Test your understanding 11

(a)   The primary objective of Cement Co, a listed company, will be to maximise shareholder wealth. The directors should, in theory, be acting in the best interests of the shareholders. The shareholders appear to be reasonably risk averse at the moment since they have expressed concern over the fall in profit.

Cement Co is open to a lot of risk and uncertainty:

–   Firstly, Q's economy is in recession which will have a direct impact on Cement Co as house building falls and government contracts are cut.

–   At the same time, the company's costs are increasing due to increases in wages and in suppliers' prices.

–   Cement Co is risking falling behind its competitors who have increased investment in research and development. There is a risk that Cement Co will not be able to meet the needs of its customers as well as its competitors.

–   Cement Co does pride itself on its approach to sustainability and safety. However, the industry is characterised by its negative impact on the environment and poor safety record and therefore it is imperative that Cement Co does not lose focus on achieving their sustainability and safety targets.

–   Finally, volatile weather conditions can have a huge impact on the building industry and on Cement Co's profitability. The weather is clearly something that cannot be controlled but the risk should be appropriately managed.

Directors can take one of three approaches to managing risk:

–   Risk averse directors – will assume the worst outcome and will seek to minimise its effect. Some of Cement Co's directors will be keen to take this approach in the hope of securing a satisfactory return for shareholders and securing their positions.

–   Risk seeking directors – will assume the best outcome and will seek to maximise its effect. Some of the directors will be risk seeking, hoping to secure an outcome that will maximise profitability and their annual bonus.

–   Risk neutral directors – these directors will be interested in the most probable outcome. This would be a sensible approach in situations where the risks remain unaltered and decisions are repeated many times.

(b) Level of cement production

Before any of the techniques for decision making under risk and uncertainty are applied, it will be necessary to construct a payoff table:

DEMAND	Weather	Probability	SUPPLY 350,000 Profit $000	280,000 Profit $000	200,000 Profit $000
350,000	Good	0.25	1,750 (W1)	1,400	1,000
280,000	Average	0.45	1,085 (W2)	1,400	1,000
200,000	Poor	0.30	325	640	1,000

Workings

Profit per bag sold in coming year = $9 – $4 = $5 Loss per bag disposed of = $4 + $0.50 = $4.50

(W1) 350,000 × $5 = $1,750,000

(W2) [280,000 × $5] – [70,000 × $(4.50)] = $1,085,000 etc.

We can now evaluate the proposed levels of cement production using four different methods:

Method 1: Expected Values

Use the probabilities provided in order to calculate the expected value of each of the supply levels.

Good: (0.25 × $1,750,000) + (0.45 × $1,085,000) + (0.30 × $325,000) = $1,023,250

Average: (0.7 × $1,400,000) + (0.3 × $640,000) = $1,172,000 Poor: 1 × $1,000,000 = $1,000,000

The expected value of producing 280,000 bags when conditions are average is the highest at $1,172,000, therefore this supply level should be chosen.

Method 2: Maximin

Identify the worst outcome for each level of supply and choose the highest of these worst outcomes.

	SUPPLY 350,000 Profit $000	280,000 Profit $000	200,000 Profit $000
Worst	325	640	1,000

The highest of these is $1,000,000 therefore choose to supply only 200,000 bags to meet poor conditions.

Method 3: Maximax

Identify the best outcome for each level of supply and choose the highest of these best outcomes.

	SUPPLY		
	350,000	280,000	200,000
	Profit $000	Profit $000	Profit $000
Best	1,750	1,400	1,000

The highest of these is $1,750,000 therefore choose to supply 350,000 bags to meet good conditions.

Method 4: Minimax Regret

For each level of demand, identify the right decision (the supply level which results in the highest profit) and the regret for the other supply levels. Choose the maximum level of regret at each possible supply level and then choose the level of supply that minimises this maximum regret.

	SUPPLY		
DEMAND	350,000	280,000	200,000
	Regret $000	Regret $000	Regret $000
350,000	Right decision	350 (W3)	750
280,000	315 (W4)	Right	400
200,000	675	360	Right decision
Maximum regret	675	360	750

(W3) Regret (opportunity cost) = $1,750,000 – $1,400,000 = $350,000

(W4) Regret (opportunity cost) = $1,400,000 – $1,085,000 = $315,000

Suitability of the different methods

The **maximin** decision rule looks at the worst possible outcome at each supply level and then selects the highest one of these. It is used when the outcome cannot be assessed with any level of certainty. The decision maker therefore chooses the outcome which is guaranteed to minimise his losses. In the process, he loses out on the opportunity of making big profits. It is often seen as the pessimistic approach to decision-making (assuming that the worst outcome will occur) and is used by decision makers who are risk averse. It can be used for one-off or repeated decisions.

The **expected value** rule calculates the average return that will be made if a decision is repeated again and again. It does this by weighting each of the possible outcomes with their relative probability of occurring. It is the weighted arithmetic mean of the possible outcomes. Since the expected value shows the long run average outcome of a decision which is repeated time and time again, it is a useful decision rule for a risk neutral decision maker. This is because a risk neutral person neither seeks risk nor avoids it; they are happy to accept an average outcome. The problem often is, however, that this rule is often used for decisions that only occur once. In this situation, the actual outcome is unlikely to be close to the long run average. For example, with Cement Co, the closest actual outcome to the expected value of $1,172,000 is the outcome of $1,085,000. This is not too far away from the expected value but many of the others are significantly different.

The **maximax** decision rule looks at the best possible outcome at each supply level and then selects the highest one of these. It is used when the outcome cannot be assessed with any level of certainty. The decision maker therefore chooses the outcome which is guaranteed to maximise his gain. In the process, he risks making a lower profit. It is often seen as an optimistic approach to decision making (assuming the best outcome will occur) and is used by decision makers who are risk seeking. It can be used for one-off or repeated decisions.

The **minimax regret** decision rule looks at the maximum regret (opportunity cost) at each level of supply and aims to choose the level of supply which minimises the maximum regret. In the process, he risks making a lower profit. It is often seen as a technique for a 'sore loser' who doesn't want to make the wrong decision.

Approaches to budgets

Chapter learning objectives

Upon completion of this chapter you will be able to:

- evaluate the strengths and weaknesses of alternative budgeting models and compare such techniques as fixed and flexible, rolling, activity based, zero based and incremental

- evaluate different types of budget variances and how these relate to issues in planning and controlling organisations

- discuss and evaluate the application of activity-based management.

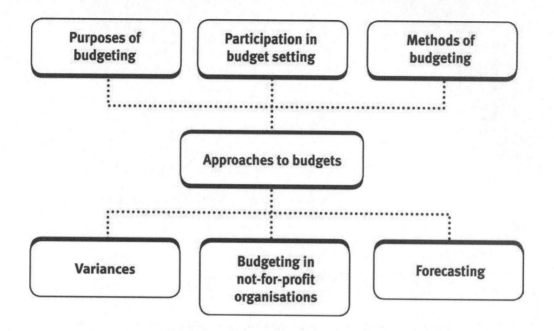

1 Assumed knowledge

Chapter 3 builds on the following knowledge from PM:

- Absorption costing and activity-based costing
- Budgeting
- Standard costing and variances
- Forecasting.

2 Introduction

In chapter 1 we said that 'performance management is any activity that is designed to improve an organisation's performance and ensure that its goals are being met'. Budgeting will assist with performance management since it is an important tool for **planning** and **control** within an organisation and contributes to performance management by providing benchmarks against which to compare actual results (through variance analysis) and develop corrective measures.

It is important that the organisation understands the relative merits of the different budgeting approaches and chooses the approach that is most suitable for them.

3 Purposes of budgeting

A **budget** is a quantitative plan prepared for a specific time period. It is normally expressed in financial terms and prepared for one year.

Budgeting serves a number of purposes:

- Planning
- Control

- Communication
- Co-ordination
- Evaluation
- Motivation
- Authorisation
- Delegation.

Purposes of budgeting

Budgeting serves a number of purposes:

Planning

A budgeting process forces the business to look into the future. This is essential for survival since it stops management from relying on ad hoc or poorly co-ordinated planning.

Control

Actual results are compared against the budget and action is taken as appropriate.

Communication

The budget is a formal communication channel that allows junior and senior staff to converse.

Co-ordination

The budget allows co-ordination of all parts of the business towards a common corporate goal.

Evaluation

Responsibility accounting divides the organisation into budget centres, each of which has a manager who is responsible for its performance. The budget may be used to evaluate the actions of a manager within the business in terms of costs and revenues over which they have control.

Motivation

The budget may be used as a target for managers to aim for. Rewards should be given for operating within or under budgeted levels of expenditure. This acts as a motivator for managers.

> ### Authorisation
>
> The budget acts as a formal method of authorisation for a manager for expenditure, hiring staff and the pursuit of plans contained within the budget.
>
> ### Delegation
>
> Managers may be involved in setting the budget. Extra responsibility may motivate managers. Management involvement may also result in more realistic targets.

4   Participation in budget setting

A **top-down** (or non-participative) budget is one that is imposed on the budget holder by senior management.

A **bottom-up** (or participative) budget involves the divisional managers of an organisation having the opportunity to participate in the setting of the budgets.

It is important that you can discuss the relative merits of these two approaches and recommend the most appropriate method for a given organisation.

Advantages of bottom-up budgeting	Advantages of top-down budgeting
• Improved motivation due to a sense of ownership and empowerment.	• Avoids budgetary slack (i.e. divisional managers may be tempted to set targets that are too easy to achieve).
• It increases divisional managers' understanding (which has an additional benefit if personal targets are set from the budget).	• Avoids dysfunctional behaviour (i.e. divisional managers lack a strategic perspective, focusing on the needs of the division and, as a result, budgets may not be in line with corporate objectives).
• Frees up senior management resource.	• Senior managers retain control.
• Improves the quality of decision making since divisional managers are close to their product markets.	• Budget setting process can be quicker.
	• Avoids the problem of bad decisions from inexperienced managers.

An organisation may use a mix of the two approaches and each approach may be used to a greater or lesser extent in different divisions. It will be up to senior management to decide on the level of central control to exercise, based on the skills and needs of the divisional managers.

5 Methods of budgeting

Different approaches to budgeting were studied in PM. In this exam it is important that you not only understand each of the techniques but that you can compare the techniques and evaluate their relative strengths and weaknesses.

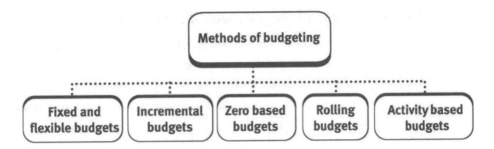

5.1 Fixed and flexible budgeting

A fixed budget is a budget prepared at a single level of activity.

A flexible budget is a budget prepared with the cost behaviour of all cost elements known and classified as either fixed or variable. The budget may be prepared at a number of activity levels and can be 'flexed' or changed to the actual level of activity for budgetary control purposes.

> **Test your understanding 1**
>
> A company has the following budgeted and actual information for a department.
>
> | | Budget | Actual |
> | --- | --- | --- |
> | Level of activity (units of output) | 1,000 | 1,200 |
> | Cost ($) | 20,000 | 23,000 |
>
> **Required:**
>
> (a) Assuming all costs are variable, has the company done better or worse than expected?
>
> (b) If $10,000 of the budgeted costs are fixed costs, the remainder being variable, has the company performed better or worse than expected?

Advantages and disadvantages of flexible budgeting

Advantages	Disadvantages
Should enable better performance evaluation as comparing like with like.	• May be perceived by some as 'moving the goal posts' resulting in demotivation – especially if bonuses are lost despite beating the original budget.
	• Difficulties splitting costs into fixed and variable elements.
	• In the long run it could be argued that all costs are variable.

Test your understanding 2

Redfern hospital is a government funded hospital in the country of Newland. Relevant cost data for the year ended 31 December 20X0 is as follows:

(1) Salary costs per staff member were payable as follows:

	Budget ($)	Actual ($)
Doctors	100,000	105,000
Nurses	37,000	34,500

Budgeted and actual staff were 60 doctors and 150 nurses.

(2) Budgeted costs for the year based on 20,000 patients per annum were as follows:

	$	Variable cost (%)	Fixed cost (%)
Other staff costs	1,440,000	100	–
Catering	200,000	70	30
Cleaning	80,000	35	65
Other operating costs	1,200,000	30	70
Depreciation	80,000	–	100

Variable costs vary according to the number of patients.

(3) The actual number of patients for the year was 23,750. Actual costs (excluding the cost of doctors and nurses) incurred during the year were as follows:

	$
Other staff costs	1,500,000
Catering	187,500
Cleaning	142,000
Other operating costs	1,050,000
Depreciation	80,000

Required:

Prepare a statement which shows the actual and budgeted costs for Redfern hospital in respect of the year ended 31 December 20X0 on a comparable basis.

5.2 Incremental budgets

An **incremental budget** starts with the previous period's budget or actual results, and adds (or subtracts) an incremental amount to cover inflation and other known changes.

Suitability

- It is suitable for stable businesses, where costs are not expected to change significantly.

- There should be good cost control.

- There should be limited discretionary costs.

Advantages	Disadvantages
• Quickest and easiest method. • Assuming that the historic figures are acceptable, only the increment needs to be justified. • Avoids 'reinventing the wheel'.	• Builds in previous problems and inefficiencies. • Uneconomic activities may be continued. • Managers may spend up to their budget to ensure that they get an increment from the highest possible base figure in the following year.

Incremental approach to budgets

AW produces two products, A and C. In the last year (20X4) it produced 640 units of A and 350 units of C incurring costs of $672,000. Analysis of the costs has shown that 75% of the total costs are variable. 60% of these variable costs vary in line with the number of A produced and the remainder with the number of C.

The budget for the year 20X5 is now being prepared using an incremental budgeting approach. The following additional information is available for 20X5:

- All costs will be 4% higher than the average paid in 20X4.

- Efficiency levels will remain unchanged.

- Expected output of A is 750 units and of C is 340 units.

Required:

What is the budgeted total variable cost of product C (to the nearest $100) for the full year 20X5?

Solution:

20X4 costs:

Total variable costs	=	75% × $672,000	=	$504,000
Proportion relating to product C	=	40% × $504,000	=	$201,600
Cost per unit of product C	=	$201,600/350	=	$576

20X5 budget costs:

Inflated cost per unit of C	=	1.04 × $576	=	$599.04
Total variable cost for product C	=	340 × $599.04	=	$203,674

i.e. $203,700 to nearest $100.

Question practice

The NW Entertainments Company (NWEC) is a privately owned organisation which operates an amusement park in a rural area within the North West region of a country which has a good climate all year round. The amusement park comprises a large fairground with high-quality rides and numerous attractions designed to appeal to people of all ages.

The park is open for 365 days in the year.

Each day spent by a guest at the park is classed as a 'Visitor Day'. During the year ended 30 November 20X3 a total of 2,090,400 visitor days were paid for and were made up as follows:

Visitor category	% of total visitor days
Adults	40
14–18 years of age and Senior Citizens	20
Under 14 years of age	40

Two types of admission pass are available for purchase, these are:

The 'One-day Visitor's pass' and the 'Two-day Visitor's pass', which entitles the holder of the pass to admission to the amusement park on any two days within the year commencing 1 December.

The pricing structure was as follows:

(i) The cost of a One-day pass for an adult was $40. Visitors aged 14–18 years and Senior Citizens receive a 25% discount against the cost of adult passes. Visitors aged below 14 years receive a 50% discount against the cost of adult passes.

(ii) The purchase of a Two-day Visitor's pass gave the purchaser a 25% saving against the cost of two One-day Visitor's passes.

(iii) 25% of the total visitor days were paid for by the purchase of One-day passes. The remainder were paid for by the purchase of Two-day passes.

Total operating costs of the park during the year amounted to $37,600,000.

KAPLAN PUBLISHING

NWEC receives income from traders who provide catering and other facilities to visitors to the amusement park. There are 30 such traders from whom payments are received. The amount of the payment made by each trader is dependent upon the size of the premises that they occupy in the amusement park as shown in the following summary:

Size of premises	No. of Annual Traders	Payment per Trader
		$
Large	8	54,000
Medium	12	36,000
Small	10	18,000

The income from each trader is received under 3 year contracts which became effective on 1 December 20X3. The income is fixed for the duration of each contract.

All operating costs of the park incurred during the year ending 30 November 20X4 are expected to increase by 4%. This has led to a decision by management to increase the selling price of all categories of admission passes by 4% with effect from 1 December 20X3. Management expect the number of visitor days, visitor mix and the mix of admission passes purchased to be the same as in the previous year.

NWEC also own a 400 bedroom hotel with leisure facilities, which is located 20 kilometres from the amusement park.

During the year ended 30 November 20X3, the charge per room on an all-inclusive basis was $100 per room, per night. The total operating costs of the hotel amounted to $7,950,000. Average occupancy during the year was 240 rooms per night. The hotel is open for 365 days in the year.

It is anticipated that the operating costs of the hotel will increase by 4% in the year ending 30 November 20X4. Management have decided to increase the charge per room, per night by 4% with effect from 1 December 20X3 and expect average occupancy will remain at the same level during the year ending 30 November 20X4.

The revenue of the hotel is independent of the number of visitors to the amusement park.

Required:

Prepare a statement showing the budgeted net profit or loss for the year to 30 November 20X4.

Answer

NWEC Budgeted Profit and Loss Statement for year to 30 November 20X4

Amusement Park – admission receipts:	$	$
One-day pass:		
Adults:	8,696,064	
14–18 years, senior citizens	3,261,024	
Under 14 years	4,348,032	
Two-day pass:		
Adults:	19,566,144	
14–18 years, senior citizens	7,337,304	
Under 14 years	9,783,072	
		52,991,640
Other revenue Income from traders		1,044,000
Total revenue – park		54,035,640
Operating costs		39,104,000
Budgeted profit of park		14,931,640
Hotel income	9,110,400	
Hotel operating costs	8,268,000	
Budgeted profit of hotel		842,400
		15,774,040

Workings:

No. of Visitor days for year to 30 November 20X4	= 2,090,400
One-day passes = 2,090,400 × 25%	= 522,600
Two-day passes (2,090,400 × 75%)/2	= 783,900

Admission fees applicable from 1 December 20X3. (increased by 4% per annum).

	One-day pass ($)	Two-day pass ($)
Adults	41.60 (40*1.04)	62.40 (41.60*2 less 25%)
14–18 years; senior citizens	31.20 (30*1.04)	46.80 (31.20*2 less 25%)
Under 14's	20.80 (20*1.04)	31.20 (20.80*2 less 25%)

Split	One-day pass revenue			Two-day pass revenue		
40%	209,040	$41.60	$8,696,064	313,560	$62.40	$19,566,144
20%	104,520	$31.20	$3,261,024	156,780	$46.80	$ 7,337,304
40%	209,040	$20.80	$4,348,032	313,560	$31.20	$ 9,783,072
	522,600			783,900		

5.3 Zero based budgets

Zero based budgeting (ZBB) is a method of budgeting that requires each cost element to be specifically justified, as though the activities to which the budget relates were being undertaken for the first time. Without approval, the budget allowance is zero.

Suitability

- Fast moving businesses/industries

- Discretionary costs such as research and development (R&D).

- Public sector organisations such as local authorities.

ZBB process

There are four distinct stages in the implementation of ZBB:

(1) Managers should specify for their responsibility centres those activities that can be individually evaluated.

(2) Each of the individual activities is then described in a decision package. The decision package should state the costs and revenues expected from the given activity. It should be drawn up in such a way that the package can be evaluated and ranked against other packages.

(3) Each decision package is evaluated and ranked usually using cost/benefit analysis.

(4) The resources are then allocated to the various packages.

ZBB

A decision package was defined by Peter Pyhrr (who first formulated the ZBB approach at Texas Instruments) as:

'A document that identifies and describes a specific activity in such a manner that senior management can:

A evaluate it and rank it against other activities competing for limited resources and

B decide whether to approve or disapprove it.'

A decision package is a document that does the following:

- Analyses the cost of the activity. (Costs may be built up from a zero base, but costing information can be obtained from historical records or last year's budget.)

- States the purpose of the activity.

- Identifies alternative methods of achieving the same purpose.

- Assesses the consequence of not doing the activity at all, or performing the activity at a different level.

- Establishes measures of performance for the activity.

Pyhrr identifies two types of package:

I   Mutually-exclusive packages. These contain different methods of obtaining the same objective.

II Incremental packages. These divide the activity into a number of different levels of activity. The base package describes the minimum effort and cost that is needed to carry out the activity. The other packages describe the incremental costs and benefits when added to the base.

ZBB exercise

A company is conducting a ZBB exercise, and a decision package is being prepared for its materials-handling operations.

- The manager responsible has identified a base package for the minimum resources needed to perform the materials-handling function. This is to have a team of five workers and a supervisor, operating without any labour-saving machinery. The estimated annual cost of wages and salaries, with overtime, would be $375,000.

- In addition to the base package, the manager has identified an incremental package. The company could lease two forklift trucks at a cost of $20,000 each year. This would provide a better system because materials could be stacked higher and moved more quickly. Health and safety risks for the workers would be reduced, and there would be savings of $5,000 each year in overtime payments.

- Another incremental package has been prepared, in which the company introduces new computer software to plan materials-handling schedules. The cost of buying and implementing the system would be $60,000, but the benefits are expected to be improvements in efficiency that reduce production downtime and result in savings of $10,000 each year in overtime payments.

The base package would be considered essential, and so given a high priority. The two incremental packages should be evaluated and ranked. Here, the forklift trucks option might be ranked more highly than the computer software.

In the budget that is eventually decided by senior management, the forklift truck package might be approved, but the computer software package rejected on the grounds that there are other demands for resources with a higher priority.

Test your understanding 3

For a number of years, the research division of Z has produced its annual budget (for new and continuing projects) using incremental budgeting techniques. The company is now under new management and the annual budget for 20X4 is to be prepared using ZBB techniques.

Required:

Explain how Z could operate a ZBB system for its research projects.

Advantages	Disadvantages
• Inefficient or obsolete operations can be identified and discontinued.	• The time involved and the cost of preparing the budget are much greater than for less elaborate budgeting methods.
• ZBB leads to increased staff involvement at all levels. This should lead to better communication and motivation.	• It may emphasise short-term benefits to the detriment of long-term benefits.
• It responds to changes in the business environment.	• The budgeting process may become too rigid and the company may not be able to react to unforeseen opportunities or threats.
• Knowledge and understanding of the cost-behaviour patterns of the organisation will be enhanced.	• There is a need for management skills that may not be present in the organisation.
• Resources should be allocated efficiently and economically.	

	• Managers may feel demotivated due to the large amount of time spent on the budgeting process.
	• It is difficult to compare and rank completely different types of activity.
	• The rankings of packages may be subjective where the benefits are of a qualitative nature.

5.4 Rolling budgets

A **rolling budget** is one that is kept continuously up to date by adding another accounting period (e.g. month or quarter) when the earliest accounting period has expired.

Suitability

- Accurate forecasts cannot be made, e.g. in a dynamic business environment or in a new business.

- For any area of business that needs tight control.

Advantages	Disadvantages
• The budgeting process should be more accurate.	• More costly and time consuming.
• Much better information upon which to appraise the performance of management.	• An increase in budgeting work may lead to less control of the actual results.
• The budget will be much more 'relevant' by the end of the traditional budgeting period.	• There is a danger that the budget may become the last budget 'plus or minus a bit'.
• It forces management to take the budgeting process more seriously.	• The budget may be demotivating because the targets are changing regularly.

Test your understanding 4

A company uses rolling budgeting and has a sales budget as follows:

	Quarter 1	Quarter 2	Quarter 3	Quarter 4	Total
	$	$	$	$	
Sales	125,750	132,038	138,640	145,572	542,000

Actual sales for Quarter 1 were $123,450. The adverse variance is fully explained by competition being more intense than expected and growth being lower than anticipated. The budget committee has proposed that the revised assumption for sales growth should be 3% per quarter for Quarters 2, 3 and 4.

Required:

Update the budget figures for Quarters 2–4 as appropriate.

Question practice

The question below is taken from a past exam and is an excellent example of how the examiner may expect you to compare the different budgeting techniques. Make sure that you attempt this question and review the recommended answer.

Test your understanding 5

The Drinks Group (DG) has been created over the last three years by merging three medium-sized family businesses. These businesses are all involved in making fruit drinks. Fizzy (F) makes and bottles healthy, fruit-based sparkling drinks. Still (S) makes and bottles fruit-flavoured non-sparkling drinks and Healthy (H) buys fruit and squeezes it to make basic fruit juices. The three companies have been divisionalised within the group structure. A fourth division called Marketing (M) exists to market the products of the other divisions to various large retail chains. Marketing has only recently been set up in order to help the business expand. All of the operations and sales of DG occur in Nordland, which is an economically well-developed country with a strong market for healthy non-alcoholic drinks.

The group has recruited a new finance director (FD), who was asked by the board to perform a review of the efficiency and effectiveness of the finance department as her first task on taking office. The finance director has just presented her report to the board regarding some problems at DG.

Extract from the finance director's Report to the Board

'The main area for improvement, which was discussed at the last board meeting, is the need to improve profit margins throughout the business. There is no strong evidence that new products or markets are required but that the most promising area for improvement lies in better internal control practices.

Control

As DG was formed from an integration of the original businesses (F, S, H), there was little immediate effort put into optimising the control systems of these businesses. They have each evolved over time in their own way. Currently, the main method of central control that can be used to drive profit margin improvement is the budget system in each business. The budgeting method used is to take the previous year's figures and simply increment them by estimates of growth in the market that will occur over the next year. These growth estimates are obtained through a discussion between the financial managers at group level and the relevant divisional managers. The management at each division are then given these budgets by head office and their personal targets are set around achieving the relevant budget numbers.

Divisions

H and S divisions are in stable markets where the levels of demand and competition mean that sales growth is unlikely, unless by acquisition of another brand. The main engine for prospective profit growth in these divisions is through margin improvements. The managers at these divisions have been successful in previous years and generally keep to the agreed budgets. As a result, they are usually not comfortable with changing existing practices.

F is faster growing and seen as the star of the Group. However, the Group has been receiving complaints from customers about late deliveries and poor quality control of the F products. The F managers have explained that they are working hard within the budget and capital constraints imposed by the board and have expressed a desire to be less controlled.

The marketing division has only recently been set up and the intention is to run each marketing campaign as an individual project which would be charged to the division whose products are benefiting from the campaign. The managers of the manufacturing divisions are very doubtful of the value of M, as each believes that they have an existing strong reputation with their customers that does not require much additional spending on marketing. However, the board decided at the last meeting that there was scope to create and use a marketing budget effectively at DG, if its costs were carefully controlled. Similar to the other divisions, the marketing division budgets are set by taking the previous year's actual spend and adding a percentage increase. For M, the increase corresponds to the previous year's growth in group turnover.'

End of extract

At present, the finance director is harassed by the introduction of a new information system within the finance department which is straining the resources of the department. However, she needs to respond to the issues raised above at the board meeting and so is considering using different budgeting methods at DG. She has asked you, the management accountant at the Group, to do some preliminary work to help her decide whether and how to change the budget methods. The first task that she believes would be useful is to consider the use of rolling budgets. She thinks that fast-growing F may prove the easiest division in which to introduce new ideas.

F's incremental budget for the current year is given below. You can assume that cost of sales and distribution costs are variable and administrative costs are fixed.

	Q1 $000	Q2 $000	Q3 $000	Q4 $000	Total $000
Revenue	17,520	17,958	18,407	18,867	72,752
Cost of sales	9,636	9,877	10,124	10,377	40,014
Gross profit	7,884	8,081	8,283	8,490	32,738
Distribution costs	1,577	1,616	1,657	1,698	6,548
Administration costs	4,214	4,214	4,214	4,214	16,856
Operating profit	2,093	2,251	2,412	2,578	9,334

The actual figures for quarter 1 (which has just completed) are:

	$000
Revenue	17,932
Cost of sales	9,863
Gross profit	8,069
Distribution costs	1,614
Administration costs	4,214
Operating profit	2,241

On the basis of the Q1 results, sales volume growth of 3% per quarter is now expected.

The finance director has also heard you talking about bottom-up budgeting and wants you to evaluate its use at DG.

Required:

Evaluate the suitability of incremental budgeting at each division.

(8 marks)

Recalculate the budget for Fizzy division (F) using rolling budgeting and assess the use of rolling budgeting at F.

(8 marks)

Recommend any appropriate changes to the budgeting method at the Marketing division (M), providing justifications for your choice.

(4 marks)

Analyse and recommend the appropriate level of participation in budgeting at Drinks Group (DG).

(6 marks)

(Total: 26 marks)

5.5 Activity-based budgeting (ABB)

Before we look at activity-based budgeting, it is useful to review the activity based models in general.

5.5.1 Activity-based costing (ABC)

Aim: the aim of ABC is to calculate the full production cost per unit. It is an alternative to absorption costing in a modern business environment.

Reasons for the development of ABC

- Absorption costing is based on the principle that production overheads are driven by the level of production. This was true in the past when businesses tended to produce only one product or a few simple and similar products. However, a higher level of competition has resulted in the diversity and complexity of the products increasing. As a result, there are a number of different factors that drive overheads, not simply the level of production.

- Production overheads are a larger proportion of total costs in modern manufacturing since manufacturing has become more machine intensive and less labour intensive. Therefore, it is important that an accurate estimate is made of the production overhead per unit.

Steps in ABC

Step 1: Group production overheads into activities (cost pools), according to how they are driven.

Step 2: Identify cost drivers for each activity, i.e. what causes the activity costs to be incurred.

Step 3: Calculate an overhead absorption rate (OAR) for each activity.

Step 4: Absorb the activity costs into the product.

Step 5: Calculate the full production cost and/or the profit or loss.

The question below recaps the calculation of the full production cost per unit using traditional absorption costing and using ABC. Make sure that you understand the calculation and that you can comment on the reasons for the differences between the full production cost per unit under the two costing methods.

Test your understanding 6

Trimake makes three main products, using broadly the same production methods and equipment for each. A conventional absorption costing system is used at present, although an activity based costing (ABC) system is being considered. Details of the three products for a typical period are:

	Hours per unit		Materials per unit	Volumes
Product	Labour	Machinery	$	Units
X	½	1½	20	750
Y	1½	1	12	1,250
Z	1	3	25	7,000

Direct labour costs $6 per hour and production overheads are absorbed on a machine hour basis. The rate for the period is $28 per machine hour (i.e. the OAR) and a total of 23,375 machine hours were worked.

Traditional absorption costing would give a full production cost per unit as follows:

	X	Y	Z
	$	$	$
Materials	20	12	25
Labour	3	9	6
Total direct cost	23	21	31
Production overhead @ $28 per hour	42	28	84
Total	64	49	115

Further analysis shows the total production overhead of $654,500 is not entirely driven by machine hours and can be divided as follows:

	%
Costs relating to set-ups	35
Costs relating to machinery	20
Costs relating to materials handling	15
Costs relating to inspection	30
	–––
Total production overhead	100

The following total activity volumes are associated with the product line for the period as a whole:

	Number of set-ups	Number of movements of materials	Number of inspections
Product X	75	12	150
Product Y	115	21	180
Product Z	480	87	670
	–––	–––	–––
Total	670	120	1,000

Required:

Calculate the cost per unit for each product using ABC principles.

Advantages and disadvantages of ABC

Advantages	Disadvantages
• Provides a more accurate cost per unit leading to better pricing, decision making and performance management.	• Limited benefit if overheads are primarily volume related or a small proportion of total costs.
• It provides a better insight into what drives overhead costs resulting in better control of costs.	• It is impossible to allocate all overheads to specific activities.
• It recognises that overhead costs are not all related to production and sales volumes.	• The choice of activities and cost drivers might be inappropriate.
• It can be applied to all overhead costs, not just production overheads.	• The benefits might not justify the costs since a large amount of data must be collected.
• It can be used just as easily in service costing as product costing.	

5.5.2 Activity based management (ABM)

Activity based management (ABM) is the use of ABC information for management purposes to improve operational and strategic decisions. Performance should improve as a result.

- By identifying the underlying drivers of activities, ABM provides an understanding of the resource implications of various courses of action and therefore **ensures that unfeasible courses of action are not taken**.

- It can assist in **re-pricing or eliminating unprofitable products**.

- It may **eliminate the need to carry out certain activities** which do not add value to the customer.

- It may identify ways to **produce a product more efficiently** by understanding what drives the costs.

- It may identify **design improvements**.

- It can assist in **improving relationships with customers and suppliers**.

- Can be used to decide which **products to develop and which strategies to pursue**.

In summary, ABM can help managers to make decisions that benefit the whole organisation, not just their activities' bottom line and ensure that the needs of the customer are being met.

Two types of ABM

```
                    ┌─────────────────────┐
                    │   Two types of ABM  │
                    └─────────────────────┘
```

Operational ABM
- Uses ABC information to improve efficiency
- Activities which add value to a product are indentified and improved
- Activities that don't add value to the product can be reduced or eliminated to cut costs without reducing product value

Strategic ABM
- Uses ABC information to decide which products to develop and sell based on profitability
- Uses ABC information to identify which customers are the most profitable and focuses more on them

Illustration 1 – Operational ABM

One of the biggest advantages of ABM is that costs are categorised by activities rather than traditional cost categories. For example:

Traditional costing system		ABM system	
Cost of sales	X	Direct material cost	X
Staff costs	X	Direct labour cost	X
Factory rent	X	**Indirect costs**	
Maintenance	X	Schedule production jobs	X
Depreciation	X	Machine set-up	X
	——	Receiving materials	X
Total costs	X	Supporting existing products	X
	——	Introducing new products	X
			——
		Total costs	X
			——

Having costs categorised by activity provides more relevant information to managers:

- There may be activities that don't add value and these could be stopped.

- There may be activities that cost more than expected and the manager can use their knowledge of the activity's cost driver to reduce the cost. For example, the cost of setting up the machines could be reduced by having longer production runs.

Test your understanding 7

Required:

Briefly discuss the potential risks associated with ABM.

Illustration 2 – The application of ABM at DHL

The international postal and logistics company, DHL saw its margins decreasing and used ABM to reverse this trend.

- Falling margins were mainly due to changes in products, destinations and customer mixes.

- The company concluded that they did not have sufficient visibility of margins to enable better pricing policies (and had different policies in different countries) so implemented ABC.

- A greater understanding of margins allowed DHL to design and implement a new pricing structure that was adopted worldwide and helped them to improve its margins.

Question practice

The question below is from a past exam and is an excellent question showing the step-up from PM to APM. Calculations may be tested but they will be used to form the basis of your decisions and will generally only be worth a small number of marks. Make sure that you attempt this question and learn from the answer. You may find it difficult to attempt a past exam question in full at this stage of your studies but it is important that you understand the level that you are expected to reach by the time you come to sit the exam.

Test your understanding 8

Navier Aerials Co (Navier) manufactures satellite dishes for receiving satellite television signals. Navier supplies the major satellite TV companies who install standard satellite dishes for their customers. The company also manufactures and installs a small number of specialised satellite dishes to individuals or businesses with specific needs resulting from poor reception in their locations.

The chief executive officer (CEO) wants to initiate a programme of cost reduction at Navier. His plan is to use activity-based management (ABM) to allocate costs more accurately and to identify non-value adding activities. The first department to be analysed is the customer care department, as it has been believed for some time that the current method of cost allocation is giving unrealistic results for the two product types.

At present, the finance director (FD) absorbs the cost of customer care into the product cost on a per unit basis using the data in table 1. He then tries to correct the problem of unrealistic costing, by making rough estimates of the costs to be allocated to each product based on the operations director's impression of the amount of work of the department. In fact, he simply adds $100 above the standard absorbed cost to the cost of a specialised dish to cover the assumed extra work involved at customer care.

The cost accountant has gathered information for the customer care department in table 2 from interviews with the finance and customer care staff. She has used this information to correctly calculate the total costs of each activity using activity-based costing in table 3. The CEO wants you, as a senior management accountant, to complete the work required for a comparison of the results of the current standard absorption costing to activity-based costing for the standard and specialised dishes.

Once this is done, the CEO wants you to consider the implications for management of the customer care process of the costs of each activity in that department. The CEO is especially interested in how this information may impact on the identification of non-valued added activities and quality management at Navier.

Navier Dishes (information for the year ending 31 March 20X3)
Customer care (CC) department

Table 1: Existing costing data

	$000
Salaries	400
Computer time	165
Telephone	79
Stationery and sundries	27
Depreciation of equipment	36
	707

Note:

1   CC cost is currently allocated to each dish based on 16,000 orders a year, where each order contains an average of 5.5 dishes.

Table 2: Activity-costing data

Activities of CC dept	Staff time	Comments
Handling enquiries and preparing quotes for potential orders	40%	relates to 35,000 enquiries/ quotes per year
Receiving actual orders	10%	relates to 16,000 orders in the year
Customer credit checks	10%	done once an order is received
Supervision of orders through manufacture to delivery	15%	
Complaints handling	25%	relates to 3,200 complaints per year

Notes:

1   Total department cost is allocated using staff time as this drives all of the other costs in the department.

2   90% of both enquiries and orders are for standard dishes. The remainder are for specialised dishes.

3   Handling enquiries and preparing quotes for specialised dishes takes 20% of staff time allocated to this activity.

4   The process for receiving an order, checking customer credit and supervision of the order is the same for both a specialised dish order and a standard dish order.

5   50% of the complaints received are for specialised dish orders.

6   Each standard dish order contains an average of six dishes.

7   Each specialised dish order contains an average of one dish.

Table 2: Activity-based costs

	Total	Standard	Specialised
Handling enquiries and preparing quotes	282,800	226,240	56,560
Receiving actual orders	70,700	63,630	7,070
Customer credit checks	70,700	63,630	7,070
Supervision of order through manufacture to delivery	106,050	95,445	10,605
Complaints handling	176,750	88,375	88,375
Total	707,000	537,320	169,680

Required:

(a) Evaluate the impact of using activity-based costing, compared to the existing costing system for customer care, on the cost of both types of product.

(13 marks)

(b) Assess how the information on each activity can be used and improved upon at Navier in assisting cost reduction and quality management in the customer care department.

Note: There is no need to make comments on the different product types here.

(12 marks)

(Total: 25 marks)

Student accountant article: visit the ACCA website, www.accaglobal.com, to review the article on 'activity-based management'.

5.5.3 Activity-based budgeting (ABB)

Now that we understand the concepts of ABC and ABM, we can review the final approach to budgeting, ABB.

Activity-based budgeting (ABB) uses the principles of ABC to estimate the firm's future demand for resources and hence can help the firm to acquire these resources more efficiently.

Illustration 3 – Steps in ABB

The operating divisions of Z have in the past always used a traditional (absorption costing) approach to analysing costs into their fixed and variable components. A single measure of activity was used which, for simplicity, was the number of units produced. The new management does not accept that such a simplistic approach is appropriate for budgeting in the modern environment and has requested that the managers adopt an activity-based approach to their budgets in the future.

Required

Explain how ABB would be implemented by the operating divisions of Z.

Solution

Step 1: Estimate the production and sales volumes of individual products or customers.

Step 2: Estimate the demand for organisational activities.

Step 3: Determine the resources that are required to perform organisational activities.

Step 4: Estimate for each resource the quantity that must be supplied to meet the demand.

Step 5: Take action to adjust the capacity of resources to match the projected supply.

Advantages	Disadvantages
• ABB draws attention to the costs of 'overhead activities' which can be a large proportion of total operating costs.	• A considerable amount of time and effort might be needed to establish an ABB system (identifying the key activities and their cost drivers).
• It recognises that it is activities that drive costs. If we can control the causes (drivers) of costs, then costs should be better managed and understood.	• ABB might not be appropriate for the organisation and its activities and cost structures.
• It provides information for the control of activity costs, by assuming that they are variable, at least in the longer-term.	• It may be difficult to identify clear individual responsibilities for activities.
• ABB can provide useful information for a total quality management (TQM) environment, by relating the cost of an activity to the level of service provided.	• It could be argued that in the short-term many overhead costs are not controllable and do not vary directly with changes in the volume of activity for the cost driver. The only cost variances to report would be fixed overhead expenditure variances for each activity.

ABB

A company has prepared an activity-based budget for its stores department. The budgeted costs are:

	Cost driver	Budgeted cost
Receiving goods	Number of deliveries	$80 per delivery
Issuing goods from store	Number of stores' requisitions	$40 per requisition
Ordering	Number of orders	$25 per order
Counting stock	Number of stock counts	$1,000 per count
Keeping records	–	$24,000 each year
Supervision	–	$30,000 each year

Activity		Actual cost
		$
Receiving goods	45 orders delivered	3,450
Issuing goods	100 requisitions	4,400
Ordering	36 orders	960
Counting	2 stock counts	1,750
Record keeping		1,900
Supervision		2,700
		———
		15,160
		———

Required:

Prepare a variance report for the month.

Solution:

Activity		Expected cost	Actual cost	Variance
		$	$	$
Receiving goods	45 orders delivered	3,600	3,450	150 F
Issuing goods	100 requisitions	4,000	4,400	400 A
Ordering	36 orders	900	960	60 A
Counting	2 stock counts	2,000	1,750	250 F
Record keeping		2,000	1,900	100 F
Supervision		2,500	2,700	200 A
		———	———	———
		15,000	15,160	160 A
		———	———	———

6   Variances

6.1 Recap of the basics of variance analysis

In PM you learnt that variance analysis was a key element of management control:

1   Targets and standards are set reflecting what should happen.

2   Actual performance is then measured.

3   Actual results are then compared with the (flexed) standards, using variance analysis.

4   "Significant" variances can then be investigated and appropriate action taken.

This process thus facilitates "management by exception".

Spend a little bit of time reviewing the variances covered in PM to ensure you are comfortable with the calculations and the meaning of each variance.

6.2 Different types of budget variance

Taking the different types of budgeting approach discussed above we can summarise the likely implications for variance analysis as follows:

Type of budget approach	Implications for variances
Fixed v flexible budgets	• Variances arising from fixed budgets are less likely to be useful for controlling a business as actual and budget figures may not be comparing like with like in volume terms. • This is why variances are usually calculated by reference to flexed budgets.
Incremental v ZBB budgets	• A problem with incremental budgeting is that managers will often spend their allowance to ensure they keep it for subsequent periods. As a result, favourable variances are likely to be small and will not reveal possible areas for further gains. • With ZBB the targets may be unrealistic since this budgeting technique is often used in areas where there is a high degree of uncertainty. Furthermore, targets may be too difficult as the culture of ZBB is to eliminate all waste. As a result the firm may have more adverse variances but these may be due more to planning issues than operational ones.

ABB	• Traditional variance analysis will have to be adapted to focus on activity costs. For example, a rate variance may become (actual rate per unit of cost driver – standard rate) × actual cost driver volume. The resulting variances should facilitate better control and planning for overheads as it focusses on what generates the costs.

6.3 Planning and operating variances

The variances calculated can be further divided into planning and operational elements if at the end of the period, with the benefit of hindsight, it is known that the original budget was unrealistic and therefore a decision is taken to amend the budget.

- The planning variance is the difference between the original standard and the revised one.

- Planning variances are thus those which arise due to inaccurate forecasts or standards in the original budget setting.

- Operational variances are then the remainder due to the decisions of operational managers.

- An operational variance is the difference between this revised standard and actual performance.

From a performance management perspective the **advantage** of this approach is that line managers can concentrate on improving operational matters for which they are genuinely responsible. For example, a sales price variance could be split to indicate how far sales prices were incorrectly estimated in the budget (planning) and how well the sales managers have done in negotiating high prices with customers (operational).

On the other hand the **disadvantage** of planning and operational variances is that too often all adverse variances are explained away as being planning errors.

Another problem is when the revised standards are harder than the original ones and managers are assessed on operating variances. They could get demotivated by moving targets, especially if they have lost a bonus that they would have achieved under the original standards.

The **calculations were covered in PM**. However, some examples have been included below for revision purposes.

Planning and operational variances for sales volume

Test your understanding 9 – Market size and share

Hudson has a sales budget of 400,000 units for the coming year based on 20% of the total market. On each unit, Hudson makes a profit of $3. Actual sales for the year were 450,000, but industry reports showed that the total market volume had been 2.2 million.

(a)   Find the traditional sales volume variance.

(b)   Split this into planning and operational variances (market size and market share). Comment on your results.

Planning and operational variances for labour efficiency

Test your understanding 10

The standard hours per unit of production for a product is 5 hours. Actual production for the period was 250 units and actual hours worked were 1,450 hours. The standard rate per hour was $10. Because of a shortage of skilled labour it has been necessary to use unskilled labour and it is estimated that this will increase the time taken by 20%.

Required:

Calculate the planning and operational labour efficiency variances.

Planning and operational variances for material price and usage

Test your understanding 11

Holmes uses one raw material for one of their products. The standard cost per unit at the beginning of the year was $28, made up as follows:

Standard material cost per unit = 7 kg per unit at $4 per kg = $28.

In the middle of the year the supplier had changed the specification of the material slightly due to problems experienced in the country of origin, so that the standard had to be revised as follows:

Standard material cost per unit = 8 kg per unit at $3.80 per kg = $30.40.

The actual output for November was 1,400 units. 11,000 kg of material was purchased and used at a cost of $41,500.

Calculate

(a)   material price and usage variances using the traditional method

(b)   all planning and operational material variances.

7 Forecasting

7.1 Introduction

A number of forecasting methods were reviewed in PM including:

- the hi-low method
- regression analysis
- time series analysis
- the learning curve model.

The learning curve model will be recapped briefly below:

7.2 The learning curve effect

As workers become more familiar with the production of a new product, the average labour time (and average labour cost) per unit will decline.

Wright's Law states that as output doubles, the average time per unit falls to a fixed percentage (referred to as the learning rate) of the previous average time.

The learning curve effect can be calculated using the following formula:

$$y = ax^b$$

where:

y = the average time (or average cost) per unit/batch

a = time (or cost) for the first unit/batch

x = output in units/batches

b = log r/log 2 (r = rate of learning, expressed as a decimal).

The formula can be used to forecast the cost of labour but would normally be examined as part of a bigger forecasting question such as the one below.

The learning curve and the steady state

The learning effect will only apply for a certain range of production. Once the steady state is reached the direct labour hours will not reduce any further.

Test your understanding 12

BFG is investigating the financial viability of a new product, the S-pro. The S-pro is a short-life product for which a market has been identified at an agreed design specification. The product will only have a life of 12 months.

The following estimated information is available in respect of the S-pro.:

1   Sales should be 120,000 in the year in batches of 100 units. An average selling price of $1,050 per batch of 100 units is expected.

2   An 80% learning curve will apply for the first 700 batches after which a steady state production time will apply, with the labour time per batch after the first 700 batches being equal to the time of the 700th batch. The labour cost of the first batch was measured at $2,500. This was for 500 hours at $5 per hour.

3   Variable overhead is estimated at $2 per labour hour.

4   Direct material will be $500 per batch for the S-pro for the first 200 batches produced. The second 200 batches will cost 90% of the cost per batch of the first 200 batches. All batches from then on will cost 90% of the batch cost for each of the second 200 batches.

5   S-pro will require additional space to be rented. These directly attributable fixed costs will be $15,000 per month.

A target net cash flow of $130,000 is required in order for the project to be acceptable.

Note: At the learning curve rate of 80% the learning factor (b) is equal to -0.3219.

Required:

Prepare detailed calculations to show whether S-pro will provide the target net cash flow.

Exam focus

The examiner is more likely to give you a completed or part completed forecast and ask you about flaws or assumptions.

Limitations of the learning curve model

The learning curve model only applies if:

- **there are no breaks in production:** a break in production may result in the learning effect being lost.

- **the product is new:** the introduction of a new product makes it more probable that there will be a learning effect.

- **the product is complex:** the more complex the product, the more probable that the learning effect will be significant and the longer it will take for the learning effect to reach the steady state.

- **the process is repetitive:** if the process is not repetitive, a learning effect will not be enjoyed.

- **the process is labour intensive:** the learning effect will not apply if machines limit the speed of labour.

8 Exam focus

Exam sitting	Area examined	Question number	Number of marks
Sept/Dec 2016	Rolling and incremental budgets	2	25
Sept/Dec 2015	ABC	3(a)	8
Mar/June 2016	ABC and ABM	3	25
Sept/Dec 2015	Weaknesses in budgeting system	2(a)	13
June 2014	Variances, budgeting evaluation, beyond budgeting	4	25
June 2013	ABC and ABM	2	25
December 2012	Budgeting	2	25
December 2010	ABC, beyond budgeting	2	25

Chapter summary

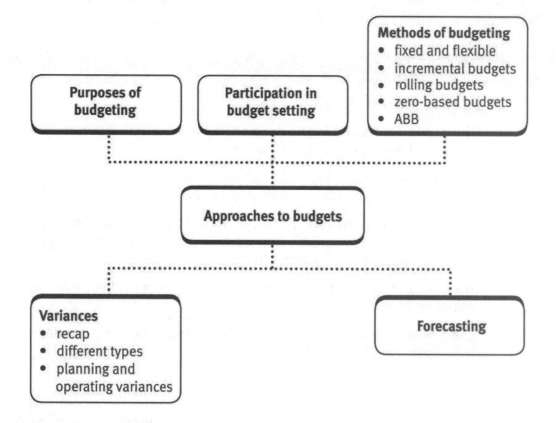

Test your understanding answers

Test your understanding 1

At first sight, the costs are higher meaning the company has done worse, from a cost control angle, but then the activity level is 20% higher than planned. If all costs are variable, we would expect costs to rise in line with activity, making expected costs 20,000 × 1.2 = $24,000. In this case the company has done better than expected.

The fixed costs of $10,000 will NOT rise in line with activity levels where as the variable costs of $10,000 will increase in line with activity levels. Therefore, the expected cost of the actual level of activity will be ($10,000 × 1.2) + $10,000 = $22,000. The actual cost is $23,000 so the company has spent more than expected.

Test your understanding 2

(W1) Actual patient numbers were 18.75% above budget, i.e. ((23,750 − 20,000) ÷ 20,000) × 100 = 18.75%. Therefore, budgeted variable costs should be increased by 18.75%.

Cost statements for the year ended 31 December 20X0

	Budget $	Actual $
Doctors	60 × $100,000 = 6,000,000	60 × $105,000 = 6,300,000
Nurses	150 × $37,000 = 5,550,000	150 × $34,500 = 5,175,000
Other staff costs	1.1875 (W1) × 1,440,000 = 1,710,000	1,500,000
Catering	(1.1875 (W1) × $200,000 × 70%) + ($200,000 × 30%) = 226,250	187,500
Cleaning	(1.1875 (W1) × $80,000 × 35%) + ($80,000 × 65%) = 85,250	142,000
Other operating costs	(1.1875 (W1) × $1,200,000 × 30%) + ($1,200,000 ×70%) = 1,267,500	1,050,000
Depreciation	80,000	80,000
Total costs	**14,919,000**	**14,434,500**

Test your understanding 3

The managers/researchers responsible for each project should decide which projects they wish to undertake in the forthcoming period. These projects will be a mixture of continued projects and new projects.

For the projects which have already been started and which the managers want to continue in the next period, we should ignore any cash flows already incurred (they are sunk costs), and we should look only at future costs and benefits. Similarly, for the new projects we should only look at the future costs and benefits.

Different ways of achieving the same research goals should also be investigated and the projects should go ahead only if the benefit exceeds the cost.

Once all the potential projects have been evaluated, if there are insufficient funds to undertake all the worthwhile projects, then the funds should be allocated to the best projects on the basis of a cost-benefit analysis.

ZBB is usually of a highly-subjective nature. (The costs are often reasonably certain, but usually a lot of uncertainty is attached to the estimated benefits.) This will be even more true of a research division where the researchers may have their own pet projects which they are unable to view in an objective light.

Test your understanding 4

The revised budget should incorporate 3% growth starting from the actual sales figure of Q1.

	Quarter 2 $	Quarter 3 $	Quarter 4 $
Sales	127,154	130,969	134,898

Workings

- Budget = $123,450 × 103%

- Budget = $127,154 × 103%

- Budget = $130,969 × 103%

Test your understanding 5

(a) The current method of budgeting at all divisions is incremental budgeting. The advantages of incremental budgeting are that it is simple and easy; therefore, it does not take up much time and resources in the finance department, which is constrained by the new information system implementation. It is suitable in organisations where the business is stable and so historic figures represent a solid base from which to consider small changes. The problems associated with incremental budgeting are that it consolidates existing practices into the targets and so tends to stifle innovation. As a result, inefficient and uneconomic activities will not be challenged and opportunity for cost savings may be missed. Also, managers may deliberately spend up to their budget limits in order to ensure that they get an increment from the highest possible base figure in the next budget.

At the different divisions

As S and H are stable businesses, it makes sense to continue to use incremental budgeting at these divisions. Change at these divisions may not seem necessary as it would create resistance from the divisional managers. However, incremental budgeting is not consistent with continuous improvement which may be required to reduce costs and improve profit margins in these divisions.

At F, the incremental budgets will be rapidly out of date in such a growing business. The current problems of management dissatisfaction and poor quality control may be resulting from divisional management trying to meet their targets with a budget that is not suitable for the growth occurring. They may be cutting corners to meet budget and so buying poorer materials or failing to increase capacity and so not making deliveries.

At M, incremental budgeting is intensifying complaints from the other divisions, who already see M as an unnecessary expense. Incremental budgeting is insufficiently critical of the existing spending and it can lead to unjustified increases.

(b) A rolling budget is one where the budget is kept up to date by adding another accounting period when the most recent one expires. The budget is then rerun using the new actual data as a basis. At Drinks Group, with its quarterly forecasting, this would work by adding another quarter to the budget and then rebudgeting for the next four quarters.

Rolling budgets are suitable when the business environment is changing rapidly or when the business unit needs to be tightly controlled.

The new budget at F would be:

	Current year Q1	Current year Q2	Current year Q3	Current year Q4	Current year Total	Next year Q1
	$000	$000	$000	$000	$000	$000
Revenue	17,932	18,470	19,024	19,595	75,021	20,183
Cost of sales	9,863	10,159	10,464	10,778	41,264	11,101
Gross profit	8,069	8,311	8,560	8,817	33,757	9,082
Distribution costs	1,614	1,662	1,712	1,764	6,752	1,817
Administration costs	4,214	4,214	4,214	4,214	16,856	4,214
Operating profit	2,241	2,435	2,634	2,839	10,149	3,051

Based on the assumptions that cost of sales and distribution costs increase in line with sales and that administration costs are fixed as in the original budget.

The budget now reflects the rapid growth of the division. Using rolling budgets like this will avoid the problem of managers trying to control costs using too small a budget and as a result, choking off the growth of the business. The rolling budgets will require additional resources as they now have to be done each quarter rather than annually but the benefits of giving management a clearer picture and more realistic targets more than outweigh this.

However, it may also be worth considering going beyond budgeting altogether in order to avoid this constraint problem.

(c) At M, as noted in part (a), incremental budgeting may not be a suitable choice of budget method. A more appropriate budgeting system for such a project-based function is zero-based budgeting (ZBB). Marketing operates around campaigns that often run for fixed periods of time and do not fit neatly into accounting periods which further undermines the use of incremental budgeting. It can be seen as a series of projects. This type of operation is best controlled by having individual budgets for each campaign that the divisional managers must justify to senior management at the start. ZBB requires each cost element to be justified, otherwise no resources are allocated. This approach would please the manufacturing divisional managers, as they will see tight control. It will not hobble M as there are few fixed overheads in marketing as it mainly involves human capital. ZBB is often used where spending is discretionary in areas such as marketing and research and development.

(d) The management style currently used at DG is top-down, budget-based with some degree of participation by divisional managers. Given the irritation being expressed by the divisional managers, the senior management could consider making the control process more participatory. This would involve shifting to more bottom-up setting of control targets. This could involve the divisions preparing budgets or else dropping budgeting altogether.

Bottom-up control involves the divisional managers at DG having an opportunity to participate in the setting of their budgets/targets. It is also known as participative control for that reason. It has the advantages of improving motivation of the divisional managers by creating a greater sense of ownership in the budget/targets. It increases the manager's understanding, which has additional benefits if personal targets are then set from the budget. Bottom-up processing frees up senior management resource as the divisional managers do more of the work. It can also improve the quality of decision making and budgeting as divisional managers are closer to their product markets.

Bottom-up control can be contrasted with top-down budgeting. A top-down budget is one that is imposed on the budget holder by the senior management. It is controlled by senior management and avoids budgets that are not in line with overall corporate objectives or that are too easily achieved.

At DG, the current approach does have involvement from the budget holders and so is participatory. This is important as the managers are set targets based on budgets, although the finance department involvement should help to avoid the issues of lack of strategic focus and slack that are noted above. The introduction of rolling budgets could be delegated to the F managers as they will be happy to take on the solution to their constraint problems. It would be wise to keep some involvement by senior finance staff in reviewing the budget – particularly, the key growth assumptions. The introduction of ZBB at M will require the involvement of budget holders as they will prepare the original proposal. These suggestions will have the advantage of encouraging innovation although it will loosen central control. Senior management will need to assess whether the managers of the stable divisions (H and S) can be relied on to drive down costs without the close oversight of the head office that is provided by a top-down approach.

Thus, some level of bottom-up budgeting fits well with both the current and future plans for financial control at Drinks Group. Although, the senior management will have to decide on the different level of central control to exercise, based on the skills of the divisional management and the degree of latitude that they require in order to improve their operations.

Test your understanding 6

(W1) Overheads

Type of overhead	%	Total overhead $
Set-ups	35	229,075
Machining	30	130,900
Material's handling	15	98,175
Inspection	30	196,350
	100	654,500

Step 1: Group production overhead into activities

Set-ups
Machining
Material's handling
Inspection

Step 2: Identify cost drivers for each activity

Number of set-ups
Number of machine hours
Number of movements of materials
Number of inspections

Step 3: Calculate an OAR for each activity

Activity cost (W1)	Cost driver	OAR = activity cost ÷ cost driver
Set-ups = $229,075	670 set ups	$341.90 per set up
Machining = $130,900	23,375 machine hours	$5.60 per machine hour
Materials handling = $98,175	120 material movements	$818.13 per movement of material
Inspection = $196,350	1,000 inspections	$196.35 per inspection

Step 4: Absorb activity costs into products

	Product X $	Product Y $	Product Z $	Total $
Set-ups	25,642.50	39,318.50	164,112.00	229,073
Machining	6,300	7,000	117,600	130,900
Materials handling	9,817.56	17,180.73	71,177.31	98,175.60
Total production overhead	71,212.56	98,842.23	484,443.81	654,498.60
Production overhead per unit	**94.95**	**79.07**	**69.21**	

Step 5: Calculate the full production cost per unit

	Product X	Product Y	Product Z
	$	$	$
Direct costs (from question)	23.00	21.00	31.00
Production overhead (step 4)	94.95	79.07	69.21
Full production cost under ABC	**117.95**	**100.07**	**100.21**
Full production cost under absorption costing	**64**	**49**	**115**

ABC has resulted in a significant change in the full production cost per unit. The cost of products X and Y have approximately doubled whereas the cost of product Z has decreased by approximately 13%.

Test your understanding 7

- Some activities will have an implicit value which is not necessarily reflected in the financial value of the product. For example:

    - A pleasant workplace can help attract/retain the best staff. A risk of operational ABM is that this activity is eliminated.

    - A low value customer may open up new leads in the market. A risk of strategic ABM is that this customer is eliminated.

- A full cost benefit analysis should be carried out to establish if the cost of the extra work required to obtain the more accurate information is less than the potential savings to be enjoyed as a result of the more accurate assessment.

Test your understanding 8

(a) **Current absorption costing**

(Workings to support quantitative results are given below.)

The CC department represents an overhead to the operations at Navier. Its costs are currently allocated in a simple fashion by dividing the total departmental cost by the number of dishes to obtain a cost of customer care for each dish as $8.03. This cost will then be added to other costs (such as materials and labour used in production) to obtain a total cost per dish. This cost can then be compared to the selling price per dish in order to obtain a figure for the profit per dish.

In addition, the FD adds a further $100 per specialised dish in order to compensate for the extra work involved. However, this leads to an over-absorption of total cost since the $8.03 will absorb fully the CC costs and an additional $160,000 (1,600 specialised dishes at $100) of costs may be incorrectly absorbed.

ABC costing

The problem at Navier is that it sells two different types of dish and these products use different amounts of the company's resources. The activity-based analysis shows that the cost of customer care per standard dish is in fact lower than the current cost allocated at $6.22 per dish. This means that these dishes are making a higher profit per unit than would be given using the existing costing system. The specialised dishes are costing $106.05 each in customer care so it is vital that their price reflects this much higher cost base. The major activities that contribute to this higher cost are dealing with initial sales enquiries and handling complaints. This is not surprising, as the specialised dishes represent a bespoke service which will not be easily reduced to a standard set of steps.

Given the size of the difference between the ABC cost ($106.05) and the current initial estimate of absorbed cost ($8.03), it is not surprising that there have been efforts to correct for this difference. The finance director's estimate of $108.03 to cover the costs of customer care for the specialised dishes is fairly accurate but, of course, the addition of this extra amount should have required the cost for the standard dishes to be reduced from $8.03 in order to compensate for the allocation of more cost to the specialised dishes. It is not clear if this is being done.

The advantage of the ABC analysis is that it shows the activities that are driving the higher costs and, therefore, this analysis opens the opportunity to consider if the customers of the specialised dishes value the additional work. If not, then ABM would require the non-value adding processes be removed/reduced. A survey of customer attitudes and a comparison with competitors' service standards would shed light on the perceived value of these activities.

A question that should arise in relation to the ABC exercise undertaken here is whether it has been worth the effort, given that the finance director does appear capable of reasonably accurately estimating the costs without undertaking the time-consuming ABC analysis. Of course, the problem of over-allocation of total costs would have to be corrected in any case.

(b) The information in the workings below shows that the main cost activities of the CC department are pre-sale preparation (handling enquiries and quotes) and post-sale complaints handling. Together, these activities consume 65% of the resources of the customer care department.

The pre-sale work is essential for the organisation and the department converts 46% (16,000/35,000) of enquiries to orders. It would be beneficial to try to benchmark this ratio to competitor performance although obtaining comparable data will be difficult, due to its commercially sensitive nature.

However, the complaints handling aspect is one which would be identified as non-value adding in an activity-based management analysis. Non-value adding activities are those that do not increase the worth of the product to the customer, common examples are inspection time and idle time in manufacturing. It is usually not possible to eliminate these activities but it is often possible to minimise them. Complaints handling is not value adding as it results from failure to meet the service standards expected (and so is already included in the price paid).

Complaints handling links directly to issues of quality management at Navier as improved quality of products should reduce these costs. These costs are significant at Navier as complaint numbers are 20% (3,200/16,000) of orders. Complaints may arise in many ways and these causes need to be identified. As far as the operation of the CC department is concerned, it may cause complaints through poor work at the quotation stage where the job is improperly understood or incorrectly specified to the manufacturing or installation teams. This leads to non-conformance costs as products do not meet expected standards and, in this case, complaints imply that these are external failure costs as they have been identified by customers.

Quality of the end product could also be affected by the supervision activity and in order to ensure that this is functioning well, the CC department will need to have the authority to intervene with the work of other departments in order to correct errors – this could be a key area for prevention of faults and so might become a core quality activity (an inspection and prevention cost).

The other activities in the department are administrative and the measures of their quality will be in the financial information systems. Order processing quality would be checked by invoice disputes and credit note issuance. Credit check effectiveness would be measured by bad debt levels.

Workings:

Customer care (CC) department

Standard absorption cost per dish

	$000
Salaries	400
Computer time	165
Telephone	79
Stationery and sundries	27
Depreciation of equipment	36
	707

Total CC cost	$707,000
Number of dishes (5.5 × 16,000)	88,000
Standard absorption cost per dish	$8.03
Finance director's adjusted cost per specialised dish	$108.03

Activity-based costs

	Total $	Standard $	Specialised $
Handling enquiries and preparing quotes	282,800	226,240	56,560
Receiving actual orders	70,700	63,630	7,070
Customer credit checks	70,700	63,630	7,070
Supervision of order through manufacture to delivery	106,050	95,445	10,605
Complaints handling	176,750	88,375	88,375
Total	707,000	537,320	169,680
Average dishes per order		6	1
No of orders		14,400	1,600
Total number of dishes		86,400	1,600
ABC absorption cost per dish		$6.22	$106.06

Test your understanding 9 – Market size and share

(a) Traditional sales volume variance

= (Actual units sold – Budgeted sales) × Standard profit per unit

= (450,000 – 400,000) × $3 = $150,000 F.

(b) Planning and operational variances The revised (ex-post) budget would show that Hudson should expect to sell 20% of 2.2 million units = 440,000 units.

Original sales × standard margin = 400,000 × $3 = $1,200,000

Market size = $120,000 F

Revised sales × standard margin = 440,000 × $3 = $1,320,000

Market share = $30,000 F

Actual sales × standard margin = 450,000 × $3 = $1,350,000

Total sales volume variance = $120,000 F + $30,000 F = $150,000 F

Comment:

Most of the favourable variance can be attributed to the increase in overall market size. However, some can be put down to effort by the sales force which has increased its share from 20% to 20.5% (450,000/2,200,000).

Managers should only be appraised on the operational variance, i.e. the market share variance.

Test your understanding 10

AH × SR	1,450 × $10	= $14,500		
			Operational variance	$500 F
RSH × SR	1,500 × $10	= $15,000		
			Planning variance	$2,500 A
SH × SR	1,250 × $10	= $12,500		
				$2,000 A

Test your understanding 11

(a) **Traditional variances**

AQAP =		$41,500
	Price variance	$2,500 F
AQSP =	11,000 × $4 =	$44,000
	Usage variance	$4,800 A
SQSP =	1,400 × 7 × $4 =	$39,200

(b) **Planning and operational variances**

Price

AQ × AP		= $41,500
	Operational variance	$300 F
AQ × RSP	11,000 × $3.80	= $41,800
	Planning variance	$2,200 F
AQ × SP	11,000 × $4	= $44,000
		$2,500 F

Usage

AQ × AP	11,000 × $4	= $44,000
	Operational variance	$800 F
AQ × RSP	11,200 × $4	= $44,800
	Planning variance	$5,600 F
AQ × SP	9,800 × $4	= $39,200
		$4,800 F

Test your understanding 12

BFG net cash flow calculation

Sales units	120,000
	$
Sales revenue	1,260,000
Costs:	
Direct material (W1)	514,000
Direct labour (W2)	315,423
Variable overhead (W3)	126,169
Rent	180,000
Net cash flow	124,408
Target cash flow	130,000

The target cash flow will not be achieved.

Workings:

W1 **Direct material**

Batches	$
First 200 @ $500	100,000
Second 200 @ $450	90,000
Remaining 800 @ $405	324,000
	————
Total	514,000

W2 **Direct labour**

$y = ax^b$

where; a = 2,500 and b = –0.3219

Total cost for first 700 batches (x = 700);	
$700 \times 2,500 \times 700^{-0.3219}$	$212,423
Total cost for first 699 batches (x = 699);	
$699 \times 2,500 \times 699^{-0.3219}$	$212,217
Cost of 700th batch ($212,423 – $212,217)	$206
Total cost of final 500 batches;	
$206 × 500	$103,000
Total labour cost ($212,423 + $103,000)	$315,423

W3 **Variable overhead**

Variable overhead is $2 per labour hour, or 40% of the direct labour cost.

Business structure and performance management

Chapter learning objectives

Upon completion of this chapter you will be able to:

- identify and discuss the particular information needs of organisations adopting a functional, divisional or network form and the implications for performance management

- discuss, with reference to performance management, ways in which the information requirements of a management structure are affected by the features of the structure

- evaluate the external and internal factors (e.g. anticipated human behaviour) which will influence the design of a management accounting system

- discuss those factors that need to be considered when determining the capacity and development potential of a system

- demonstrate how the type of business entity will influence the recording and processing methods

- discuss the problems encountered in planning, controlling and measuring performance levels, e.g. productivity, profitability, quality and service levels, in complex business structures

- discuss the impact on performance management of the use of business models involving strategic alliances, joint ventures and complex supply chain structures

- assess the changes to management accounting systems to reflect the needs of modern service orientated businesses compared with the needs of a traditional manufacturing industry

- assess the influence of business process re-engineering (BPR) on systems development and improvements in organisational performance

- analyse the role that performance management systems play in business integration using models such as the value chain and McKinsey's 7S's

- discuss how changing an organisation's structure, culture and strategy will influence the adoption of new performance measurement methods and techniques.

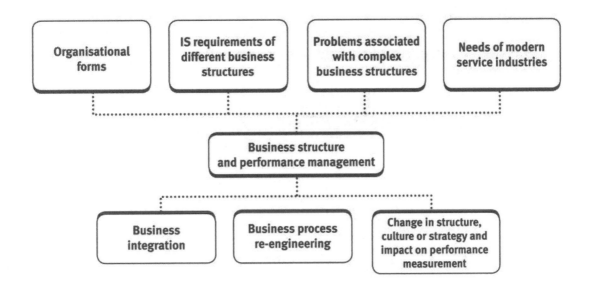

1 Knowledge from other ACCA exams

Chapter 4 builds on the knowledge of organisational structure and the value chain from the SBL exam.

2 Introduction

In this chapter we will look at the information and information system requirements of **different business structures**. We will also discuss the implications of a particular structure for performance management.

An important element of structure is **business integration**. Performance management can improve as a result of linkages between people, operations, strategy and technology. Section 7 of this chapter reviews two important frameworks for understanding business integration; Porter's value chain and McKinsey's 7s model.

The chapter then introduces the topic of **business process re- engineering**. This is the fundamental redesign of business processes and, amongst other things, it can result in a change of structure.

3 Organisational forms

3.1 Functional, divisional and network (virtual) structures

In the exam, you may be asked to discuss the particular information needs of an organisation adopting a functional, divisional or network structure and the implications of these structures for performance management.

3.2 Functional structure

Functional organisations group together employees that undertake similar tasks into departments.

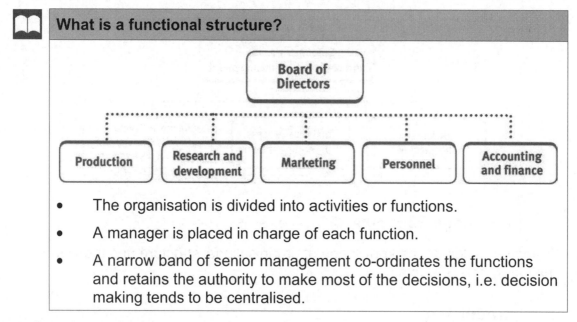

What is a functional structure?

- The organisation is divided into activities or functions.
- A manager is placed in charge of each function.
- A narrow band of senior management co-ordinates the functions and retains the authority to make most of the decisions, i.e. decision making tends to be centralised.

Information needs

The centralised structure results in:

- Data being passed from the functional level to the upper level.
- Data is then aggregated and analysed at the upper level for planning and control purposes.
- Feedback is then given at functional level.

Performance management

There are a number of advantages and disadvantages of a functional structure for performance management:

Advantages	Disadvantages
• Lower costs since roles are not duplicated.	• Unsuitable for diversified or growing organisations since it is hard to assess the performance of an individual product or market.
• Better control due to standardisation of outputs/ systems etc.	• Functional managers may make decisions that are good for themselves and their function but do not optimise organisational performance.
• Greater levels of employee motivation since specialists are grouped together so don't feel isolated and due to the defined career path that often exists within the function.	• Decision making slow due to the long chain of command.

3.3 Divisional structure

In a divisional structure the organisation is split into several divisions (sometimes referred to as strategic business units or subsidiaries) – each one autonomously overseeing a product or geographic region.

Information needs

The decentralised structure results in:

- Information being required lower down the hierarchy due to the high level of autonomy that exists.

- For example, information will be required by the divisions for budgeting purposes.

Implications for performance management

There are a number of advantages and disadvantages of a divisional structure for performance management:

Advantages	Disadvantages
• Easier for an organisation to grow and diversify.	• Inefficiencies due to duplication of functions.
• Easier to assess the performance of individual products or markets.	• Potential loss of goal congruence if the division makes decisions that benefit itself to the detriment of the overall organisation.
• There is clear responsibility for the performance of each division.	
• Performance management systems can be tailored to meet divisional needs.	• Cost arising from development and maintenance of appropriate information and control systems.
• Top management should be free to concentrate on strategic matters.	• Difficult to set a transfer price to fairly reflect the performance of the divisions.

> **Test your understanding 1**
>
> Company A is a diversified business with strategic business units (SBUs) in very different business areas. It is organised with each SBU being a separate division.
>
> Company B is a multinational with different parts of the supply chain in different countries. It is also divisionalised.
>
> **Required:**
>
> Comment on the differences in performance management issues for each company.

3.4 Network (virtual) structures

A network (or virtual) organisation occurs when an organisation outsources many of its functions to other organisations and simply exists as a network of contracts, with very few, if any, functions being kept in-house.

Characteristics include:

- The organisation has little or no physical premises.

- Employees and managers work remotely (often from home) and are connected using IT such as emails, video conferencing, intranets and extranets.

- Suppliers and customers are linked using IT systems which can add to the impression that they all form part of the same organisation.

- The organisation appears to the outside world to be just like any traditional organisation.

Illustration 1 – Network structures

Amazon.com

Many internet companies are examples of networks – Amazon being perhaps one of the best known on-line retailers.

- Amazon operates its website but relies on external suppliers, warehouses, couriers and credit card companies to deliver the rest of the customer experience. Most orders placed on Amazon's website are forwarded to suppliers, who then send the goods directly to the customer.

- These partners are also expected to provide Amazon with information on, for example, stock availability, delivery times and promotional material.

- The customer feels that they are dealing with one organisation, not many.

Information needs

With network structures, targeted information is needed to make decisions:

- Each party needs to have feedback as to how it is performing in relation to expectations and to others.

- Those responsible for regulating the performance of the organisation will also need information for decision making to enable them to make resource allocation decisions.

- Control is normally exercised via shared goals and, in the case of inter-organisational collaborations, contractual agreements.

Test your understanding 2

The idea of the network organisation emphasises:

- the decentralisation of control

- the creation of more flexible patterns of working

- a greater empowerment of the workforce

- the displacement of hierarchy by team working

- the development of a greater sense of collective responsibility

- the creation of more collaborative relationships among co-workers.

Required:

Comment on the importance of information to such an organisation.

Implications for performance management

Advantages:

- The organisation has the flexibility to meet the specific needs of a project.

- It can compete with large, successful organisations – they look and feel bigger than they are.

- It can assemble the components needed to exploit market opportunities.

- Lower costs, for example due to low investment in assets.

Disadvantages:

- It may be difficult to reach agreement over common goals and measures.

- Planning and control may be difficult – a traditional system of standard costing and variance analysis is less relevant since the core organisation does not need detailed information regarding the costs incurred by its business partners. Instead, they will require financial information (such as the prices that partners will charge) and non-financial information from partners (such as the quality of the goods/services, delivery times and ethical behaviour).

- This loss of control may result in a number of problems, for example a fall in quality or a greater/lesser degree of risk taking than would be desired.

- Confidentiality of information is a risk since the core organisation will share information with its partners (some of these partners may also work with competitor' organisations).

- Monitoring of the workforce may be difficult since the core organisation will not employ many of the virtual organisation's workforce and those that it does employ will often work remotely.

- It may be difficult to capture and share information if the systems are not integrated or are not compatible.

- Partners may work for competitors thus reducing competitive advantage. (The retention of the organisation's core competencies in-house should help to minimise this issue).

Many of the problems identified above can be addressed through the use of a robust **service level agreement** (SLA). This is a negotiated, legal agreement between the core organisation and its partners regarding the level of service to be provided. It should include the following:

- An agreement of common goals and measures.

- Areas of responsibility should be identified. Action to be taken if KPIs are not met should be stated (for example, the use of fines).

- The activities expected of each partner together with the minimum standards expected, for example with regards to quality.

- A confidentiality agreement.

- An agreement of the standards and procedures to be adhered to by the workforce. It is worth noting that other actions outside those stated in the SLA may be used to effectively manage the workforce, for example the use of payment by results or the creation of cultural controls and a climate of trust.

- The information and reporting procedures to be followed. It is worth noting that the core organisation may put a common interface system in place to assist with information gathering.

Student accountant article: visit the ACCA website, www.accaglobal.com, to review the article on 'complex business structures'.

4 Information system requirements of different business structures

The information system requirements will be driven by the characteristics of the organisational structure. For example:

Characteristics of organisation structure	Information system
Large, complex structure.	A sophisticated system will be necessary and beneficial and should be cost effective.
High level of interaction between business units.	System should aid communication between managers.
Responsibility centres in place, i.e. the business is split into parts which are the responsibility of a single manager. The area of responsibility may be a cost centre, profit centre or investment centre (see chapter 9).	Management accounting systems should be designed to reflect the responsibility structure in place and ensure that costs and revenues can be traced to those responsible. Managers of responsibility centres will require: • the correct information • in the correct form • at the correct intervals.

Responsibility centres

Responsibility accounting is a system of accounting based upon the identification of individual parts of a business which are the responsibility of a single manager.

Budgetary control and responsibility accounting are inseparable.

- An organisation chart must be drawn up in order to implement a budgetary control system satisfactorily. It may even be necessary to revise the existing organisation structure before designing the system.

- The aim is to ensure that each manager has a well-defined area of responsibility and the authority to make decisions within that area, and that no parts of the organisation remain as 'grey' areas where it is uncertain who is responsible for them.

- This area of responsibility may be simply a cost centre, or it may be a profit centre (implying that the manager has control over sales revenues as well as costs) or an investment centre (implying that the manager is empowered to take decisions about capital investment for his department). Appropriate performance measures for such structures are discussed in later chapters.

- Once senior management have set up such a structure, with the degree of delegation implied, some form of responsibility accounting system is needed.

- Each centre will have its own budget, and the manager will receive control information relevant to that budget centre.

- Costs (and possibly revenue, assets and liabilities) must be traced to the person primarily responsible for taking the related decisions, and identified with the appropriate department.

- Some accountants would go as far as to advocate charging departments with costs that arise strictly as a result of decisions made by the management of those departments.

Management accounting systems should be designed to reflect the responsibility structure in place and ensure that costs and revenues can be traced to those responsible.

Controllability

The principal of controllability is very important in responsibility accounting. Whilst controllability refers mainly to costs, it is important to remember that its principles can also apply to revenues and investments.

- Controllability can depend on the time scale being considered.

  – Over a long enough time-span, most costs are controllable by someone in the organisation.

  – In the short-term some costs, such as rent, are uncontrollable even by senior managers, and certainly uncontrollable by managers lower down the organisational hierarchy.

- There may be no clear-cut distinction between controllable and non-controllable costs for a given manager, who may also be exercising control jointly with another manager.

- The aim under a responsibility accounting system will be to assign and report on the cost to the person having primary responsibility. The most effective control is thereby achieved, since immediate action can be taken.

- Some authorities would favour the alternative idea that reports should include all costs caused by a department, whether controllable or uncontrollable by the departmental manager. The idea here is that, even if he has no direct control, he might influence the manager who does have control.

5 Problems associated with complex business structures

Complex business structures may include those discussed in section 3 (i.e. divisional and network structures) but may also include structures such as:

- joint ventures
- strategic alliances
- franchising
- licensing
- multinationals and
- complex supply chains.

There are a number of problems in planning, controlling and measuring performance in these complex business structures. For example:

Business structure	Problems in planning control
Joint venture (JV) – a separate business entity whose shares are owned by two or more business entities. Useful for sharing costs, risks and expertise.	• In terms of measuring performance, the primary difficulty is establishing the objectives of the JV. The different partners may have different goals, risk appetites and timescales. Hence a large variety of performance measures will be required and there will have to be some agreement on common goals. • Attributing accountability for performance is difficult since each JV partner will bring different skills and knowledge to the venture. This accountability should be established at the outset. • Reporting of joint profits/losses difficult if partners are unwilling to share information or do not have an integrated system. • Quality, cost control and risk management difficult if partners have different opinions. • The JV partners may be reluctant to share too much information about their own business with the other JV partner. However, in order to succeed a climate of trust must exist which will rely on compatible management styles and cultures.

Strategic alliance – similar to a joint venture but a separate business entity is not formed.	Many of the difficulties above also apply but more specifically: • Independence is retained making it difficult to put common performance measures in place and to collect and analyse management information. • Security of confidential information a concern.
Multinationals – have subsidiaries or operations in a number of countries.	• Co-ordination of subsidiaries or operations to ensure they are working towards the overall mission and objectives can be difficult. • Cultural, language, currency and time zone differences may make planning and control difficult. • Measuring and reporting performance may be difficult if common systems don't exist. • Open to greater levels of uncertainty, for example due to exchange rate movements, changes in government policy and recession.

Question practice with additional assistance

The question below is taken from a past exam. It is an excellent test of your ability to add depth to your answer and to use the scenario since there is only one requirement worth 17 marks.

Additional guidance has been included within both the question and the answer. Take the time to read this guidance and use the advice given when attempting future questions.

This is an excellent question to learn from. Ensure that you attempt it and take time to review the answer before sitting the exam.

Test your understanding 3

Callisto Retail (Callisto) is an on-line reseller of local craft products related to the historic culture of the country of Callistan. The business started ten years ago as a hobby of two brothers, Jeff and George. The brothers produced humorous, short video clips about Callistan which were posted on their website and became highly popular. They decided to use the website to try to sell Callistan merchandise and good initial sales made them believe that they had a viable business idea.

Callisto has gone from strength to strength and now boasts sales of $120m per annum, selling anything related to Callistan. Callisto is still very much the brothers' family business. They have gathered around themselves a number of strategic partners into what Jeff describes as a virtual company. Callisto has the core functions of video clip production, finance and supplier relationship management. The rest of the functions of the organisation (warehousing, delivery and website development) are outsourced to strategic partners.

The brothers work from their family home in the rural North of Callistan while other Callisto employees work from their homes in the surrounding villages and towns. These employees are involved in video editing, system maintenance, handling customer complaints and communication with suppliers and outsourcers regarding inventory. The employees log in to Callisto's systems via the national internet infrastructure. The outsourced functions are handled by multinational companies of good reputation who are based around the world. The brothers have always been fascinated by information technology and so they depend on email and electronic data interchange to communicate with their product suppliers and outsourcing partners.

Recently, there have been emails from regular customers of the Callisto website complaining about slow or non-delivery of orders that they have placed. George has commented that this represents a major threat to Callisto as the company operates on small profit margins, relying on volume to drive the business. He believes that sales growth will drive the profitability of the business due to its cost structure.

Jeff handles the management of outsourcing and has been reviewing the contracts that exist between Callisto and its strategic partner for warehousing and delivery, RLR Logistics. The current contract for warehousing and delivery is due for renewal in two months and currently, has the following service level agreements (SLAs):

1 RLR agree to receive and hold inventory from Callisto's product suppliers.

2 RLR agree to hold 14 days inventory of Callisto's products.

3 RLR agree to despatch from their warehouse any order passed from Callisto within three working days, inventory allowing.

4 RLR agree to deliver to customers anywhere in Callistan within two days of despatch.

Breaches in these SLAs incur financial penalties on a sliding scale depending on the number and severity of the problems. Each party to the contract collects their own data on performance and this has led to disagreements in the past over whether service levels have been achieved although no penalties have been triggered to date. The most common disagreement arises over inventory levels held by RLR with RLR claiming that it cannot be expected to deliver products that are late in arriving to inventory due to the product suppliers' production and delivery issues.

Required:

Assess the difficulties of performance measurement and performance management in complex business structures such as Callisto, especially in respect of the performance of their employees and strategic partners.

(Total: 17 marks)

Question assistance

Step 1 – Review the requirements

Assessment = is an alternative to 'evaluate' where both pros and cons are needed and final judgement on their balance is required.

Performance measurement AND performance management – so need to go further than just the measures and think about how to improve performance.

'Complex business structures such as Callisto' – what constitutes a complex business structure and how does Callisto meet this definition?

Ensure employees and strategic partners are specifically addressed.

Step 2 – Review scenario for relevant information relating to requirements

Examples here include:

- 'on-line reseller'

- 'They have gathered around themselves a number of strategic partners into what Jeff describes as a virtual company'

- 'The rest of the functions of the organisation (warehousing, delivery and website development) are outsourced to strategic partners'

- 'The employees log in to Callisto's systems via the national internet infrastructure'

- 'outsourced functions are handled by multinational companies of good reputation'

- 'so they depend on email and electronic data interchange to communicate with their product suppliers and outsourcing partners'

- 'complaining about slow or non-delivery of orders'

- 'the company operates on small profit margins'

- The current contract for warehousing and delivery is due for renewal in two months'

- 'Each party to the contract collects their own data on performance and this has led to disagreements in the past'.

Step 3 – Plan the answer

You need to plan your answer identifying sufficient points for each part of the requirement. Use headings to structure your plan – this will help you keep focused when you write your answer.

Difficulties for Performance Measurement

- Employees

- Strategic partners.

For each heading you need to be identifying the difficulties for a virtual organisation (the 'textbook' answer) and combine this with relevant examples and information regarding Callisto. Both of these elements are essential for your answer otherwise you are either just describing the scenario or merely repeating textbook content.

Step 4 – Check requirements

Quick recap of requirements – have you covered everything?

Step 5 – Write your answer

Use space, headings and short paragraphs to clearly signpost to the marker that you have covered all the necessary parts. If you have planned properly this will be the easiest part of the whole question.

6 The needs of modern service industries

6.1 Introduction

Although not strictly a type of structure, it makes sense to look at service industries as part of this chapter.

Traditional manufacturing companies have been replaced by modern service industries, e.g. insurance, management consultancy and professional services.

The differences between the products of manufacturing companies and those of service businesses:

- can create **problems in measuring and controlling performance**
  and

- this, in turn, **affects the information needs of service organisations**.

6.2 Characteristics of services

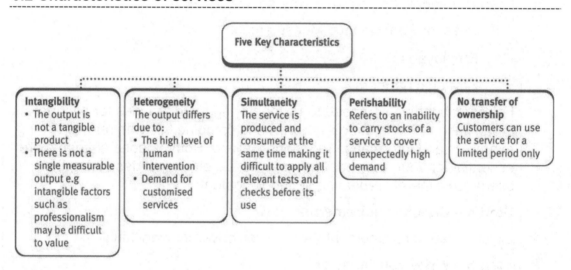

6.3 Measuring service quality

Service providers do not have a physical product so base competitive advantage on less tangible customer benefits such as:

- soundness of advice given

- attitude of staff

- ambience of premises

- speed of service

- flexibility/responsiveness

- consistent quality.

Test your understanding 4

Required:

State the performance measures that may be used in order to assess the surgical quality provided by a hospital indicating how each measure may be addressed.

7 Business integration

7.1 What is business integration?

An important aspect of business structure is business integration.

Business integration means that all aspects of the business must be aligned to secure the most efficient use of the organisation's resources so that it can achieve its objectives effectively.

Rather than focusing on individual parts of the business in isolation, the whole process from the initial order to final delivery of the product and after sales service needs to be considered.

Hammer and Davenport

Modern writers such as **Hammer** and **Davenport** argue that many organisations have departments and functions that try to maximise their own performance and efficiency at the expense of the whole.

Their proposed solution is twofold:

1   Processes need to be viewed as complete entities that stretch from initial order to final delivery of a product.

2   IT needs to be used to integrate these activities.

Four aspects in particular need to be linked:

*   people

*   operations

*   strategy

*   technology.

Test your understanding 5

Required:

XYZ has a conventional functional structure. Assess how many different people in the organisation may have to deal with customers, and the problems this creates.

There are two frameworks for understanding integrated processes and the linkages within them:

- Porter's value chain model.

- McKinsey's 7S model.

7.2 Porter's value chain

The value chain model is based around **activities** rather than traditional functional departments (such as finance). It considers the organisation's activities that create value and drive costs and therefore the organisation should focus on improving those activities. The activities are split into **primary** ones (the customer interacts with these and can 'see' the value being created) and **secondary** (or support) activities which are necessary to support the primary activities.

Margin, i.e. profit will be achieved if the customer is willing to pay more for the product/service than the sum of the costs of all the activities in the value chain.

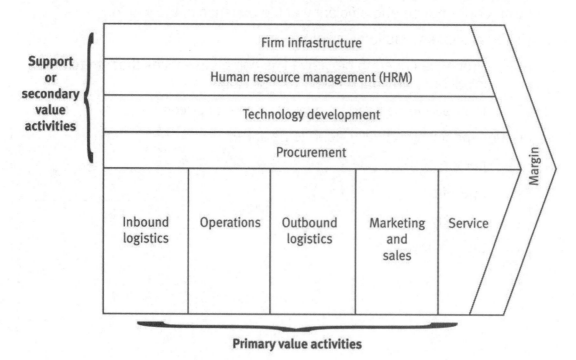

Illustration 2 – Value chain activities

Primary activity	Description	Example
Inbound logistics	Receiving, storing and handling raw material inputs	A just-in-time stock system could give a cost advantage (see chapter 13)
Operations	Transformation of raw materials into finished goods and services	Using skilled craftsmen could give a quality advantage
Outbound logistics	Storing, distributing and delivering finished goods to customers	Outsourcing activities could give a cost advantage
Marketing and sales	Market research and the marketing mix (product, price, place, promotion)	Sponsorship of a sports celebrity could enhance the image of a product
After sales service	All activities that occur after the point of sale, such as installation, training and repair	A flexible approach to customer returns could enhance a quality image

Secondary (support) activity	Description	Example
Firm infrastructure	How the firm is organised	Centralised buying could result in cost savings due to bulk discounts
Technology development	How the firm uses technology	Modern computer-controlled machinery gives greater flexibility to tailor products to meet customer specifications
Human resource management	How people contribute to competitive advantage	Employing expert buyers could enable a supermarket to purchase better wine than their competitors
Procurement	Purchasing, but not just limited to materials	Buying a building out of town could give a cost advantage over High Street competitors

Illustration 3 – Value chain

Value chain analysis helps managers to decide how individual activities might be changed to reduce costs of operation or to improve the value of the organisation's offerings. Such changes will increase margin.

For example, a clothes manufacturer may spend large amounts on:

buying good quality raw materials (inbound logistics)

hand-finishing garments (operations)

building a successful brand image (marketing)

running its own fleet of delivery trucks in order to deliver finished clothes quickly to customers (outbound logistics).

All of these should add value to the product, allowing the company to charge a premium for its clothes.

Another clothes manufacturer may:

- reduce the cost of its raw materials by buying in cheaper supplies from abroad (inbound logistics)

- making all its clothes using machinery that runs 24 hours a day (operations)

- delaying distribution until delivery trucks can be filled with garments for a particular location (outbound logistics).

All of these should enable the company to gain economies of scale and to sell clothes at a cheaper price than its rivals.

Evaluation of the value chain

Advantages of the value chain model

- Particularly useful for focusing on how each activity in the process adds to the firm's overall competitive advantage.

- Emphasises CSFs within each activity and overall.

- Examines both primary activities (e.g. production) and support activities, such as HRM, which may otherwise be dismissed as overheads.

- Highlights linkages between activities.

Disadvantages of the value chain model

- It is more suited to a manufacturing environment and can be hard to apply to a service provider.

- It is intended as a quantitative analysis tool but this can be time consuming since it often requires recalibrating the system to allocate costs to individual activities.

Test your understanding 6

Many European clothing manufacturers, even those aiming at the top end of the market, outsource production to countries with lower wage costs such as Sri Lanka and China.

Required:

Comment on whether you feel this is an example of poor integration (or poor linkage in Porter's terminology).

Uses in performance management

- Used as part of **strategic analysis** to identify strengths or weaknesses and to focus on how each activity does or could add to the firms competitive advantage.

- Used for **ongoing performance management**. It emphasises the CSFs within each activity and targets can then be set and monitored in relation to these.

- In addition to examining primary activities (for example, production) it **looks at support activities** (for example, HRM), which may have otherwise have been dismissed as overheads.

- It highlights the linkages between activities. The idea of a **chain** is important. Value will be created by linking activities and hence:

  - information systems should allow the free flow of information between activities and across departmental boundaries.

  - job descriptions and reporting hierarchies should reflect activities.

Test your understanding 7

Kudos Guitar Amplifiers (KGA)

Kudos Guitar Amplifiers (KGA) was set up by Phil Smith two years ago in the UK. Phil, an electrical engineer and musician, started repairing and then building guitar amplifiers for himself and friends. Initially Phil based his amplifiers around existing classic circuits but soon discovered a potential to tweak these to produce modern variations and improved tones. Partly as a result of the excellent sound but also the low prices compared to established brands, Phil soon found himself inundated with requests and so started the business and employed more staff.

The big break came when a number of high profile professional musicians started using KGA amplifiers. Despite operating in a highly competitive market sector, Phil has struggled to meet demand since and has waiting lists for the hand-built, top of the range models, even having increased prices considerably.

Phil is looking to expand the business further, extend the range of products offered to include cheaper models and look to sell into additional markets. He has recruited more staff, built a state of the art, dedicated factory and appointed managers. To ensure the longevity of his business Phil commissioned a strategic consultant who advised him to adopt a competitive strategy of differentiation.

Extracts from the value chain analysis produced by the consultant are as follows:

- Inbound logistics

  As well as Phil's proprietary circuit designs, part of the sound of KGA amplifiers comes from the use of rare "new old stock" (NOS) components, some originally manufactured in the 1960s. Locating sufficient numbers of such components to the required quality is a major challenge and it is felt that KGA's relationship with two key suppliers is vital.

- Operations

  The top of the range models are hand built by master craftsmen with point to point wiring and specialist components. Given normal variations in some of these, different elements are tested and matched by ear to optimise tonal characteristics. Extensive quality control tests are done before an amplifier is ready for sale. Newer, cheaper models use pre-assembled circuit boards bought from a SE Asian supplier.

The factory also uses "clean room" technologies and fume extraction safety processes that far exceed current industry requirements and add to the factory running costs.

- Outbound logistics

  Originally selling direct to customers, Phil has now agreed distribution contracts with two national UK retailers and is hoping to secure similar deals in Germany and the USA.

- Marketing and sales

  Marketing currently consists of word of mouth, advertising in guitar magazines and sponsorship of high profile musicians. The company will also be setting up a website and Facebook page. It is felt that continued publicity from famous guitarists and online exposure are vital to achieving growth targets.

  The new ranges have the same brand name as the original hand-built products.

> - Service
>
>   Phil offers a lifetime warranty on his top of the range amplifiers with a guaranteed turnaround of 5 days, although he did have a problem repairing an amplifier in time for a rock band headlining at a major festival. Cheaper ranges have an industry standard 12 months' warranty.
>
> **Required**
>
> Identify the performance management issues arising from the above analysis.

Value system

More recently, organisations have started to consider supply chain partnerships. The value system looks at linking the value chains of suppliers and customers to that of the organisation. A firm's performance depends not only on its own value chain, but on its ability to manage the value system of which it is part.

 Illustration 4

> In Chapter 2 we looked at an illustration on the UK supermarket giant, Tesco and its high wastage levels of products such as bagged salads. Tesco's 'farm to fork' methodology has engaged with producers, suppliers and customers to collect data on the levels and causes of food waste and to give an overall waste 'footprint' for a selection of products. This has shown where waste 'hotspots' have occurred and has enabled Tesco to develop a waste reduction action plan and targets for each product. For example, 'display until' dates have been removed from fruit and vegetables.
>
> This emphasis on reduced wastage should help Tesco to cut costs and should contribute to meeting its objective of being a socially responsible retailer.

7.3 McKinsey's 7s model

The **McKinsey 7S model** describes an organisation as consisting of seven interrelated internal elements.

A change in one element will have repercussions on the others. All seven elements must be aligned to ensure organisational success.

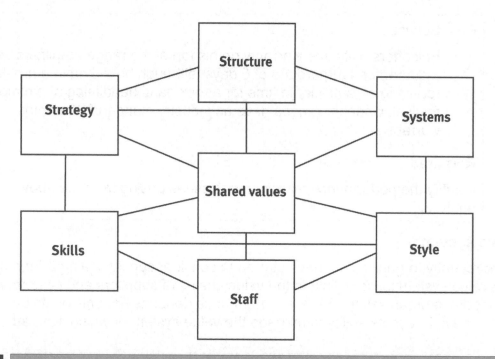

 McKinsey's 7S model

There are three **hard** elements of business behaviour

- Strategy – what will the company do?

- Structure – how should it be organised?

- Systems – what procedures need to be in place (few or many)?

Hard elements are easier to define or identify and management can directly influence them.

There are four **soft** elements.

- Staff – what staff will we require?

- Style – what management style will work best?

- Shared values – what culture (attitudes) will be most suitable?

- Skills – what skills will our staff/company need?

Soft elements are more difficult to describe, less tangible and are more influenced by culture.

8 Business Process Re-engineering (BPR)

8.1 What is BPR?

The discussion of BPR follows on from the value chain. As discussed, the value chain shows the way in which the various activities of an organisation work together to add value. The ways these activities function and interrelate constitute an organisation's processes. This process perspective is the emphasis of BPR.

BPR is the **fundamental rethinking and radical redesign of business processes** to achieve dramatic improvements in critical, contemporary measures of performance, such as cost, quality, service and speed. Improved customer satisfaction is often the primary aim.

Illustration 5 – IBM and BPR

Prior to re-engineering, it took IBM Credit between one and two weeks to issue credit, often losing customers during this period.

- On investigation it was found that performing the actual work only took 90 minutes. The rest of the time (more than seven days!) was spent passing the form from one department to the next.

- The solution was to replace specialists (e.g. credit checkers) with generalists – one person (a deal 'structurer') processes the entire application from beginning to end.

- Post re-engineering, the process took only minutes or hours.

Test your understanding 8

A business process is a series of activities that are linked together in order to achieve given objectives. For example, materials handling might be classed as a business process in which the separate activities are scheduling production, storing materials, processing purchase orders, inspecting materials and paying suppliers.

Required:

Suggest ways in which materials handling might be re-engineered.

8.2 The influence of BPR on the organisation

BPR cuts across traditional departmental lines in order to achieve more efficient delivery of the final product.

- This change to a process view will require a change in **culture** with a move towards process teams rather than functional departments.

- Employees will need to **retrain** in order to gain additional skills.

- The change will require much **communication and leadership** from senior management as a result.

- BPR results in more **automation and greater use of IT/IS** to integrate processes. The rise of BPR in the 1990s coincided with the widespread adoption of new IT systems based on personal computers, networks and the internet.

8.3 Does BPR improve organisational performance?

Advocates of BPR would argue that **organisational performance will improve**:

- BPR encourages a long-term strategic view by asking questions about how core processes can be honed in order to achieve corporate goals more effectively.

- BPR revolves around customer needs; the fulfilment of which is vital for sustaining competitive advantage.

- BPR can help reduce organisational complexity by eliminating unnecessary activities.

- A process should be made cheaper and more responsive to customer needs by stripping away the peripheral activities and bureaucratic layers that sometimes emerge from excessive focus on functional boundaries.

However, the approach does have a number of **weaknesses** which may make it ill-suited to an organisation today. BPR often produced a quick fix to perceived problems but at a long-term cost. Practical problems include:

- A decline in morale due to staff cuts and a perception that BPR is all about cost cutting.

- Staff may feel devalued when their current role is fundamentally changed with a re-organisation into new teams with different goals and expectations.

- BPR often strips out different layers of middle management. This may lead to a loss of co-ordination and communication.

- BPR often utilised outsourcing; farming out business processes and elements of production. However, this sometimes had adverse consequences on quality and flexibility.

- In many cases, business processes were not redesigned but merely automated.

Numerous organisations have attempted to redesign their business processes but have failed to enjoy the enormous benefits promised. It is now widely accepted that BPR may be a backward-looking approach. It takes what has happened in the past and seeks to improve it, but with limited regard for what will happen in the future.

8.4 The influence of BPR on systems development

Remember 'what gets measured gets done'. Therefore, the systems will have to be redesigned to capture new performance measurement data, focusing on factors such as:

- quality
- innovation
- ability to work as a team
- on time delivery.

It is also said that 'what gets rewarded gets repeated' so the reward system (for example, the payment of a bonus) should be aligned to these new measures. The basic part of the remuneration may also increase to reflect the increased skills base, autonomy and responsibility of employees.

9 The impact of a change in structure, culture and strategy on performance measurement

A change in organisational structure, culture or strategy may result in a requirement for new performance measurement techniques and methods:

Organisational change	Examples of impact on performance measurement
Structure	• Highly centralised and/or functional structures will require a performance measurement system that enables data to be collected at functional level, analysed at the upper level and then fed back to the functional levels. These structures tend to inhibit a manager's discretion to try out new performance measurement techniques. • A task centred and/or decentralised structure will require a performance measurement system that allows data to be collected and analysed lower down the hierarchy. Managers will have more discretion to try out new performance measurement techniques.

Culture	• An innovative or creative culture will be willing to embrace new performance measurement techniques. Measurement techniques will need to focus on the performance of the innovations.
	• A restrictive, bureaucratic culture will be less open to the adoption of new performance measurement techniques.
Strategy	• The performance measurement techniques adopted should be aligned to the strategy the organisation is pursuing.
	• For example, an organisation that focuses on quality and has adopted a TQM approach will need performance measures that focus on factors such as the quality of the product or service, the cost of prevention and speed of response (quality is discussed in Chapter 13).

10 Exam focus

Exam sitting	Area examined	Question number	Number of marks
Mar/June 2016	BPR	2	25
June 2015	Value chain	1(v)	6
June 2014	BPR	2(a)(b)	17
June 2014	Complex business structures	3(c)	8
June 2013	Differences between services and manufacturing organisations	1(i)	5
June 2013	Change in divisional structure	4(c)	9
June 2012	Performance management and measurement in complex business structures	5	17
June 2012	Complex business structures	5	17

Chapter summary

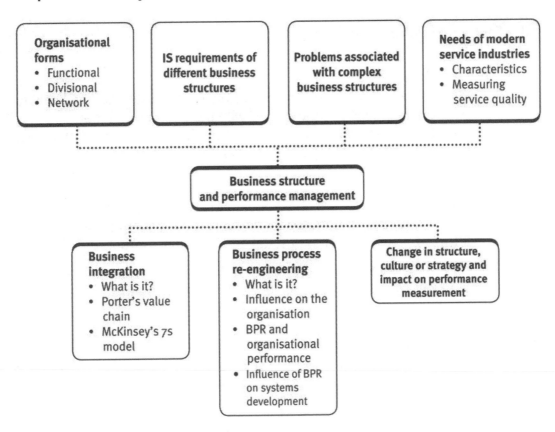

Test your understanding answers

Test your understanding 1

Company A

- Given that business units are in unrelated markets, there is likely to be more devolved management, with the use of divisional performance measures and reliance on the measurement systems, particularly financial reporting, for control.

Company B

- There is a need for a high level of interaction between business units, so senior management control is more important, whether in terms of standardisation or detailed operational targets.

- The performance measurement system may aid communication between managers and provide a common language.

Test your understanding 2

Information is key to a successful network organisation:

- This is mainly through the systems that facilitate co-ordination and communication, decision making and the sharing of knowledge, skills and resources.

- Information systems can reduce the number of levels in the organisation by providing managers with information to manage and control larger numbers of workers spread over greater distances and by giving lower-level employees more decision-making authority.

- It is no longer necessary for these employees to work standard hours every day, nor work in an office or even the same country as their manager. With the emergence of global networks, team members can collaborate closely even from distant locations. Information technology permits tight co-ordination of geographically dispersed workers across time zones and cultures.

Test your understanding 3

> *Tutor tip: Splitting your answer into the measurement and management sections is a good start. You can break it down further by separating employees, strategic partners and other issues.*

Performance measurement problems at Callisto

In a virtual organisation such as Callisto, performance measurement can be difficult due to the fact that key players in the business processes and in the supply chain are not 'on site'. Callisto has the problem of collecting and monitoring data about its employees working from home and the outsourcing partners.

> *Tutor tip: This identifies the key issue relating to the 'virtual' nature of a company like Callisto.*

At Callisto, there is a reliance placed on information technology for handling these remote contacts. Collecting and monitoring performance should therefore be done automatically as far as possible. A large database would be required that can be automatically updated from the activities of the remote staff and suppliers. This will require the staff and supplier systems to be compatible.

> *Tutor tip: Another specific issue relating to virtual organisations that has been linked to information regarding Callisto. This paragraph goes further than just identifying the issue and explains the implications.*

Employees

The employees can be required to use software supplied by Callisto and in fact, at Callisto, they use the internet to log in remotely to Callisto's common systems. Although this solution requires expenditure on hardware and software, it is within the control of Callisto's management.

> *Tutor tip: Part of 'assessing' the difficulty may involve explaining why it is not too much of an issue – so here identifying the fact that Callisto still have control over their employees.*

Even with reviews of system logs to identify the hours that staff spend logged in to the systems, there is still the difficulty of measuring staff outputs in order to ensure their productivity. These outputs must be clearly defined by Callisto's managers, otherwise there will be disputes between staff and management.

> *Tutor tip: Again, the implication of the problem has been described.*

One further outstanding issue is the need to ensure that such communication is over properly secured communication channels, especially if it contains customer or financial data. There are likely to be significant penalties if data protection regulations are breached, not to mention the reputational impact.

Strategic partners

The strategic partners, such as RLR, will have their own systems. A problem for Callisto is that there is disagreement over the measurement of the key SLAs. In order to resolve such disputes, lengthy reconciliations between Callisto's and RLR's systems will have to be undertaken otherwise there are no grounds for enforcement of the SLAs and the SLAs represent Callisto's key control over the relationship.

Tutor tip: The implication has been explained with specific reference to information in the scenario. This ensures your answer is not just a generic 'textbook' answer.

The solution would be for the partners to agree a standard reporting format for all data that relates to the SLAs which would remove the need for such reconciliations.

Tutor tip: Part of 'assessing' a difficulty may involve thinking about how it can be resolved.

Finally, there is the problem that Callisto and the partner organisation may have differing objectives – the obvious conflict over price between supplier and customer being one. However, at Callisto, this is being addressed by the use of detailed SLAs which both organisations can use to develop performance measures such as inventory levels and delivery times.

Performance management problems at Callisto

Tutor tip: Performance management goes a step further than merely measuring output and considers how improvements can be made.

Employees

The performance management of employees is complicated due to the inability of management to 'look over their shoulder' since they are not present in the same building. However, employees will enjoy the advantages of home-working, such as lower commuting times, more contact with family and greater flexibility in working hours. The disadvantages are the difficulties in measuring outputs mentioned above and ensuring motivation and commitment.

Tutor tip: This nicely combines an identification of the problem, the implications of the problem along with an upside to the situation.

The motivation and commitment can be addressed through suitable reward schemes which would have to be tied to agreed outputs and targets for each employee. Work could be divided into projects where the outputs are more easily identified and pay and bonuses related to these.

Tutor tip: Further assessment of the problem considers the possible solutions.

Strategic partners

When managing the performance of the strategic partners it is crucial that there is a balance between consideration of security and control issues and encouraging a positive and collaborative relationship.

> *Tutor tip: This introduces the difficulty faced regarding performance management of strategic partners.*

One difficulty which may arise concerns confidentiality as the partners will have access to commercially sensitive information about customers' locations and suppliers' names and lead times. Callisto must control access to this information without affecting the relationship. Leakage of such data will have a detrimental effect on the company's reputation. However interface between the organisations can create wasteful activity if there is not an atmosphere of trust. At Callisto, this is illustrated by the problem of reconciliation of performance data.

> *Tutor tip: The problem is further explained and the possible implications considered.*

It is also important to consider reliability where the partner is supplying a business critical role (as for RLR with Callisto) such that it would take considerable time to replace such a relationship and affect customer service while this happened.

Finally Callisto must carefully consider profit sharing. The collaborative nature of the relationship and the difficulty of breaking it combine to imply that it will be in the interest of both parties to negotiate a contract that is motivating and profitable for both sides. For Callisto, the business aim is to increase volume and this will require customer loyalty so the quality of service is important.

> *Tutor tip: The 'difficulty' identified here is how to determine the appropriate split of profit between Callisto and its partners.*

Test your understanding 4

- The percentage of satisfied patients which could be measured by using the number of customer complaints or via a patient survey.

- The time spent waiting for non-emergency operations which could be measured by reference to the time elapsed from the date when an operation was deemed necessary until it was actually performed.

- The number of successful operations as a percentage of total operations performed which could be measured by the number of remedial operations undertaken.

- The percentage of total operations performed in accordance with agreed schedules which could be measured by reference to agreed operation schedules.

- The standards of cleanliness and hygiene maintained which could be measured by observation or by the number of cases of hospital bugs such as MRSA.

- The staff to patient ratio which could be measured by reference to personnel and patient records.

- The responsiveness of staff to requests of patients which could be measured via a patient survey.

Test your understanding 5

1   Sales staff to make the original sale.

2   Delivery staff to arrange delivery.

3   Accounts staff chasing up payment if invoices are overdue.

4   Customer service staff if there is a problem with the product.

Possible problems include:

- delivery staff may be unaware of any special delivery requirements agreed by the sales staff

- accounts staff may be unaware of any special discounts offered

- aggressive credit controllers could damage sales negotiations for potential new sales

- credit controllers might not be aware of special terms offered to the client to win their business

- customers may resent having to re-explain their circumstances to each point of contact

- customer service may be unaware of the key factors in why the client bought the product and hence not prioritise buying.

Customer service could be improved by having one customer-facing point of contact.

Test your understanding 6

Firms following a cost leadership strategy have found that outsourcing to China, say, has cut costs considerably, even after taking into account distribution costs.

Differentiators have, on the whole, found that they have saved costs without compromising quality. Thus the apparent conflict between low cost production and high quality branding has not been a problem. Furthermore the perceived quality of Chinese garments is rising with some manufacturers claiming that quality is higher than in older European factories.

Note: Commercial awareness – given that many firms do it, be wary of criticising the approach too heavily! They must have their reasons.

Test your understanding 7

Introduction

Generally, the value chain is a model of business integration showing the way that business activities are organised. This model is based around activities rather than traditional functional departments (such as finance). A key idea is that it is activities which create value and incur costs. The activities are split into two groups: primary ones which the customer interacts with directly and can 'see' the value being created and secondary ones which are necessary to support the primary activities. By identifying how value is created, the organisation can then focus on improving those activities through its performance measurement system.

Context – competitive strategy *(note: this aspect of the analysis has considerable overlap with the SB: case study)*

If KGA is going to adopt a strategy of differentiation as recommended, then it needs to ensure that all aspects of the value chain are coordinated to support this.

In particular the following issues are relevant:

- There is a risk that the cheaper range could undermine the brand perception as the inherent quality will be lower than the hand-built models. Whether this is a significant risk is unclear as the cheaper models may still offer exceptional sound quality compared to rival products within their price range. If there is a risk, then it might be worth considering using a different brand strategy for them.

- Non value-added activities should be discontinued. In particular, excessive spending on clean room and extraction processes seems unnecessary as it does not add to the perceived quality of the amplifiers and does not appear to be valued by customers.

- Activities that are vital for the high sound quality – sourcing NOS components, being hand built and tested by craftsmen and the publicity gained from being used by famous guitarists – need to be strengthened and consolidated.

Performance management – establishing CSFs and KPIs

Based on the above analysis, KGA will need to establish a system of CSFs and KPIs, which could include the following:

CSF	Comment	KPIs
Securing sufficient volumes of high quality NOS components	The NOS components are a vital part of the final sound quality for the hand built amplifiers.	• Number of each component in stock • % returns back to suppliers due to quality problems • Lead times by component and supplier
Ensuring build and sound quality of top of the range amplifiers	KGA's success is underpinned by the sound quality of its amplifiers. If this suffers for any reason then customers will by competitors' offerings instead.	• % rejected by quality control • % requiring reworking or repair • Average scores in online reviews • Staff turnover of master craftsmen
Meeting sponsored guitarists' needs	Many customers are drawn to KGA products because they see guitar heroes using the products. If these guitar players chose to use different brands then sales would drop and the brand be undermined.	• Turnaround time on repairs and servicing • No (%) of returns • Time taken to build new equipment for them

Effective website sales and marketing	The website is seen as key to new growth.	<ul><li>No of hits</li><li>Average length of visit</li><li>% of hits that translate into sales</li><li>Average purchase value</li><li>% down time</li></ul>

Performance management – MIS issues

Another feature of the value chain is the idea of a chain. This is the thought that value is built by linking activities and so there must be a flow of information between the different activities and across departmental boundaries. In performance management terms, this will affect:

- information systems which will have to ensure good communication across functional boundaries and

- job descriptions and reporting hierarchies as these will have to reflect activities.

The chain does not stop at the organisation's boundaries. This is likely to be obvious to KGA given the importance of supply chain management but the value chain will allow the organisation to focus on those relationships on which value most depends.

Specifically for KGA, the value chain would emphasise the importance of supplier management to obtain suitable NOS components, leading through to operations in the form of testing and matching components, resulting in finished amplifiers.

Test your understanding 8

In the case of materials handling, the activity of processing purchase orders might be re-engineered by:

- integrating the production planning system with that of the supplier (an exercise in supply chain management (or SCM)) and thus sending purchase orders direct to the supplier without any intermediate administrative activity

- joint quality control procedures might be agreed thus avoiding the need to check incoming materials. In this manner, the cost of material procurement, receiving, holding and handling is reduced.

The impact of information technology

Upon completion of this chapter you will be able to:

- highlight the ways in which contingent (internal and external) factors influence management accounting and its design and use

- discuss the principal internal and external sources of management accounting information, their costs and limitations

- explain how information systems provide instant access to previously unavailable data that can be used for benchmarking and control purposes and help improve performance (for example, through the use of enterprise resource planning systems and data warehouses)

- evaluate the external and internal factors (e.g. anticipated human behaviour) which will influence the design of a management accounting system

- evaluate the compatibility of management accounting objectives and management accounting information systems

- discuss the integration of management accounting information within an overall information system, for example the use of enterprise resource planning systems

- demonstrate how the information might be used in planning and controlling activities, e.g. benchmarking against similar activities

- discuss how IT developments, e.g. unified corporate databases, RFIDs and network technology may influence management accounting systems

- discuss the integration of management accounting information within an overall information system, for example the use of enterprise resource planning systems

- discuss the development of Big Data and its impact on performance measurement and management, including the risks and challenges it presents.

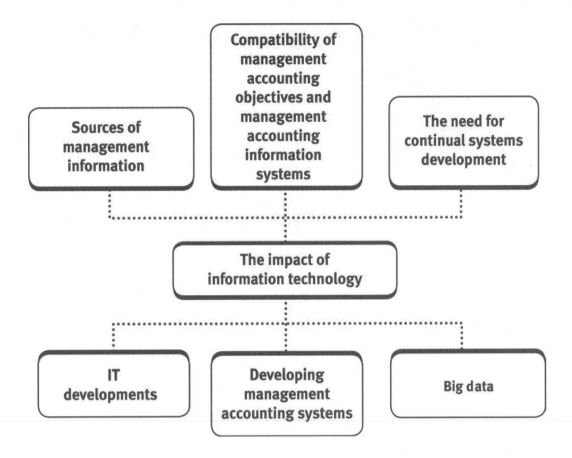

1 Introduction

Managers need access to good information in order to be able to effectively plan, direct and control the activities that they are responsible for. The first part of this chapter focuses on the sources of management information and on the development and importance of an effective management accounting information system.

The chapter then goes on to look at some IT developments and discusses how advancements in technology have allowed managers instant access to data and have enabled remote input of data.

2 Sources of management information

2.1 Introduction

Managers need information for planning and decision making and in order to manage and control their organisations effectively. As a result, managers will need a range of **internal and external information**.

2.2 Internal sources

Internal sources of information may be taken from a variety of areas such as the sales ledger (e.g. volume of sales), payroll system (e.g. number of employees) or the fixed asset system (e.g. depreciation method and rate).

Examples of internal sources of information

Examples of internal data:

Source	Information
Sales ledger system	• Number and value of invoices • Volume of sales • Value of sales, analysed by customer • Value of sales, analysed by product
Purchase ledger system	• Number and value of invoices • Value of purchases, analysed by supplier
Payroll system	• Number of employees • Hours worked • Output achieved • Wages earned • Tax deducted
Fixed asset system	• Date of purchase • Initial cost • Location • Depreciation method and rate • Service history • Production capacity
Production	• Machine breakdown times • Number of rejected units
Sales and marketing	• Types of customer • Market research results

2.3 External sources

In addition to internal information sources, there is much information to be obtained from external sources such as suppliers (e.g. product prices), customers (e.g. price sensitivity) and the government (e.g. inflation rate).

Examples of external sources of information

External source	Information
Suppliers	• Product prices • Product specifications
Newspapers, journals	• Share price • Information on competitors • Technological developments • National and market surveys
Government	• Industry statistics • Taxation policy • Inflation rates • Demographic statistics • Forecasts for economic growth
Customers	• Product requirements • Price sensitivity
Employees	• Wage demands • Working conditions
Banks	• Information on potential customers • Information on national markets
Business enquiry agents	• Information on competitors • Information on customers
Internet	• Almost everything via databases (public and private), discussion groups and mailing lists

Test your understanding 1

Required:

What are the limitations of using externally generated information?

2.4 Use of internal and external information in performance management

The internal and external information may be used in **planning** and **controlling** activities. For example:

- Newspapers, the Internet and business enquiry agents (such as Dun and Bradstreet) may be used to obtain external competitor information for benchmarking purposes.

- Internal sales volumes may be obtained for variance analysis purposes.

Test your understanding 2

Required:

Briefly explain the use of customer data for control purposes.

2.5 The costs of internal and external information

The benefit of management information must exceed the cost (benefit > cost) of obtaining the information.

Benefits and costs of information

The design of management information systems should involve a cost/benefit analysis. A very refined system offers many benefits, but at a cost. The advent of modern IT systems has reduced that cost significantly. However, skilled staff have to be involved in the operation of information systems, and they can be very expensive to hire.

Let us illustrate this with a simple example. Production costs in a factory can be reported with varying levels of frequency ranging from daily (365 times per year) to annually (once per year). Costs or benefits of reporting tend to move as follows in response to increasing frequency of reporting.

- Information has to be gathered, collated and reported in proportion to frequency and costs will move in line with this. Experience suggests that some element of diseconomy of scale may set in at high levels of frequency.

- Initially, benefits increase sharply, but this increase starts to tail off. A point may come where 'information overload' sets in and benefits actually start to decline and even become negative. If managers are overwhelmed with information, then this actually starts to get in the way of the job.

KAPLAN PUBLISHING

The position may be represented graphically as follows:

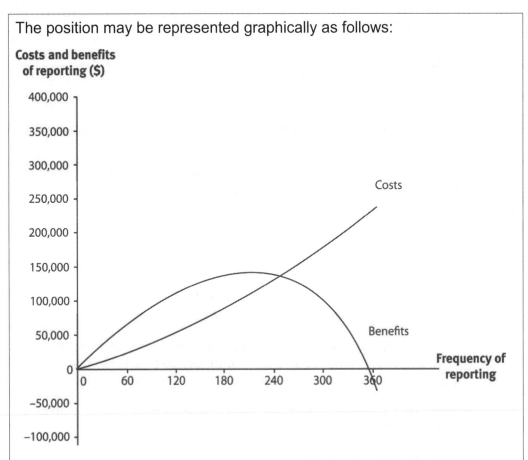

Costs and benefits of reporting ($)

An information system is just like any part of a business operation. It incurs costs and it offers benefits. In designing an information system, the accountant has to find some means of comparing the two for different options and determining which option is optimal. In this sense, system design follows the same practices for investment appraisal and decision making which are explored later in this text.

In the above case it can be seen that net benefits (benefits less costs) are maximised at around 120 reports per year – suggesting an optimal information cycle of about 3 days. The system should be designed to gather, collate and report information at three-day intervals. This is an over-simplified example but it serves to illustrate a general logic which can be applied to all aspects of information system design.

The costs of information can be classified as follows:

Costs of internal information	Costs of external information
Direct data capture costs, e.g. the cost of barcode scanners in a supermarket.	Direct costs, e.g. newspaper subscriptions.
Processing costs, e.g. salaries paid to payroll processing staff.	Indirect costs, e.g. wasted time finding useful information.
Indirect costs, e.g. information collected which is not needed or is duplicated.	Management costs, e.g. the cost of processing information.
	Infrastructure costs, e.g. of systems enabling Internet searches.

3 Compatibility of management accounting objectives and management accounting information systems

Management accounting systems must be capable of producing performance and control information that is consistent with the objectives of the management accountant. Management accounting information may be used to:

- **assess the performance** of the business as a whole or of individual divisions or products

- **value inventories**

- **make future plans** – the provision of management accounting information may assist in making future business plans

- **control the business** – for example, through variance reporting

- **make decisions** – for example, through the provision of summary information (which can be used to make strategic decisions) or through the provision of more detailed information (which can be used to make tactical and operational decisions).

The information is only useful to the management accountant if it is:

- **aligned** to the objectives of the management accountant

- **relevant** – to the needs of the user

- **accurate and complete** – to inspire confidence in the user

- **timely** – in the right place at the right time

- **appropriately communicated** – using a suitable format and communication medium

- **cost < benefit**.

Illustration 1

Many organisations are aiming to improve efficiency and minimise wastage through the adoption of a lean philosophy (see Chapter 13 for further discussion). This organisational objective will directly impact the objectives of the management accountant (since alignment of objectives is necessary). As a result, the management accountant will require an information system that has been simplified, is efficient and keeps wastage down to a minimum. This may, for example, result in the provision of information to the management accountant which is simple to read and is instantly accessible.

4 Developing management accounting systems

4.1 What is a management information system?

A management information system (MIS) converts internal and external data into useful information which is then communicated to managers at all levels and across all functions to enable them to make timely and effective decisions for planning, directing and controlling activities.

4.2 What makes an effective MIS?

An effective MIS will:

- define the areas of control within the organisation and the individuals who are responsible for those areas

- ensure that the relevant information is communicated and flows to the managers in charge of those areas.

4.3 Types of MIS

There are a number of key types of MIS:

Type of MIS	Explanation
Executive information system (EIS)	An EIS gives senior executives access to internal and external information. Information is presented in a user-friendly, summarised form with the option to 'drill down' to a greater level of detail.
Decision support system (DSS)	A decision support system aids managers in making decisions. The system predicts the consequences of a number of possible scenarios and the manager then uses their judgement to make the final decision.
Expert system	Expert systems hold specialist knowledge, e.g. on law and taxation, and allow non-experts to interrogate them for information, advice and recommended decisions. Can be used at all levels of management.

Test your understanding 3

CB publishing is considering the impact of a new system based on an integrated, single database which would support an executive information system (EIS) and a decision support system (DSS). A network update would allow real time input of data.

Required:

Evaluate the potential impact of the introduction of the new system on performance management.

Test your understanding 4

Required:

Discuss the factors that need to be considered when determining the capacity and development potential of a management information system.

5 The need for continual systems development

Information and management accounting systems need to be developed continually otherwise they will become out of date either because of advances in technology or because of environmental changes.

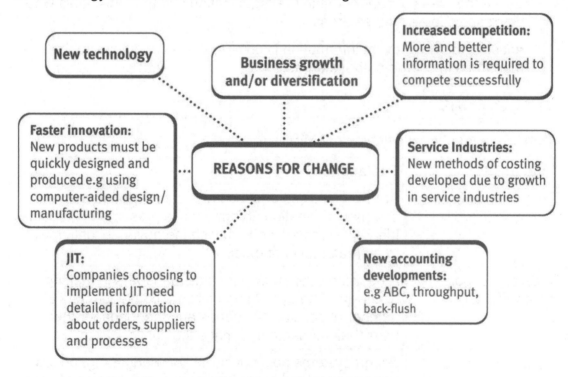

Change will be required to maintain or improve the performance of the system in an increasingly competitive and global market.

Test your understanding 5

Blueberry is a quoted hotel resort chain based in Europe. It is considering the use of an activity-based management approach and has identified five activity areas (cost pools) and cost drivers.

The company has recently invested in a 'state of the art' IT system which has the capability to collate all of the data necessary for budgeting in each of the activity areas.

Required:

Explain the problems that Blueberry might experience in the successful implementation of an activity-based costing system using its recently acquired 'state of the art' IT system.

Test your understanding 6

Lead times are becoming increasingly important within the clothing industry. An interesting example of a company going against the conventional wisdom is Zara International, part of the Inditex group (Spain).

- Zara produces half of its garments in-house, whereas most retailers outsource all production. Although manufacturing in Spain and Portugal has a cost premium of 10 to 15%, local production means the company can react to market changes faster than the competition.

- Instead of predicting months before a season starts what women will want to wear, Zara observes what is selling and what is not and continuously adjusts what it produces on that basis. This is known as a 'design-on-demand' operating model.

- Rather than focusing on economies of scale, Zara manufactures and distributes products in small batches.

- Instead of using outside partners, Zara manages all design, warehousing, distribution, and logistics functions itself.

- The result is that Zara can design, produce, and deliver a new garment to its 600-plus stores worldwide in a mere 15 days.

By comparison a typical shirt manufacturer may take 30 days just to source fabric and then a further ten days to make the shirt. For some firms overall lead time could be between three and eight months from conception to shelf.

Required:

Comment on the importance of IT systems to Zara's competitive strategy.

6   IT developments

There has been a wealth of IT developments. These include:

Data warehouses

A data warehouse is a:

- **Database:** data is combined from multiple and varied sources (internal and external) into one comprehensive, secure and easily manipulated data store. A unified corporate database allows all users to access the same information, to see an overall picture of performance and helps inform business decisions.

- **Data extraction tool:** data can be extracted from the database to meet the individual user's needs.

- **A decision support system:** data mining is used to analyse the data and unearth unknown patterns or correlations in data.

Illustration 2 – Influence of IT on Sainsbury plc

Sainsbury plc, the UK supermarket giant, has a data warehouse with information about purchases made by the company's eight million customers.

Transactional details are tied to specific customers through the company's Nectar loyalty programme, producing valuable information about buying habits.

Initial analysis of the information quickly showed Sainsbury's how ineffective its traditional mass-mailing approaches were – where large numbers of coupons were widely distributed in an attempt to get customers through its doors. Rather than buying more, many customers would cherry-pick the specials and go to its competitors for other items. This meant many advertising campaigns were running at a loss.

Since those initial findings, a concerted focus on timely data analysis and relevant marketing has helped Sainsbury to design far more effective direct marketing campaigns based on customers' actual purchasing habits.

In one campaign designed to increase the value of customers' shopping baskets, Sainsbury's analysed purchases and identified the product category from which each customer purchased most frequently. A coupon for that category would then be sent, along with five other coupons for areas in which it was hoping to boost sales – to encourage customers to buy other types of products. The response rate was 26%, a tremendous amount in retail.

The data warehouse will bring the benefit of removing possible **duplication** of files and **reducing storage** requirements. However, the centralisation of data may make a **loss more catastrophic** although backup procedures will reduce the risk. The cost of such an upgrade should also be **less than the benefit**.

Data mining

This is the analysis of data contained within a data warehouse to unearth relationships between them.

Illustration 3 – Data mining relationships

Data mining results may include:

- **Associations** – when one event can be correlated to another, e.g. beer purchasers buy peanuts a certain percentage of the time.

- **Sequences** – one event leading to another event, e.g. a rug purchase followed by a purchase of matching curtains.

- **Classifications** – profiles of customers who make purchases can be set up.

These relationships can be used to help an organisation focus on the things that the customer enjoys and desires. Marketing can be targeted to a group of customers and the organisation will focus on the more profitable product offerings.

Networks

Most organisations connect their computers together in local area networks (LANs), enabling them to share data (e.g. via email) and to share devices such as printers. Wide area networks (WANs) are used to connect LANs together, so that computer users in one location can communicate with computer users in another location. Improvements in broadband speed and security have eased communication across sites and from home.

A network should **facilitate the transfer of information** between different parts of the business.

Intranet

This is a private network contained within an organisation. It allows company information and computing resources to be shared among employees.

Extranet

This is a private, secure extension of an Intranet. It allows the organisation to share information with suppliers, customers and other business partners.

Internet

This is a global system of interconnected networks carrying a vast array of information and resources.

By connecting the network to the internet (or intranet/extranet), **communication with key stakeholders** will be improved and it may be possible to share data with organisations which could assist in a **benchmarking** exercise.

However, the opening of the organisation's network to the internet will provide additional opportunities for the spread of viruses and possibly open the network to **hackers**.

Illustration 4 – The internet and management information	

An Internet site that allows customers to place orders on-line can provide the following useful management accounting information:

Data	Use
Customer details	For delivery purposes; also to build up a record of customer interests and purchases.
Product details accessed and products bought	For delivery purposes; also to build up patterns such as products that are often bought together.
Value of products bought	Sales accounting and customer profiling.
Product details accessed but product not bought	Other items that the customer might be interested in. Why were they not bought? Has a rival got better prices?
Date of purchase	Seasonal variations; tie in with special offers and advertising campaigns.
Time of purchase	Some web-sites might be particularly busy at certain times of the day. Why that pattern? Avoid busy times when carrying out web-site maintenance.
Delivery method chosen	Most Internet sellers give a choice of delivery costs and times. Analysis of this information could help the company to increase its profits.

The use of intranets to enhance performance

HI is a large importer of cleaning products; HI has its head office situated in the centre of the capital city. This head office supports its area branches; a branch consists of an area office and a warehouse. The branches are spread geographically throughout the country; a total of seven area branches are supported.

Currently each HI area office and warehouse supports and supplies its own dealers with the required products. When stocks become low they place a Required Stock Form (RSF) with head office. On receipt of the RSF, head office despatch the goods from their central warehouse to the appropriate area office. When the central warehouse becomes low on any particular item(s) HI will raise purchase orders and send them to one of their many international suppliers.

Typically, each area office has its own stock recording system, running on locally networked personal computer systems (PCs). RSFs are e-mailed to head office.

Required:

How would the introduction of an Intranet enhance performance within HI?

Solution:

An Intranet could provide an excellent opportunity for HI to link all the areas in a number of ways: i.e. allowing access to a central database would be a substantial improvement on the current system, where updates are faxed or e-mailed to head office. This may possibly lead to the development of an integrated database system.

An automatic stock replenishment system could be introduced for the branches, replacing RSFs. If some branches were short of specific items and other branches had ample stocks, then movement between branches may be possible. Currently head office may order goods from suppliers when the organisation has sufficient stocks internally.

Dissemination of best practice throughout the organisation can be encouraged and savings in terms of printing and distributing paper based manuals, catalogues and handbooks. All the current internal documentation can easily be maintained and distributed.

The Intranet would enable the establishment of versatile and standard methods of communication throughout the company.

The Intranet could encourage group or shared development, currently several area offices have their own IT systems working independently on very similar projects.

An Intranet could also enable automatic transfer of information and data i.e. the quarterly figures could be circulated. Monthly returns of business volumes could be calculated on an as required basis.

Information can be provided to all in a user-friendly format.

Enterprise resource planning system (ERPS)

An ERPS is an example of a **unified database of corporate information**. Rather than data existing in isolation in different parts of the business, it integrates the data from many aspects of operations (for example, manufacturing, inventory, distribution, invoicing and accounting) and support functions (such as human resource management and marketing) into **one single system**.

Benefits to the organisation include:

- identification and planning of the use of resources across the organisation to ensure customers' needs are fulfilled

- the free flow of information between all functions and improved communication between departments

- aids the management decision making process due to decision support features

- can be extended to incorporate supply chain management (SCM) and customer relationship management (CRM) software, thus helping to manage connections outside the organisation.

Software companies like SAP and Oracle have specialised in the provision of ERPS across many different industries.

Test your understanding 7

Required:

Explain how the introduction of an ERPS could impact on the role of management accountants.

Radio frequency identification (RFID)

Organisations can use small radio receivers to tag items and hence to keep track of their assets. It can be used for a variety of purposes, for example:

- to track inventory to retail stores

- to tag livestock on farms

- to track the location of doctors in a hospital.

Illustration 5 – RFID

Many clothing retailers began the phased rollout of item-level radio frequency identification (RFID) tags in 2007 following extensive testing of the technology. Stock accuracy has improved and stores and customers have commented on the more consistent availability of sizes in the pilot departments.

The tags allow staff to carry out stocktaking 20 times faster than bar code scanners by passing an RFID reader over goods. At the end of each day, stock on the shop floor will be scanned and the data collected will be compared with information in a central database containing each store's stock profile, to determine what products need to be replaced. This has led to improved sales through greater product availability.

The introduction of RFID can bring about a number of **benefits**:

- Information on the location and quantity of items can be provided in real time meaning that less time is spent looking for items.

- This information should be more accurate since it will be less reliant on physical checks.

- Performance reporting should improve due to the provision of real time information.

- Control should be easier. This is firstly due to the provision of real time information and, secondly, since the location and quantity of items will be known, the risk of theft and obsolescence will be reduced.

The benefits must outweigh the costs. **Costs** will include the cost of hardware, software, ongoing running and maintenance costs and training costs.

Test your understanding 8

Required:

Discuss the impact of recent IT developments on management accounting and on business performance.

7 Big Data

7.1 What is Big Data?

There are several definitions of Big Data. The most common refer to:

Extremely large collections of data that may be analysed to reveal patterns, trends and associations.

Data collections so large that conventional methods of storing and processing that data will not work.

Big Data is a big buzzword at the moment and some say that it will be even bigger than the Internet. The ability to harness these vast amounts of data will transform our ability to understand the world and will lead to huge advances, for example, in understanding customer behaviour, foiling terrorist attacks, preventing diseases and pinpointing marketing efforts.

Illustration 6 – The use of Big Data by supermarkets

A supermarket is able to take data from a your past buying patterns, its internal inventory information, your mobile phone location data, social media as well as weather information to send you a voucher for barbeque food; but only if you own a barbeque, the weather is nice, you are within 3 miles of one of their stores and the barbeque food is in stock.

7.2 The 3Vs

Big Data is **characterised** by the 3Vs:

- **Volume:** organisations now hold huge volumes of data. For example:

    - A **supermarket** will have a data store of all purchases made, when and where they were made, how they were paid for and the use of coupons via loyalty cards swiped at the checkout.

    - An **online retailer** will have a data store of every product looked at and bought and every page visited.

    - **Mobile phone providers** will have a data store of texts, voice mails, calls made, browsing habits and location.

    - **Social media companies**, such as Facebook, will have a data store of all the postings an individual makes (and where they were made), photos posted and contacts.

- **Variety:** Big Data can include much more than simply financial information and can include other organisational data which is operational in nature as well as other internal and external information. This data can be both structured and unstructured in nature:

    - **Structured data** – for example, a bank will hold a record of all receipts and payments (date, amount and source) for a customer.

    - **Unstructured data** – can make up 80% of business data but is more difficult to store and analyse.

- **Velocity:** The data must be turned into useful information quickly enough to be of use in decision making and performance management (in real time if possible). The sheer volume and variety of data makes this task difficult and sophisticated methods are required to process the huge volumes of non-uniform data quickly.

A fourth 'v', **veracity** is sometimes included, i.e. is the data accurate enough to be relied upon?

7.3 Processing Big Data

The ability to manage Big Data successfully will drive innovation (and potentially competitive advantage) to reduce the time taken to answer key business questions and hence make decisions.

The processing of Big Data is known as **Big Data analytics**. For example, Google Analytics tracks many features of website traffic.

Hadoop software allows the processing of large data sets by utilising multiple servers simultaneously.

7.4 Big Data and performance management

Big Data is relevant to performance management in a number of ways, such as:

- It can help the organisation to **understand its customers' needs and preferences** which can then be used to improve marketing and sales.

- It can **improve forecasting**, for example of future customer spending or of machine replacement cycles, so that more appropriate decisions can be made.

- It can help the organisation to **automate business processes** resulting in improved efficiency.

- It can help to provide more **detailed, relevant and up to date performance measurement**.

7.5 Examples of how Big Data is used

- **Consumer facing organisations** monitor social media activity to gain insight into customer behaviour and preferences. This source can also be used to identify and engage brand advocates and detractors, and assess responsiveness to advertising campaigns and promotions.

- **Sports teams** can use data of past fixtures to track tactics, player formations, injuries and results to inform future team strategies.

- **Manufacturing companies** can monitor data from their equipment to determine usage and wear. This allows them to predict the optimal replacement cycle.

- **Financial Services organisations** can use data on customer activity to carefully segment their customer base and therefore accurately target individuals with relevant offers.

- **Politicians** are using social media analytics to establish where they have to campaign the hardest to win the next election.

- **Humanitarian agencies**, such as the United Nations, use phone data to understand population movements during relief operations and outbreaks of disease, meaning they can allocate resources more efficiently and identify areas at risk of new disease outbreaks.

More examples of Big Data in the real world

UPS's delivery vehicles are equipped with sensors which monitor data on speed, direction, braking performance and other mechanical aspects of the vehicle. This information is then used to optimise maintenance schedules and improve efficiency of delivery routes saving time, money and reducing wastage.

Data from the vehicles is combined with customer data, GPS information and data concerning the normal behaviour of delivery drivers. Using this data to optimise vehicle performance and routes has resulted in several significant improvements:

- Over 15 million minutes of idling time were eliminated in one year. This saved 103,000 gallons of fuel.

- During the same year 1.7 million miles of driving was eliminated, saving 183,000 gallons of fuel.

It is widely reported that **Walmart (Asda)** tracks data on over 60% of adults in the US. Data gathered includes online and in store purchasing pattern, Twitter interactions and trends, weather reports and major events. This data, according to the company, ensures a highly personalised customer experience. Walmart detractors criticise the company's data collection as a breach of human rights and believe the company uses the data to make judgements and conclusions on personal information such as sexual orientation, political view and even intelligence levels.

Tesco has sophisticated sensors installed on all refrigeration units to monitor the temperature at regular intervals and to send the information over the internet to a central data warehouse. The data collected is used to identify units that are operating at temperatures that are too low (resulting in energy wastage) or too high (resulting in potential stock obsolescence and a safety risk). Engineers can monitor the data remotely and can then visit the store to rectify any problem that is identified. Previously, store managers may have overlooked a problem or only identified a problem once it had escalated into something more serious.

Netflix has over 100 million users worldwide. The company uses information gathered from analysis of viewing habits to inform decisions on which shows to invest in. Analysing past viewing figures and understanding viewer populations and the shows they are likely to watch allows the analysts to predict likely viewing figures before a show has even aired. This can help to determine if the show is a viable investment.

Test your understanding 9

MC is a mobile phone network provider, offering mobile phones and services on a range of different tariffs to customers across Europe. The company enjoyed financial success until three years ago but increasing competitive pressure has led to a recent decline in sales. There has also been an increase in the level of complaints regarding the customer service provided, and the company's churn rate (number of customers leaving the company within a given time frame) is at an all-time high.

Required:

Discuss how Big Data could help drive the strategic direction of MC company.

7.6 Risks associated with Big Data

- The **availability of skills** to use Big Data systems, which is compounded by the fact that many of the systems are rapidly developing and support is not always easily and readily available. There is also an increasing need to combine data analysis skills with a deep understanding of the industry being analysed and this need is not always recognised.

- The **security of data** is a major concern in the majority of organisations and if the organisation lacks the resources to manage data then there is likely to be a greater risk of leaks and losses. There can be a risk to the data protection of organisations as they collect a greater range of data from increasingly personal sources (for example, Facebook).

- It is important to recognise that just because something CAN be measured, this does not necessarily mean it should be. There is a risk that **valuable time is spent measuring relationships that have no organisational value**.

- **Incorrect data** (poor veracity) may result in incorrect conclusions being made.

- There may be **technical difficulties** associated with integrating existing data warehousing and, for example, Hadoop systems.

- The **cost** of establishing the hardware and analytical software needed.

Student accountant article: visit the ACCA website, www.accaglobal.com, to review the articles on 'Big Data and performance management' and 'Big Data'.

8   Exam focus

Exam sitting	Area examined	Question number	Number of marks
Mar/June 2016	RFID	2(a)	14
Mar/June 2016	Data warehouse, loyalty cards	1(v)	8
Sept/Dec 2015	ERPS	1(iv)	10
June 2015	ERPS	2(a)	10
December 2013	RFID	3(a)	12
December 2011	Control and development of IS	3	20
June 2011	EIS	1(c)	5
December 2010	Impact of KPIs on system design	1(d)	9

Chapter summary

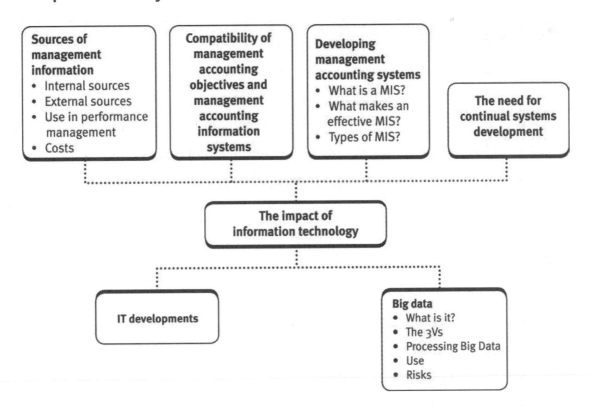

Test your understanding answers

Test your understanding 1

- External information may not be accurate.

- External information may be out of date.

- The company publishing the data may not be reputable.

- External information may not meet the exact needs of the business.

- It may be difficult to gather external information, e.g. from customers or competitors.

Test your understanding 2

Historical customer data will give information about:

- product purchases and preferences

- price sensitivity

- where customers shop

- who customers are (customer profiling).

For a business that prioritises customer satisfaction this will give important control information. Actual customer data can be compared with plans and control action can be taken as necessary, e.g. prices may be changed or the product mix may be changed.

KAPLAN PUBLISHING

Test your understanding 3

Advantages	Disadvantages
• Benefit of real time data input and access.	• Cost of real time data input.
• Improved decision making, e.g. the EIS should allow drill- down access of data to operational level but presentation of data should be based on the KPIs of the company.	• Cost of linking the EIS to new, external data sources.
	• Cost of implementation and training.
• The EIS will link to external data sources thus reducing the risk of ignoring issues from the wider environment.	• Risk that the system does not work properly or that training is inadequate.
	• Increased security threat since the data is only held in one place.
• The database will reduce/eliminate the problem of data redundancy since data is only held in one place.	• Potential information overload, especially for senior management.
• Improved data integrity. Data is only held in one place and therefore time and effort will be taken to ensure it is of high quality.	

Test your understanding 4

A management information system can be developed to varying levels of refinement. Specifically:

- **Reporting frequency**– information can be collected and reported with varying levels of frequency, e.g. for example, the management accounting system of a manufacturer can report actual production costs on a daily, weekly, monthly or even annual basis.

- **Reporting quantity and level of detail** – information can be collected and reported at varying levels of detail e.g. in absorbing overheads into product costs one can use a single factory overhead absorption rate (OAR) or one can operate a complex ABC system. The information requirements of the latter are far more elaborate than those of the former.

- **Reporting accuracy and back-up** – subtle qualitative factors can be incorporated into information systems at varying levels, e.g. information can be rigorously checked for accuracy or a more relaxed approach can be adopted.

Broadly, **the more refined the MIS** is, then **the more expensive it is** to establish and operate. The organisation has to decide if the increased benefits outweigh the increased costs.

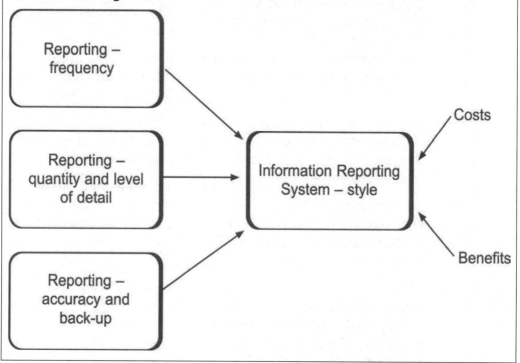

Test your understanding 5

- A large amount of data will need to be collected initially on each activity. Therefore, the cost of buying, implementing and maintaining a system of activity-based costing will be high.

- Incorrect identification of cost pools and cost drivers would result in inaccurate information being produced by the ABC system and hence incorrect decisions by managers.

Test your understanding 6

IT systems are critical to Zara's short lead times.

Zara needs comprehensive information in the following areas:

- which garments are selling, at what price points and in what quantities – key information will relate to both Zara stores and those of competitors

- detailed product specifications for these garments to enable design of new products

- compatibility between reporting and design software systems

- supply chain management

- order and delivery systems.

Test your understanding 7

The introduction of ERPS has the potential to have a significant impact on the work of management accountants.

- The use of ERPS causes a substantial reduction in the gathering and processing of routine information by management accountants.

- Instead of relying on management accountants to provide them with information, managers are able to access the system to obtain the information they require directly via a suitable electronic access medium.

- ERPS perform routine tasks that not so long ago were seen as an essential part of the daily routines of management accountants, for example perpetual inventory valuation. Therefore, if management accountants are not to be diminished then it is of necessity that management accountants should seek to expand their roles within their organisations.

- Management accountants may be involved in interpreting the information generated from the ERPS and to provide business support for all levels of management within an organisation.

Test your understanding 8

- IT developments, such as networks and databases, provide the opportunity for instant access to management accounting information.

- It is possible to directly access and manipulate information from both internal and external sources.

- Information is relatively cheap to collect, store and manipulate.

- Many of the modern forms of management accounting have been developed in conjunction with IT systems, e.g. it may be difficult to run a meaningful ABC system without IT support.

- Data mining techniques can be used to uncover previously unknown patterns and correlations and hence improve performance.

Test your understanding 9

Big Data management involves using sophisticated systems to gather, store and analyse large volumes of data in a variety of structured and unstructured formats. Companies are collecting increasing volumes of data through everyday transactions and marketing activity. If managed effectively this can lead to many business benefits although there are risks involved.

A company like MC will already collect a relatively large amount of data regarding its customers, their transactions and call history. It is likely that a significant proportion of their customers are also fairly digitally engaged and therefore data can be gathered regarding preferences and complaints from social media networks. This will be particularly useful to MC as they have seen an increase in complaints and have a high churn rate so engaging with customers will be highly beneficial.

Recent competitive pressure has led to a decline in sales and so MC need to consider the strategic direction which is most appropriate for them to improve performance.

Analysing the large amounts of data available to them will inform decisions on areas such as:

- The type of handsets currently most in demand and therefore the prices required when bundling with tariffs; Main areas of complaint and therefore the areas of weakness which need to be resolved

- Which types of communication are most popular (e.g. data, call minutes, text messages) to ensure the tariffs have the right combinations

- Usage statistics for 'pay as you go' customers, to drive the most appropriate offers and marketing activity

- Most popular competitor offerings with reasons.

Performance reports for management

Chapter learning objectives

Upon completion of this chapter you will be able to:

- discuss the difficulties associated with recording and processing data of a qualitative nature

- advise on common mistakes and misconceptions in the use of numerical data used for performance measurement

- evaluate the output reports of an information system in the light of:

  - best practice in presentation

  - the objectives of the report/organisation – the needs of the readers of the reports

  - avoiding the problem of information overload.

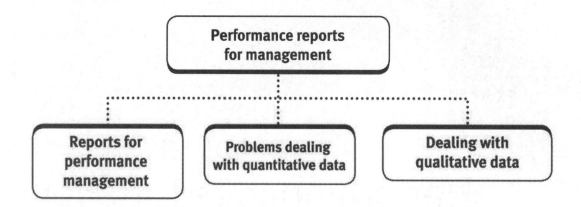

1   Assumed knowledge

This chapter builds on your knowledge of performance reports from PM.

2   Introduction

In the previous chapter we discussed the managers' requirement to access good information in order to be able to effectively plan, direct and control the activities that they are responsible for.

An important component of this good information will be the performance reports (output reports) produced for management. The output reports produced from a management information system might include overall performance reports for managers (e.g. a monthly management account report) or they may be more specific and tailored to the manager in question, e.g. an inventory report may be produced for the production manager. Importantly, the performance reports need to be tailored to suit the needs of the users of those reports. The qualities of a good performance report are discussed in the first part of this chapter.

The second part of the chapter looks at the common mistakes and misconceptions that people make when using numerical data for performance measurement.

Finally, the chapter discusses qualitative information. Qualitative information is highly subjective and hard to pin down and is therefore often ignored to the detriment of the quality of the performance report. However, although it is difficult to record and process data of a qualitative nature these factors still need to be considered when making a decision.

3 Reports for performance management

3.1 Introduction

The design of performance reports (output reports) is regularly examined in APM.

Before discussing what makes a good performance report, it is worth noting that performance means different things to different organisations and therefore there is no single correct way of measuring or presenting performance. For example, a profit-seeking organisation may be interested in sales growth or gross margins where as a charity may be interested in the efficient and effective use of its funds. In addition, within a single organisation different aspects of performance will be examined at different times.

3.2 Designing a good performance report

When designing a good performance report there are four key considerations:

1   What is the purpose of the report?
2   Who is the audience for which the report is being produced?
3   What information is needed (as a result of points 1 and 2 above)?
4   What layout is suitable?

Each of these will be examined in turn.

3.3 Purpose

A common mistake in performance reports is that the focus is primarily on profit. However, successful performance depends on the achievement of the organisation's mission and objectives. The performance report should therefore reflect the mission and objectives.

3.4 Audience

The audience of the report may range from skilled and experienced managers (who will be sophisticated enough to understand the information without much detailed explanation) to, say, the local community who may have fewer skills and require further explanation. It is important to consider the scenario given in the exam to determine whether the right amount and type of information has been given.

Care must be taken to ensure that the performance report is relevant to the needs of the user, is easy to use, is understandable and is adaptable to their needs.

3.5 Information

The information provided must match the purpose of the performance report. A range of information should be included:

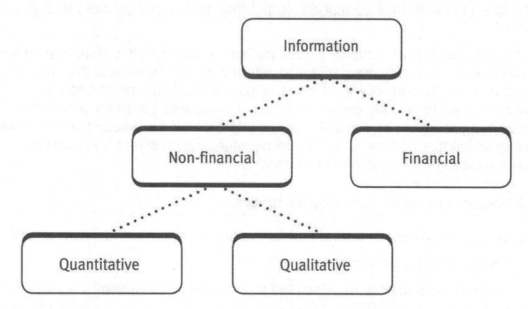

A common theme in exam questions is that the organisation's performance report focuses solely on financial performance. Although important in the short-term, the sole focus on financial performance may be detrimental to the achievement of the organisation's mission and objectives in the long term. Non-financial factors focusing on areas such as customer satisfaction, product innovation and employee productivity will be equally as important.

Some of this non-financial information may be quantitative (i.e. can be expressed in numerical terms) but much of this information will be qualitative (non-numerical). This qualitative information is highly subjective and hard to pin down and is therefore often ignored to the detriment of the quality of the performance report.

(Qualitative information is explored in more detail in the next section).

3.6 Layout

Information overload is a common theme in exam questions. The layout of the report needs to help the user to quickly understand the organisation's results, the key trends and the reasons for these.

Rather than solely including a large volume of figures the layout could be complemented through the inclusion of:

- graphs, charts or other visual displays making the performance report easily understandable and easy to use.

- narrative explanation drawing attention to important matters and causes.

Qualities of performance reports

The output reports from an information system should allow the organisation to run the business effectively both today and in the future. Output reports should have the following characteristics:

Characteristic	Explanation
Accurate	For example, figures should add up and there should be no typos.
Complete	The reports should include all the information that is needed by the readers of the report and should be aligned to the overall objectives of the report or of the organisation.
Cost < benefit	The benefit of having the information must be greater than the cost of providing it.
Understandable	The readers of the report must be able to understand the contents and use the contents to fulfil their needs. Presentation should be clear and in line with best practice.
Relevant	Information that is not needed by the reader(s) of the report should be omitted. Information overload can be a huge problem and can detract from the usefulness of the report. The problem of information overload may be overcome using, for example, drill-down reports (provide users with the capability to look at increasingly detailed information about a particular item) and exception reports (which are only triggered when a situation is unusual or requires management action).
Adaptable	The output reports should have the capability of being adapted to meet the needs of the user or the organisation.
Timely	The information should be provided when needed and should not be provided too frequently (this can result in information overload and the cost of providing the information exceeding the benefit).
Easy to use	Information should be presented in a form recommended by the industry or organisation's best practice. It should not be too long (to prevent information overload) and it should be sent using the most appropriate communication channel to ensure user needs are met.

> **Test your understanding 1**
>
> **Required:**
>
> Discuss the weaknesses in an information system that could result in poor output reports.

Question practice

The question below is an extract from a past exam question. Take the time to complete and review this question. It will help to give you a broader understanding of some of the areas covered above.

> **Test your understanding 2**
>
> Metis is a restaurant business in the city of Urbanton. Metis was started three years ago by three friends who met at university while doing courses in business and catering management. Initially, their aim was simply to 'make money' although they had talked about building a chain of restaurants if the first site was successful.
>
> The three friends pooled their own capital and took out a loan from the Grand Bank in order to fit out a rented site in the city. They designed the restaurant to be light and open with a menu that reflected the most popular dishes in Urbanton regardless of any particular culinary style. The dishes were designed to be priced in the middle of the range that was common for restaurants in the city. The choice of food and drinks to offer to customers is still a group decision amongst the owners.
>
> Other elements of the business were allocated according to each owner's qualifications and preferences. Bert Fish takes charge of all aspects of the kitchen operations while another, Sheila Plate, manages the activities in the public area such as taking reservations, serving tables and maintaining the appearance of the restaurant. The third founder, John Sum, deals with the overall business issues such as procurement, accounting and legal matters.
>
> Competition in the restaurant business is fierce as it is easy to open a restaurant in Urbanton and there are many competitors in the city both small, single-site operations and large national chains. The current national economic environment is one of steady but unspectacular growth.

The restaurant has been running for three years and the founders have reached the point where the business seems to be profitable and self-sustaining. The restaurant is now in need of refurbishment in order to maintain its atmosphere and this has prompted the founders to consider the future of their business. John Sum has come to you as their accountant looking for advice on aspects of performance management in the business. He has supplied you with figures outlining the recent performance of the business and the forecasts for the next year (see the performance report below). This table represents the quantitative data that is available to the founders when they meet each quarter to plan any short-term projects or initiatives and also, to consider the longer-term future. Bert and Sheila have often indicated to John that they find the information daunting and difficult to understand fully.

Metis Performance Report

	Actual 20X0 ($)	Actual 20X1 ($)	Actual 20X2 ($)	Forecast 20X3 ($)	Latest quarter to 31 March 20X2 (Q4 20X2) ($)	Previous quarter (Q3 20X2) ($)
Revenue						
Food	617,198	878,220	974,610	1,062,180	185,176	321,621
Wine	127,358	181,220	201,110	219,180	38,211	66,366
Spirits	83,273	118,490	131,495	143,310	24,984	43,394
Beer	117,562	167,280	185,640	202,320	35,272	61,261
Other beverages	24,292	34,850	38,675	42,150	7,348	12,763
Outside catering	9,797	13,940	15,470	16,860	2,939	5,105
Total	979,680	1,394,000	1,547,000	1,686,000	293,930	510,510
Cost of sales						
Food	200,589	284,422	316,748	345,209	60,182	104,527
Wine	58,585	83,361	92,511	100,821	17,577	30,528
Spirits	21,651	30,807	34,189	37,261	6,496	11,283
Beer	44,673	63,566	70,543	76,882	13,403	23,279
Other beverages	3,674	5,228	5,801	6,323	1,102	1,914
Outside catering	3,135	4,461	4,950	5,395	941	1,634
Total	332,307	472,845	524,742	571,891	99,701	173,165
Gross profit	647,373	921,155	1,022,258	1,114,109	194,229	337,345
Staff costs	220,428	313,650	348,075	379,350	66,134	114,865

Other operating costs						
Marketing	25,000	10,000	12,000	20,000	3,000	3,000
Rent/ mortgage	150,800	175,800	175,800	193,400	43,950	43,950
Local property tax	37,500	37,500	37,500	37,500	9,375	9,375
Insurance	5,345	5,585	5,837	6,100	1,459	1,459
Utilities	12,600	12,978	13,043	13,173	3,261	3,261
Waste removal	6,000	6,180	6,365	6,556	1,591	1,591
Equipment repairs	3,500	3,658	3,822	3,994	956	956
Depreciation	120,000	120,000	120,000	120,000	30,000	30,000
Building upgrades				150,000		
Total	360,745	371,701	374,367	550,723	93,592	93,592
Manager salary	35,000	36,225	37,494	38,806	9,373	9,373
Net profit/ loss before interest and corporate taxes	31,200	199,579	262,322	145,230	25,130	119,515
Net margin	3.2%	14.3%	17.0%	8.6%	8.5%	23.4%

Required:

Critically assess the existing performance report and suggest improvements to its content and presentation.

(12 marks)

Student accountant article: visit the ACCA website, www.accaglobal.com, to review the article on 'reports for performance management'.

4 Problems dealing with quantitative data

There are a number of common mistakes and misconceptions that people make when using numerical data for performance measurement. These include the following:

Collection of data

An organisation often uses sampling to collect data and establish statistics. However, it is difficult to collect a random sample and a sample that is big enough to be representative of the whole population.

Failing to look for underlying causes

For example, an internet retailer may report that the number of hits to their website has increased by 50% over the last two weeks. This does not seem as impressive if it turns out that the manager has advertised some heavily discounted products.

Looking at figures in isolation

Continuing the previous example, a better approach to assess internet sales might be to consider number of hits, what % of customers then bought something and the average purchase value.

Data processing

Care should be taken when processing data. For example, when choosing an average to report, the mean can be skewed by extreme values (however, the mode and median also have limitations).

Presentation of data

The choice of, say, graph or chart may be inappropriate. For example, a graph may indicate dramatic changes but only because of the scale chosen.

Failing to evaluate figures using a suitable comparator or benchmark

A manager may report an increase in sales of 20% on the last year but this may indicate poor performance if the market grew by 30% over the same period.

Failing to understand underlying samples

A divisional manager may claim 90% customer satisfaction, but this is misleading if, say, only ten out of five thousand customers were consulted.

Similarly any samples that are self-selecting are notoriously unreliable. For example, the scores on websites where customers can post feedback and rate products may be distorted by false positives paid for by sellers or false negatives paid for by rivals.

Failing to understand percentages

Suppose quality control reject rates increase from 5% to 6% of total items made. This should be reported as a 20% increase but some managers may state that rejects have only increased by 1%.

It may also be misleading to quote a percentage figure, rather than an absolute figure. For example, a business may boast that eating one of its yogurts every day results in a 50% reduction in a certain disease. However, looking at the absolute figures this decrease is only from a two in a million chance of catching the disease to a one in a million chance.

Selective use of figures

Detailed performance measurement often reveals a mixed picture but, unless KPIs are set in advance, some managers may select only the positive indicators when reporting performance. For example, a manager may boast about revenue growth but fail to report a reduction in profit.

Confusing correlation and causality

Suppose a new manager has invested heavily in their division and, at the same time, revenues have increased. It is very easy to assume that the increase in revenue was caused by the investment, whereas it may be due to a different cause altogether, such as an up run in the economy.

Student accountant article: visit the ACCA website, www.accaglobal.com, to review the article on 'common mistakes and misconceptions in the use of numerical data used for performance measurement'.

5 Problems dealing with qualitative data

 Qualitative information is information that cannot normally be expressed in numerical terms (whereas quantitative information can).

Qualitative information is often in the form of opinions, for example:

- **employees** – who will be affected by certain decisions which may threaten their continued employment, or cause them to need re-training

- **customers** – who will be interested to know about new products, but will want to be assured that service arrangements, etc. will continue for existing products

- **suppliers** – who will want to be aware of the entity's plans, e.g. a move to a just-in-time (JIT) environment.

The fact that qualitative information is often in the form of opinions presents a problem since the information is **subjective** in nature. For example, in assessing quality of service, customers have different expectations and priorities and so are unlikely to be consistent in their judgements. One way to reduce the effect of subjectivity is to look at **trends** in performance since the biases will be present in each individual time period but the trend will show relative changes in quality.

It is difficult to record and process data of a qualitative nature but qualitative factors still need to be considered when making a decision. These include:

- **The effects on the environment:** certain decisions may affect emissions and pollution of the environment. The green issue and the entity's responsibility towards the environment may seriously affect its public image.

- **Legal effects:** there may be legal implications of a course of action, or a change in law may have been the cause of the decision requirement.

- **Political effects:** government policies, in both taxation and other matters, may impinge on the decision.

- **Timing of decision:** the timing of a new product launch may be crucial to its success.

These factors must be considered before making a final decision. Each of these factors is likely to be measured by opinion. Such opinions must be collected and coordinated into meaningful information. Qualitative data will often be transformed into quantitative information (for example, by applying a 1 to 5 scale when assessing customer satisfaction). However, it will never escape from the problem of being judgemental and subjective.

Illustration 1 – Dealing with qualitative data

Here are some examples of qualitative effects.

- The impact of a decreased output requirement on staff morale is something that may be critical but it is not something that an information system would automatically report.

- The impact of a reduction in product range may have a subtle impact on the image that a business enjoys in the market – again something that an information system may not report.

Test your understanding 3

Information and Investment

Moffat commenced trading on 01/12/X2, it supplies and fits tyres and exhaust pipes and services motor vehicles at thirty locations. The directors and middle management are based at the Head Office of Moffat.

Each location has a manager who is responsible for day-to-day operations and is supported by an administrative assistant. All other staff at each location are involved in the fitting and servicing operations.

The directors of Moffat are currently preparing a financial evaluation of an investment of $2 million in a new IT system for submission to its bank. They are concerned that sub-optimal decisions are being made because the current system does not provide appropriate information throughout the organisation. They are also aware that not all of the benefits from the proposed investment will be quantitative in nature.

Required:

(a) Explain the characteristics of **three** types of information required to assist in decision-making at different levels of management and on differing timescales within Moffat, providing two examples of information that would be appropriate to each level.

(b) Identify and explain **three** approaches that the directors of Moffat might apply in assessing the **qualitative** benefits of the proposed investment in a new IT system.

(c) Identify **two qualitative** benefits that might arise as a consequence of the investment in a new IT system and explain how you would attempt to assess them.

6 Exam focus

Exam sitting	Area examined	Question number	Number of marks
Sept/ Dec 2017	Evaluation of performance report	1(i)	15
Mar/June 2017	Evaluation of performance report	1(iii)	8
Mar/June 2016	Evaluation of performance report	1(i)	14
December 2014	Qualitative factors	2(c)	7
June 2014	Evaluation of performance report	1(i)	15
December 2013	Wrong signals and dysfunctional behaviour	2(b)	10
June 2013	Evaluation of strategic performance report	1(ii)	8
June 2012	Assessment of performance report	1(i)	12
December 2011	Suitability of branch information given	4(a)	8

Chapter summary

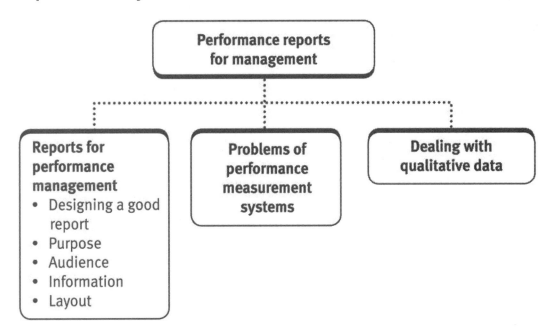

Test your understanding answers

Test your understanding 1

- **Unreliable information:** Information must be sufficiently reliable (e.g. accurate and complete) so that managers trust it to make judgements and decisions.

- **Presentation:** The information system may not be capable of presenting the information in a user-friendly format.

- **Appropriate information:** The information produced by the system should assist in meeting the organisation's objectives and should meet the needs of the users.

- **Timeliness:** Information must be available in time for managers to use it to make decisions.

- **Responsibility and controllability:** Information systems might fail to identify controllable costs, or indicate management responsibility properly. Information should be directed to the person who has the authority and the ability to act on it.

- **Information overload:** In some cases, managers might be provided with too much information, and the key information might be lost in the middle of large amounts of relatively unimportant figures.

- **Cost and value:** The cost of providing the information should not exceed the benefits obtained.

Test your understanding 2

Current performance report

The existing performance report has some good elements and many weaknesses. The current report shows clearly the calculation of profit and the profit margin from the business and shows how this has changed over the past three years along with a forecast of the next year. There is also a breakdown of the performance in the last two quarters which gives a snapshot of more immediate performance. The report breaks revenue and costs into product categories and so might allow a review of selling and procurement activities.

However, there are a number of weaknesses with the existing report. Firstly, the report only clearly answers the question 'what was the profit?' The owners have indicated that their aim is to 'make money' and it is possible that making money and profit may not be entirely compatible in the short term. For example, there are no cash measures of performance on the report. These are likely to assume greater importance given the planned improvements and any long-term expansion of the business. The owners might wish to consider refining their long-term goal in order to make it a more precise statement.

The current report does not present its information clearly. There is too much unnecessary information (e.g. the detail on operating costs). The style of presentation could easily be confusing to a non-accountant as it shows a large table of numbers with few clear highlights. The use of more percentage figures rather than absolute numbers may help (e.g. gross margins, change on comparative period percentages). Also, the numbers are given to the last $ where it would probably be sufficient to work in thousands of dollars.

The current report does not break down conveniently according to the functional areas over which each owner-manager has control. It summarises the overall build-up of profit but, for example, it cannot be easily used to identify performance of the service staff except indirectly through growth in total revenue. In order to improve this aspect of the report, the critical success factors associated with each functional area will need to be identified and then suitable performance measures chosen. For example, Sheila's area is customer-facing and so a measure of customer satisfaction based on number of complaints received or changes over time in average scores in customer surveys would be helpful. Bert's area is kitchen management and so staff efficiency (measured by number of meals produced per staff hour) and wastage control (measured by gross margin) may be critical factors. In your own financial and legal areas, costs are mostly fixed and so absolute measures such as the cost of capital may be helpful. In the area of procurement, purchasing the appropriate quality of food and drink for the lowest price is critical and so a gross margin for each product category would aid management.

The timescales reported in the current format are possibly not helpful for quarterly meetings. The existing report shows evidence of seasonality in the large change between Q3 and Q4 performance (42% fall in revenue). The figures for two years ago may not be particularly relevant to current market conditions and will not reflect recent management initiatives. It may be useful to consider reporting the last quarter's monthly performance giving comparative figures from the previous year and drop the use of the detailed 20X0 and 20X1 figures in favour of just supplying net profit figures for those years in order to give an overview of long-term performance.

The current report does not give much benchmark data to allow comparisons in order to better understand the results. It would be helpful to have budget figures for internal comparison and competitor figures for an external comparison of performance. Such external data is often difficult to obtain although membership of the local trade association may give access to a suitably anonymised database provided Metis is willing to share its data on the same basis.

Finally, the current document only reports financial performance. I have already indicated that this may not be sufficient to capture the critical factors that drive the business. A restaurant will be judged on the service and quality of its products as well as its pricing. It would be an improvement to include this style of reporting although gathering reliable data on these non-financial areas is more demanding.

Test your understanding 3

Information and Investment – Moffat

(a)   The management of an organisation need to exercise control at different levels within an organisation. These levels are often categorised as being strategic, tactical and operational. The information required by management at these levels varies in nature and content.

Strategic information

Strategic information is required by the management of an organisation in order to enable management to take a longer term view of the business and assess how the business may perform during the period. The length of this long term view will vary from one organisation to another, being very much dependent upon the nature of the business and the ability of those responsible for strategic decisions to be able to scan the planning horizon.

Strategic information tends to be holistic and summary in nature and would be used by management, when for example, undertaking SWOT analysis.

In Moffat strategic information might relate to the development of new services such as the provision of a home-based vehicle recovery service or the provision of 24hr servicing. Other examples would relate to the threats posed by Moffat's competitors or assessing the potential acquisition of a tyre manufacturer in order to enhance customer value via improved efficiency and lower costs.

Tactical information

Tactical Information is required in order to facilitate management planning and control for shorter time periods than strategic information. Such information relates to the tactics that management adopt in order to achieve a specific course of action. In Moffat this might involve the consideration of whether to open an additional outlet in another part of the country or whether to employ additional supervisors at each outlet in order to improve the quality of service provision to its customers.

In Moffat the manager at each location within Moffat would require information relating to the level of customer sales, the number of vehicles serviced and the number of complaints received during a week. Operational information might be used within Moffat in order to determine whether staff are required to work overtime due to an unanticipated increase in demand, or whether operatives require further training due to excessive time being spent on servicing certain types of vehicle.

Operational information

Operational information relates to a very short time scale and is often used to determine immediate actions by those responsible for day-to-day management.

Perhaps the preferred approach is to **acknowledge the existence of qualitative benefits and attempt to assess them in a reasonable manner acceptable to all parties including the company's bank**. The financial evaluation would then not only incorporate 'hard' facts relating to costs and benefits that are qualitative in nature, but also would include details of qualitative benefits which management consider exist but have not attempted to assess in financial terms. Such benefits might include, for example, the average time saved by location managers in analysing information during each operating period.

(b) One approach that the directors of Moffat could adopt would be to **ignore the qualitative benefits** that may arise on the basis that there is too much subjectivity involved in their assessment.

The problem that this causes is that the investment will probably look unattractive since all the costs will be included in the valuation where as significant benefits and savings will have been ignored. This approach lacks substance and would not be recommended.

An alternative approach would involve **attempting to attribute values to each of the identified benefits that are qualitative in nature**. Such an approach will necessitate the use of management estimates in order to derive the cash flows to be incorporated in a cost benefit analysis. The problems inherent in this approach include gaining consensus amongst interested parties regarding the footing of the assumptions from which estimated cash flows have been derived. Furthermore, if the proposed investment does take place then it may well prove impossible to prove that the claimed benefits of the new system have actually been realised.

Alternatively, the management of Moffat could attempt to express qualitative benefits in specific terms linked to a hierarchy of organisational requirements.

For example, qualitative benefits could be categorised as being:

(1) Essential to the business.

(2) Very useful attributes.

(3) Desirable, but not essential.

(4) Possible, if funding is available.

(5) Doubtful and difficult to justify.

(c) One of the main qualitative benefits that may arise from an investment in a new IT system by Moffat is the **improved level of service to its customers in the form of reduced waiting times** which may arise as a consequence of better scheduling of appointments and inventory management. This could be assessed via the introduction of a questionnaire requiring customers to rate the service that they have received from their recent visit to a location within Moffat according to specific criteria such as adherence to appointed times, time taken to service a vehicle, cleanliness of the vehicle and attitude of staff.

Alternatively a follow-up telephone call from a centralised customer services department may be made by Moffat personnel in order to gather such information.

Another qualitative benefit may arise in the form of competitive advantage. **Improvement in customer specific information and service levels may give Moffat a competitive advantage.**

Likewise **improved inventory management may enable costs to be reduced** thereby enabling a 'win-win' relationship to be enjoyed with customers.

Chapter

7

Human resource aspects of performance management

Chapter learning objectives

Upon completion of this chapter you will be able to:

- advise on the relationship of HR management to performance measurement (performance rating) and suitable remuneration methods

- discuss and evaluate different methods of reward practices

- assess the potential beneficial and adverse consequences of linking reward schemes to performance measurement, for example, how it can affect the risk appetite of employees

- assess the statement 'What gets measured gets done'

- discuss the accountability issues that might arise from performance measurement systems

- demonstrate how management style needs to be considered when designing an effective performance measurement system.

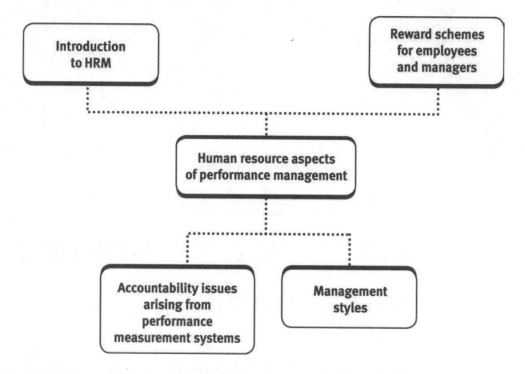

Student accountant articles: visit the ACCA website, www.accaglobal.com to review the article on 'reward schemes for employees and management'.

1 Assumed knowledge

Chapter 7 builds on your knowledge of Hopwood's management styles from PM.

2 Introduction

This chapter looks at the link between human resource management and performance measurement and considers the impact of the employee reward system on the behaviour of employees and on the performance of the organisation as a whole. It also discusses the accountability issues that might arise from performance measurement systems and looks at how management style needs to be considered when designing an effective performance measurement system.

3 Introduction to human resource management (HRM)

3.1 Definition of HRM

HRM is the strategic and coherent approach to the management of an organisation's most valued assets: the people working there who individually and collectively contribute to the achievement of its objectives for sustainable competitive advantage (Armstrong).

HRM includes the recruitment of employees, the development of policies relating to human resources (e.g. reward systems) and the management and development of employees (e.g. through training and development and through the appraisal system).

3.2 Importance of human resources

Human resource management has grown in importance from the traditional view of the personnel department, whose role was primarily seen as that of hiring and firing employees. Today, employees are seen less as an expensive necessity but as a strategic resource that may provide the organisation with competitive advantage.

Illustration 1 – Importance of human resources

In service industries, such as restaurants, employees have direct contact with customers. Having employees that are friendly and helpful has a large impact on how customers will view the business. Teams must be passionate about delivering an amazing guest experience to each and every customer and they should be provided with the right tools and training to deliver this brilliant experience.

An organisation uses HRM to ensure that it has the correct people in place to fulfil its strategic and operational objectives.

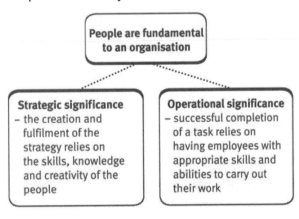

Illustration 2 – HM and competitive advantage

Some examples of the link between HRM and strategy are as follows:

If competitive advantage is sought through differentiation then HRM needs to ensure that high quality, skilled staff are recruited, that these staff are given the freedom to be creative and innovate, that a culture of service and quality is prevalent, and that rewards are geared towards long-term success and beyond short-term financial measures.

On the other hand, if a strategy of cost leadership was pursued, then HRM needs to focus on recruiting low skilled workers, providing repetitive, simple tasks, minimising staff numbers, providing strict controls, and focusing appraisals and rewards on short-term cost measures.

> ### Test your understanding 1
>
> **Required:**
>
> If an organisation planned to grow through acquisition, how might HRM contribute to the achievement of this strategy?

The problem with human resources is that they require more management than other resources since humans are complex, emotional creatures.

4 Reward schemes for employees and managers

4.1 Introduction

A reward system refers to all the monetary, non-monetary and psychological payments that an organisation provides for its employees in exchange for the work they perform.

4.2 The importance of target selection

It is important that appropriate targets (performance measures) are set for the employee. Targets should be:

- **Relevant** to the organisation's overall objective, e.g. if the organisation has an objective of 100% quality then an individual production worker may be set a target to produce products with zero defects. (It is worth noting that quality initiatives are often undermined by targets that focus on short-term profits).

- **Achievable** – employees may be unmotivated if they consider targets are very difficult or impossible to achieve, e.g. zero defects may be seen as impossible. However, it is worth noting that the same may be true if targets are too easy to achieve.

- **Controllable** – the individual will be unmotivated if they feel they can't control the target set, e.g. a production worker may not be responsible for defects if poor quality materials are purchased.

- **Prioritised** – employees will be overwhelmed and hence unmotivated if they are set a large number of targets.

- **Rewarded** – employees should be rewarded for achieving the target (s) set.

4.3 The purpose of reward systems

There are a number of purposes of reward systems:

- To further the organisation's objectives through the achievement of the employee's objectives. The two sets of objectives should be aligned. Importantly:
    - 'What gets measured gets done'.
    - 'What gets measured and fed back gets done well'.
    - 'What gets rewarded gets repeated'.

Illustration 3 – Alignment of goals

The reward scheme should support the organisation's goals and must be consistent with its strategy. For example, the UK supermarket Waitrose has a strategy of differentiation. Staff receive generous pay and benefits which are linked to the achievement of certain skills and pre-agreed targets. The supermarket, Lidl, on the other hand has a strategy of cost leadership. It has a simple reward scheme offering fairly low wages as staff are less skilled and new staff are easy to recruit and need little training.

- To ensure the recruitment and retention of appropriately skilled staff.

- To provide a fair and consistent basis for rewarding employees.

- To motivate staff and maximise performance.

Illustration 4 – Vroom's expectancy theory

Motivated staff are more likely to achieve targets and organisational goals.

Vroom believed that people will be motivated to do things to reach a goal if they believe in the worth of that goal and if they can see that what they do will help them in achieving it. **Vroom's expectancy model is stated as:**

Force = valence × expectancy

where:

Force = the strength of a person's motivation.

Valence = the strength of an individual's desire for an outcome.

Expectancy = the probability that they will achieve that outcome.

Reward schemes and employee motivation

A well known theory of motivation is Maslow's hierarchy of needs.

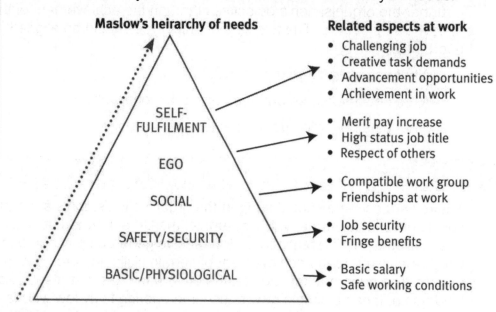

Maslow stated that people's wants and needs follow a hierarchy. As employees become progressively more highly paid, monetary rewards become less important as other needs such as recognition and an ability to achieve one's potential become more important.

- To reward performance through promotion or progression.
- To control salary costs.
- To comply with legal requirements and ethical obligations.

Illustration 5 – Reward systems and ethics

Awarding huge salaries and large bonuses to the senior executives of big companies may be seen as unethical when the economy is in recession and there is a climate of job cuts and pay freezes. However, others would argue that in order for a company to survive and thrive, the best senior executives must be attracted and retained. Therefore, executives must be offered a competitive and attractive reward package.

- To ensure the employees' attitude to risk is aligned with that of the organisation.

Illustration 6 – Reward schemes and risk appetite

As mentioned above, one of the problems associated with linking reward schemes to performance is that employees will prioritise the achievement of their reward which may impact their risk appetite.

UK banking executive's pay has received widespread political and media coverage since the 2008 financial crisis. It is argued that performance related bonuses have incentivised excessive risk taking and short-termism and there are widespread concerns that remuneration policies may have been a contributory factor to the financial crisis.

4.4 Methods of reward

Employee rewards fall into four categories:

- **Basic pay** – this is the minimum amount that an employee receives for working in an organisation and is determined in a number of ways such as market rates or job evaluation. Hourly rates or fixed annual salaries may be paid. Basic pay may be supplemented by other types of remuneration.

- **Performance-related pay** – pay is based on the level of performance. Rewards may be based on individual, group or organisational performance, all of which aim to motivate employees to work harder. (The types of performance-related pay are discussed below).

- **Benefits** – a wide range of rewards other than wages or pensions, such as company cars or health insurance. These can provide additional incentives at a lower cost and can be designed in a flexible way to suit the individual employee.

- **Share options** – these give employees the right to purchase shares at a specified exercise price at a specified time in the future. Share options will generally be exercisable on a specific date. They are often given to senior managers and should motivate them to increase share price. However, there is an argument that many of the factors that influence share price will be outside of the manager's control or that (previously risk averse) managers could be tempted to take risks in the hope of increasing the share price.

Test your understanding 2

Required:

Evaluate the four different reward methods.

4.5 Types of performance-related pay

There are a number of different types of performance-related pay:

- **Piecework schemes** – a price is paid for each unit of output. Often viewed as a fair system but quality control will be required.

- **Individual performance-related pay** – a pay rise or bonus is given to an employee on achievement of pre-agreed objectives or based on the assessment by a manager. Advantages include the ability to align individual objectives with organisational goals and the controllability of rewards by the employee. However, such schemes may result in a lack of teamwork and in tunnel vision (sole concentration on areas which are measured and rewarded).

- **Group performance-related pay** – rewards are based on the achievement of group targets. Encourages teamwork but may not be seen as fair by employees.

- **Knowledge contingent pay** – for example, an accountant may receive a bonus or pay rise on passing their ACCA exams.

- **Commission** – normally used for sales staff and is based on a percentage of their sales. Can motivate staff but may lead to short termism and manipulation of results.

- **Profit-related pay** – part of the employee's remuneration is linked to organisational profit. Can motivate employees to increase company profit and increase loyalty but may lead to short termism and lack of motivation if employees feel they have no control over organisational profit.

4.6 Benefits and problems of linking reward schemes to performance measurement

Benefits of linking reward schemes to performance	Potential problems of linking reward schemes to performance
• It gives individuals an incentive to achieve a good performance level since they know that this will be rewarded. • Schemes based on shares can motivate employees/managers to act in the long-term interests of the organisation. • Effective schemes also attract and keep the employees valuable to an organisation. • By tying an organisation's key performance indicators to a scheme, it is clear to all employees that performance creates organisational success. • By rewarding performance, an effective scheme creates an organisation focused on continuous improvement.	• Employees will prioritise the achievement of their reward which may impact their risk appetite. Employees may become too cautious and risk averse or conversely they may take bigger risks. • Employees may be unmotivated if they feel that they were penalised financially for circumstances outside of their control, e.g. an employee may have hit their quality target but did not receive a reward because the company's annual performance was poor. • Employees may become highly stressed if a significant proportion of their income is performance related. • Employees will have an extra incentive towards the dysfunctional behaviour, i.e. making decisions that are not in the best interests of the business. • Should targets be based on individual, team, division or group performance?

Question practice

The question below is an extract from a past exam question. Make sure that you take the time to attempt the question and review the answer.

Test your understanding 3

Lincoln & Lincoln Advertising (LLA) is an advertising agency based in Veeland, which is a large well-developed country considered to be one of the wealthiest in the world. LLA operates out of three regional offices (North, East and West) with its head office functions based in the East offices. The business offers a wide range of advertising services:

Strategic: Advising on an overall advertising campaign (mix of advertising channels and overall themes)

Buying: Advising and buying advertising space (on television, radio, websites and in newspapers and magazines); and

Creative: Designing and producing specific adverts for the customers' use.

The company is one of the three largest agencies in Veeland with many years of experience and many awards won. Competition in advertising is fierce, as advertising spending by businesses has suffered recently during a general economic downturn. Most new business is won in tender competitions between different advertising agencies.

Remuneration policy and regional offices

There are broadly five grades of staff at each regional office. The following is an outline of their remuneration packages. (The head office staff are treated separately and are not part of this exercise.)

Senior management

All staff at this level are paid a basic fixed salary, which reflects industry norms over the last few years, plus a bonus dependent on the net income of their office.

Creative staff

The 'creatives' are on individual packages which reflect the market rates in order to recruit them at the time that they were recruited. Some are fixed salary and some have a fixed element plus a bonus based on their office's revenues.

Buying staff

The buyers are paid a fixed salary plus a bonus based on the prices for advertising space that they negotiate compared to the budgeted cost of space. The budget is set by the finance team at head office based on previous years' experience and their forecast for supply and demand in the year in question.

Account management staff

Account management handles relationships with clients and also develops new clients. They are paid a fixed market-based salary.

Administration staff

These staff are paid the market rate for their jobs as a fixed salary based on hours worked.

Required:

Using the information provided, evaluate LLA's remuneration policy suggesting changes as appropriate.

(10 marks)

5 Accountability issues arising from performance measurement systems

In order to ensure that an employee is motivated to meet the performance measures (targets set), the targets need to be:

- clear (SMART) and
- linked to controllable factors.

As mentioned previously, employees will be unmotivated if they feel they are penalised for circumstances outside of their control.

Illustration 7 – Berry, Broadbent and Otley

There are many ways in which poorly designed performance measurement can result in wrong signals and dysfunctional behaviour. Berry, Broadbent and Otley identified the following problem areas:

- **Misrepresentation** – 'creative' reporting to suggest that a result is acceptable. For example, a manager may report that 98% of customers were 'satisfied' or 'more than satisfied' with the level of service they were provided with. However, on further investigation it may be found that feedback was only sought from a small selection of customers.

- **Gaming** – is dysfunctional behaviour where an individual manager is trying to meet their individual targets while ignoring the good of the whole organisation. For example, a manager may decide to cut divisional investment to boost divisional return on investment but this may result in a long-term fall in profits.

- **Misinterpretation** – failure to recognise the complexity of the environment in which the organisation operates. For example, looking at the financial aspects of performance a manager may be assessed as performing well. However, on further investigation it may be discovered that non-financial factors such as customer satisfaction are less favourable and therefore performance has been misinterpreted.

- **Short-termism (myopia)** – leading to the neglect of longer-term objectives. Financial measures such as return on capital employed (ROCE) may lead to short-termism. The use of a mix of financial and non-financial measures may lead to an improved focus on long term success.

- **Measure fixation** – measures and behaviour in order to achieve specific performance indicators which may not be effective. For example, an excessive focus on cost cutting to the detriment of quality and long term performance.

- **Tunnel vision** – undue focus on stated performance measures to the detriment of other areas. For example, an undue focus on ROCE to the detriment of employee satisfaction due to their needs, for say training or competitive remuneration, not being met.

- **Sub-optimisation** – focus on some objectives so that others are not achieved. For example, a focus on winning new customers may result in a reduced focus on the satisfaction of existing customers.

- **Ossification** – an unwillingness to change the performance measurement scheme once it has been set up, especially when it shows that good or adequate results are being achieved. The example of customer surveys being sent to only a select group of customers is also relevant here.

A number of actions might be taken in order to minimise the impact of imperfections that may exist within the performance measurement system. These methods will be explored in later chapters.

6 Management styles

Hopwood identified three distinct management styles of performance appraisal. The style needs to be considered when designing an effective performance measurement system.

Hopwood styles

Budget constrained style

The manager's performance is primarily evaluated upon the basis of his ability to continually meet the budget on a short-term basis. The manager will receive unfavourable feedback from his superior if, for instance, his actual costs exceed the budgeted costs, regardless of other considerations.

Profit-conscious style

The manager's performance is evaluated on the basis of his ability to increase the general effectiveness of his unit's operations in relation to the long-term purposes of the organisation.

Non-accounting style

The budgetary information plays a relatively unimportant part in the superior's evaluation of the manager's performance.

	Budget constrained	Profit-conscious	Non-accounting
Characteristics	Pressure to hit short-term financial targets.	Focus on longer-term performance.	• Little emphasis on financial performance. • Look at non-financial aspects instead.
Performance measurement systems	Short-term financial performance is measured using, say, ROCE or annual gross profit.	Measures of long- term profitability may be used. For example, the net present value (NPV) of a project over its entire life may be used when making decisions.	Non-financial measures such as customer satisfaction, employee morale or innovation may be used.
Advantages	Should ensure short- term targets are met.	Give flexibility to go 'off plan' if justifiable.	• Focus on causes rather than effects. • Targets may be more meaningful to staff.
Disadvantages	• Short-termism (e.g. cost cutting). • Results may be 'distorted'. • Stress for employees and difficult working relationships. • Lack of flexibility. • Stifles ingenuity.	Loss of short-term control.	Financial implications of behaviour may be neglected.

7 Exam focus

Exam sitting	Area examined	Question number	Number of marks
Sept/ Dec 2017	Management styles	3(c)	10
Mar/June 2016	Reward scheme assessment	1(v)	12
Mar/June 2016	Reward systems	2(b)	11
June 2015	Management styles	4(c)	10
June 2015	Reward systems	3(c)	9
June 2014	Appraisals	2(c)	8
December 2012	Reward schemes	1(iii)	10
December 2011	Performance appraisal system, Hopwood	4(b) and (c)	12

Chapter summary

Reward schemes for employees and managers
- definition
- importance of target selection
- purpose of reward systems
- methods
- performance-related pay
- linking performance and rewards

Introduction to HRM
- definition
- importance

Human resource aspects of performance management

Accountability issues arising from performance measurement systems

Management styles

Test your understanding answers

Test your understanding 1

HRM may have to:

- plan potential redundancies when staff are measured

- facilitate and manage the changes in culture and performance that are necessary

- ensure that corporate goals and missions are understood and communicated

- unify reward systems

- redesign jobs

- plan training.

This is just one further example of the link between HRM and strategy, but it should illustrate how HRM plays a role in contributing to the achievement of an organisation's objectives.

Test your understanding 2

	Advantages	Disadvantages
sick pay	• Easy to administer. • Basic employee needs taken care of.	• Does not motivate employees to achieve strategy. • Does not motivate employees to improve performance.
Performance-related pay	• Motivates employees to achieve strategy. • Motivates employees to improve performance.	• Can be subjective and inconsistent. • Can be viewed as unfair if based on team/company performance. • Stressful for employee if they rely on this to pay for basic needs.

Benefits	• Can be tailored to the individual employee.	• Employees may not want. • Does not motivate employees to achieve strategy. • Big additional cost.
Share options	• Should motivate employees to increase share price.	• Factors that influence share price may be outside of employee's control. • May tempt managers to take excessive risks.

Test your understanding 3

Remuneration packages

Generally, using industry norms as a basic benchmark will help to ensure that staff are kept broadly happy, although it will not motivate them to outperform their peers.

Taking each of the staff levels in turn:

Senior management

Their basic salary reflects historic norms and the bonus should motivate performance. It is notable that no account is taken of the different economic conditions that each office may find itself in and so there may be resentment from those in offices where the general economy is doing poorly to those who are in a region with good performance and so profits are growing easily. It may be worthwhile trying to benchmark the performance of each office against its regional competitors, although it can be hard to obtain such detailed information.

Creative staff

The creatives' packages are set when recruited. This could lead to a loss of motivation, especially for those who get only a fixed salary. If a bonus is paid, then it is currently based on revenue and not profits and so there is no mechanism to control costs on projects with these employees. There will be tension between the need for imaginative ideas and cost efficient ones. Overall, it is likely that each staff member should have a personalised package with a performance element that would be based on the assessment of a superior manager. In order to maintain some sense of objectivity, the criteria that the manager might use to judge performance should be agreed across the firm and could include, primarily, winning new business in tender competitions and, secondarily, winning industry awards.

Buying staff

The packages for the buying staff appear to be based on appropriate performance, although the setting of such targets depends heavily on the expertise of the finance team and, as they are based in the East office, they may lack the local knowledge to set the budget accurately. It may be wise to maintain the bulk of the buyers' remuneration as a fixed salary element as a result.

Account management staff

It is surprising that this group of client-facing staff are not paid on performance. It would seem that their performance could be directly measured by client retention and new business won, so it would be common for such staff to have a high percentage of their remuneration based on performance and not be wholly fixed. Measures such as numbers of clients and total client revenues would be appropriate for these posts.

Administration staff

This is a common method of remuneration for these types of jobs and in line with the general market. A small bonus based on the overall performance of the firm may help to create a culture of loyalty throughout the business. It is unlikely to be efficient to set individual targets for such employees, given that there will probably be a large number of them.

Financial performance measures in the private sector

Chapter learning objectives

Upon completion of this chapter you will be able to:

- demonstrate why the primary objective of financial performance should be primarily concerned with the benefits to shareholders

- discuss the appropriateness of, and apply the following as measures of performance:

    - gross profit and operating profit

    - return on capital employed (ROCE) – earnings per share (EPS)

    - earnings before interest, tax & depreciation adjustment (EBITDA)

    - net present value (NPV)

    - internal rate of return and modified internal rate of return (IRR, MIRR)

- discuss why indicators of liquidity and gearing need to considered in conjunction with profitability

- compare and contrast short and long run financial performance and the resulting management issues

- assess the appropriate benchmarks to use in assessing performance.

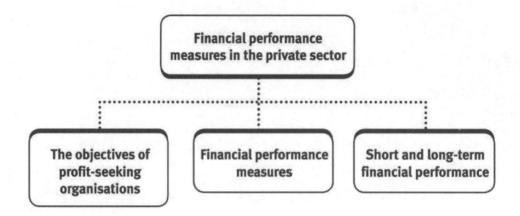

1 Assumed knowledge

Chapter 8 builds on your knowledge of financial performance measures from PM.

2 Introduction

In the exam, you may be required to look at performance measures in a variety of contexts. In this chapter we focus on the principal measures used by the private sector. The emphasis will be on financial measures (non–financial measures will be reviewed in Chapter 11).

3 The objectives of profit-seeking organisations

3.1 Maximising shareholder wealth

- The primary objective of a profit seeking organisation is to maximise shareholder wealth.

- This is based on the argument that shareholders are the legal owners of a company and so their interests should be prioritised.

- Shareholders are generally concerned with the following: – current earnings

  - future earnings

  - dividend policy

  - relative risk of their investment.

All of these are driven by financial performance.

Test your understanding 1
Required:
What will be the primary objective of a commercial bank? What might be some of its subsidiary or secondary objectives?

Objectives according to Drucker

Peter Drucker has suggested that profit-seeking organisations typically have objectives relating to the following:

- market standing

- innovation

- productivity

- physical and financial resources

- profitability

- manager performance and development

- worker performance and attitude

- public responsibility.

3.2 The relationship between profits and shareholder value

Rather than focusing on achieving higher profit levels, companies are under increasing pressure to look at the long-term value of the business. This is due to the following factors:

- research has suggested a poor correlation between shareholder return and profits

- investors are increasingly looking at long-term value

- reported profits may not be comparable between companies.

ZBB

Total shareholder return (TSR) is the return shareholders receive both in dividends and capital growth.

Studies have found that there is little correlation between TSR and earnings per share (EPS) growth, and virtually no relationship at all with return on equity, yet many companies are still using profit as their only measure of performance.

Even where companies state that their objective is to maximise shareholder value, often directors' bonuses are still based on short-term profitability or EPS targets.

However strong evidence has been found between shareholder value and future cash flows.

While these issues have been known for some time, they have come into sharp focus due to the performance of new technology/communications companies.

Illustration 1 – Profits and shareholder value

Timescales

In calculating shareholder value it is customary to make a distinction between the 'planning' period (usually less than 5 years), and the 'continuing period' beyond. Results for different industries show the following:

Industry	% of value in the planning period	% of value in the continuing period
Tobacco	40	60
Sporting goods	20	80
Skin care	5	95
High tech	−20	120

High tech companies, such as Apple, need to make decisions based on the long-term value of the business since these companies tend to make initial losses due to the high level of research and development required.

3.3 How to measure the long-term value of a business

A **value based management** (VBM) approach aligns the strategic, operational and management processes to focus management decision making on what activities create wealth for shareholders (VBM will be explored in more detail in Chapter 9).

4   Financial performance measures

4.1 Introduction

This chapter is concerned with measuring:

*   the financial performance of the organisation as a whole

*   the performance of the key projects.

Chapter 9 will cover divisional performance and Chapter 11 will cover non-financial performance.

Although most of these indicators will be familiar to you from PM, there will be a different emphasis in APM questions. A common problem of APM candidates is that they throw every indicator that they can remember at a problem in an uncritical fashion. APM is all about the critical approach. It is about selecting from the range of indicators that you know from PM and using those which are most appropriate to the scenario. In addition, the examiner will not only expect you to calculate the numbers but to also give performance management advice based on what you have calculated.

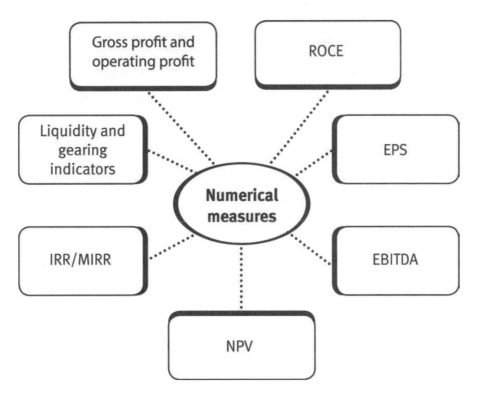

Each of these measures will be reviewed in turn.

 Performance measurement systems

A good performance measurement system should have the following characteristics:

- Support corporate strategy, its communication and implementation.

- Measure performance from a financial, non-financial, quantitative and qualitative perspective.

- Attuned to the needs of decision makers and their activities.

- Reporting is produced at sufficient regularity to properly support decision-making.

- Attention to the accuracy of data and calculation of measures is important for trust in the information.

Any performance measurement system requires the identification of indicators which can identify past, current or potential future outcomes.

The aim:

- Report past outcomes, both good and bad.

- Identify where improvements should be made and what resources are required.

- Determine the quality and robustness of business processes; and

- Allow stakeholders to independently judge an organisation's performance.

By embodying the key measures that are important for the organisation's strategy they can indicate to the organisation what is important. (Often incorporated in strategic frameworks such as scorecards).

NB: As a general rule these measures are only meaningful when compared with:

- other time periods
- other measures of performance
- other companies
- other industries
- budget.

4.2 Gross and operating profit

Despite concerns over the poor correlation between profit and shareholder value, many business use profit based targets. This is primarily for the following reasons:

- The information is readily available internally as it is needed for statutory reporting
- Most managers feel they understand it
- It makes comparisons between companies easier as they also have to produce statutory reports.

Evaluation of gross versus operating profit

The relative pros and cons of using gross compared with operating profit are as follows:

Gross profit	Operating profit
• Focusses purely on whether the process of making and selling products is profitable – i.e. does the price cover the manufacturing cost, before considering selling, distribution and admin costs.	• Also considers selling, distribution and admin costs, so indicates whether gross profit is sufficient to cover wider costs.

• Useful for highlighting product profitability issues – for example, if gross profit has fallen, is this due to cost rises, pressure to drop prices or a mixture of both? Management response will depend on the underlying causes.	• Useful for highlighting wider cost efficiency issues – for example, a division may have improving gross profit but worsening operating profit indicating underlying good products but poor control over distribution and/or admin.
• For short term decision making it could be argued that contribution would be a more useful metric.	

Neither operating profit nor gross profit consider variables that management may have little control over, such as taxes or interest charges, which will be based on financing used. This allows those who review the income statement to judge management's efficiency in running the business.

The gross profit margin and operating profit margin are often calculated: (Gross profit ÷ Sales) × 100%

(Operating profit ÷ Sales) × 100%

4.3 Return on capital employed (ROCE)

ROCE is a key measure of **profitability**. It shows the operating profit that is generated from every $1 of assets employed.

$$ROCE = \frac{\text{Operating profit}}{\text{Capital employed}} \times 100$$

Note:

- If the operating profit is not given in the exam question, use the profit figure that is closest to it.

- Capital employed = total assets less current liabilities or total equity plus long-term debt.

- Capital employed may be based on net book value (NBV), gross book value or replacement cost (be guided by the exam question). It may be the average figure (if information for two periods is given), the figure at the start of the period (if an average can't be calculated) or the figure at the end of the period (if this is all that is given in the question).

A high ROCE is desirable. An increase in ROCE could be achieved by:

- Increasing operating profit, for example through an increase in sales price or better control of costs.

- Reducing capital employed, for example through the repayment of its debt.

Advantages	Disadvantages
• Easy to calculate. • Figures are readily available. • Measures how well a business is utilising the funds invested in it. • Often used by external analysts/investors.	• Research shows a poor correlation between ROCE and shareholder value. • Care must be taken to ensure that like is compared with like, when comparing with different companies – e.g. inclusion of intangibles in capital employed. • Can be distorted by accounting policies. • ROCE can be improved by cutting back investment – this may not be in the company's long-term best interest.

Test your understanding 2

	Company A $	Company B $
Profit from operations	20,000	1,000,000
Sales	200,000	2,000,000
Capital employed	100,000	10,000,000

Required:

For companies A and B, which of the following statements are true?

(1)　Company A has a higher ROCE than company B.

(2)　Company B has a higher ROCE than company A.

(3)　Company A is more profitable than company B.

(4)　Company A is better utilising the funds invested in it than company B.

Choose:

A　(1), (3) and (4)

B　(2) only

C　(1) and (4)

D　None of these

4.4 EPS

EPS is a measure of the profit attributable to each ordinary share.

$$EPS = \frac{\text{Profit after tax less preference dividends}}{\text{Weighted average number of ordinary shares in issue}}$$

As is the case for other ratios, for EPS to be truly meaningful, it must be set in context.

- Is EPS growing or declining over time?

- Is there likely to be significant dilution of EPS?

- Is it calculated consistently?

Advantages	Disadvantages
• Easily understood by shareholders. • Calculation is precisely defined by accounting standards. • Figures are readily available. • Often used as a performance measure between companies, sectors, periods within the same organisation.	• Research shows a poor correlation between EPS growth and shareholder value. • Accounting treatment may cause ratios to be distorted.

Test your understanding 3

A company's share capital is as follows:

Ordinary shares ($1 each) $6,000,000

9% Preference shares $1,000,000

The company made profits before tax of $5,500,000. Corporation tax on this is calculated as $2,100,000.

Required:

Calculate the company's EPS.

4.5 EBITDA

EBITDA is earnings before interest, tax, depreciation, amortisation and write-offs (such as goodwill).

Advantages	Disadvantages
• It is a measure of underlying performance since it is a proxy for cash flow generated from operating profit. • Tax and interest are externally generated and therefore not relevant to the underlying success of the business. • Depreciation and amortisation represent a write off of expenditure over a number of years and might therefore be excluded when examining the performance of a particular year. • Easy to calculate. • Easy to understand.	• Poor correlation to shareholder wealth. • Comparison between organisations difficult due to potential differences in accounting policies and the calculation of an absolute figure. • It ignores changes in working capital and their impact on cash flow. • It fails to consider the amount of fixed asset replacement needed by the business. • It can easily be manipulated by aggressive accounting policies related to income recognition and capitalisation of expenses.

4.6 Other profitability measures

Measure	Calculation
Asset turnover	Sales ÷ Capital employed
Dividend cover	PAT ÷ Dividends paid during the year
Dividend yield	(Dividend per share ÷ Current share price) × 100%
P/E ratio	Share price ÷ EPS
Earnings yield	(EPS ÷ Share price) × 100%
Return on equity	Net profit after tax ÷ average shareholders' equity

One additional measure of performance is economic value added (EVA). This will be discussed in Chapter 9.

4.7 Liquidity and risk indicators

Liquidity ratios

These ratios measure the ability of the company to meet its short-term obligations:

Measure	Calculation
Current ratio	Current assets ÷ Current liabilities
Acid test or quick ratio	(Current assets – inventories) ÷ Current liabilities
Raw material period	(Ave. value of raw materials ÷ Purchases) × 365
WIP period	(Ave. value of WIP ÷ Cost of sales) × 365
Finished goods period	(Ave. value of finished goods ÷ Cost of sales) × 365
Receivables period	(Ave. receivables ÷ Sales) × 365
Payables period	(Ave. payables ÷ Purchases) × 365

There is often a trade-off between liquidity and profitability. Companies can be highly profitable but get into trouble when they run out of cash (overtrading).

Therefore liquidity needs to be considered alongside profitability when appraising a company's financial situation.

Risk ratios

These ratios measure the ability of the company to meet its long-term liabilities:

- Financial gearing = (Long-term debt/Shareholder funds) × 100% **or**

- Financial gearing = (Long-term debt/(Long-term debt + Shareholders funds)) × 100%

- Operating gearing = (Fixed costs/Variable costs)

- Interest cover = (PBIT/Interest charges).

4.8 Appraising individual projects

We will now review some of the techniques that are available for appraising individual projects. These include:

- Net present value (NPV)

- Internal rate of return (IRR)

- Modified internal rate of return (MIRR).

4.9 Net present value (NPV)

The **NPV** is the present value (PV) of all cash inflows less the PV of all cash outflows of a project.

NPV represents the increase or decrease in the value of an organisation today as a result of accepting the project being reviewed.

Decision rule: any project that generates a positive NPV is viable.

Advantages	Disadvantages
• Strong correlation with shareholder value. • It considers the time value of money. • Risk can be allowed for by adjusting the cost of capital. • Cash flows are less subject to manipulation and subjective decisions than accounting profits. • Considers all cash flows of a project. • Superior measure to IRR for mutually exclusive projects.	• Difficult to calculate/understand. • It does not easily allow two projects of very different scales to be compared. • It is based on assumptions about cash flows, the timing of those cash flows and the appropriate cost of capital. • Many firms use NPV for investment appraisal and then switch to profit-based measures to motivate managers.

Test your understanding 4

Oracle invests in a new machine at the beginning of Year 1 which costs $15,000. It is hoped that the net cash flows over the next five years will correspond to those given in the table below.

Year	1	2	3	4	5
Net cash flow ($)	1,500	2,750	4,000	5,700	7,500

Required:

(i) Calculate the NPV assuming a 15% cost of capital.

(ii) Calculate the NPV assuming a 10% cost of capital.

(iii) Draw a conclusion based on your findings.

Sensitivity analysis

Sensitivity analysis calculates the percentage change in a variable, for example sales volume, that would have to occur before the original investment decision is reversed, i.e. the project NPV changes to $0.

$$\text{Sensitivity} = \frac{\text{NPV}}{\text{PV of flows under consideration}} \times 100$$

Benchmarking

Benchmarking has already been covered in chapter 1. In the exam, you may be required to assess the relative financial performance of a project or an organisation compared to appropriate benchmarks.

Test your understanding 5

JDL manufactures a range of solar panel heating. They have recently developed the new EF solar panel. The directors of JDL recently spent $20,000 on market research, the findings of which led them to believe that a market exists for the EF panels.

The finance director of JDL has gathered relevant information and prepared the following evaluation relating to the proposed manufacture and sale of the EF solar panels:

(1) Sales are expected to be 2,700 units per annum at a selling price of $3,000 per unit.

(2) Variable material, labour, and overhead costs are estimated at $1,580 per unit.

(3) In addition, a royalty of $250 per unit would be payable to EF (Environmental Friends), for the use of their brand name.

(4) Fixed overheads are estimated at $900,000 per annum. These overheads cannot be avoided until the end of the year in which the EF solar panels is withdrawn from the market.

(5) An initial investment of $7 million would be required. A government grant equal to 50% of the initial investment would be received on the date the investment is made. No tax allowances would be available on this initial investment. The estimated life cycle of the EF solar panels is six years.

(6) Corporation tax at the rate of 30% per annum is payable in the year in which profit occurs.

(7) The cost of capital is 12%.

Required:

(a) Calculate the net present value (NPV) of the EF solar panels proposal and recommend whether it should be undertaken by the directors of JDL.

(b) Using sensitivity analysis, estimate by what percentage each of the under-mentioned items, taken separately, would need to change before the recommendation in (a) above is varied:

   (i)   Initial outlay of $3,500 (i.e. initial investment of $7,000 minus grant of $3,500).

   (ii) Annual contribution.

(c) Comment on THREE factors other than NPV that the directors of JDL should consider when deciding whether to manufacture the EF solar panels.

(d) Explain the term 'benchmarking' and briefly discuss the potential benefits that JDL can obtain as a result of undertaking a successful programme of benchmarking.

4.10 Internal rate of return (IRR)

When presented with uncertainty about the cost of capital, some managers prefer to assess projects by reference to the IRR.

Decision rule: the project should be accepted if the IRR is greater than the firm's cost of capital.

The **IRR** is the discount rate when the NPV = 0.

$$IRR = L + \frac{NPVL}{NPVL - NPVH} \times (H - L)$$

where:

L = lower cost of capital

H = higher cost of capital

NPVL = the NPV at the lower cost of capital

NPVH = the NPV at the higher cost of capital

Test your understanding 6

A project's predicted cash flows give:

- a NPV of $50,000 at a cost of capital of 10%

- a NPV of ($10,000) at a cost of capital of 15%.

Required:

Calculate the IRR.

4.11 Modified internal rate of return (MIRR)

One drawback of IRR is that it is possible to get multiple rates of return.

MIRR eliminates this possibility.

The **MIRR** represents the actual return generated by a project.

The MIRR assumes that funds will be reinvested at the investor's required return (cost of capital). It is calculated as follows:

Method:

Step 1: The cash inflows after the initial investment are converted to a single cash inflow at the end of the last year of the project by assuming that the cash inflows are reinvested at the investor's required rate of return (cost of capital).

Step 2: The present value of the cash outflows is then calculated.

Step 3: The MIRR is calculated as the return which equates to the present value of the outflows to this single inflow, using present value tables.

Illustration 2 – MIRR

The following information is available for a project:

Year	0	1	2	3	4
Cash flow ($)	(5,000)	2,000	(1,000)	3,500	3,800

The cost of capital is 10%.

Required:

Calculate the MIRR of the project.

Solution:

Step 1: Find the value of the cash inflows at the end of the project

Year	Cash inflows ($)	Value at the end of year 4 ($)
1	2,000	$2,000 \times (1.10)^3 = 2,662$
3	3,500	$3,500 \times 1.10 = 3,850$
4	3,800	$= 3,800$
		Total = 10,312

Step 2: Find the present value of the cash outflows

Year	Cash outflows ($)	Value in year 0 ($)
0	5,000	5,000
2	1,000	$1,000 \div (1.10)^2 = 826$
		Total = 5,826

Step 3: Calculate the MIRR

$10,312 \times$ Discount factor $_{\text{yr 4 @ MIRR}} = 5,826$

Discount factor $_{\text{yr 4 @ MIRR}} = 5,826 \div 10,312$

$= 0.565$

From tables, MIRR is approximately **15%**

Alternatively, a formula can be used to calculate the MIRR:

(Present value of inflows ÷ present value of outflows)$^{1/n} \times$ (1 + cost of capital) − 1

where n = the life of the project in years

Illustration 3 – MIRR alternative solution

Required:

Using the information from the previous illustration, calculate the MIRR using the formula.

Solution:

Start by calculating the present value of the cash inflows:

Year	Cash inflows ($)	DF 10%	Present value ($)
1	2,000	0.909	1,818
3	3,500	0.751	2,629
4	3,800	0.683	2,595
			Total = 7,042

Next, calculate the present value of the cash outflows:

Year	Cash outflows ($)	DF 10%	Present value ($)
0	5,000	1	5,000
2	1,000	0.826	826
			Total = 5,826

Finally, use the formula to calculate the MIRR:

$$\text{MIRR} = (7{,}042 \div 5{,}826)^{1/4} \times 1.1 - 1$$

MIRR = **15.3%** (as per illustration 3)

Decision rule: the project should be accepted if the MIRR is greater than the firm's cost of capital.

4.12 Assessing performance and giving performance management advice

The examiner will expect you to be able to assess and comment on the financial performance of an organisation using a range of appropriate measures. In the APM exam it is more important that you can give performance management advice rather than just being able to calculate a long list of ratios. Bear this in mind when attempting the questions below.

Test your understanding 7

AK is a privately owned manufacturing company and has been experiencing difficulties.

Required:

You have been asked to assess the current position of AK using appropriate performance measures:

	20X6	20X5
	$000	$000
Receivables	5,200	3,120
Inventory	2,150	2,580
Cash	350	1,350
	———	———
Total current assets	7,700	7,050
Non-current assets	14,500	14,500
Total payables	4,500	3,150
Sales	17,500	16,625
Operating costs	14,000	12,950
	———	———
Operating profit	3,500	3,675
	———	———
Earnings	2,625	2,756

There are 2.5 million shares in issue.

Additional example on assessing financial performance

BPG is a Telecommunications company that commenced trading in 20X1 in the country of Brean. In 20X6 it created a similar division in the country of Portlet.

Required:

Assess the financial performance of BPG and its operations in Brean and Portlet during the years ended 20X8 and 20X9. Using the data provided below.

Note: you should highlight any information that would be required to make a more comprehensive assessment of financial performance.

Summary Income Statements

| | 20X9 | | | 20X8 | | |
	Brean	Portlet	Company	Brean	Portlet	Company
	$000	$000	$000	$000	$000	$000
Revenue	14,400	2,900	17,300	14,040	1,980	16,020
Salaries	4,450	1,340	5,790	4,125	1,185	5,310
Consumables	2,095	502	2,597	1,950	380	2,330
Other operating costs	2,921	695	3,616	2,754	620	3,374
	9,466	2,537	12,003	8,829	2,185	11,014
Marketing	2,456	600	3,056	2,092	480	2,572
Interest			850			900
Depreciation and amortisation	400	160	560	400	100	500
	2,856	760	4,466	2,492	580	3,972
Total costs	12,322	3,297	16,469	11,321	2,765	14,986
Profit/(loss)	2,078	(397)	831	2,719	(785)	1,034

Statement of financial position

| | 20X9 | | | 20X8 | | |
	Brean	Portlet	Company	Brean	Portlet	Company
	$000	$000	$000	$000	$000	$000
Assets						
Non-current assets	9,000	1,600	10,600	8,000	1,000	9,000
Current assets	4,550	1,000	5,550	5,000	800	5,800
Total assets	13,550	2,600	16,150	13,000	1,800	14,800
Equity and liabilities						
Share capital			9,150			7,800
Non-current liabilities						
Long term borrowings			4,000			4,500
Current liabilities	2,400	600	3,000	2,000	500	2,500
			16,150			14,800

Solution:

Company		20X9	20X8
ROCE =	PBIT/D+E	12.8%	15.7%
EBITDA =	EBITDA	2,241	2,434
Gearing =	D/E	43.7%	57.7%
or gearing =	D/D+E	30.4%	36.6%

Each operation

		20X9 Brean	20X9 Portlet	20X8 Brean	20X8 Portlet
Sales margin =	Profit/revenue (%)	14.4	(13.7)	19.4	(39.6)
Non-current asset turnover =	Revenue/non-curr assets	1.6	1.8	1.76	1.98

	Brean	Portlet	Company
% Revenue growth	2.6	46.5	8
% Profit growth	(23.6)	49.4	
% Increase in costs:			
Salaries	7.9	13.1	
Marketing	7.4	32.1	
Operating costs	6.1	12.1	

The turnover in Brean has increased by 2.6% whilst in Portlet turnover has increased by 46.5% which is excellent since the business only commenced trading in 20X6. The overall growth amounted to 8% which is an acceptable level.

The profits in Brean are down by nearly 24% whilst in Portlet the loss has fallen by 49%. Portlet will need to make further growth in sales and monitor costs in order to become more profitable.

The costs within Brean have risen by 8% for salaries, 7% for marketing and 6% for operating costs yet sales have only increased by 2.6%.

The costs within Portlet have risen substantially more than in Brean. Marketing for example has risen by 32%. This may be due to the fact that this is a necessary cost to develop the growth in revenue within the newly established operation.

Salaries and operating costs have risen by between 12 and 13%, yet sales have increased by 46%. These costs should be monitored as the business grows further.

The EBITDA has fallen by 8% from $2,434,000 to $2,241,000 and ROCE has also fallen from 13.1 % to 10.4%. This is not a very good sign for the company.

The non-current asset utilisation ratios of Brean show a decrease from 20X8 to 20X9. Portlet also shows a decrease from 2 to 1.8, this is less surprising given that the operation has only recently been established. Portlet is clearly in a rapid growth phase hence the need for investment in non-current assets.

It would be useful to have previous years data for Brean to observe longer term trends for revenue and costs. Data for Portlet from its first year of operation in 20X6 would enable a complete picture to be taken.

Competitor information would allow us to establish the market share and establish how well the operations are performing in comparison to competitors.

It is clear that long term borrowings have decreased from 20X8 to 20X9 and that BPG has sufficient cash flow to repay some of the debt finance. However it would be useful to have a breakdown of working capital for each operation.

It would also be useful to have future market and financial projections for Brean and Porlet, which should reflect the actual results in 20X8 and 20X9.

Budgeted data would be useful to see if they have managed to meet the targets set.

Note: You may be tempted to review the cash flows. This is not required in the question and the examiner is unlikely to expect this from you in this type of question.

Test your understanding 8

Water Supply Services (WSS) and Enterprise Activities (EA) are two wholly-owned subsidiaries of Aqua Holdings. You have recently qualified as an accountant and have joined the finance team of Aqua Holdings at headquarters. Your finance director is not satisfied with the performance of these two subsidiaries and has asked you to prepare a report covering the following issues:

(1) The profitability of the two subsidiaries.

(2) The competence of the EA manager to make financial decisions.

(3) The consequences of having a common management information system serving both companies.

The finance director has also provided you with the following background information on the two companies.

WSS

The company holds a licence issued by the government to be the sole supplier of drinking water to a large town. The business necessitates a considerable investment in infrastructure assets and is therefore highly capital intensive. To comply with the licence the company has to demonstrate that it is maintaining guaranteed service standards to its customers. WSS is extensively regulated requiring very detailed annual returns concerning costs, prices, profits and service delivery standards. The government enforces a price-capping regime and therefore the company has limited freedom in tariff determination – the government will normally only sanction a price increase following a demonstrable rise in costs.

EA

In contrast to WSS, EA operates in a very competitive market offering a plumbing service to domestic properties. The business has the following characteristics:

- rapidly changing market conditions
- a high rate of new entrants and business failures
- occasional shortages of skilled plumbers
- fluctuating profits.

In addition to this background information you also have summarised income statements and statements of financial position for the last two years for both companies.

Water Supply Services

Summary income statement

	Year 20X9 $m	20X8 $m
Turnover	31	30
Less: Staff costs	3	2
General expenses	2	2
Depreciation	12	9
Interest	5	5
Profit	9	12

Summary statement of financial position

	Year	
	20X9	**20X8**
	$m	$m
Non-current assets	165	134
Current assets	5	6
Total assets	170	140
Current liabilities	(3)	(6)
Debentures	(47)	(47)
Net assets	120	87
Shareholders' equity	120	87

Enterprise activities – summary income statement

	Year	
	20X9	**20X8**
	$m	$m
Turnover	20	35
Less: Staff costs	5	6
General expenses	10	10
Materials	3	6
Depreciation	1	1
Profit	1	12

Summary statement of financial position

	Year	
	20X9	**20X8**
	$m	$m
Non-current assets	22	22
Current assets	13	12
Total assets	35	34
Current liabilities	(4)	(4)
Net assets	31	30
Shareholders' equity	31	30

Required:

Prepare a report on the comparative financial performance of Water Supply Services and Enterprise Activities from the above financial statements. Your report should incorporate an assessment of the potential limitations of undertaking such a comparison.

5 Short and long-term financial performance

5.1 Introduction

Short-term financial performance measures are used for:

- control purposes, e.g. variance analysis is carried out comparing actual and budgeted results and investigating any differences.

- determining executive rewards – rewards may be linked to the achievement of short-term targets.

- assessing the quality of past decisions and assessing the impact of decisions yet to be made.

5.2 Problems of using short-term targets to appraise performance

A focus on short-term performance (and the measurement of manager's performance based on short-term results) can threaten a company's ability to create long-term value for its shareholders. Managers may feel the pressure to achieve short-term targets (such as a target ROCE or gross profit margin) and, as a result, long-term performance may be compromised. For example:

- Investment in new assets is cut. This may lead to a short-term boost in profits but long-term profitability may suffer as a result of old, and potentially inefficient, assets being used.

- The development and training budget may be cut to boost short-term profitability. However, employees are a vital resource for many organisations and a lack of investment in this area could lead to a loss of competitive advantage and a resultant fall in long-term profits.

5.3 Steps to reduce short termism

- **Use financial and non-financial measures:** these should focus manager's attention on long-term financial performance. Methods such as the balanced scorecard can be used (these methods will be discussed in detail in chapter 11).

- **Switch from a budget-constrained style:** a switch should be made to a profit-conscious or non-accounting style (Hopwood). Both of these approaches have a more long-term focus.

- **Share options:** if these are given to management they should focus their attention on improving share price and hence long-term performance.

- **Bonuses:** these should be linked to profits over timescales greater than one year.

- **NPV and IRR:** should be used to appraise investments. Discounted cash flow techniques recognise the future economic benefits of current investments.

- **Reduce decentralisation:** this should increase central control and reduce the problem of dysfunctional behaviour.

- **Value-based techniques:** focus on the key drivers of shareholder wealth. These techniques can be incorporated and will be discussed in more detail in chapter 9.

5.4 Should a short-term approach ever be taken?

It is generally accepted that a focus on long-term performance is superior. However, there are some situations when it is important to measure the achievement of short-term targets and to link rewards to these targets.

The best example of this would be an organisation which is fighting to survive. It is only by overcoming short-term hurdles and building short-term profits that long-term survival (and profitability) can be achieved. Cash flow measures may be more important than profit measures at this stage.

6 Exam focus

Exam sitting	Area examined	Question number	Number of marks
Sept/ Dec 2017	ROCE, EBITDA	2(a)	16
Sept/Dec 2016	Evaluation of performance measures, ROCE	1(ii)(iii)	23
June 2014	Fixed and variable costs	1(ii)	6
June 2013	Evaluation of strategic performance report and metrics	1(ii)	8
December 2012	ROCE	3(b)	7
December 2012	Financial performance evaluation and choice of measures	1(i)(ii)	20
June 2012	Evaluation of performance measures	1(ii)(iii)	24

Chapter summary

```
┌─────────────────────────────┐
│   Financial performance     │
│ measures in the private sector │
└─────────────────────────────┘
```

The objectives of profit-seeking organisations
- maximising shareholder wealth
- survival and growth
- relationship between profits and shareholder value
- measuring the long-term value of a business

Financial performance measures
- ROCE
- other profitability measures
- EPS
- EBITDA
- NPV
- IRR
- MIRR
- liquidity and gearing ratios
- assessing performance and giving performance management advice

Short and long-term financial performance
- problems of using short-term targets
- steps to reduce short termism
- should a short-term approach ever be taken?

Test your understanding answers

Test your understanding 1

A bank's primary objective will be **profit maximisation** for the benefit of the shareholders.

Secondary objectives may include:

- market share
- customer satisfaction
- revenue growth
- employee satisfaction.

Test your understanding 2

Answer is C.

Company A has a ROCE of 20% ($20k ÷ $100k) compared with only 10% for Company B ($1 m ÷ $10m). A higher ROCE means that the company is better at utilising the funds invested in it.

Test your understanding 3

Profits before tax	$5,500,000
Less tax	$2,100,000
Less preference dividends (9% × 1,000,000)	$90,000
	————
Earnings	$3,310,000
	————
Number of ordinary shares	6,000,000

EPS = (Profit after tax, − preference dividends)/Weighted average number of ordinary shares in issue

= $3.31 m/6m

= 55.2 cents

Test your understanding 4

Year	Cash flow $	DF 15%	PV $	DF 10%	PV $
0	(15,000)	1.00	(15,000)	1.00	(15,000)
1	1,500	0.870	1,305	0.909	1,364
2	2,750	0.756	2,079	0.826	2,272
3	4,000	0.658	2,632	0.751	3,004
4	5,700	0.572	3,260	0.683	3,893
5	7,500	0.497	3,727	0.621	4,657
NPV			**(1,997)**		**190**

(i) NPV @ 15% = ($1,997)

(ii) NPV @ 10% = $190

(iii) If the company's cost of capital is 10% the project would be accepted, if it were 15% it wouldn't.

Test your understanding 5

(a)

All figures in $000	0	1	2	3	4	5	6
Sales revenue		8,100	8,100	8,100	8,100	8,100	8,100
Variable costs		(4,266)	(4,266)	(4,266)	(4,266)	(4,266)	(4,266)
Royalties		(675)	(675)	(675)	(675)	(675)	(675)
Fixed costs		(900)	(900)	(900)	(900)	(900)	(900)
Cash inflow from operations		2,259	2,259	2,259	2,259	2,259	2,259
Tax payable (30%)		(678)	(678)	(678)	(678)	(678)	(678)
Initial investment	(7,000)						
Government grant received	3,500						
	(3,500)	1,581	1,581	1,581	1,581	1,581	1,581
Discount factor @ 12%	1	0.893	0.797	0.712	0.636	0.567	0.507
	(3,500)	1,412	1,260	1,126	1,006	897	802
NPV	**3,002**						

Alternatively, an annuity approach can be taken:

Time	Narrative	CF	DF	PV
0	Investment	(7,000)	1	(7,000)
0	Grant	3,500	1	3,500
1 – 6	Net inflow (see above)	2,259	4.111	9,287
1 – 6	Tax 30%	(678)	4.111	(2,787)
NPV				**3,000**

(b)   (i)

$$\text{Sensitivity} = \frac{\text{NPV}}{\text{PV of initial outlay}} \times 100$$

$$= \frac{3,002}{3,500} \times 100$$

= 85.8% i.e. the initial outlay would have to increase by 85.8% before decision is reversed

(ii)

Figures in $000	1	2	3	4	5	6
Sales revenue	8,100	8,100	8,100	8,100	8,100	8,100
Variable costs	(4,266)	(4,266)	(4,266)	(4,266)	(4,266)	(4,266)
Royalties	(675)	(675)	(675)	(675)	(675)	(675)
Contribution before tax	3,159	3,159	3,159	3,159	3,159	3,159
Tax payable (30%)	(948)	(948)	(948)	(948)	(948)	(948)
Contribution after tax	2,211	2,211	2,211	2,211	2,211	2,211
Discount factor @ 12%	0.893	0.797	0.712	0.636	0.567	0.507
	1,975	1,762	1,574	1,406	1,254	1,121

NPV contribution = **9,089**

Or using annuities:

Time	Narrative	CF	DF	PV
1 – 6	Contribution	3,159	4.111	12,987
1 – 6	Tax @ 30%	(948)	4.111	3,897
PV contribution				
				9,089

Sensitivity = NPV/PV of contribution = 3002/9089 = 33% i.e. the annual contribution would have to decrease by 33% before the project was rejected.

(c) Factors that should be considered by the directors of JDL include:

– How the cash flows are estimated. How accurate they are requires detailed consideration.

– The cost of capital used by the finance director might be inappropriate. For example if the EF solar panels proposal is less risky than other projects undertaken by JDL then a lower cost of capital should be used.

  - How strong is the EF brand name? The directors are proposing to pay royalties equivalent to 8% of sales revenue during the six years of the anticipated life of the project. Should they market the EF solar panels themselves?

  - Would competitors enter the market and what would be the likely effect on sales volumes and selling prices?

N.B: Only three factors were required.

(d) Benchmarking is the use of a yardstick to compare performance. The yardstick for benchmarking is based on best in class.

A major problem facing the management of JDL lies in the accessing of information regarding the activities of a competitor firm that may be acknowledged to display best practice. Internal benchmarking i.e. using another function within the same firm as the standard can help in the avoidance of the problems of information access, but that clearly limits the scope of what can be achieved. The most common approach is process benchmarking, where the standard of comparison is a firm which is not a direct competitor but is best in practice for a particular process or activity.

The objective is to improve performance. This is best achieved by means of the sharing of information which should prove of mutual benefit to both parties to the benchmarking programme. As a result of receiving new information each party will be able to review their policies and procedures. The very process of comparing respective past successes and failures can serve as a stimulus for greater innovation within each organisation.

To evaluate the performance JDL they need to establish a basis for targets which reflects the performance of an organisation which displays 'Best Practice'. As a direct consequence of a comparison of existing standards with the 'Best Practice' organisation, managers can focus upon areas where improvements can be achieved and evaluate measures to help attain those improvements.

A principal benefit that will be derived by JDL as a result of undertaking a successful programme of benchmarking will be the identification of areas where cost savings are possible. Hence the levels of cost of sales and operating expenses can be reduced leading to increased profitability.

Test your understanding 6

$$IRR = 10\% + \frac{50,000}{50,000 + 10,000} \times (15\% - 10\%)$$

$$= 14.17\%$$

Test your understanding 7

	20X6	20X7
Current ratio	7,700 ÷ 4,500 = 1.7	7,050 ÷ 3,150 = 2.2
Acid test ratio	5,550 ÷ 4,500 = 1.2	4,470 ÷ 3,150 = 1.4
Receivable days	(5,200 ÷ 17,500) × 365 = 108 days	(3,120 ÷ 16,625) × 365 = 68 days
Inventory days	(2,150 ÷ 14,000) × 365 = 56 days	(2,580 ÷ 12,950) × 365 = 73 days
Asset turnover	17,500 ÷ 17,700 = 1.0 times	16,625 ÷ 18,400 = 0.9 times
ROCE	(3,500 ÷ 17,700) × 100 = 19.8%	(3,675 ÷ 18,400) × 100 = 20.0%
EPS	2,625 ÷ 2,500 = 1.05	2,756 ÷ 2,500 = 1.10

The company has high receivables, low inventories, a low cash balance and high trade payables.

The philosophy is to chase sales by offering lax trade credit to customers, while attempting to maintain adequate liquidity by taking extensive credit from suppliers.

This is a risky policy since it involves the risk of:

- long-standing receivables balances going bad

- discouraging potential customers since low inventory means an increased risk of goods being out of stock.

The low cash balance means that unexpected expenditures cannot be paid for out of cash. Specific funds would have to be organised.

The high trade payables will upset the suppliers; they may even stop supply until the balance outstanding is paid.

Test your understanding 8

Report on the comparative financial performance of WSS and EA.

(i) Summary of financial ratios

	WSS		EA	
	20X9	**20X8**	**20X9**	**20X8**
Profitability (W1)				
ROCE	8.4%	12.7%	3.2%	40.0%
Profit margin	45.2%	56.7%	5.0%	34.3%
Asset utilisation	18.6%	22.4%	64.5%	116.7%
Liquidity				
Current ratio	1.7	1.0	3.25	3.0
Risk				
Gearing (W2)	39.2	54.0	0	0
Growth				
Turnover	3.3%		(42.9%)	
Profit	(25%)		(91.7%)	
Capital employed	24.6%		3.3%	

(ii) Comments on ratios

Both companies have shown a significant fall in profits. The ratios show that this is due to both a reduction in margins and falling asset utilisation. Capital employed has grown (especially for WSS) and it may be that this extra investment needs more time to generate additional profit.

EA has witnessed a dramatic reduction in sales. Costs seem to be largely fixed as these have only fallen by 17%. Turnover for the regulated monopoly appears to be more stable.

Financial risk (gearing) is high in WSS (although no comparisons with similar companies are available), but the gearing ratio has fallen in the year. High gearing magnifies the effect of volatile turnover on profit. Although it would seem EA has high operating gearing (fixed to total costs), this is somewhat compensated by the fact that it has no financial gearing.

Liquidity for both companies has improved, although no benchmarks against respective industry averages are available.

(iii) **Limitations**

Accuracy of the figures – are the two years under review representative?

Short versus long term – longer-term trends would be useful. Certain events in 20X9 (i.e. expenditure on fixed assets) will reduce short-term performance but fuel longer-term growth (and profit).

The two companies cannot really be compared – one is a regulated monopoly, the other has to compete in a competitive market based on the perception of its products, quality and value for money. As such, comparison may be better carried out using industry benchmarks.

Profitability can only be fully appraised when compared against required returns of the shareholders. This, in turn, reflects the perceived risks they take when investing in each company. This may be lower for a regulated monopoly, and thus ROCEs lower, although the monopoly does have a higher level of gearing.

Workings

(W1) **Profitability ratios (20X9 shown)**

	WSS	EA
ROCE*	14/167 × 100 = 8.4%	1/31 × 100 = 3.2%
Profit margin	14/31 × 100 = 45.2%	1/20 × 100 = 5.0%
Asset utilisation	31/167 × 100 = 18.6%	20/31 × 100 = 64.5%

*Note: profit before interest used as the objective is to measure internal efficiency rather than return to external shareholders.

(W2) **Gearing ratios (20X9 shown)**

	WSS	EA
Debt/Equity	47/120 = 39.2	0

Divisional performance appraisal and transfer pricing

Chapter learning objectives

Upon completion of this chapter you will be able to:

- Discuss the appropriateness of, and apply the following as measures of performance:

    - return on investment (ROI)

    - residual income (RI)

    - economic value added (EVA)

- describe, compute and evaluate performance measures relevant in a divisionalised organisation structure including ROI, RI and Economic value added (EVA)

- discuss the need for separate measures in respect of managerial and divisional performance

- discuss the circumstances in which a transfer pricing policy may
be needed and discuss the necessary criteria for its design

- demonstrate and evaluate the use of alternative bases for transfer pricing

- explain and demonstrate issues that require consideration when setting transfer prices in multinational companies

- evaluate and apply the value-based management approaches to performance management

- discuss the problems encountered in planning, controlling and measuring performance levels, e.g. productivity, profitability, quality and service levels, in complex business structures.

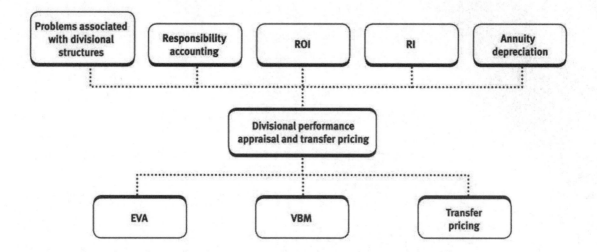

1 Assumed knowledge

Chapter 9 builds on the following knowledge from PM:

- Divisional performance measures

- Transfer pricing.

2 Introduction to divisional performance management

A feature of modern business management is the practice of splitting a business into semi-autonomous units with devolved authority and responsibility. Such units could be described as 'divisions', subsidiaries or strategic business units (SBUs) but the principles are the same.

It is common in APM to have to apply your knowledge of performance management to more complex business structures such as divisional structures.

This chapter will review some of the methods available for appraising divisional performance.

3 Problems associated with divisional structures

Before looking at the methods for divisional performance appraisal it is worth noting that divisional structures may result in the following **problems**:

- **Co-ordination** – how to co-ordinate different divisions to achieve overall corporate objectives.

- **Goal congruence** – managers will be motivated to improve the performance of their division, possibly at the expense of the larger organisation.

- **Controllability** – divisional managers should only be held accountable for those factors that they can control. The performance of a division's manager must be appraised separately to the performance of the division. It may be difficult to determine exactly what is and what is not controllable.

- **Inter-dependence of divisions** – the performance of one division may depend to some extent on others, making it difficult to measure performance levels.

- **Head office costs** – whether/how head office costs should be reapportioned.

- **Transfer prices** – how transfer prices should be set as these effectively move profit from one division to another.

Illustration 1 – Inter-dependence of divisions

Suppose division A makes components that are subsequently used in division B to make the finished item that is then sold to customers. The following are examples of areas where the performance of B will be affected by problems in A.

- **Productivity** – suppose some staff in division A are ill, slowing down the supply of components to division B. This will slow down division B as well, unless adequate inventories are held.

- **Profitability** – suppose the transfer pricing system includes an element of actual cost. Cost overruns in A would be passed on to B.

- **Quality** – poor quality work in A will ultimately compromise the quality of the finished product.

- **Service levels** – customer queries to B could involve A's component in which case they need to be re-directed. Division A may not be as customer-focused as B, compromising customer goodwill.

Management of a division

The management of a division are normally remunerated on a basis linked to the performance they achieve. Typically, they are given performance targets and only if they achieve those targets do they get a salary bonus.

The central idea is that the manager of a division is in the same position as an independent entrepreneur. If he experiences the risks and rewards of business ownership, then he/she will act in a manner calculated to maximise the value of the division – or that is the theory. The modern variation on this theme is to give management 'share options' – the right to buy shares at a given price. If the share price performs well, (and the stock market is a good judge of business performance), then the manager benefits. The theory is that this promotes goal congruence between managers and shareholders.

> Having decentralised, it is essential that senior management monitor and control the performance of the divisions and of those people with direct responsibility for those divisions. An accounting information system (a management control system) must be in place to allow for divisional assessment. The system used must have a close bearing on divisional goals and must recognise that some costs of a division will be controllable by its managers and some will not.

4 Responsibility accounting

Responsibility accounting is based on the principle of **controllability**, i.e. managers should only be made accountable and be assessed on those aspects of performance they can control.

The controllability principle may result in the establishment of different performance measures for the division and its manager.

In practice, it can be difficult to establish which items are controllable and which are uncontrollable. For example, an increase in supplier's prices may be seen as something that the divisional manager cannot control. However, it could be argued that the cost is controllable since the divisional manager may be able to change the source or type of supply.

Types of responsibility centres

There are three types of responsibility centre.

When assessing divisional performance it is vital that the measures used match the type of division:

Type of division	Description	Typical measures
Cost centre	• Division incurs costs but has no revenue stream.	• Total cost • Cost variances • Cost per unit and other cost ratios • Non-financial performance indicators (NFPIs), for example related to quality, productivity, efficiency.

Type of division	Description	Typical measures
Profit centre	• Division has both costs and revenue. • Manager **does not** have the authority to alter the level of investment in the division.	All of the above plus: • sales • profit • sales variances • margins • market share • working capital ratios (depending on the division concerned) • NFPIs related to customer satisfaction.
Investment centre	• Division has both costs and revenue. • Manager **does** have the authority to invest in new assets or dispose of existing ones.	All of the above plus: • return on investment (ROI) • residual income (RI) • economic value added (EVA). These are discussed in more detail below.

5 Return on investment (ROI)

5.1 What is ROI?

ROI is the divisional equivalent of ROCE. It shows the operating profit that is generated for every \$1 of assets employed. If ROI is used to appraise the performance of the divisional manager then only the controllable elements of operating profit and capital employed should be included (as discussed in the previous section).

$$\text{ROI} = \frac{\text{Controllable operating profit}}{\text{Controllable capital employed}} \times 100$$

Decision rule: If ROI > cost of capital (required return), then accept the project or appraise the division as performing favourably.

5.2 Advantages and disadvantages of ROI

Advantages	Disadvantages
• Widely used and accepted since it is in line with ROCE which is frequently used to assess overall business performance. • As a relative measure it enables comparisons to be made with divisions or companies of different sizes. • It can be broken down into secondary ratios for more detailed analysis, i.e. profit margin and asset turnover.	• May lead to dysfunctional decision making (see below). • Increases with age of asset if net book values (NBVs) are used (see below). • Different accounting policies can confuse comparisons. • Exclusion from capital employed of intangible assets, such as brands and reputation. • The corporate objective of maximising total shareholders' wealth is not achieved by making decisions on the basis of ROI. • It may encourage the manipulation of profit and capital employed figures to improve results and, for example, to obtain a bonus payment.

Dysfunctional decision making

There is a risk that if ROI is used as a performance measure, management may only take decisions which will increase divisional ROI, regardless of wider corporate benefits.

The test your understanding below illustrates the problem of dysfunctional behaviour.

Test your understanding 1

Managers within MV are appraised on the ROI of their division. The company's cost of capital is 15%.

Jon, a divisional manager, has the following results:

	$
Annual profit	30,000
Investment	100,000

Within his division, the purchase of a new piece of equipment has been proposed. This equipment would cost $20,000, would yield an extra $4,000 of profit per annum and would have many other non-financial and environmental benefits to the division and the company as a whole.

Required:

Will Jon invest in the new equipment? Is this the correct decision for the company?

Age of assets

The ROI will increase with the age of the asset. This may encourage divisional managers to hold onto old, and potentially inefficient, assets rather than investing in new ones.

The test your understanding below illustrates this problem.

Test your understanding 2

McKinnon Co sets up a new division in Blair Atholl investing $800,000 in fixed assets with an anticipated useful life of 10 years and no scrap value. Annual profits before depreciation are expected to be a steady $200,000.

Required:

You are required to calculate the division's ROI for its first three years based on the opening book value of assets. Comment on your results.

6 Residual income

6.1 Introduction

The problems of dysfunctional behaviour and holding onto old assets can be addressed by using residual income (RI) to appraise divisional performance.

6.2 What is residual income (RI)?

Controllable operating profit	X
Less imputed interest (controllable capital employed × cost of capital)	(X)
	———
RI	X
	———

Decision rule: if the RI is positive:

- accept the project or

- appraise the division as performing favourably.

6.3 Advantages and disadvantages of RI

Advantages	Disadvantages
<ul><li>It reduces the problems of ROI, i.e. dysfunctional behaviour and holding onto old assets.</li><li>Interpreting the result is simple; if the RI is positive then the division is generating a return above that required by the finance providers.</li><li>The cost of financing a division is brought home to divisional managers.</li><li>Different cost of capitals can be applied to different divisions based on their risk profiles.</li></ul>	<ul><li>It is difficult to decide upon an appropriate cost of capital.</li><li>It does not facilitate comparisons between divisions since the RI is driven by the size of the divisions and their investment.</li><li>It does not always result in decisions that are in the best interests of the company (EVA is a superior measure to RI in this respect).</li><li>Different accounting policies can confuse comparisons (as for ROI).</li><li>It may encourage the manipulation of profit and capital employed figures to improve results and, for example, to obtain a bonus payment (as for ROI).</li></ul>

6.4 Comparison of ROI and RI

Test your understanding 3

Division Z has the following financial performance:

Operating profit	$40,000
Capital employed	$150,000
Cost of capital	10%

Required:

Would the division wish to accept a new possible investment costing $10,000 which would earn an annual operating profit of $2,000 if the evaluation was on the basis of:

(a) ROI

(b) RI?

Is the division's decision in the best interests of the company?

Test your understanding 4

KM is considering a new project and has gathered the following data:

The initial investment is $66 million which will be required at the beginning of the year. The project has a three year life with a nil residual value. Depreciation is calculated on a straight-line basis.

The project is expected to generate revenue of $85m in year 1, $90m in year 2 and $94m in year 3. These values may vary by 6%.

The direct costs will be $50m in year 1, $60m in year 2 and $70m in year 3. These may vary by 8%.

Cost of capital may also vary from 8% to 10% for the life of the project.

Use the written down value of the asset at the start of each year to represent the value of the asset for the year.

Ignore tax.

Required:

Prepare two tables for:

(a) the best outcome and

(b) the worst outcome

showing the annual operating profit, residual income and return on investment for each year of the project and the NPV.

7   Annuity depreciation

Annuity depreciation

- As discussed, the use of ROI and RI does not always result in decisions that are in the best interests of the company.

- Specifically, a project with a positive net present value (NPV) at the company's cost of capital may show poor ROI or RI results in early years, leading to its rejection by the divisional manager.

- Annuity depreciation is one attempt to resolve this problem.

Example:

Division X is currently generating a ROI of 12%. It is considering a new project. This requires an investment of $1.4 million and is expected to yield net cash inflows of $460,000 per annum for the next four years. None of the initial investment will be recoverable at the end of the project.

The company has a cost of capital of 8%. Annual accounting profits are to be assumed to equal annual net cash inflows less depreciation, and tax is to be ignored.

Required:

(a)   Calculate and comment on the NPV of the project.

(b)   Calculate and comment on the ROI and RI of the project.

(c)   Calculate and comment on the ROI and RI of the project using annuity depreciation.

(d)   Calculate and comment on the ROI and RI of the project at the project IRR of 12%.

Solution:

(a)   **NPV calculation**

Time	CF ($)	DF 8%	PV ($)
0	(1,400,000)	1	(1,400,000)
1 – 4	460,000	3.312	1,523,520

NPV = 123,520

Conclusion: the project has a positive NPV and is therefore worthwhile accepting from the company's point of view.

(b) ROI and RI

	Year 1 $000	Year 2 $000	Year 3 $000	Year 4 $000
NBV at start of year	1,400	1,050	700	350
Net cash inflow	460	460	460	460
Depreciation	(350)	(350)	(350)	(350)
Profit	110	110	110	110
Imputed interest @ 8%	(112)	(84)	(56)	(28)
RI	(2)	26	54	82
ROI	7.9%	10.5%	15.7%	31.4%

Conclusion: If the manager's performance is measured (and rewarded) on the basis of RI or ROI, he is unlikely to accept the project. The first year's RI is negative, and the ROI does not exceed the company's cost of capital until year 2, or the ROI currently being earned until year 3. Divisional managers will tend to take a short-term view. More immediate returns are more certain, and by year 3 he may have moved jobs.

(c) ROI and RI using annuity depreciation

Annuity depreciation is calculated as follows:

Step 1: Calculate the equivalent annual cost (EAC) of the initial investment

EAC = Initial investment ÷ cumulative discount factor at the company's cost of capital

= $1.4m ÷ 3.312

= $422,705

Step 2: Calculate annual depreciation

Annual depreciation = EAC – interest on opening NBV

e.g. for year 1 = 422,705 – (1,400,000 × 8%)

= $310,705

The ROI and RI can now be calculated as follows:

	Year 1 $000	Year 2 $000	Year 3 $000	Year 4 $000
NBV at start of year	1,400	1,089.3	753.7	391.3
Net cash inflow	460	460	460	460
Depreciation	(310.7)	(335.6)	(362.4)	(391.4)
Profit	149.3	124.4	97.6	68.6
Imputed interest @ 8%	(112)	(87.1)	(60.3)	(31.3)
RI	**37.3**	**37.3**	**37.3**	**37.3**
ROI	**10.7%**	**11.4%**	**12.9%**	**17.5%**

Conclusion: The project now has an equal, positive, RI over its life, which will encourage the manager to invest, a decision compatible with that using NPV.

However, there is still a problem if ROI is used as the performance measure, in that the short-term low rate of return may not encourage investment in what is, in fact, a worthwhile project. A way round this is to use annuity depreciation at a different rate that will ensure a level ROI over the project life. The rate to be used will be the IRR of the project.

(d) ROI and RI using annuity depreciation at the project IRR

12% is now used instead of 8% in computing both the EAC of the investment and the interest on capital, yielding the following results:

	Year 1 $000	Year 2 $000	Year 3 $000	Year 4 $000
NBV at start of year	1,400	1,108	781	414.7
Net cash inflow	460	460	460	460
Depreciation	(292)	(327)	(366.3)	(410.2)
Profit	168	133	93.7	49.8
Imputed interest @12%	(168)	(133)	(93.7)	(49.8)
RI	0	0	0	0
ROI	12%	12%	12%	12%

Conclusion:

The ROI and the RI is now level over the project life, ensuring a consistent decision whether the short-term or long-term view is taken. Using 12% as an appraisal rate for the project yields consistent results under all three methods (NPV, ROI and RI) i.e. the project is at break-even.

This somewhat contrived approach is probably less useful than the one above when RI is used to assess performance.

In addition, the use of annuity depreciation does not produce helpful results when cash flows are uneven.

8 Economic value added

8.1 What is economic value added (EVA)?

- EVA is a measure of performance similar to residual income. However, adjustments are made to financial profits and capital to truly reflect the economic value generated by the company.

- It is a measure of performance that is directly linked to shareholder wealth.

- It is important to note that EVA can be used to appraise organisation-wide performance as well as divisional performance.

Calculating EVA

	$
Net operating profit after tax (NOPAT)	X
Less: adjusted value of capital employed at beginning of the year × WACC	(X)
EVA	X/(X)

Decision rule: a positive EVA is favourable, since the organisation is providing a return greater than that required by the providers of finance.

8.2 Adjustments required to operating profit and capital employed

	Change to operating profit	Change to capital employed
Depreciation and non-current assets	**Add** back depreciation. **Deduct** economic depreciation which reflects the true value of assets during the period.	Adjust value to reflect economic depreciation and not accounting depreciation. In addition, adjust value to reflect replacement cost of non-current assets rather than the book value.
Provisions	**Add** increase in provisions in the period, e.g. debt provisions, deferred tax provisions. **Deduct** reduction in provisions in the period. These represent over-prudence in the financial accounts.	**Add** back the value of provisions in the period.
Non-cash expenses	**Add** back since they do not represent cash paid and may be as a result of profit manipulation and not real costs.	**Add** to retained profit at the end of the year.
Interest paid net of tax, i.e. interest × (1 – tax rate)	Interest payments are taken into account in WACC.	

Expenditure on advertising, research and development and employee training	**Add** back, i.e. capitalise the entire expense. **Deduct** amortisation for the period (if mentioned).	**Increase** capital employed at the end of the year. **Increase** capital employed in respect to similar add backs in previous year's investments.
Operating leases	**Add** lease payments. **Deduct** depreciation on operating lease assets.	Add present value of future lease payments. Operating leases should be treated in the same way as financial leases (i.e. capitalised) to prevent firms from using operating leases to reduce capital employed and hence increase EVA.

Summary NOPAT calculation

	$
Controllable operating profit	X
Add:	
accounting depreciation	X
increase in provisions	X
non-cash expenses	X
advertising, research and development and employee training costs	X
operating lease payments	X
Deduct:	
economic depreciation	(X)
decrease in provisions	(X)
amortisation of advertising, research and development and employee training	(X)
depreciation of operating lease assets	(X)
tax paid plus tax relief on interest (interest × tax rate)	(X)
= NOPAT	**X**

8.3 What is the WACC?

WACC = (proportion of equity × cost of equity) + (proportion of debt × post tax cost of debt)

For example, suppose that a company is 60% financed by equity which has a cost of 10% pa and 40% financed by debt which has an after tax cost of 6%

WACC = (0.60 × 0.10) + (0.40 × 0.06) = 0.084 therefore 8.4%

8.4 Evaluation of EVA

EVA assesses the value created by managers, so is a more appropriate tool for measuring performance than a profit based measure. However, it is not without its drawbacks.

Advantages	Disadvantages
Maximisation of EVA will create real wealth for shareholders.	Requires numerous adjustments to profit and capital employed figures which can be cumbersome. (The full version requires more than 100 adjustments to the information in the financial statements).
The adjustments made mean the measure is closer to cash flow than to accounting profit avoiding the distortion of results by the accounting policies in place.	Does not facilitate comparisons between divisions since EVA is an absolute measure (as is RI).
The cost of financing a division is bought home to the division's manager.	There are many assumptions made when calculating the WACC, making its calculation difficult and potentially inaccurate. In addition, the WACC is for the company as a whole whereas the cost of capital chosen when calculating RI can reflect the risk of the division.
Long-term value-adding expenditure can be capitalised, removing any incentive that managers may have to take a short-term view.	Based on historical data whereas shareholders are interested in future performance.
Interpreting the result is simple; if the EVA is positive then the division is generating a return above that required by the finance providers.	

Rationale behind the required adjustments for EVA

Accounting adjustments

Stern Stewart argues that profits calculated in accordance with financial reporting principles do not reflect the economic value generated by the company and so need adjusting.

There are three main reasons for these adjustments:

(1) To convert from accrual to cash accounting.

(2) Spending on 'market building' items such as research, staff training and advertising costs should be capitalised to the extent that they have not been in the financial statements. Stern Stewart believes that financial reporting standards are too strict in this regard, and discourage managers from investing in items that bring long-term benefits.

(3) Unusual items of profit or expenditure should be ignored.

This can result in 160 adjustments being necessary in calculating NOPAT. The APM examiner will test only the most common adjustments, which are as follows:

(1) Expenditure on promotional activities, research and development and employee training should be capitalised where they generate long term benefit.

Marketing activities for long-term benefit generate future value for the business, so are added back to profit and should also be added to capital employed in the year in which the expenses were incurred. This also means any prior year expenditure is also added in to capital employed.

(2) The accounting depreciation charge is replaced with a charge for economic depreciation.

Economic depreciation reflects the true change in value of assets during the period, unlike accounting depreciation. If no detail is given on economic depreciation then candidates should assume that accounting depreciation represents a reasonable approximation for it.

(3) Items such as provisions, allowances for doubtful debts, deferred tax provisions and allowances for inventory should be added back to capital employed.

These are considered to represent over-prudence on the part of financial accountants, and this understates the true value of capital employed. Any expenses or income recognised in the income statement in respect of movements in such items should also be removed from NOPAT.

(4) Non-cash expenses should be added back to profits, and to capital employed.

Non-cash expenses are correctly added back to profit as such costs are treated as unacceptable accounting adjustments on a cash-based view.

(5) Changing the treatment of operating leases to match finance leases.

Under IAS 17 operating leases are treated differently from finance leases in the financial statements, with finance leases being capitalised and operating leases being excluded from the statement of financial position. This inconsistency means that firms can take advantage of operating leases to reduce the reported capital employed and, therefore, increase the calculated EVA^{TM}.

When calculating EVA^{TM} therefore, operating leases should be capitalised and added to capital employed. On the income statement side, operating lease charges should be added back. In principle, interest and depreciation should then be charged on the assets acquired under finance leases. However, any interest would then be added back to profit in calculating NOPAT, and accounting depreciation would be replaced with economic depreciation.

(6) The tax charge.

The tax cost should be the amount paid adjusted for lost tax on interest and not the adjusted amount of tax charged in the accounts. These "cash taxes" are calculated as follows:

Cash taxes = tax charge per income statement – increase (add reduction) in deferred tax provision + tax benefit of interest

Note: no further adjustments are made in respect of the tax on the other items adjusted for during the calculation of NOPAT.

Illustration 2 – Adjusting for operating leases

Division A is calculating EVA for the first time. It has operating leases on equipment, for which it pays annual rental charges of $40,000. The current value of the operating leases is estimated at $150,000. The economic life of the leased asset is 5 years.

Calculating NOPAT

- Add back the operating lease charge of $40,000.

- Deduct the annual 'economic' depreciation of $30,000 (assume equal annual depreciation of $150,000 ÷ 5 years).

- NET IMPACT – add back $10,000 (the implied interest charge on the lease).

Calculating the adjusted value of capital employed

- The net book value of the operating leases should be added back, i.e. $150,000.

- The annual economic cost of these assets is $30,000 ($150,000 ÷ 5) and so the capital employed would be depreciated by this amount each year thereafter.

Test your understanding 5

Division B has a reported operating profit of $8.4 million, which includes a charge of $2 million for the full cost of developing and launching a new product that is expected to generate profits for 4 years.

The company has an after tax weighted average cost of capital of 10%.

The operating book value of the division's assets at the beginning of the year is $60 million, and the replacement cost has been estimated at $75 million.

Assume the tax charge is $0.

Required:

Calculate division B's EVA.

Student accountant articles: visit the ACCA website, www.accaglobal.com, to review the two articles on 'economic value added versus profit based measures of performance'.

9 Value-based management

This is a slight aside but it is worth covering here since it follows on from our discussion of EVA.

As mentioned in the previous chapter, businesses (and the divisions within them) are under increasing pressure to look at the long-term value of the business since this is what investors will be interested in.

Value-based management (VBM) is an approach to management whereby the company's strategy, objectives and processes are aligned to help the company focus on the key drivers of shareholder wealth and hence the maximisation of this value.

Measuring shareholder value

Traditionally, financial measures such as EPS and ROCE were used to quantify shareholder value. However, none of these measures directly correlates with the market value of the company (i.e. shareholder value).

VBM is an approach which takes the interests of the shareholders as its primary focus.

VBM begins from the view that the value of a company is measured by its **discounted cash flows**. The idea being that value is only created when companies generate returns which beat their cost of capital.

VBM then focuses the management of the company on those areas which create value. A key to this process is the identification of the drivers of value and then a concentration of effort at all levels (strategic, tactical and operational) on these drivers in order to increase the value of the firm.

Illustration 3 – Value drivers

There are seven key strategic drivers of shareholder value:

- revenue
- operating margin
- cash tax rate
- incremental capital expenditure
- investment in working capital
- cost of capital
- growth period.

Each level of management will be able to link its activities to one or more of these value drivers. For example, a key value driver at operational level may be departmental service levels. This will link to the strategic drivers of revenue and operating margin.

Implementing VBM

The implementation of VBM will involve four steps:

- **Step 1** – a strategy is developed to maximise value.

- **Step 2** – key value drivers are identified and performance targets (both short and long term) are defined for those value drivers. Targets may be developed by benchmarking against competitors.

- **Step 3** – a plan is developed to achieve the targets.

- **Step 4** – performance metrics and reward systems are created that are compatible with these targets. Staff at all levels of the firm should be motivated to achieve the new targets set.

Measures used in VBM

Measures include:

- **EVA** – this is the primary measure used. A positive EVA indicates value creation while a negative one indicates destruction.

- **Market value added** (MVA) – this is the accumulated EVAs generated by an organisation since it was formed.

- **Shareholder value analysis** – this is the application of a discounted cash flow technique to valuing the whole business rather than a single potential investment.

MVA and shareholder value analysis

As well as EVA, consultants have produced a number of other value based measures, with each claiming its own merits.

(1) **Market value added (MVA)**

MVA is the value added to the business by management since it was formed, over and above the money invested in the company by shareholders and long term debt holders. A positive MVA means value has been added and a negative MVA means value has been destroyed.

MVA can effectively be seen as the accumulated EVAs generated by an organisation over time. As such it should be highly correlated with EVA values. If year after year a company has a positive EVA then these will add up to give a high MVA.

(2) **Shareholder value analysis**

SVA is an application of discounted cash flow techniques to valuing the whole business rather than a potential investment.

One problem in the estimation of future values is that theoretically the cash flows go to infinity. A practical way to resolve this is to take free cash flows for a few years into the future (the 'competitive advantage period') and then estimate the residual value of the organisation using either some market multiple or book value. The valuation of the company and hence the individual shares can be directly derived from the SVA.

One criticism of the above is that the estimation of the terminal value is subjective. There is a problem in determining how many years' cash flows can be realistically projected into the future and therefore at which point the terminal value should be calculated. However, all valuation methods depend upon estimating future dividends, earnings or cash flows and hence they all contain some element of subjectivity.

The techniques available for increasing and monitoring value will be/have been covered in other chapters and include (amongst others):

- the balanced scorecard
- business process re-engineering
- TQM
- JIT
- ABC and ABM
- benchmarking.

VBM evaluation

VBM focuses on value as opposed to profit, thus focusing on the long-term rather than purely the short-term. This makes the organisation more forward looking.

However, VBM can become an exercise in valuing everything and changing nothing.

In addition, management information systems may need to be adapted to take account of the need to measure non-financial indicators.

Since EVA is one of the key measures used in VBM, the advantages and disadvantages of EVA will also be relevant here.

Question practice

Take the time to review and attempt the scenario-based question below. It contains an exam standard EVA calculation and also requires an explanation of VBM.

Test your understanding 6

EcoHomes is an innovative company that was born from the demand of customers for high quality, bespoke homes at affordable prices. The company is based in the country of Geeland and is divided into three geographical areas; North, East and West. The company's mission is 'to make environmentally sound homes available to the general public in a way that ensures accessibility and quality of the product'.

EcoHomes is an off-site timber frame manufacturer, producing the shell of the house in their state of the art factory using sustainably sourced, certified timber. The controlled environment assures customers of the best quality available. EcoHomes prides itself on being a 'one-stop shop' providing the customer with a full design and build and a fixed price quotation which includes all the planning, demolition, ground works, house build and landscaping.

EcoHomes is starting to lose market share and its key goal of 'being the number one bespoke house builder in Geeland' is starting to slip away. The fall in market share is primarily due to the entry of two new competitors into the market. The first of these, Dream Homes, provides cutting edge house designs and premium quality builds (but at prices to match). The second new competitor, Bespoke Homes 4all, undercuts EcoHomes on price but is not able to provide the same quality, design, build or finish.

EcoHomes has just released a profit warning for the first quarter of the current year, 20X2. This has caused the board to reconsider its position and to take action to address the changed environment. Some cost cutting has already begun, such as the commencement of a voluntary redundancy programme and the introduction of a pay freeze for all employees. However, the board recognises that it will need to take more radical steps to fully address the issues it is facing.

EcoHomes has traditionally used EPS and ROCE to quantify shareholder value. The CEO understands that a number of EcoHomes' rivals are now using a value-based management (VBM) approach to performance management and he thinks that it may be a useful development for EcoHomes given the tough competitive environment. Financial data for EcoHomes for the last two years is provided in appendix 1. The CEO has come to you to advise him on the implications of a switch to VBM.

Appendix: Financial data for EcoHomes

	20X1	**20X0**
	$m	$m
Operating profit	130	110
Interest	20	18
Profit before tax	110	92
Tax @ 25%	27.5	23
Profit after tax	82.5	69

Further information is as follows:

(1)   The allowance for doubtful debts was $6 million at 1 January 20X0, $5 million at 31 December 20X0 and $7 million at 31 December 20X1.

(2)   Research and development costs of $10 million were incurred during each of the year's 20X0 and 20X1 on a new project, Project Light which is part completed. These costs were expensed in the income statement.

(3)　At 1 January 20X0, the company had completed another research project, Project Glass. Total expenditure on this project was $30 million, none of which had been capitalised in the financial statements. The product developed by Project Glass went on sale on 1 January 20X0. The product has a two year lifecycle and no further sales of this product are expected after 31 December 20X1.

(4)　The company incurred non-cash expenses of $0.3 million in both years.

(5)　Capital employed was $670 million at 1 January 20X0 and $740 million at 1 January 20X1.

(6)　The pre-tax cost of debt was 5% in each year. The estimated cost of equity was 12% in 20X0 and 14% in 20X1. The rate of corporation tax was 25% in both years.

(7)　The company's capital structure was 60% equity and 40% debt.

(8)　There was no provision for deferred tax.

Required:

Write a report to the CEO of EcoHomes addressing the following:

(a)　Perform an assessment of EcoHomes using economic value added (EVA). Briefly comment on the results of your calculations.

(14 marks)

(b)　Evaluate the use of value-based management (VBM) approaches to performance management.

(7 marks)

(Total: 21 marks)

10　Transfer pricing

10.1 Introduction

The **transfer price** is the price at which goods or services are transferred from one division to another within the same organisation.

The transfer price chosen will have a direct impact on the performance of the divisions.

Characteristics of a good transfer price

- **Goal congruence** – the transfer price that is negotiated and agreed upon by the buying and selling divisions should be in the best interests of the company overall.

- **Fairness** – the divisions must perceive the transfer price to be fair since the transfer price set will impact divisional profit and hence performance evaluation.

- **Autonomy** – the system used to set the transfer price should seek to maintain the autonomy of the divisional managers. This autonomy will improve managerial motivation.

- **Bookkeeping** – the transfer price chosen should make it straightforward to record the movement of goods or services between divisions.

- **Minimise global tax liability** – multinational companies can use their transfer pricing policies to move profits around the world and thereby minimise their global tax liability.

10.2 The general rules for setting transfer prices

Scenario 1: There is a perfectly competitive market for the product/service transferred

Transfer price = market price

A perfect market means that there is only one price in the market, there are no buying and selling costs and the market is able to absorb the entire output of the primary division and meet all the requirements of the secondary division.

Scenario 2: The selling division has surplus capacity

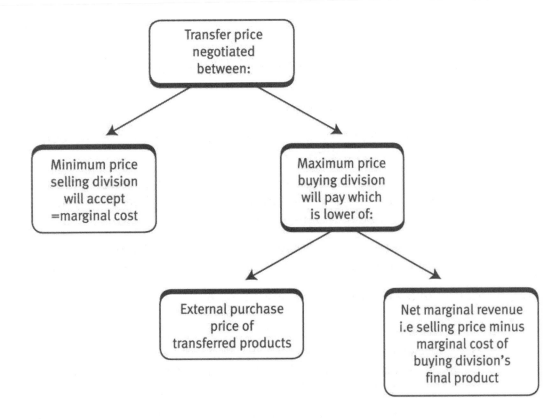

Scenario 3: The selling division does not have any surplus capacity

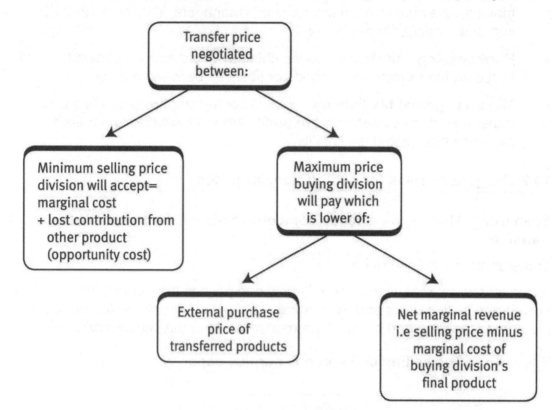

10.3 Practical considerations when setting the transfer price

Considerations when using the market price

- As mentioned, if a perfectly competitive market exists for the product, then the market price is the best transfer price.

- However, care must be taken to ensure the division's product is the same as that offered by the market (for example, quality and delivery terms are the same). If not, an adjusted market price should be used.

- In addition, the market price should be adjusted for costs not incurred on an internal transfer, for example, delivery costs and marketing costs.

Considerations when using a cost based approach

- The cost may be:

  - **the marginal cost** – as mentioned, this will be the very minimum the selling division will accept. This will be preferred by the buying division, i.e. they will consider the price to be fair.

  - **the full cost** – this will be preferred by the selling division, i.e. they will consider the price to be fair.

  - **the opportunity cost** – if there is no spare capacity in the selling division, the opportunity cost should be added to the marginal cost/full cost.

- The selling division will want to recognise an element of profit on its transfer (since it will most probably be a profit centre). Therefore, the final transfer price can be set at **cost + % profit**.

- **Standard cost** should be used rather than actual cost to avoid inefficiencies being transferred from one department to another and to aid planning and budgeting.

- **'Fairness'** is one of the key characteristics of a good transfer price. Two alternative approaches that may be perceived as fair by both the buying and the selling divisions are:

  - **marginal cost plus a lump sum (two part tariff)** – the selling division transfers each unit at marginal cost and a periodic lump sum charge is made to cover fixed costs.

  - **dual pricing** – the selling division records one transfer price (e.g. full cost + % profit) and the buying division records another transfer price (e.g. marginal cost). This will be perceived as fair but will result in the need for period-end adjustments in the accounts.

Illustration 4 – Practical methods of transfer pricing

Manuco

Manuco has been offered supplies of special ingredient Z at a transfer price of $15 per kg by Helpco, which is part of the same group of companies. Helpco processes and sells special ingredient Z to customers external to the group at $15 per kg. Helpco bases its transfer price on total cost-plus 25% profit mark-up. Total cost has been estimated as 75% variable and 25% fixed.

Required:

Discuss the transfer prices at which Helpco should offer to transfer special ingredient Z to Manuco in order that group profit maximising decisions may be taken on financial grounds in each of the following situations.

(a) Helpco has an external market for all its production of special ingredient Z at a selling price of $15 per kg. Internal transfers to Manuco would enable $1.50 per kg of variable packing cost to be avoided.

(b) Conditions are as per (i) but Helpco has production capacity for 3,000 kg of special ingredient Z for which no external market is available.

(c) Conditions are as per (ii) but Helpco has an alternative use for some of its spare production capacity. This alternative use is equivalent to 2,000 kg of special ingredient Z and would earn a contribution of $6,000.

Solution

(a) Since Helpco has an external market, which is the opportunity foregone, the relevant transfer price would be the external selling price of $15 per kg. This will be adjusted to allow for the $1.50 per kg avoided on internal transfers due to packing costs not required, i.e. the transfer price is $13.50 per kg.

(b) In this situation Helpco has no alternative opportunity for 3,000 kg of its special ingredient Z. It should, therefore, offer to transfer this quantity at marginal cost. This is variable cost less packing costs avoided = $9 – $1.50 = $7.50 per kg (note: total cost = $15 × 80% = $12; variable cost = $12 × 75% = $9). The remaining amount of special ingredient Z should be offered to Manuco at the adjusted selling price of $13.50 per kg (as above).

(c) Helpco has an alternative use for some of its production capacity, which will yield a contribution equivalent to $3 per kg of special ingredient Z ($6,000/2,000 kg). The balance of its spare capacity (1,000 kg) has no opportunity cost and should still be offered at marginal cost. Helpco should offer to transfer: 2,000 kg at $7.50 + $3 = $10.50 per kg; 1,000 kg at $7.50 per kg (= marginal cost); and the balance of requirements at $13.50 per kg.

Test your understanding 7

X, a manufacturing company, has two divisions: Division A and Division B. Division A produces one type of product, ProdX, which it transfers to Division B and also sells externally. Division B has been approached by another company which has offered to supply 2,500 units of ProdX for $35 each.

The following details for Division A are available:

	$
Sales revenue:	
Sales to division B @ $40 per unit	400,000
External sales @ $45 per unit	270,000
Less:	
Variable cost @$22 per unit	352,000
Fixed costs	100,000
Profit	218,000

External sales of Prod X cannot be increased, and division B decides to buy from the other company.

Required:

(a) Calculate the effect on the profit of division A.

(b) Calculate the effect on the profit of company X.

KAPLAN PUBLISHING

Test your understanding 8

A company operates two divisions, Able and Baker. Able manufactures two products, X and Y. Product X is sold to external customers for $42 per unit. The only outlet for product Y is Baker.

Baker supplies an external market and can obtain its semi-finished supplies (product Y) from either Able or an external source. Baker currently has the opportunity to purchase product Y from an external supplier for $38 per unit. The capacity of division Able is measured in units of output, irrespective of whether product X, Y or a combination of both are being manufactured.

The associated product costs are as follows:

	X	Y
Variable costs per unit	32	35
Fixed overheads per unit	5	5
	—	—
Total unit costs	37	40

Required:

(a) Using the above information, provide advice on the determination of an appropriate transfer price for the sale of product Y from division Able to division Baker under the following conditions:

    (i)   when division Able has spare capacity and limited external demand for product X

    (ii)   when division Able is operating at full capacity with unsatisfied external demand for product X.

(b) The design of an information system to support transfer pricing decision making necessitates the inclusion of specific data. Identify the data that needs to be collected and how you would expect it to be used.

Question practice

Take the time to review and attempt the scenario-based question below. It contains an exam standard transfer pricing calculation and also requires an explanation of transfer pricing.

Test your understanding 9

The Thornthwaite division is a member of the Kentmere group, and manufactures a single product, the Yoke.

It sells this product to external customers, and also to Froswick, another division in the group. Froswick further processes the Yoke and then sells it on to external customers.

The divisions have the freedom to set their own transfer prices, and also to choose their own suppliers.

The Kentmere group uses Residual Income (RI) to assess divisional performance, and each year it sets a target RI for each division. The group uses a cost of capital of 12%.

Each divisional manager receives a salary, plus a bonus equal to that salary for hitting its RI target.

There has recently been much discussion at board level about the impact of internal transfers and their impact on reported performances. In part this was prompted by a comment from a retired shareholder, Mr Brearley, at the recent shareholder meeting. He said that he had read a lot in the press about bonus schemes and their dysfunctional impact on corporate performance. The directors want to know whether or not Kentmere has any such issues.

The managers of both divisions have provided you with the following information for the next quarter (quarter 3):

Thornthwaite division
Budgeted information for quarter 3:
Maximum production capacity 200,000 units
External demand 170,000 units
External selling price $45
Variable cost per unit $30
Fixed production costs $2,500,000
Capital employed $6,000,000
Target RI $250,000

Froswick division

Froswick has found an external supplier willing to supply Yokes at a price of $42 per unit.

Required:

(a) Froswick requires 50,000 Yokes. Calculate the transfer price that Thornthwaite would set to achieve its target RI.

(6 marks)

(b) What prices should Thornthwaite set in order to maximise group profits? Explain the basis of your calculations.

(4 marks)

(c) Is Mr Brearley correct to be concerned about the bonus scheme? Draft some briefing notes for the board so that they can prepare their response, including supporting calculations and suggested improvements to the transfer pricing and bonus policies.

(10 marks)

(Total: 20 marks)

10.4 International transfer pricing

Almost two thirds of world trade takes place within multi-national companies. Transfer pricing in multi-national companies has the following complications:

Taxation

The selling and buying divisions will be based in different countries. Different taxation rates in these countries allows the manipulation of profit through the use of transfer pricing.

Illustration 5 – Taxation and transfer pricing

Rosca Coffee is a multinational company. Division A is based in Northland, a country with a tax rate of 50%. This division transfers goods to division B at a cost of $50,000 per annum. Division B is based in Southland, a country with a tax rate of 20%. Based on the current transfer price of $50,000 the profit of the divisions and of the company is as follows:

	Division A $	Division B $	Company $
External sales	100,000	120,000	220,000
Internal transfers to div B	50,000	–	50,000
Fixed and variable costs	(70,000)	(40,000)	(110,000)
Transfer costs from div A	–	(50,000)	(50,000)
Profit before tax	80,000	30,000	110,000
Profit after tax	40,000	24,000	64,000

Rosca Coffee want to take advantage of the different tax rates in Northland and Southland and have decided to reduce the transfer price from $50,000 to $20,000. This will result if the following revised profit figures:

	Division A $	Division B $	Company $
External sales	100,000	120,000	220,000
Internal transfers to div B	20,000	–	20,000
Fixed and variable costs	(70,000)	(40,000)	(110,000)
Transfer costs from div A	–	(20,000)	(20,000)
Profit before tax	50,000	60,000	110,000
Profit after tax	25,000	48,000	73,000

Conclusion: the manipulation of the transfer price has increased the company's profits from $64,000 to $73,000.

Remittance controls

- A country's government may impose restrictions on the transfer of profits from domestic subsidiaries to foreign multinationals.

- This is known as a 'block on the remittances of dividends' i.e. it limits the payment of dividends to the parent company's shareholders.

- It is often done through the imposition of strict exchange controls.

- Artificial attempts at reducing tax liabilities could, however, upset a country's tax authorities. Many tax authorities have the power to alter the transfer price and can treat the transactions as having taken place at a fair arm's length price and revise profits accordingly.

Test your understanding 10

Required:

Discuss how a multinational company could avoid the problem of blocked remittances.

Additional example on international issues

A multinational organisation, C, has 2 divisions each in a different country – Divisions A and B. Suppose Division A produces a product X where the domestic income tax rate is 40% and transfers it to Division B, which operates in a country with a 50% rate of income tax. An import duty equal to 25% of the price of product X is also assessed. The full cost per unit is $190, the variable cost $60.

Required:

The tax authorities allow either variable or full cost transfer prices. Determine which should be chosen.

Solution

Effect of transferring at $190 instead of $60:

	$
Income of A is $130 higher and so A pays $130 × 40% more income tax	(52)
Income of B is $130 lower and so C pays $130 × 50% less income tax	65
Import duty is paid by B on an additional $130, and so C pays $130 × 25% more duty	(32.5)
Net effect (cost) of transferring at $190 instead of $60	(19.5)
Additional example on international issues	

Conclusion: C should transfer at variable cost.

Student accountant article: visit the ACCA website, www.accaglobal.com, to review the article on 'transfer pricing'.

11   Exam focus

Exam sitting	Area examined	Question number	Number of marks
Mar/June 2017	Divisional performance measurement including the use of net profit and EVA	4	25
Sept/Dec 2016	Transfer pricing	4(b)(c)	17
Mar/June 2016	Divisional performance appraisal	1(ii) – (iv)	24
Sept/Dec 2015	Responsibility centres	3(b)(ii)	4
Sept/Dec 2015	EVA	1(i)	15
June 2015	EVA, ROI and RI, responsibility centres	4	25
June 2014	EVA and VBM	1(iii)(iv)	19
June 2013	Transfer pricing	4	25
December 2012	EVA	3(a)	13
June 2012	EVA	1(ii)	3
June 2011	RI, ROI, EVA, transfer pricing	1(a)(b)	24
December 2010	EVA and VBM	3	20

Chapter summary

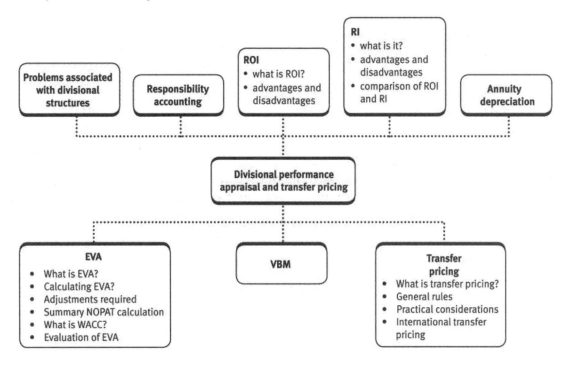

Test your understanding answers

Test your understanding 1

	Before	After	Investment
Profit ($)	30,000	34,000	4,000
Investment ($)	100,000	120,000	20,000
ROI	30%	28%	20%

- Jon's decision – from a personal point of view, the ROI of Jon's division will go down and his bonus will be reduced or lost as a result. Therefore, Jon will reject the investment.

- However, the new equipment has a ROI of 20%. This is higher than the company's cost of capital (required return) of 15% and therefore Jon should accept the new investment.

Conclusion: dysfunctional behaviour has occurred.

Test your understanding 2

Year	Opening book value of assets	Annual book depreciation	Closing value of assets	Pre-dep'n profits	Post dep'n profits	ROI
	$000	$000	$000	$000	$000	
1	800	80	720	200	120	15%
2	720	80	640	200	120	17%
3	640	80	560	200	120	19%

Conclusion: The ROI increases, despite no increase in annual profits, merely as a result of the book value of assets falling. Therefore, the divisional manager will be rewarded for holding onto old, and potentially inefficient, assets.

Test your understanding 3

(a) **ROI**

Current ROI = ($40k/$150k) × 100	26.7%
ROI with new investment = ($42k/$160k) × 100	26.3%
ROI of the new investment = ($2k/$1 0k) × 100	20%

Decision: The division would not accept the investment since it would reduce the division's ROI.

However, this is not in the best interests of the company since the ROI (20%) is greater than the company's cost of capital (10%).

(b) **RI**

Current RI = $40k – (10% × $150k)	$25k
RI with new investment = $42k – (10% × $160k)	$26k

Decision: The division would accept the investment since it generates an increase in RI of $1,000.

This decision is in the best interests of the company.

Test your understanding 4

(a) **Best outcome**

	Year 1	Year 2	Year 3
RI and ROI	$m	$m	$m
NBV @ start of year	(66.0)	(44.0)	(22.0)
Revenue (add 6%)	90.1	95.4	99.6
Less direct cost (minus 8%)	(46.0)	(55.2)	(64.4)
Net cash flow	44.1	40.2	35.2
Less depreciation	(22.0)	(22.0)	(22.0)
Operating profit	**22.1**	**18.2**	**13.2**
Less imputed interest @ 8%	(5.3)	(3.5)	(1.8)
RI	**16.8**	**14.7**	**11.4**
ROI	**33.5%**	**41.4%**	**60.0%**

NPV @ 8% discount factor

Timing	CF	DF	PV
t_0	(66.0)	1.000	(66.0)
t_1	44.1	0.926	40.8
t_2	40.2	0.857	34.5
t_3	35.2	0.794	28.0
NPV			**37.3**

(b) **Worst outcome**

RI and ROI	Year 1	Year 2	Year 3
	$m	$m	$m
NBV @ start of year	(66.0)	(44.0)	(22.0)
Revenue (minus 6%)	79.9	84.6	88.4
Less direct cost (add 8%)	(54.0)	(64.8)	(75.6)
	———	———	———
Net cash flow	25.9	19.8	12.8
Less depreciation	(22.0)	(22.0)	(22.0)
Operating profit	**3.9**	**(2.2)**	**(9.2)**
Less imputed interest @ 10%	(6.6)	(4.4)	(2.2)
RI	**(2.7)**	**(6.6)**	**(11.4)**
ROI	**5.9%**	**–5.0%**	**–41.8%**

NPV @ 10% discount factor

Timing	CF	DF	PV
t_0	(66.0)	1.000	(66.0)
t_1	25.9	0.909	23.5
t_2	19.8	0.826	16.4
t_3	12.8	0.751	9.6
	———	———	———
NPV			**(16.5)**

Test your understanding 5

NOPAT

	$m
Controllable operating profit	8.4
Add back items that add value: development costs	2
Deduct amortisation of development costs ($2m ÷ 4 years)	(0.5)
	———
NOPAT	9.9

Adjusted value of capital employed

	$m
Opening book value of assets	60
Adjustment to reflect the replacement cost of assets ($75m – $60m)	15
	———
Adjusted value of capital employed	75

EVA

	$m
NOPAT	9.9
Less: adjusted value of capital employed × WACC ($75m × 10%)	(7.5)
	———
EVA	**2.4**
	———

Test your understanding 6

REPORT

To: CEO

From: A accountant

Date: April 20X2

Subject: EVA calculation and evaluation of VBM

Introduction

This report performs an assessment of EcoHomes using economic value added (EVA) and evaluates the use of value-based management as a tool for managing performance.

(a) **EVA calculation**

(W1) **Calculation of NOPAT**

	20X1 $m	20X0 $m
Operating profit	130	110
Add research costs expensed (Project Light)	10	10
Less amortisation of prior year expenses (Project Glass)	(15)	(15)
Add increase in allowance for doubtful debts	2	(1)
Add non-cash expenses	0.3	0.3
Less cash taxes (W3)	(32.5)	(27.5)
	———	———
NOPAT	94.8	76.8

(W2) Calculation of adjusted capital employed at 1 January

	20X1 $m	20X0 $m
Capital at 1 January per statement of financial position	740	670
Add allowance for bad and doubtful debts	5	6
Add capitalisation of research and development (Project Light)	10	
Add capitalisation of research and development (Project Glass)	15	30
Add non-cash expenses incurred during 20X0	0.3	
Adjusted capital employed at 1 January	770.3	706

(W3) Calculation of net tax

	20X1 $m	20X0 $m
Tax charge per income statement	27.5	23
Add tax relief on interest (interest × 25%)	5	4.5
Cash taxes	32.5	27.5

(W4) Weighted average cost of capital (WACC)

20X1: $(60\% \times 14\%) + ((40\% \times 5\% \times (1 - 25\%)) =$ 9.9%

20X0: $(60\% \times 12\%) + ((40\% \times 5\% \times (1 - 25\%)) =$ 8.7%

EVA = NOPAT – (WACC × adjusted capital employed)

20X1: $94.8 - (9.9\% \times 770.3) = \$18.54$ million

20X0: $76.8 - (8.7\% \times 706) = \$15.38$ million

Conclusion:

EVA is positive in both 20X0 and 20X1 showing that EcoHomes is adding value in both periods. The EVA increased by 20.5% year on year from $15.38 million in 20X0 to $18.54 million in 20X1. This is particularly pleasing given the level of competition within the industry. However, it will be necessary to closely monitor the EVA to ensure that there is no reduction in the figure in 20X2.

(b)   Evaluation of value-based management

Value-based management (VBM) is an approach to management whereby the company's strategy, objectives and processes are aligned to help the company focus on the key drivers of shareholder wealth and hence the maximisation of value.

Traditionally, EcoHomes used the financial measures of ROCE and EPS to quantify shareholder value. However, neither of these measures directly correlates with the market value of the company (shareholder value).

VBM takes the interests of shareholders as its primary objective. EVA is the primary measure used, (other methods include market value added and shareholder value analysis). A positive EVA indicates value creation (as in 20X0 and 20X1 in EcoHomes) while a negative one indicates destruction. EVA is consistent with net present value (NPV). Maximisation of EVA will create real wealth for shareholders.

Although EVA is calculated using the profit figure, the profit is adjusted in order to bring it closer to a cash flow measure of performance which is less affected by various accounting adjustments such as depreciation. Long-term value added expenditure can be capitalised, removing any incentive that managers may have to take a short-term view.

EVA will also bring the cost of financing home to EcoHomes' managers.

A major disadvantage of VBM measures such as EVA, compared to say EPS or ROCE, is the unfamiliarity and complexity of the calculation. Staff will need to be trained and shareholders educated in order to overcome this.

Another disadvantage of EVA is the large number of assumptions made when calculating the WACC. It should also be remembered that calculations such as EVA are based on historical data whereas shareholders are interested in future performance.

Test your understanding 7

(a) Division A will lose the contribution from internal transfers to Division B. Contribution foregone = 2,500 × $(40 – 22) = $45,000 reduction.

(b)

	$ per unit
Cost per unit from external supplier	35
Variable cost of internal manufacture saved	22
	——
Incremental cost of external purchase	13
	——
Reduction in profit of X	= $13 × 2,500 units
	= $32,500

Test your understanding 8

(a) (i)   The transfer price should be set between $35 (minimum price Able will sell for) and $38 (maximum price Baker will pay). Able has spare capacity, therefore the marginal costs to the group of Able making a unit is $35. If the price is set above $38, Baker will be encouraged to buy outside the group, decreasing group profit by $3 per unit.

(ii)   If Able supplies Baker with a unit of Y, it will cost $35 and they (both Able and the group) will lose $10 contribution from X. Therefore, the minimum price able will sell for is $45. So long as the bought-in external price of Y to Baker is less than $45, Baker should buy from that external source.

(b)   The following are required.

– Marginal costs (i.e. unit variable costs) and incremental fixed costs for various capacity levels for both divisions.

– External market prices if appropriate.

– External bought-in prices from suppliers outside the group. – Opportunity costs from switching products.

– Data on capacity levels and resource requirements.

Test your understanding 9

(a)   We must assume that Thornthwaite can divert sales away from existing customers, as it only has 30,000 units of spare capacity. This may not be possible because of existing contractual arrangements, or the adverse impact on goodwill and future sales.

Target Residual Income = $250,000.

Charge for capital employed = $6,000,000 × 12% = $720,000.

So, required profit = 250 + 720 = $970,000

As fixed costs are $2,500,000, the required contribution is 2,500 + 970 = $3,470,000

If we transfer 50,000 units to Froswick, we can sell 150,000 units externally at a contribution of (45 – 30) = $15/unit.

So, contribution from external sales = 150,000 × $15 = $2,250,000

We therefore require contribution of 3,470 – 2,250 = $1,220,000 from internal transfer of 50,000 units. Contribution required per unit = $1,220,000/50,000 = $24.40 per unit.

Therefore transfer price Thornthwaite would set = 24.4 + 30 = $54.40.

(b)   The transfers should be made on an opportunity cost basis.

Thornthwaite has spare capacity of 30,000 units, and since the variable cost of production is less than the price at which Froswick can buy in from an external supplier, it should use this capacity.

The transfer price should be at least equal to Thornthwaite's marginal cost of $30, but less than the external price that Froswick can buy in at of $42.

Once this spare capacity has been used up, we do not want Thornthwaite to turn away external customers paying $45/unit as this would only save $42/unit from Froswick buying in. Hence, when there is no spare capacity the transfer price should be set at the external selling price of $45/unit. This would encourage Froswick to buy in externally.

Summary:

Transfer 30,000 units at >marginal cost of $30 (but less than the buy-in price of $42).

Set a transfer price of $45 for units in excess of 30,000, to encourage Froswick to buy externally.

(c)   **Briefing notes on the potential dysfunctional effect of the bonus scheme at Kentmere**

The first thing to note is that the bonus is material – the divisional manager can double his/her pay by hitting the RI target. It is likely that this will influence decisions that the manager takes.

A decentralised structure encourages local managers to optimise their own reported performance. They are not necessarily that concerned with corporate performance overall, especially as this is not linked to their rewards. This may well encourage dysfunctional behaviour since a decision that looks good for an individual division may not be in the best interests of the company overall. This is indeed the case here.

We can use the figures given to illustrate this:

If Thornthwaite sets the transfer price calculated of $54.40, Froswick will exercise its right to buy from the external supplier at a price of $42. This is clearly dysfunctional as Thornthwaite could have used its spare capacity to manufacture 30,000 units internally at a marginal cost of $30/unit.

This causes a net cost to the group of 30,000 × (30 – 42) = $360,000.

Using the opportunity costs for the transfer price as calculated in part (b) would avoid this dysfunctional behaviour, but would of course mean that Thornthwaite misses its RI target.

Improvements to transfer pricing policy:

A transfer pricing policy should have the following attributes:

–   The transfer price should motivate the correct decision for the company as a whole.

–   It should preserve the local autonomy rather than being imposed.

–   It should provide a margin to both parties.

–   It should be simple to operate and understand.

Clearly our current system, whilst being simple, does not meet these criteria. Allowing Thornthwaite to set the transfer price means that it will seek to meet its own objectives, which will in turn mean that Froswick rejects the transfer and buys from outside. This is dysfunctional and causes a loss to the group as a whole.

One solution would be to use a two – part system. Goods could be transferred at marginal cost during the period, with a lump sum period end recharge to cover Thornthwaite's fixed costs and to allocate profit. This would require Head Office intervention as the two divisions would clearly disagree on what the lump sum should be!

Improvements to the bonus scheme:

The problem with the current bonus scheme is that it is based on the achievement of a single target figure, which it seems can readily be manipulated by setting a higher transfer price. It provides a classic example of "what you measure is what you get", and so dysfunctional behaviour results.

We need a scheme that encourages a corporate view rather than a parochial divisional view, so Thornthwaite's bonus should be linked to the overall Company performance and not its own result. This in turn means that it should incorporate measures like quality, efficiency improvements and staff welfare.

This is more difficult, because as models such as Fitzgerald and Moon's Building Blocks tell us, rewards should be based on principles such as clarity, motivation and controllability. A divisional manager may feel that overall company performance is outside their direct control, and lacks the necessary clarity.

So, in conclusion Mr Brearley is correct to be concerned. There are fundamental weaknesses in linking the bonus to a single measure, and particularly one that can be manipulated by adjusting the transfer price.

Test your understanding 10

Blocked remittances might be avoided by means of:

- increasing transfer prices paid by the foreign subsidiary to the parent company (see below)

- lending the equivalent of the dividend to the parent company

- making payments to the parent company in the form of:

  – royalties

  – payments for patents

  – management fees and charges

- charging the subsidiary company additional head office overheads.

Note: The government of the foreign country might try to prevent many of these measures being used.

Performance management in not-for-profit organisations

Chapter learning objectives

Upon completion of this chapter you will be able to:

- highlight and discuss the potential for diversity in objectives depending on organisation type

- discuss the difficulties in measuring outputs when performance is not judged in terms of money or an easily quantifiable objective

- discuss how the combination of politics and the desire to measure public sector performance may result in undesirable service outcomes – e.g. the use of targets

- assess 'value for money' service provision as a measure of performance in not-for-profit organisations and the public sector

- discuss the use of benchmarking in public sector performance (league tables) and its effects on operational and strategic management and client behaviour.

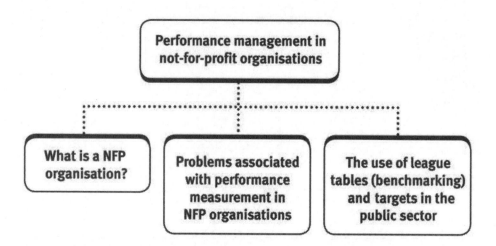

Student accountant articles: visit the ACCA website, www.accaglobal.com, to review the two articles on 'not-for-profit organisations'.

1 Assumed knowledge

Chapter 10 builds on your knowledge of performance measurement in not-for-profit organisations (NFP) from PM.

2 Introduction

NFP organisations display the following characteristics:

- Most do not have external shareholders and hence the maximisation of shareholder wealth is not the primary objective.

- They do not distribute dividends.

- Their objectives normally include some social, cultural, philanthropic, welfare or environmental dimension which would not be readily provided in their absence.

There are a number of types of NFP organisation:

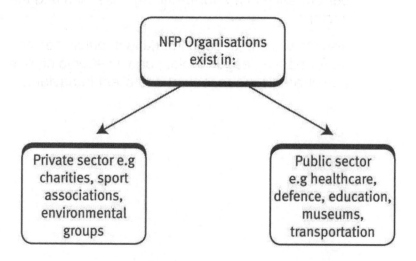

There are a number of **problems associated with performance management in NFP organisations**; the first part of this chapter will explore these problems and will also discuss possible solutions.

The second part of the chapter focuses on the use of **benchmarking in public sector organisations** and its effect on strategic management and behaviour. It also discusses the issues surrounding the **use of targets in the public sector**.

3 Problems associated with performance management in NFP organisations

Problem 1: Non-quantifiable costs and benefits

Introduction

Many of the benefits arising from expenditure by these bodies are non-quantifiable in monetary terms. The same can be true of costs. This is because:

- **No readily available scale exists**

  For example, how to measure the impact of a charity providing a help line to people suffering from depression?

- **How to trade off cost and benefits measured in a different way**

  For example, suppose funds in a hospital are reallocated to reduce waiting lists (a benefit) but at the expense of the quality of patient care (a cost). Is the time saved enough to compensate for any potential additional suffering?

- **Timescale problems**

  Benefits often accrue over a long time period and therefore become difficult to estimate reliably. For example, a school may invest in additional sports facilities that will benefit pupils over many decades.

- **Externalities**

  Suppose a council decides to grant planning permission for new houses to be built. The new residents will increase the number of cars on local roads, resulting in greater congestion and pollution, affecting other residents.

Illustration 1 – Non-quantifiable costs and benefits

Non-quantifiable benefits

In 2001, the British government scrapped admission charges to some of the country's most famous museums and galleries. The policy has attracted tens of millions of extra people to the nation's great artistic and cultural collections. Subjects such as history, art and geography have been enlivened by being able to go to a museum or gallery and see and touch the exhibitions. However, it is difficult to quantify the benefits.

Non-quantifiable costs

A hospital has decided to save money by using a cheaper cleaning firm. However, this decision may create problems in a number of areas:

- It may lead to the spread of infection.

- The general public may lose confidence in the quality of the cleaning.

- Medical staff may become demotivated because they are unable to carry out their work effectively.

However, it is difficult to measure these costs.

Test your understanding 1

In an attempt to improve people's quality of life the UK government has introduced a range of performance measures to measure quality of life, including the following:

- the local bird population

- the stock of 'decent' housing

- traffic volumes.

Required:

A town planning office is considering whether to approve a plan to build new houses on farmland. Assess the plan by reference to the three indicators given.

Solution = cost benefit analysis (CBA)

Some NFP organisations, particularly in the public sector, attempt to resolve the above difficulties by quantifying **in financial terms** all of the costs and benefits associated with a decision.

Illustration 2 – CBA

Suppose a local government department is considering whether to lower the speed limit for heavy goods vehicles (HGVs) travelling on a particular road through a residential area. The affected stakeholders may be identified as follows:

Stakeholder	Cost	Benefit
HGV operators	• Extra journey time • Potential speeding fines	• Fewer accidents
Other road uses	• Extra journey times	• Fewer accidents
Local residents	• Higher noise levels and pollution	• Fewer accidents
Local authority	• Cost of new signs, speed cameras • Cost of enforcement	• Fines collected

These costs and benefits then need to be quantified financially.

Factor	How to measure
Time	• For HGV operators this can be quantified as additional wages, overtime premiums, additional fuel costs, etc. • For other road users we need to quantify how much people value their time. One way this can be done is by comparing the costs of different modes of transport (e.g. coach versus rail versus air) to see the premium travellers will pay to save time. • Another approach is to compare property prices as they get further away from train stations as this will in part reflect longer journey times.
Noise	• Cost of installing double glazing to reduce noise levels. • Difference in house prices between houses next to the busy road and those set further back.

Pollution	•	Cost of cleaning off soot and other pollutants.
	•	Comparison of house prices near/away from main roads.
Accidents	•	Impact on insurance premiums for drivers.
	•	For victims of accidents the value of not breaking a leg, say, or not being killed, is estimated in many ways, e.g. the present value of future earnings affected.

Once these have been quantified, it is relatively straightforward to compare overall costs and benefits to see the net impact on society.

Problem 2: Assessing the use of funds

Introduction

Many NFP organisations, particularly public sector organisations, do not generate revenue but simply have a fixed budget for spending within which they have to keep. The funding in public sector organisations tends to come directly from the government.

The government will be keen to ensure that the funding is put to the best use. However, it can be difficult to assess whether or not this is the case.

Illustration 3 – Funding

An ineffective or inefficient police force will not be closed down, but is likely to justify and obtain additional funding.

Solution = assess value for money

Value for money (VFM) is often quoted as an objective in NFP organisations, i.e. have they gained the best value from the limited funds available?

VFM can be assessed in a number of ways:

- by the analysis of **economy, efficiency** and **effectiveness** (the **3Es**). This is the standard and most useful criteria for assessing value for money (see detailed discussion below)

- by using appropriate performance indicators/measures (see below)

- by benchmarking an activity against similar activities in other organisations. The organisation should seek out and then adopt recognised good practice where this can be adapted to the institution's circumstances

- by conducting VFM studies (possibly in conjunction with other institutions) or through internal VFM audit work.

Using performance measures to assess VFM

When assessing VFM using performance measures, it is important to tailor your choice of indicators to the scenario given, focusing on the most relevant measures (for example, measures relating to the organisation's mission or objectives). Once you have calculated the relevant measures you must be prepared to discuss the performance management response to each measure. Statements of which indicator have gone up or gone down will not be adequate in the exam.

Test your understanding 2

Maple Council is concerned about the performance of St George's School, one of the primary schools within its jurisdiction and, in order to substantiate this concern, the Council's Education Department has collected the following information regarding the last two years.

	20X7	20X8
School Roll (no of pupils)	502	584
Number of teaching staff	22	21
Number of support staff	6	6
Number of classes	20	20
Possible teaching days in a year	290	290
Actual teaching days in a year	279	282
Total pupil absences (in pupil teaching days)	2,259	3,066
Total teaching staff absences (in pupil teaching days)	132	189

	$	$
Budgeted expenditure	2,400,000	2,600,000
Actual expenditure	2,200,000	2,900,000

The data has been sent to the council's finance department in which you work for analysis.

Required:

Calculate relevant performance measures for St George's School for each of the last two years.

Based on your calculations analyse the school's performance in terms of value for money and explain the possible management responses to your findings.

Value for money and the 3Es

Value for money is interpreted as providing an economic, efficient and effective service. Appropriate performance indicators should be chosen for each 'E'.

Economy – an input measure. Are the resources the cheapest possible for the quality desired? For example, the organisation could measure the cost of buying equipment or the cost of staff.

Effectiveness – an output measure looking at whether objectives are being met. Different NFP organisations will have different objectives and therefore the performance indicators will have to be tailored to the individual organisation.

Efficiency – here we link inputs and outputs. Is the maximum output being achieved from the resources used? For example, the productivity per staff member may be measured and perhaps benchmarked against an average figure.

Test your understanding 3

Required:

Explain the meaning of economy, efficiency and effectiveness for a university, incorporating specific examples and performance indicators for each of the 3Es.

Test your understanding 4

A local government housing department (LGHD) has funds which it is proposing to spend on the upgrading of air conditioning systems in its housing inventory.

It is intended that the upgrading should enhance the quality of living for the occupants of the houses.

Preferred contractors will be identified to carry out the work involved in the upgrading of the air conditioning systems, with each contractor being responsible for upgrading of the systems in a proportion of the houses. Contractors will also be required to provide a maintenance and operational advice service during the first two years of operation of the upgraded systems.

Prior to a decision to implement the proposal, LGHD has decided that it should carry out a value for money (VFM) audit.

You have been given the task of preparing a report for LGHD, to help ensure that it can make an informed decision concerning the proposal.

Required:

Prepare a detailed analysis which will form the basis for the preparation of the final report. The analysis should include a clear explanation of the meaning and relevance of each of (a) and (b) below and should incorporate specific references to examples relating to the upgrading proposal.

(a) Value for Money (VFM) audit (including references to the roles of principal and agent).

(6 marks)

(b) Economy, efficiency and effectiveness as part of the VFM audit.

(6 marks)

(Total: 12 marks)

Other methods of evaluating performance

In addition to assessing value for money and the 3Es the following approaches can be used to assess the performance of NFP organisations:

- The 'goal approach' looks at the ultimate objectives of the organisation, i.e. it looks at output measures.

  For example for a hospital: Have waiting lists been reduced? Have mortality rates gone down? How many patients have been treated?

- The 'systems resources approach' looks at how well the organisation has obtained the inputs it needs to function.

  For example, did the hospital manage to recruit all the nurses it needed?

- The 'internal processes approach' looks at how well inputs have been used to achieve outputs – it is a measure of efficiency.

  For example, what was the average cost per patient treated?

Problem 3: Multiple and diverse objectives

Diverse objectives

As mentioned, NFP organisations are unlikely to have an objective of maximisation of shareholder wealth. Instead they are seeking to satisfy the particular needs of their members or sections of society, which they have been set up to benefit.

Illustration 4 – Diverse objectives

Diverse objectives in NFP organisations include:

- A hospital's objective is to treat patients.

- A council's objective is care for the local community.

- A charity's objective may be to provide relief for victims of a disaster.

Multiple objectives

Multiple stakeholders in NFP organisations give rise to multiple objectives. This can be problematic when assessing the performance of these organisations.

Solution

The problem of multiple and diverse objectives can be overcome by prioritising objectives or making compromises between objectives.

Illustration 5 – The problem of multiple objectives

A hospital will have a number of different groups of stakeholders, each with their own objectives. For example:

*   Employees will seek a high level of job satisfaction. They will also aim to achieve a good work-life balance and this may result in a desire to work more regular daytime hours.

*   Patients will want to be seen quickly and will demand a high level of care.

There is potential conflict between the objectives of the two stakeholder groups. For example, if hospital staff only work regular daytime hours then patients may have to wait a long time if they come to the hospital outside of these hours and the standard of patient care will fall dramatically at certain times of the day.

The hospital must prioritise the needs of different stakeholder groups. In this case, the standard of patient care would be prioritised above giving staff the regular daytime working hours that they would prefer. However, in order to maintain staff morale an element of compromise should also be used. For example, staff may have to work shifts but will be given generous holiday allowances or rewards to compensate for this.

Test your understanding 5

Required:

Describe the different groups of stakeholders in an international famine relief charity. Explain how the charity might have conflicting objectives and the impact this conflict may have on the effective operation of the organisation.

Problem 4: The impact of politics on performance measurement

The combination of politics and performance measurement in the public sector may result in undesirable outcomes.

*   The public focus on some sectors, such as health and education, make them a prime target for political interference.

*   Long-term organisational objectives are sacrificed for short-term political gains.

KAPLAN PUBLISHING

Illustration 6 – Impact of politics

Politicians may promise 'increased funding' and 'improved performance' as that is what voters want to hear, but it may result in undesirable outcomes.

Increased funding:

- may be available only to the detriment of other public sector organisations

- may be provided to organisations in political hot-spots, not necessarily the places that need more money

- may not be used as efficiently or effectively as it could be

- may only be available in the short-term, as a public relations exercise.

Improved performance:

- may be to the detriment of workers and clients

- may come about as the result of data manipulation, rather than real results

- may be a short-term phenomenon

- may result in more funds being spent on performance measurement when it might better be used on improvements, e.g. hospitals under increasing pressure to compete on price and delivery in some areas may result in a shift of resources from other, less measurable areas, such as towards elective surgery and away from emergency services.

Test your understanding 6 – Long practice question on NFPOs

Public versus private sector

The objective of a health authority (a public sector organisation) is stated in its most recent annual report as:

'To serve the people of the region by providing high-quality health care within expected waiting times'.

The 'mission statement' of a large company in a manufacturing industry is shown in its annual report as:

'In everything the company does, it is committed to creating wealth, always with integrity, for its shareholders, employees, customers and suppliers and the community in which it operates.'

Required:

(a) Discuss the main differences between the public and private sectors that have to be addressed when determining corporate objectives or missions.

(10 marks)

(b) Describe three performance measures which could be used to assess whether or not the health authority is meeting its current objective.

(3 marks)

(c) Explain the difficulties which public sector organisations face in using such measures to influence decision making.

(5 marks)

(Total: 18 marks)

4 The use of league tables (benchmarking) and targets in the public sector

4.1 Introduction

A **league table** is a chart or list which compares one organisation with another by ranking them in order of ability or achievement.

Benchmarking will be used to rank the organisations in the league table.

League tables have become a popular performance management tool in the public sector in recent years, for example in hospitals and schools.

Illustration 7 – The use of league tables in schools

In 2016 the secondary schools league tables showed that London is the highest performing region in England at GCSE level (exams sat by students at the age of 16) with over 70% of pupils achieving the benchmark at GCSE of five A* to C grades including English and mathematics. This is a striking turnaround in the last 20 years. In 1997 only 29.9% of London pupils reached this level.

4.2 Advantages of league tables

- Implementation stimulates competition and the adoption of best practice. As a result, the quality of the service should improve.

- Monitors and ensures accountability of the providers.

- Performance is transparent.

- League tables should be readily available and can be used by consumers to make choices.

4.3 Disadvantages of league tables

Test your understanding 7

Required:

Discuss the disadvantages of using league tables in the public sector.

Test your understanding 8

A government has decided to improve school performance by the use of league tables with schools assessed on the following:

- percentage pass rates in examinations

- absenteeism.

It has been proposed that funding be linked to these measures.

Required:

Suggest some potentially negative outcomes of this system.

4.4 Benchmarking and league tables

As mentioned, benchmarking will be used to rank the organisations in the league table.

This is a key technique but is not without its problems:

- Dysfunctional behaviour – managers focus on achieving targets to the detriment of overall performance.

- Poor results may lead to users switching to alternative providers resulting in a downward spiral in the quality of the service provided.

- Benchmarking is often a measuring exercise, not a learning exercise.

- Benchmarking will not lead to improvements if pressure is not exerted by stakeholders.

Student accountant article: visit the ACCA website, www.accaglobal.com, to review the article on 'benchmarking and the use of targets in the public sector'.

4.5 The use of targets in public sector organisations

Introduction

 'A **performance target** represents the level of performance that the organisation aims to achieve for a particular activity. Such targets should be consistent with the SMART criteria' (Government and Audit Commission).

The results from the benchmarking process (discussed above) can be used to set attainment targets for public sector organisations such as schools, hospitals and the police force.

Advantages and disadvantages of targets

Targets should act as an invaluable tool for improvement:

- improving the efficiency and effectiveness of public expenditure
- reducing overall expenditure
- increasing accountability and transparency
- increasing responsiveness to stakeholder needs.

However, there are a number of **issues** associated with the use of targets:

- **Central control** – most targets are set centrally by government. It may be more appropriate for targets to be drawn up locally by professionals who are aware of the challenges faced in different parts of the country.

- **Difficulty level** – targets that are too difficult tend to debilitate rather than motivate and those that are too easy lead to complacency.

- **All or nothing** – not meeting the target can be seen as a sign of failure. However, if an aspirational target is set it may not be met but may still result in improvements and act as a motivator.

- **Too many targets** – there is a tendency to set too many targets to try to measure every aspect of service delivery. However, a manager responsible for service delivery will be unable to concentrate on more than a handful of targets at any one time.

- **Targets not always appropriate** – it is not always appropriate to set targets, e.g. if the activity is not within the control of the person responsible for meeting the target or it is difficult to quantify the outputs of the organisation.

- **Cost** – the cost of setting the target may outweigh the benefit.

- **Lack of ownership of targets** – each target should have a named person who is accountable for the performance and achievement of the objective.

- **Gaming** – there may be a tendency for people to 'play the system' rather than using the targets as a tool for improvement, i.e. people want to look good rather than be good.

- **Conflict** – conflict between targets may occur, e.g. a reduction in the number of children on the Child Protection Register may coincide with an increase in child abuse cases.

5 Exam focus

Exam sitting	Area examined	Question number	Number of marks
Sept/ Dec 2017	NFPIs, VFM	3(a)(b)	15
Mar/June 2016	VFM and league tables	4	25
December 2014	VFM and performance indicators	2(b)	12
December 2013	League tables	4	25
June 2012	Public sector benchmarking	4	17

Chapter summary

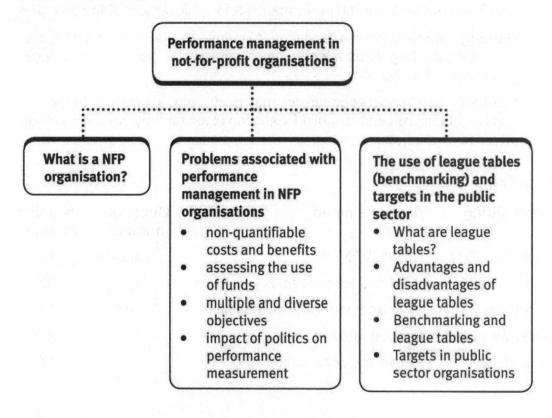

Test your understanding answers

Test your understanding 1

	The local bird population	The stock of 'decent' housing	Traffic volumes
Improved quality of life		X	
Reduced quality of life	X		X
Reason	Fewer feeding and nesting areas	New houses should be reasonably habitable!	New homes will result in a higher local population and more traffic

Test your understanding 2

	20X7	20X8
Measure 1		
Possible pupil teaching days		
(school roll × possible teaching days in the year)	145,580	169,360
Actual pupil teaching days		
(school roll × actual teaching days in the year)	140,058	164,688
Actual to possible teaching days as a %	**96.2%**	**97.2%**
Measure 2		
Pupils absences as a % of total actual teaching days	2,259	3,066
	————	————
	140,058	164,688
	1.6%	**1.9%**
Measure 3		
Staff absences as a % of total actual teaching days	132	189
	————	————
	140,058	164,688
	0.1%	**0.1%**
Measure 4		
Pupil teacher ratio	502:22	584:21
	22.8:1	**27.8:1**

Measure 5

Pupil to non-teaching staff ratio	502:6	584:6
	83.7:1	**97.3:1**

Measure 6

Average class size	502	584
	———	———
(school/number of classes)	20	20
	25.1	**29.2**

Measure 7

	20X7	20X8
Budgeted expenditure per pupil	2,400,000	2,600,000
	———	———
	502	584
	$4780.88	$4452.05
Actual expenditure per pupil	2,200,000	2,900,000
	———	———
	502	584
	4382.47	4965.75

Comments

In certain circumstances, the schools performance has been fairly consistent over the two years. Staff and pupil absences as a percentage of total actual pupil teaching days have deteriorated marginally (but the fall may not merit investigation by management), whilst actual to possible total teaching days has shown a slight improvement (managers may investigate the reasons for this improvement and take steps to improve this figure further next year).

The major area of concern is the number of pupils on the school roll is roughly 16% higher than last year. This may have an impact on performance. Management must investigate the reasons for the increase and establish whether the trend is set to continue. Action may be taken if a link to a deterioration in performance is established, e.g. through the recruitment of more teaching staff, building additional classrooms and investing in extra resources such as IT resources and books. However, the increase in student numbers may actually indicate more efficient use of resources and hence value for money. Pupil to teaching staff, pupil to non-teaching staff, and average class size has worsened. Whether this is enough to effect the quality of provision is impossible to say without further investigation.

Expenditure per pupil has fallen but this is a function of the increased pupil numbers.

Overall, it is not really possible to arrive at a firm conclusion about the schools performance. This is partly due to a lack of data from the school, and partly because of a lack of data from other schools against which to compare it.

Test your understanding 3

Value for money for a university would comprise three elements:

Economy – this is about balancing the cost with the quality of resources. Therefore, it will review areas such as the cost of books, computers and teaching compared with the quality of these resources. It recognises that the organisation must consider its expenditure but should not simply aim to minimise costs, e.g. low cost but poor quality teaching or books will hinder student performance and will damage the reputation of the university.

Effectiveness – this measures the achievement of the organisation's objectives, for example:

- The % of students achieving a target grade.

- The % of graduates who find full time employment within 6 months of graduating.

Efficiency – this focuses on the efficient use of any resources acquired, for example:

- How often are the library books that are bought by the university taken out by students?

- What is the utilisation of IT resources?

- What % of their working time does academic staff spend lecturing and researching?

Test your understanding 4

(a) Value for money audits may be seen as being of particular relevance in not-for-profit organisations where they are an important performance assessment tool. The VFM audit focuses on the achievement of objectives of the organisation in a way that ensures the most economic, efficient and effective manner. This may be complicated by the inter-relationship of objectives.

In the scenario the principal objective is the provision of the upgrade of the air-conditioning systems, ensuring that the quality of the system is satisfactory to LGHD. A subsidiary objective is to ensure satisfaction of the occupants of the premises with the quality and ease of use of the upgraded system.

An extension of the objectives is to ensure that the upgrade is seen to satisfy cost-benefit criteria, both in terms of the upgrade and the subsequent maintenance and operational advice to be provided by the contractors.

The principals are LGHD as the provider of funds and the house occupiers as recipients of the improved service.

The agents are the contractors who are tasked with the installation and maintenance of the upgrade plus the advice to users (occupants) during the initial two year period.

(b) The focus on the achievement of the objectives of the proposed improvements will benefit from consideration of the relevance of each of Economy, Efficiency and Effectiveness. The three Es are likely to be seen as possibly being in conflict with each other in terms of the achievement of objectives.

Economy will be seen as being achieved by aiming at minimising the average cost per house for the upgrade and subsequent maintenance and advice. This may be aimed at choosing the lowest quote per house for the proposed upgrades. A possible problem with this approach is that the quality of the work done may be compromised resulting in dissatisfaction of occupants.

Efficiency may be seen as the maximisation of the input/output ratio. In this exercise, this may be measured through maximising the number of houses that can have the air-conditioning upgrade with the funds available.

Effectiveness requires the achievement of the objectives (both principal and subsidiary) of the proposal. This may be measured by focusing on factors such as:

– The quality of upgrade obtained

– The level of improvement in air-conditioning achieved

– The extent to which external noise is eliminated

– Whether residents' feedback indicates that the benefits will outweigh any inconvenience caused by the upgrading work

– LGHD considers that 'value for money' has been achieved.

Test your understanding 5

The stakeholders will include donors, people needing aid, voluntary staff, paid staff, the governments of the countries granting and receiving aid.

There may be conflicting objectives. Donors and people needing aid will want all of the funds to be spent on famine relief. Management staff may require a percentage of the funds to be spent on administration and promotion in order to preserve the long-term future of the charity. Donors may have their own views about how donations should be spent which conflict with management staff.

The charity may wish to distribute aid according to perceived need. Governments in receiving countries may have political reasons for distorting information relating to need. These conflicts may make it difficult to set clear objectives on which all stakeholders agree.

Test your understanding 6 – Long practice question on NFPOs

(a) The main differences between the public and private sector regarding corporate objectives are:

The objectives of a public sector body are usually set out in the Act of Parliament or legal document that brought the body into existence. They are therefore difficult to change, even as environmental conditions change around the body. The directors of a private sector body have more freedom in making up the objectives of the company as they go along, and can change the objectives rapidly in response to changing conditions.

The value of the output of a private sector body can be easily determined in an unbiased way, by looking at the sales revenue achieved. Such numbers can therefore be part of the objectives to be achieved. There is no easy way for determining the economic value of the output of a public sector body; placing a value on the achievements of a country's Navy last year is almost impossible.

The mission statement of the company in the question recognises the role of the company in having responsibilities to different groups of stakeholders: shareholders, customers, the community at large, etc. Some public sector bodies appear to ignore the interests of certain stakeholders; you might for example be able to think of bodies that appear to be run more for the employees of the body itself rather than the public it is supposed to be serving. Private sector bodies that ignore stakeholders go bust and leave the marketplace. Failing public sector bodies often are rewarded with greater slices of public money to finance their inadequacies.

Private sector companies can attract finance in a free marketplace if they wish to expand. Public sector bodies are constrained by short-term cash limits set by the government depending on the state of the public finances. This acts against the construction of long-term strategic plans in the public sector.

The public sector has historically had little understanding of capital as a scarce resource. In the objective quoted in the question for the health authority, there is no mention of giving value for money to the taxpayers who finance the services. Private sector companies have to give value for money to their shareholders; otherwise the shareholders will sell their shares and the share price will fall, making future capital issues more expensive.

(b) In terms of the health authority's current objective, three performance measures that could be used are:

Number of patients who survive serious surgery: this would give a measure of the quality of emergency health care provided, and could be calculated as an absolute figure and a percentage, and compared with the figures for the previous year and nationally.

Length of time (on average) before an ambulance arrives after an emergency call is made: this could be compared with the figure for the previous year and for other similar regions of the country.

Length of waiting list for serious operations, i.e. the average time period between a patient being recommended for an operation by his doctor and the operation actually taking place: this figure could be compared with the figure for the previous year and with national figures.

(c) Decisions have to be made at both a local level (the tactical and operational decisions in running the public sector organisation) and a national level (mainly in terms of the amount of money to be made available to the service).

If insufficient funds have been made available to a health authority, the only way it can maintain standards is to let the waiting list increase. This might reflect badly on the local managers, but the responsibility for the problem really lies with the politicians who have decided to inadequately finance the organisation.

Similar problems exist in other public sector areas. Consider the police, for example. If they arrest more criminals, is this good or bad? Some people would say it is a good thing in that they are detecting more crime; others would say it is a failure of their crime prevention measures. If the statistical percentage of successful prosecutions brought was to be used as a performance measure, this might pressure the police to release on caution all those suspects against whom the police felt they did not have a watertight case. This is surely not in the public interest.

The recommended solution is for public sector organisations to rephrase their statements of objectives to bring more stakeholders into view, and then to construct a range of performance measures, which takes into account the wishes of each of these stakeholders.

Test your understanding 7

- Encourages providers to focus on performance measures rather than the quality of the service.

- Costly and time consuming.

- May encourage creative reporting.

- The value of any performance indicator depends on the quality of any data in the calculation. The data management systems in the public sector do not always provide quality data.

- Many of the outcomes valued by society are not measurable but many of the performance indicators have been selected on the basis of what is practical rather than what is meaningful.

- Differences between public sector organisations may make comparisons meaningless, e.g. a school in a deprived area will be at a natural disadvantage. This may result in employees being held responsible for things over which they have no control.

- A poor ranking may have a negative impact on public trust and employee morale.

- A poor ranking may lead to a worsening of future performance, e.g. gifted children are no longer sent to a poorly performing school and this results in an even lower ranking in future years.

Test your understanding 8

- Children with special needs/disabilities will find it harder to gain school places as they may be perceived as having less chance of passing examinations reducing school performance and funding. (The irony here is that schools which are willing to accept children with disabilities often need more funding, not less.)

- Truants are likely to be expelled at the school's first realistic opportunity. This may result in the school performing better but only transfers the 'problem' somewhere else.

- Schools may focus on examination performance to the detriment of other educational goals, e.g. art, sports.

- Schools facing difficulties will receive less funding to help overcome those problems.

- There will be increased competitiveness and decreased collaboration between schools.

Non-financial performance indicators

Chapter learning objectives

Upon completion of this chapter you will be able to:

- discuss the interaction of non-financial performance indicators with financial performance indicators

- identify and discuss the significance of non-financial

- performance indicators in relation to product/service quality, e.g. customer satisfaction reports, repeat business ratings, access and availability

- discuss the difficulties in interpreting data on qualitative issues

- discuss the significance of brand awareness and company profile and their potential impact on business performance

- apply and evaluate the 'balanced scorecard' approach as a way in which to improve the range and linkage between performance measures

- evaluate how models such as SWOT analysis, Boston Consulting Group, balanced scorecard, Porter's generic strategies and 5 Forces may assist with the performance management process

- apply and evaluate the 'performance pyramid' as a way in which to link strategy, operations and performance

- apply and evaluate the work of Fitzgerald and Moon that considers performance measurement in business services using building blocks for dimensions, standards and rewards

- advise on the link between achievement of the corporate strategy and the management of human resources (e.g. through the Building Block model).

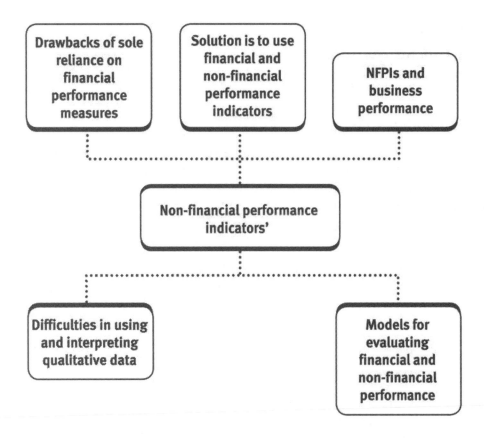

1 Assumed knowledge

Chapter 11 builds on your knowledge of financial and non-financial performance measurement from PM.

2 Introduction

In Chapters 8 and 9 we looked at a wide range of financial performance measures. However, in order to fully appraise the performance of an organisation, and to understand if the best techniques are being used to drive its success, it is useful to use a range of financial performance indicators (FPIs) and non-financial performance indicators (NFPIs) to evaluate performance.

3 Drawbacks of sole reliance on financial performance measures

There are a number of problems associated with the sole use of FPIs to monitor performance:

Short-termism

The problem of short-termism was discussed in Chapter 8. Linking rewards to financial performance may tempt managers to make decisions that will improve short-term financial performance but may have a negative impact on long-term profitability. For example, a manager may decide to delay investment in order to boost the short-term profits of their division.

Internal focus

Financial performance measures tend to have an internal focus. In order to compete successfully it is important that external factors (such as customer satisfaction and competitors' actions) are also considered.

Manipulation of results

Most managers will act in good faith and have an honest approach to performance management. However, in order to achieve target financial performance (and hence their reward), some managers may be tempted to manipulate results, e.g. costs recorded in the current year may be wrongly recorded in the next year's accounts in order to improve current year performance.

It is important to point out that NFPIs can also be open to manipulation by managers (in fact they may be even more open to manipulation due to their subjective nature). However, using a comprehensive range of FPIs and NFPIs should assist in achieving a true and fair view of organisational performance and any problems associated with manipulation of results should be minimised.

Do not convey the whole picture

The use of FPIs has limited benefit to the company since they do not convey the full picture regarding the factors that drive long-term success and maximisation of shareholder wealth, e.g. customer satisfaction, ability to innovate, quality.

Backward looking

Financial performance measures are traditionally backward looking. This is not suitable in today's dynamic business environment.

4 Solution = use financial and non-financial performance indicators

In order to overcome the problems discussed in section 3, a broader range of measures should be used.

The optimum system for performance measurement and control will include:

- Financial performance indicators (FPIs) – it is still important to monitor financial performance, e.g. using ROCE, EBITDA, EVA.

- Non-financial performance indicators (NFPIs) – these measures will reflect the long-term viability and health of the organisation.

The measures used should be tailored to the circumstances in the organisation.

By focusing on the examination and improvement of upstream determinants (e.g. quality, flexibility, resource utilisation and innovation), improvements in downstream results (e.g. competitiveness and financial performance) should occur.

The models used to evaluate financial and non-financial performance will be reviewed in detail in section 7.

FPIs and NFPIs

The following table gives examples of possible FPIs and NFPIs:

Financial performance	• cost
	• profitability
	• liquidity
	• budget variance analysis
	• market ratios
	• level of bad debts
	• return on capital employed (ROCE).
Competitiveness	• sales growth by product or service
	• measures of customer base
	• relative market share and position.
Activity	• sales units
	• labour/machine hours
	• number of passengers carried
	• number of material requisitions serviced
	• number of accounts reconciled
	• whichever measurement is used it may be compared against a pre-set target.
Productivity	• efficiency measurements of resources planned against consumed
	• measurements of resources available against those used
	• productivity measurements such as production per person or per hour or per shift.
Quality of service	• quality measures in every unit
	• evaluate suppliers on the basis of quality
	• number of customer complaints received
	• number of new accounts lost or gained
	• rejections as a percentage of production or sales.

Customer satisfaction	• speed of response to customer needs • informal listening by calling a certain number of customers each week • number of customer visits to the factory or workplace • number of factory and non-factory manager visits to customers.
Quality of working life	• days' absence • labour turnover • overtime • measures of job satisfaction.
Innovation	• proportion of new products and services to old ones • new product or service sales levels.

5 NFPIs and business performance

5.1 Introduction

There are a number of areas that are particularly important for ensuring the success of a business and where the use of NFPIs plays a key role. These include:

- product and service quality
- brand awareness and company profile.

Each of these will be reviewed in turn.

5.2 Product and service quality

Problems with product or service quality can have a long-term impact on the business and they can lead to customer dissatisfaction and loss of future sales.

NFPIs are particularly useful when assessing product and service quality. Measures may focus on:

- the **quality of incoming supplies**, e.g. a sample of incoming supplies may be inspected to determine the level of quality
- the **quality of work completed** – again, a sample of output may be checked to verify the levels of quality
- **customer satisfaction** – one definition of quality is 'the ability of a product or service to meet customers' needs'. Customer satisfaction, loyalty and repeat business go hand in hand and it is important to measure customer satisfaction, e.g. using customer surveys.

Product and service quality

- A product (or service) and its components should be critically and objectively compared both with competition and with customer expectation and needs, for example:
  - Is it good value?
  - Can it really deliver superior performance?
  - How does it compare with competitor offerings?
  - How will it compare with competitor offerings in the future given competitive innovations?

- Product and service quality are usually based on several critical dimensions that should be identified and measured over time. Performance on all these dimensions needs to be combined to give a complete picture. For example:
  - an automobile firm can have measures of defects, ability to perform to specifications, durability and ability to repair
  - a bank might be concerned with waiting time, accuracy of transactions, and making the customer experience friendly and positive
  - a computer manufacturer can examine relative performance specifications, and product reliability as reflected by repair data.

- The relative importance of different factors will vary from company to company and between customers, but achieving high quality means ensuring all the factors of the product or service package meet customer requirements.

- Measures should be tracked over time and compared with those of competitors. It is the relative comparisons and changes that are most important.

- One of the most important assets of many firms is the loyalty of the customer base. Measures of sales and market share are useful but are crude indicators of how customers really feel about a firm.

- Often the most sensitive and insightful information comes from those who have decided to leave a brand or firm. Thus, 'exit interviews' for dissatisfied customers who have 'left' a brand can be very productive.

- Another key area is access and availability of products and services, as failure in these areas can cause a loss of customers.

- Other possible sources of non-financial information related to product and service quality and customer satisfaction are:
  - repeat business ratings, which is useful as a complement to measurements of absolute sales
  - general customer satisfaction surveys
  - monitoring of the number and type of complaint.

Illustration 1 – Quality of service at Heathrow Airport

Heathrow Airport Holdings Limited owns and runs London Heathrow Airport, one of the world's busiest airports. It uses regular customer surveys for measuring customer perceptions of a wide variety of service quality attributes, including, for example, the cleanliness of its facilities, the helpfulness of its staff and the ease of finding one's way around the airport. Public correspondence is also analysed in detail, and comment cards are available in the terminals so that passengers can comment voluntarily on service levels received. Duty terminal managers also sample the services and goods offered by outlets in the terminals, assessing them from a customer perspective.

They check the cleanliness and condition of service facilities and complete detailed checklists which are submitted daily to senior terminal managers. The company has also a wealth of internal monitoring systems that record equipment faults and failures, and report equipment and staff availability. These systems are supported by the terminal managers who circulate the terminals on a full-time basis, helping customers as necessary, reporting any equipment faults observed and making routine assessments of the level of service provided by Heathrow Airport Holdings Limited.

Heathrow Airport Holdings Limited

Quality characteristic	Measures	Mechanisms
Access	Walking distance/ease of finding way around	Surveys/operational data
Aesthetics	Staff appearance/airport appearance/quality of catering	Surveys/inspection
Availability	Equipment availability	Internal fault monitors
Cleanliness	Environment and equipment	Surveys/inspection
Comfort	Crowdedness	Surveys/inspection
Communication	Information clarity/clarity of labelling and pricing	Surveys/inspection
Competence	Staff efficiency	Management inspection
Courtesy	Courtesy of staff	Surveys/inspection
Friendliness	Staff attitude	Surveys/inspection
Reliability	Equipment faults	Surveys/inspection
Responsiveness	Staff responsiveness	Surveys/inspection
Security	Efficiency of security checks/number of urgent safety reports	Surveys/internal data

5.3 Brand awareness and company profile

Brand awareness is an indicator of the strength of a product's/service's place in the customers' minds.

Developing and maintaining a brand and/or a company profile can be expensive. However, it can also enhance performance due to customer loyalty which results in repurchasing and continued use of the products. The value of a brand/company profile is based on the extent to which it has:

- high loyalty
- name awareness
- perceived quality
- other attributes such as patents or trademarks.

A range of FPIs and NFPIs will assist in measuring customer loyalty.

FPIs may focus on areas such as:

- marketing spend against sales
- market share
- elasticity of demand to price (i.e. the change in demand as a result of a change in price) and
- profit margins compared to other companies who make similar products but whose brand strength is much stronger/weaker.

NFPIs may focus on areas such as:

- customer awareness and
- consumer opinions.

Brand awareness and company profile

- If potential customers do not know about a company, they will not purchase from it. Therefore, one of the main goals of any business should be to build brand awareness.

- Assessment of brand awareness means identifying the product or company's associations in the minds of customers, and its perceived quality. This is related to but can be very different from actual quality – but ultimately it is the consumer who decides what a brand is really worth.

- Associations can be monitored in an effective way by talking to groups of customers informally on a regular basis. The identification of changes in important associations is likely to emerge from such efforts. More structured tools are also available.

- A brand or firm can be scaled on its key dimensions using a representative sample of customers. Key dimensions can then be tracked over time.

- For companies with a high company profile it is particularly important that brand awareness is positive.

- Measures of brand awareness can either look at the direct link between the brand and overall results, e.g. by considering the price premiums which the company obtains, or monitor the more intangible aspects such as awareness and consumer opinion.

Test your understanding 1

Required:

How are the measures of product and service quality related to brand awareness and company profile?

6 Difficulties in using and interpreting qualitative data

In Chapter 6 we discussed the difficulties in recording and processing data of a qualitative nature and looked at how a business can deal with qualitative data.

Most NFPIs are in qualitative terms. These qualitative factors can often:

- be difficult to measure. For example, two separate customers may be provided with an identical product or service but may have different perceptions as to how well it satisfied their needs

- be difficult to express in quantitative terms. This problem can be addressed, for example, by using a scoring system on a customer survey for the level of customer satisfaction.

Qualitative data

Difficulties in using and interpreting qualitative information

Particularly at higher levels of management, non-financial information is often not in numerical terms, but qualitative, or soft, rather than quantitative. Qualitative information often represents opinions of individuals and user groups. However there are issues related to its use:

- Decisions often appear to have been made on the basis of quantitative information; however qualitative considerations often influence the final choice, even if this is not explicit.

- Conventional information systems are usually designed to carry quantitative information and are sometimes less able to convey qualitative issues. However the impact of a decreased output requirement on staff morale is something that may be critical but it is not something that an information system would automatically report.

- In both decision making and control, managers should be aware that an information system may provide a limited or distorted picture of what is actually happening. In many situations, sensitivity has to be used in interpreting the output of an information system.

- Information in the form of opinions is difficult to measure and interpret. It also requires more analysis.

- Qualitative information may be incomplete.

- Qualitative aspects are often interdependent and it can be difficult to separate the impact of different factors.

- Evaluating qualitative information is subjective, as it is not in terms of numbers – there are no objective formulae as there are with financial measures.

- The cost of collecting and improving qualitative information may be very high.

- Difficulties in measurement and interpretation mean that qualitative factors are often ignored.

Working with qualitative information

Despite the challenges it presents, there may be ways of improving the use of qualitative information.

- Where it is important to make use of qualitative information, it is essential to ensure that users are aware of any assumptions made in analysis and of the difficulties involved in measuring and counting it.

- It is sometimes possible to quantify issues which are initially qualitative, by looking at its impact. For example, when looking at service quality, considering the cost of obtaining the same quality of service elsewhere.

Even if it is not possible to quantify issues precisely, attempting to do so is likely to improve decision making as the issues are likely to have been thought through more thoroughly.

Test your understanding 2

Required:

Your company is considering replacing its current products with a new range which will use different production techniques. What qualitative issues will you need to consider?

7 Models for evaluating financial and non-financial performance

7.1 Introduction

There are three key models that an organisation can use to evaluate its financial and non-financial performance.

- Kaplan and Norton's balanced scorecard

- Fitzgerald and Moon's building block model

- The performance pyramid.

These are highly examinable. Each one will be reviewed in turn but remember that questions may ask you to compare and contrast the methods rather than just discussing each one in isolation.

7.2 The balanced scorecard

What is the balanced scorecard?

Kaplan and Norton's balanced scorecard was designed to be used as strategic performance measurement and management framework. It provides a framework which can be utilised to develop a multi-dimensional set of performance measures for strategic control of the business.

The balanced scorecard includes:

- financial measures (these reveal the results of actions already taken)

- non-financial measures (these are drivers of future financial performance)

- external as well as internal information.

The balanced scorecard allows managers to look at the business from four important perspectives:

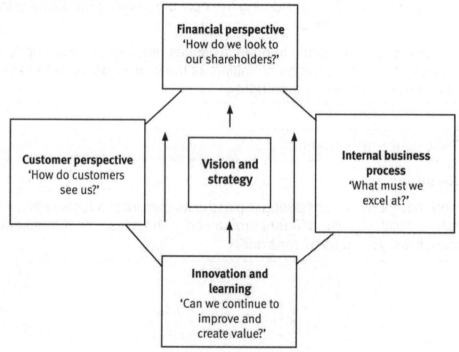

KAPLAN PUBLISHING

Within each of these perspectives a business should seek to:

- identify a series of goals (i.e. CSFs) and
- to establish appropriate measures (KPIs).

These should be in line with the overall strategic objectives and vision of the organisation.

Illustration 2 – Examples of goals and measures

A balanced scorecard for an electronics company could include the following goals and measures:

	Goals (CSFs)	Measures (KPIs)
Customer perspective	Low cost	Benchmark cost vs competitor's cost
	High quality	% defects
	Responsive service	% on-time deliveries
Internal perspective	Operational excellence	Production cycle time, rectification time, % of production completed on time and within budget
	Employee satisfaction	Staff turnover
Innovation and learning	Innovation	% of income from new products
	Internal learning	Number of employee suggestions and % implemented, % of time spent on staff development
Financial perspective	Growth and development	Quarterly sales growth
	Survival	Cash flow
	Profitability	ROCE

It would be beneficial to rank the goals and measures in order of importance.

Test your understanding 3

Required:

Using the four perspectives of the balanced scorecard, suggest some performance measures for a building company involved in house building and commercial property and operating in a number of different countries.

Evaluation of the balanced scorecard as a performance management tool

- The balanced scorecard provides a balanced view of organisational performance in that:

    - it includes a mixture of financial and non-financial measures – it covers internal and external matters

    - it links the fulfilment of long-term and short-term objectives to the achievement of overall strategy and vision. Success in the four key areas should lead to the long-term success of the organisation.

- 'What gets measured gets done'. If managers know they are being appraised on various aspects of performance, they will pay attention to these areas.

- Managers are unlikely to be able to distort performance as bad performance is difficult to hide if multiple measures are used.

- It is flexible, as what is measured can be changed over time to reflect changing priorities.

However, the balanced scorecard is not without its problems.

Test your understanding 4

Required:

Discuss the disadvantages of the balanced scorecard.

Implementing the balanced scorecard

There are four essential activities which have to be executed rigorously if the implementation of the balanced scorecard is to succeed:

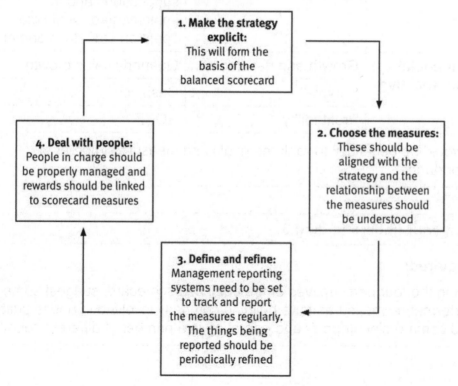

Steps involved in implementing the scorecard

(1) Make the strategy explicit

The starting point in producing a balanced scorecard is identifying the strategic requirements for success in the firm. Typically, those strategic requirements will relate to products, markets, growth and resources (human, intellectual and capital).

For example, businesses like Dell may want to be low-cost producers achieving competitive advantage from selling undifferentiated products at lower prices than those of competitors, or a business may have a product development strategy to become a leader in technology and command a premium like Apple. Their strategy may also be to develop and maintain market share, like Microsoft, or their strategy may be to occupy the number-one or number-two position in their lines of business.

(2) Choose the measures

Performance measures have to be selected that clearly relate to the achievement of the strategies identified in the earlier process. As has been seen throughout the discussion of performance measures in this text, the selection of appropriate indicators and measures is critical. The selected measures form the goals that management communicates to staff as being important. Those goals are what staff will strive to achieve. If the wrong goals are selected then the firm may find itself doing the wrong things.

The general problem is that performance measures that relate to limited parts of the business can be very prone to inducing dysfunctional behaviour. For example, a firm might minimise its inventory holding in order to meet some inventory holding target – but at the expense of total operating costs.

(3) Define and refine

Management reporting systems and procedures need to be set up to track and report the measures regularly. This involves all the issues relating to the processing of data and the reporting of information discussed earlier in this text.

The precise requirements of reporting associated with the use of the balanced scorecard will make demands on both the management accounting and IT systems in an organisation. Fully satisfying those demands has a cost and sometimes compromises may have to be made in order to contain that cost.

All sorts of practical problems may be encountered in reporting on an indicator. For example, when reporting on revenue:

– How is revenue calculated and when is it recorded?

– Should it include the non-core business activity?

– Should revenue be reported under product, region or customer headings?

– How should interdivisional transactions be reported?

Operating the management accounting system associated with the balanced scorecard requires that the things being reported should be defined and periodically refined.

(4) **Deal with people**

The balanced scorecard is an exercise in modifying human behaviour. It is its interaction with people that determines whether or not it will work.

Balanced scorecards can easily become a confusing mass of measures, some of which even contradict each other. There may be too many measures and action to achieve some of them may contribute to failure to achieve others. The measures may not always be prioritised.

To be effective, the measures contained in the scorecard should be limited in number, reasonably consistent and ranked in some order of priority. Further, performance measures should be aligned with the management structure. Career progression and remuneration should be appropriately linked to scorecard measure linked performance. Organisations which adopt a balanced scorecard but continue to reward managers on the basis of a narrow range of traditional financial measures are likely to be disappointed by the results.

Practical example of scorecard implementation

One example reported in management literature of how the balanced scorecard might be applied is the US case of Analog Devices (a semi-conductor manufacturer) in the preparation of its five-year strategic plan.

Analog Devices had as its main corporate objective: 'Achieving our goals for growth, profits, market share and quality creates the environment and economic means to satisfy the needs of our employees, stockholders, customers and others associated with the firm. Our success depends on people who understand the interdependence and congruence of their personal goals with those of the company and who are thus motivated to contribute towards the achievement of those goals.'

Three basic strategic objectives identified by the company were market leadership, sales growth and profitability.

The company adopted targets as follows:

Customer perspective

- Percentage of orders delivered on time: a target was set for the five-year period to increase the percentage of on-time deliveries from 85% to at least 99.8%.

- Outgoing defect levels: the target was to reduce the number of defects in product items delivered to customers, from 500 per month to fewer than 10 per month.

- Order lead time: a target was set to reduce the time between receiving a customer order to delivery from 10 weeks to less than three weeks.

Internal perspective

- Manufacturing cycle time: to reduce this from 15 weeks to 4 to 5 weeks over the five-year planning period.

- Defective items in production: to reduce defects in production from 5,000 per month to fewer than 10 per month.

Learning and innovation perspective

- Having products rated 'number one' by at least 50% of customers, based on their attitudes to whether the company was making the right products, performance, price, reliability, quality, delivery, lead time, customer support, responsiveness, willingness to co-operate and willingness to form partnerships.

- The number of new products introduced to the market.

- Sales revenue from new products.

- The new product sales ratio: this was the percentage of total sales achieved by products introduced to the market within the previous six quarters.

- Average annual revenues for new products in their third year.

- Reducing the average time to bring new product ideas to market.

Financial targets were set for revenue, revenue growth, profit and return on assets, but the idea was that the financial targets would flow from achieving the other targets stated above.

Analog Devices sought to adopt financial and non-financial performance measures within a single system, in which the various targets were consistent with each other and were in no way incompatible.

Strategy mapping

Strategy mapping was developed by Kaplan and Norton as an extension to the balanced scorecard and to make the implementation of the scorecard more successful.

The steps involved are:

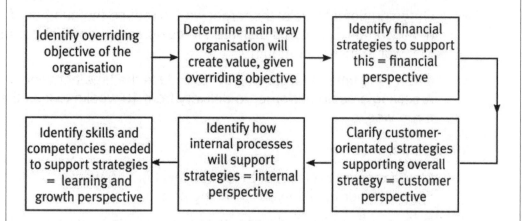

- At the head of the strategy map is the overriding objective of the organisation which describes how it creates value. This is then connected to the organisation's other objectives, categorised in terms of the four perspectives of the balanced scorecard, showing the cause-and-effect relationships between them.

- The strategy map helps organisations to clarify, describe and communicate the strategy and objectives, both within the organisation and to external stakeholders by presenting the key relationships between the overall objective and the supporting strategy and objectives in one diagram.

Issues when implementing the strategy map:

- Organisations have often found it difficult to translate the corporate vision into behaviour and actions which achieve the key corporate objectives.

- In practice, many employees do not understand the organisation's strategy, and systems such as performance management and budgeting are not linked to the strategy.

Question practice

The following question is of the same standard and style as the real exam. It examines the balanced scorecard, amongst other areas, and effectively demonstrates the linkages between different performance management techniques. Take the time to attempt the question in full and learn from the answer, considering both content and style.

Test your understanding 5

Jump is a listed business operating a chain of quality health clubs in a European country. The company has a strong reputation for the quality of its service but there are a number of other health clubs operating in the country and the market is fiercely competitive.

The country in which Jump is located is currently in recession. Consumer spending is falling throughout the economy and there is no immediate likelihood of a resumption of growth. Appendix 1 shows the financial data for Jump for the past two years.

Jump's Chief Executive Officer (CEO) has recently conducted a strategic review of the business in the context of the current economic recession. He has identified the following strategy as critical for Jump's success:

(1)   Focus on key customers.

(2)   Ensure Jump's offerings meet the needs of these customers.

(3)   Reduce or eliminate costs which do not address the needs of these customers.

(4)   Build for the future using a programme of sustainable development.

Jump recognises that it operates in a highly competitive environment and periodically monitors its share of the market and compares its prices with those of its competitors. The CEO has identified the need to operate a more systematic method of performance improvement. To this end, he believes that competitor benchmarking is necessary and has information that at least one of Jump's main competitors benchmark already.

Appendix 2 contains data analysing Jump and its two main competitors; Fitness Matters and Active First.

Appendix 1: Financial data for Jump

	20X0	20X1
	€m	€m
Operating profit	51.9	42.7
Interest	4.2	6.1
Profit before tax	47.7	36.6
Profit for the year	37.2	26.3
EVA	20.6	7.2

	20X0	20X1
Average number of shares in issue	140 million	140 million

Stock market information:

	20X0	20X1
Country's market index	1,020.7	704.3
Health club sector index	1,711.3	1,320.3
Jump's average share price	€1.22	€1.03

Appendix 2: Comparative data

	Fitness Matters		Active First		Jump	
	20X0	**20X1**	**20X0**	**20X1**	**20X0**	**20X1**
Revenue €m	246	239	521	508	483	522
Profit for the year €m	19.3	17.4	40.4	25.9	37.2	26.3
No. of health clubs	18	20	26	35	20	21
Market share	12.4%	12.2%	16.9%	15.6%	16.0%	16.0%
Revenue per health club €m	13.7	12.0	20.0	14.5	24.2	24.9

Required:

(a) Describe the different perspectives of the balanced scorecard showing how the new strategy as outlined by the CEO links to these perspectives. Suggest appropriate performance measures for Jump for each of the detailed points within the strategy.

(8 marks)

(b) Assess the financial performance of the company using share price, EPS and EVA. Critically evaluate the use of these performance metrics and how they may affect management behaviour.

(11 marks)

(c) Prepare a report for the board on a bench marking exercise using the information given in appendix 2.

   (i) Evaluate the benefits and difficulties of benchmarking in this situation.

   (ii) Evaluate the performance of Jump using the data given in the question. Conclude as to the performance of the company.

(13 marks)

Professional marks for appropriateness of format, style and structure of the report.

(3 marks)

(Total: 35 marks)

Student accountant articles: visit the ACCA website, www.accaglobal.com, to review the article on 'performance measures to support competitive advantage'.

7.3 The building block model

Fitzgerald and Moon have developed an approach to improving the performance measurement system in **service organisations**. It suggests that the performance measurement system should be based on the three building blocks of dimensions, standards and rewards.

Dimension
Competitiveness
Financial performance
Quality of service
Flexibility
Resource utilisation
Innovation

Standards
Ownership
Achievability
Fairness

Rewards
Clarity
Motivation
Controllability

Dimensions

The dimensions are the CSFs for the business. Suitable metrics must be developed to measure each performance dimension.

Dimensions fall into two categories: downstream results (competitiveness and financial performance) and upstream determinants (quality of service, flexibility, resource utilisation and innovation).

Dimension	Type of measure
Competitiveness	Relative market share
Financial performance	Turnover growth
Quality of service	Product reliability
Flexibility	Delivery time
Resource utilisation	Productivity
Innovation	New product numbers

Dimensions of performance

The table above identifies the dimensions of performance. The first two of these relate to downstream results, the other four to upstream determinants. For example, a new product innovation will not impact on profit, cash flow and market share achieved in the past – but a high level of innovation provides an indicator of how profit, cash flow and market share will move in the future. If innovation is the determinant of future performance, it is a key success factor.

Standards

The standards are the targets (KPIs) set for the metrics chosen from the dimensions measured. The standards set should have the following characteristics:

- **Ownership:** Managers who participate in the setting of standards are more likely to accept and be motivated by the standards than managers on whom standards are imposed.

- **Achievability:** An achievable, but challenging, standard is a better motivator than an unachievable one.

- **Fairness:** When setting standards across an organisation, care should be undertaken to ensure that all managers have equally challenging standards.

Rewards

Rewards are the motivators for the employees to work towards the standards set. Remember:

- what gets measured gets done

- what gets measured and fed back gets done well

- what gets rewarded gets repeated.

To ensure that employees are **motivated** to meet standards, the standards need to be **clear** (e.g. the target is to 'achieve four product innovations per year' rather than to simply 'innovate') and linked to **controllable** factors. The actual means of motivation may involve performance related pay, a bonus or a promotion.

The building block model thus makes an explicit link between achievement of the corporate strategy and the management of human resources.

Fitzgerald and Moon example

Fitzgerald and Moon applied to a Washing Machine Manufacturer:

Dimension = CSF	Flexibility – On time delivery	Quality of service	Financial performance
Standard = KPI	Delivery speed	Reliability	Profitability
Reward	Points for each on time delivery – leading to a bonus	% commission for repair engineers from fee or warranty paid	Management profit related bonuses

Test your understanding 6

FL provides training on financial subjects to staff of small and medium-sized businesses. Training is at one of two levels – for clerical staff, instructing them on how to use simple financial accounting computer packages, and for management, on management accounting and financial management issues.

Training consists of tutorial assistance, in the form of workshops or lectures, and the provision of related material – software, texts and printed notes.

Tuition days may be of standard format and content, or designed to meet the client's particular specifications. All courses are run on client premises and, in the case of clerical training courses, are limited to 8 participants per course.

FL has recently introduced a 'helpline' service, which allows course participants to phone in with any problems or queries arising after course attendance. This is offered free of charge.

FL employs administrative and management staff. Course lecturers are hired as required, although a small core of technical staff is employed on a part-time basis by FL to prepare customer-specific course material and to man the helpline.

Material for standard courses is bought in from a group company, who also print up the customer-specific course material.

Required:

Suggest a measure for each of the six dimensions of the building block model.

Question practice

The question below is an extract from a past exam question. It is a great question to attempt to ensure that you fully understand the building block model and that you can apply your knowledge in the context of the scenario.

Test your understanding 7

The Sentinel Company (TSC) offers a range of door-to-door express delivery services. The company operates using a network of depots and distribution centres throughout the country of Nickland. The following information is available:

(1)   Each depot is solely responsible for all customers within a specified area. It collects goods from customers within its own area for delivery both within the specific area covered by the depot and elsewhere in Nickland.

(2) Collections made by a depot for delivery outside its own area are forwarded to the depots from which the deliveries will be made to the customers.

(3) Each depot must therefore integrate its deliveries to customers to include:

   (i) goods that it has collected within its own area; and

   (ii) goods that are transferred to it from depots within other areas for delivery to customers in its area.

(4) Each depot earns revenue based on the invoiced value of all consignments collected from customers in its area, regardless of the location of the ultimate distribution depot.

(5) Depot costs comprise all of its own operating costs plus an allocated share of all company costs including centralised administration services and distribution centre costs.

(6) Bonuses for the management team and all employees at each depot are payable quarterly. The bonus is based on the achievement of a series of target values by each depot.

(7) Internal benchmarking is used at TSC in order to provide sets of absolute standards that all depots are expected to attain.

(8) The Appendix shows the target values and the actual values achieved for each of a sample group of four depots situated in Donatellotown (D), Leonardotown (L), Michaelangelotown (M), and Raphaeltown (R). The target values focus on three areas:

   (i) depot revenue and profitability

   (ii) customer care and service delivery; and

   (iii) credit control and administrative efficiency.

   The bonus is based on a points system, which is also used as a guide to the operational effectiveness at each depot. One point is allocated where the target value for each item in the Appendix is either achieved or exceeded, and a zero score where the target is not achieved.

Appendix: Target and actual value statistics for Donatellotown (D), Leonardotown (L), Michaelangelotown (M), and Raphaeltown (R) for the Quarter ended 31 October 20X1.

Revenue and Profit Statistics:

	Revenue (1)		Profit (2)	
	Target	Actual	Target	Actual
	$m	$m	$m	$m
Company overall	200	240	30	32
Selected depots:				
D	16	15	2.4	2.3
L	14	18	2.1	2.4
M	12	14	1.8	2.2
R	18	22	2.7	2.8

Note: For the purpose of calculation of each depot's points it is essential that actual profit as a percentage of actual revenue must exceed the target profit (%).

Customer Care and Service Delivery Statistics:

	Target	Actual			
Selected Depots:		D	L	M	R
	%	%	%	%	%
Measure (% of total):					
(3) Late collection of consignments	2.0	1.9	2.1	1.8	2.4
(4) Misdirected consignments	4.0	4.2	3.9	3.3	5.1
(5) Delayed response to complaints	1.0	0.7	0.9	0.8	1.2
(6) Delays due to vehicle breakdown	1.0	1.1	1.4	0.3	2.0
Measure (% of revenue):					
(7) Lost items	1.0	0.6	0.9	0.8	1.9
(8) Damaged items	2.0	1.5	2.4	1.5	1.8

Credit Control & Administration Efficiency Statistics:

	Target	D	L	M	R
(9) Average debtor weeks	5.5	5.8	4.9	5.1	6.2
(10) Debtors in excess of 60 days (% of total)	5%	?	?	?	?
(11) Invoice queries (% of total)	5%	1.1%	1.4%	0.8%	2.7%
(12) Credit notes as a % of revenue	0.5%	?	?	?	?

Other information:

	D	L	M	R
Aged Debtor analysis (extract):	$000	$000	$000	$000
Less than 30 days	1,300	1,500	1,180	2,000
31 – 60 days	321	133	153	552
Value of credit notes raised during the period ($000)	45	36	28	132

Note: TSC operates all year round.

> **Required:**
>
> Prepare a report for the directors of TSC which:
>
> (a) contains a summary table which shows the points gained (or forfeited) by each depot. The points table should facilitate the ranking of each depot against the others for each of the 12 measures provided in the Appendix
>
> **(9 marks)**
>
> (b) evaluates the relative performance of the four depots as indicated by the analysis in the summary table prepared in (a)
>
> **(5 marks)**
>
> (c) assesses TSC in terms of financial performance, competitiveness, service quality, resource utilisation, flexibility and innovation and discusses the interrelationships between these terms, incorporating examples from within TSC; and
>
> **(10 marks)**
>
> (d) critiques the performance measurement system at TSC.
>
> **(5 marks)**
>
> **Note:** this requirement includes 4 professional marks.
>
> **(Total: 33 marks)**

Evaluation of the building block model

The building block model has a number of advantages:

- All key determinants of success (financial and non-financial) in performance will be measured.

- It covers internal and external matters.

- It differentiates between downstream results and upstream determinants.

- It is specifically tailored to the service industry.

- The reward system will operate in a way to optimally motivate the individual staff members, i.e. rewards should be clear and linked to controllable factors.

- Targets are set in such a way to engage and motivate staff, i.e. through ownership, achievability and fairness.

- Managers are unlikely to be able to distort performance.

However, it is not without its drawbacks:

- It is not suitable for non-service companies.

- It can be difficult to see how the building blocks link to the strategic objectives.

In addition, many of the drawbacks discussed in TYU4 are also relevant here.

7.4 Performance pyramid

- The performance pyramid, developed by Lynch and Cross, includes a hierarchy of financial and non-financial performance measures.

- The aim is to produce a set of performance measures which are comprehensive in examining the results and the determinants of those results for the organisation.

- It is based on the belief that each level of the organisation has different concerns but they must support each other in order to achieve the overall objective of the organisation.

- The pyramid shape is to emphasise that the measures from the operational up to the strategic levels should support the corporate vision.

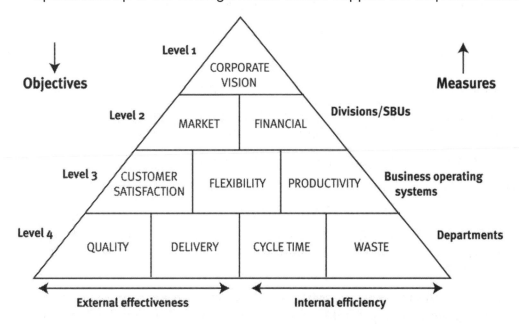

Level 1: At the top of the organisation is the corporate vision through which the organisation describes how it will achieve long-term success and competitive advantage.

Level 2: This focuses on the achievement of an organisation's CSFs in terms of market-related measures and financial measures. The marketing and financial success of a proposal is the initial focus for the achievement of corporate vision.

Level 3: The marketing and financial strategies set at level 2 must be linked to the achievement of customer satisfaction, increased flexibility and high productivity at the next level. These are the guiding forces that drive the strategic objectives of the organisation.

Level 4: The status of the level 3 driving forces can be monitored using the lower level departmental indicators of quality, delivery, cycle time and waste.

The left hand side of the pyramid contains measures which have an external focus and which are predominantly non-financial. Those on the right are focused on the internal efficiency of the organisation and are predominantly financial.

Test your understanding 8

Required:

Suggest two measures (KPIs) for each of the three categories at the business operating systems level, i.e. customer satisfaction, flexibility and productivity.

Student accountant article: visit the ACCA website, www.accaglobal.com, to review the article on 'the pyramids and pitfalls of performance measurement'.

Evaluation of the performance pyramid

Many of the strengths covered for the balanced scorecard and the building block model also apply for the performance pyramid, i.e.

- It includes a mixture of financial and non-financial measures.

- It covers internal and external matters.

- Managers are unlikely to be able to distort performance.

- If managers know they are being appraised on certain aspects of performance, they will pay attention to these.

- It is flexible and measures can change over time.

Supporters of the performance pyramid claim that it is better than the balanced scorecard and the building block model since:

- **It is hierarchical**, requiring senior managers to set objectives for each level of the organisation. The performance measures will then be specific to each level.

- **It is process focused**. It considers how processes combine to achieve the organisation's goals. Measures interact both horizontally (for example, cutting production cycle time should shorten delivery time) and vertically (for example, cutting production cycle time should increase productivity).

- **It recognises that financial and non-financial measures can support each other**. For example, improved flexibility should improve market position by meeting customer's needs, while also improving financial performance by increasing revenue and reducing fixed costs.

However, there are a number of **drawbacks**:

- Implementation of the performance pyramid will use vital management time and resource.

- Some measures may conflict, for example there will be a trade-off between quality and cost.

- In addition, many of the drawbacks discussed in TYU4 are relevant here.

8 Exam focus

Exam sitting	Area examined	Question number	Number of marks
Mar/June 2017	Building block model	1(iv)	6
Sept/Dec 2016	Balanced scorecard	1(i)	8
Sept/Dec 2015	Balanced scorecard	4	25
June 2015	Balanced scorecard	3(a),(b)	16
December 2014	NFPIs in the public sector	2(a)	6
December 2013	Performance pyramid	2(a)	15
June 2013	Balanced scorecard and building block model	1(iii)(iv)(v)	33
December 2011	Performance pyramid	2(b)(c)	18
June 2011	Building block model	3	20
June 2011	Balanced scorecard	2(a)(b)(d)	21

Chapter summary

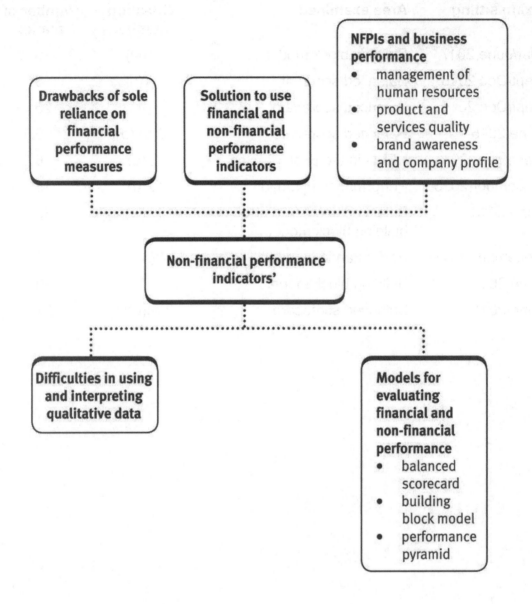

Test your understanding answers

Test your understanding 1

The experience of existing customers and their perception of the quality of the products or services will help to determine whether the company profile is positive or negative. This is particularly important for a high profile company, about which everyone will have an opinion whether or not they have any experience as a customer. This will be based on the opinions of customers with whom they have contact, and on press reports which discuss the quality of the company's offering.

Test your understanding 2

- The impact on and the views of employees. Any decision which affects working practices will have a morale effect on employees. Some decisions, such as to close a department, will have a greater effect than others, for example an increase in production, but both will affect employees.

- The impact on and opinion of customers who will be affected by any decision which changes the finished product or its availability. For example, the deletion of a product will force customers to choose an alternative item.

- Suppliers will be affected by changes to production which require different raw materials or delivery schedules. For example, an increase in production may cause the supplier to increase production of the raw material.

- The response of competitors. Any decision to changes in product specification or pricing will affect competitors who will then choose whether or not to respond.

- The impact on demand for scarce resources. A change in production as a result of the decision may alter the demand for individual resources and the result of the decision may alter availability.

- Any social and environmental effects.

Test your understanding 3

Financial perspective

- ROCE and RI – overall and by SBU.
- Margins – overall and by product/customer/country.
- Different costs as a percentage of sales – e.g. labour costs/sales, sub-contractor costs/sales.
- Sales growth.
- Cash flow targets.
- Market share.

Customer perspective

- Percentage of scheduled targets met – especially whether contracts are finished on time.
- Percentage of repeated business.
- Number of complaints received.
- Targets for new customers won.
- Percentage of apartments sold off-plan.

Internal business perspective

- Percentage of tenders won.
- Percentage of utilisation of fixed assets – vehicles, plant and machinery.
- Percentage of contracts with cost overruns.
- Cost overrun as percentage of budgeted cost.
- Targets for employee productivity.

For staffing, environmental and health and safety measures.

Innovation and learning perspective

- Number of patents established for new methods/technologies.
- Percentage of new materials used compared with total materials.
- Percentage of total revenue coming from new buildings using new structural innovations in their design.

Test your understanding 4

The disadvantages are as follows:

- It is **difficult to record and process data of a non-financial**, i.e. qualitative, **nature**.

- **Information overload** due to the large number of measures that may be chosen. However, Kaplan and Norton recommended that only a handful of measures are used.

- Potential **conflict between measures**, e.g. profitability may increase in the short-term through a reduction in product development.

- The **measures chosen may not align with the strategy and/or vision** of the organisation.

- **Poor communication to employees/managers** – organisations which adopt the balanced scorecard but continue to reward managers on the basis of a narrow range of traditional financial measures are likely to be disappointed with the results.

- **Lack of commitment by senior management** will lead to an inevitable failure of the scorecard.

- The **lack of some key perspectives**. For example, Tesco introduced a fifth perspective focusing on CSR.

- The **cost** involved in establishing suitable measures and in measuring the performance of all four perspectives.

- It focuses on the **strategic level**. However, a similar approach can be implemented at the tactical or operational level.

Test your understanding 5

(a) The balanced scorecard allows managers to look at the business from four important perspectives:

Customer – how do our customers see us and how do we present ourselves to them?

Internal business process – what processes must we excel at in order to meet the needs of our customers and shareholders?

Innovation and learning – can we continue to improve and create value?

Financial – how do we look to our shareholders and how do we optimally serve their interests?

Cost cutting – this focuses mainly on the internal business process perspective and seeks to focus the business on value added activities.

Appropriate performance measures may include efficiency savings generating by removing or reducing unnecessary processes or products.

Build for the future using sustainable development – the future focus ties into the innovation and learning perspective but may also have a knock on impact on the other three perspectives.

In terms of appropriate performance measures, Jump may monitor its energy efficiency.

The new strategy focuses on four key areas which will address the balanced scorecard perspectives in different ways:

Focus on key customers – this will directly address the customer perspective but will also have implications for the other three perspectives.

In terms of appropriate performance measures, Jump should begin by segmenting the market, e.g. by age, gender, income or the family lifecycle. Jump should then analyse each segment in terms of profitability and changing market share and should then target the most profitable segment(s) of the market.

Ensure Jump's offerings meet the needs of these customers – this will directly address the customer perspective but may also result in a change in internal business processes and an increase in innovation and learning. This, in turn, should have a knock on impact on the financial perspective.

In terms of appropriate performance measures, from a customer perspective, Jump should monitor levels of customer satisfaction (e.g. via surveys) and repeat business. Internal business processes could be benchmarked against competitors or could be monitored internally, again through the review of customer satisfaction. Innovation and learning could be monitored by looking at the number of new products and staff training time, e.g. are target customers satisfied with a range of new aerobics classes offered and the competence of the staff leading these classes? The financial perspective could be monitored using, say, ROCE, EPS or profit margin.

(b) **Assessment of financial performance**

The year on year performance has declined. EPS (W1) has fallen by 29% which would normally result in a fall in shareholder satisfaction. However, when reviewing the share price it would seem that Jump's shareholders would be encouraged by the company's future prospects. Although Jump's share price has fallen by 16% year on year, the market as a whole has fallen by 31% and more importantly the health sector has fallen by 23%.

Furthermore, even though Jump's EVA has fallen by 65% year on year it has remained positive so the company continues to create value for its shareholders.

(W1) EPS

	20X0	20X1
EPS = PAT ÷ average number of = shares in issue	€37.2m ÷ 140m = €0.266	€26.3m ÷ 140m = €0.188

Evaluation of performance metrics

	Advantages	Disadvantages
EPS	• Widely used measure. • Important to shareholders since relates to dividend growth.	• Based on accounting profit which is subject to manipulation. • Comparison is only between two years which can be misleading.
Share price	• Widely used by shareholders to monitor investments.	• Volatile • Subject to fluctuations outside of manager's control. • Managers may be encouraged to make decisions which boost short term share price.
EVA	• Widely used and measured. • Adjustments are made to profit.	• Numerous adjustments to profit must be made.

Conclusion as to impact of metrics on management

Both EPS and share price may encourage managers to make decisions which improve short term financial performance but may impact on long term profitability. EVA aims to partially tackle this issue through the adjustment of accounting figures but the large number of adjustments can make this measure unwieldy.

(c)   **To:** Board of Jump

From: A Accountant

Date: Today

Subject: Benchmarking performance

This report describes the benefits and problems associated with benchmarking the company's performance. Then, the performance of Jump and its two main competitors is calculated and evaluated.

Benchmarking is the use of a yardstick to compare performance. The yardstick, or benchmark, is based upon the best in class. Competitor benchmarking uses a direct competitor with the same or similar processes as the benchmark.

(i) **Advantages of benchmarking**

Improved performance

Benchmarking could be a key tool in enabling Jump to improve its performance and increase profitability in this highly competitive market. There should be improvements across all areas, e.g. quality, customer service.

Achievability

The improvements will be seen as achievable since the new methods have actually been used in another organisation. This should encourage managers and employees to buy-in to the change process.

Improved understanding of environmental pressures

The benchmarking process should enable Jump to get back in touch with the needs of its customers and to better understand its competitors. The industry is highly competitive and so this greater awareness will be essential for future success.

Eliminates complacency

Benchmarking can help Jump to overcome complacency and to drive organisational change.

Continuous improvement

Benchmarking can be carried out at regular intervals and can therefore drive continuous improvement in the business.

Disadvantages of benchmarking

Identifying best practice

It may prove difficult to identify the organisations that are best in class.

Cost

The actual benchmarking exercise will be costly for Jump. It is essential that the benefits of the exercise are greater than the associated costs.

Impact on motivation

If comparisons are unfavourable the information could have a negative impact on employee motivation and this would result in further inefficiencies.

Deciding which activities are to be benchmarked

This is a difficult process. Jump may not realise that there are better ways of doing things until they have seen their competitors carrying out certain processes.

Managers become too target driven

Benchmarking can result in managers becoming obsessed with hitting targets. This could sometimes be counterproductive.

Collection of data

The actual collection of data can be time consuming and costly. Data may not be readily accessible for all areas of performance measurement and competitors may be unwilling to share details.

(ii) Comparing Jump to its competitors, it is clear that Jump has done well to increase its total revenue (8% increase) but this comes at the cost of a significant fall in profit compared with Fitness matters (Fitness Matter's fall in profit was 10% compared with a 29% fall for Jump). Jump should look into its pricing policy since it may have been buying sales by offering heavy discounts and these may not be sustainable in the long term.

Active Matters drop in profit is greatest of all but this may be explained by problems in the range and quality of its services. Active matters opened nine new health clubs in the period but there has been an overall fall in revenue of 2%. Jump could analyse Active Matter's offerings to its customers in order to avoid making the same mistakes.

In terms of market share, Jump has maintained its position against slight falls in its competitors.

In revenue per health club, Jump has outperformed its competitors. However, this may be due to Jump having a larger average health club. The average club area for the three companies should be investigated.

Conclusion

In conclusion, Jump seems to be performing well with increased revenues and the maintenance of market share during the decline. The company must guard against the danger of eroding margins too far.

Test your understanding 6

Possible measures include:

Financial performance

- Fee levels.
- Material sales.
- Costs.
- Net profit.
- Outside lecturer costs.

Competitiveness

- Market share.
- Sales growth.
- Success rate on proposals.

Quality of service

- Repeat business levels.
- Number of customer complaints.
- Help-line use may be related to tuition quality.

Flexibility

- Availability and use of freelance staff.
- Breadth of skills and experience of lecturers.

Resource utilisation

- Use of freelance lecturers.
- Levels of non-chargeable staff time.

Innovation

- Number of new in-company courses.
- Time to develop new courses.
- New course formats.

Note: only one measure was required for each dimension.

Test your understanding 7

Report:

To: The Directors of TSC

From: Management Accountant

Subject: The performance of our depots

Date: 5 December 20X1

(a) **Summary analysis of points gained (1) or forfeited (0) for quarter ended 31 October 20X1**

	D	L	M	R
Revenue and Profit Statistics:				
Revenue	0	1	1	1
Profit (see note below)	1	0	1	0
Customer Care and Service Delivery Statistics:				
Late collection of consignments	1	0	1	0
Misdirected consignments	0	1	1	0
Delayed response to complaints	1	1	1	0
Delays due to vehicle breakdown	0	0	1	0
Lost items	1	1	1	0
Damaged items	1	0	1	1
Credit Control & Administration Efficiency Statistics:				
Average debtor weeks	0	1	1	0
Debtors in excess of 60 days	1	1	1	1
Invoice queries (% of total)	1	1	1	1
Credit notes as a % of revenue	1	1	1	0
Total points gained	**8**	**8**	**12**	**4**

Workings:

(i) **Profit point calculation:**

Actual results, e.g. Donatellotown = 2.3/15 = 15.3% (1 point) and Leonardotown = 2.4/18 = 13.3% (0 point)

(ii) **Debtors in excess of 60 days (% of total)**

	D	L	M	R
Revenue ($000)	15,000	18,000	14,000	22,000
Debtor weeks	5.8	4.9	5.1	6.2
Therefore debtors	1,673	1,696	1,373	2,623
Less than 30 days	(1,300)	(1,500)	(1,180)	(2,000)
31–60 days	(321)	(133)	(153)	(552)
More than 60 days	52	63	40	71
Debtors in excess of 60 days (% of total)	3.1	3.7	2.9	2.7

(iii) **Value of credit notes raised as a % of revenue**

e.g. Donatellotown = $45,000/$15,000,000 = 0.3%

(b) The summary analysis in (a)(i) shows that using overall points gained, Michaelangelotown has achieved the best performance with 12 points. Donatellotown and Leonardotown have achieved a reasonable level of performance with eight points each. Raphaeltown has underperformed, however, gaining only four out of the available 12 points.

Michaelangelotown is the only depot to have achieved both an increase in revenue over budget and an increased profit revenue percentage.

In the customer care and service delivery statistics, Michaelangelotown has achieved all six of the target standards,

Donatellotown four; Leonardotown three. The Raphaeltown statistic of achieving only one out of six targets indicates the need for investigation.

With regard to the credit control and administrative efficiency statistics, Leonardotown and Michaelangelotown achieved all four standards and Donatellotown achieved three of the four standards. Once again, Raphaeltown is the 'poor performer' achieving only two of the four standards.

(c) The terms listed may be seen as representative of the dimensions of performance. The dimensions may be analysed into results and determinants.

The results may be measured by focusing on financial performance and competitiveness. **Financial performance** may be measured in terms of revenue and profit as shown in the data in the appendix of the question in respect of TSC. The points system in part (a) of the answer shows which depots have achieved or exceeded the target set. In addition, liquidity is another aspect of the measurement of financial performance. The points total in part (a) showed that Leonardotown and Michaelangelotown depots appear to have the best current record in aspects of credit control.

Competitiveness may be measured in terms of sales growth but also in terms of market share, number of new customers, etc. In the TSC statistics available we only have data for the current quarter. This shows that three of the four depots listed have achieved increased revenue compared to target.

The **determinants** are the factors which may be seen to contribute to the achievement of the results. Quality, resource utilisation, flexibility and innovation are cited by Fitzgerald and Moon as examples of factors that should contribute to the achievement of the results in terms of financial performance and competitiveness. In TSC a main **quality** issue appears to be customer care and service delivery. The statistics in the points table in part (a) of the answer show that the Raphaeltown depot appears to have a major problem in this area. It has only achieved one point out of the six available in this particular segment of the statistics.

Resource utilisation for TSC may be measured by the level of effective use of drivers and vehicles. To some extent, this is highlighted by the statistics relating to customer care and service delivery. For example, late collection of consignments from customers may be caused by a shortage of vehicles and/or drivers. Such shortages could be due to staff turnover, sickness, etc or problems with vehicle maintenance.

Flexibility may be an issue. There may, for example, be a problem with vehicle availability. Possibly an increased focus on sources for short-term sub-contracting of vehicles/collections/deliveries might help overcome delay problems.

The 'target v actual points system' may be seen as an example of **innovation** by the company. This gives a detailed set of measures that should provide an incentive for improvement at all depots. The points system may illustrate the extent of achievement/non-achievement of company strategies for success. For example TSC may have a customer care commitment policy which identifies factors that should be achieved on a continuing basis. For example, timely collection of consignments, misdirected consignments re-delivered at no extra charge, prompt responses to customer claims and compensation for customers.

(d) The performance measurement system used by TSC appears simplistic. However, it may be considered to be measuring the right things since the specific measures used cover a range of dimensions designed to focus the organisation on factors thought to be central to corporate success, and not confined to traditional financial measures.

Internal benchmarking is used at TSC in order to provide sets of absolute standards that all depots are expected to attain. This should help to ensure that there is a continual focus upon the adoption of 'best practice' at all depots. Benchmarks on delivery performance place an emphasis upon quality of service whereas benchmarks on profitability are focused solely upon profitability!

Incentive schemes are used throughout the business, linking the achievement of company targets with financial rewards. It might well be the case that the profit incentive would act as a powerful motivator to each depot management team. However, what is required for the prosperity of TSC is a focus of management on the determinants of success as opposed to the results of success.

(Alternative relevant discussion would be acceptable)

Test your understanding 8

Possible measures (KPIs)

Customer satisfaction

- Repeat purchases.

- Numbers of complaints.

- Value of refunds.

- Sales growth by market segment.

Flexibility

- Product/service introduction time.

- Product/service mix flexibility.

- Internal setup times – the time taken to switch production from one product to another.

- Delivery response time – the time taken to meet customer delivery requests.

Productivity

- Revenue per employee.

- Sales and administration costs as a percentage of sales revenue.

- Units of output per unit of resource.

- Capital asset utilisation.

Note: only two measures were required for each category.

Corporate failure

Chapter learning objectives

Upon completion of this chapter you will be able to:

- assess the potential likelihood of corporate failure, utilising quantitative and qualitative performance measures and models (such as Z-scores and Argenti)

- assess and critique quantitative and qualitative corporate failure prediction models

- identify and discuss performance improvement strategies that may be adopted in order to prevent corporate failure

- discuss how long-term survival necessitates consideration of life-cycle issues

- identify and discuss operational changes to performance management systems required to implement the performance improvement strategies.

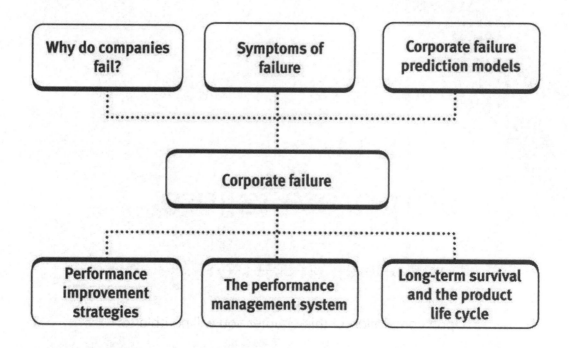

1 Introduction

So far we have focused on how effective performance management and measurement can help an organisation in achieving its goals. However, not all businesses will achieve their goals successfully. If left unchecked, these businesses are at risk of corporate failure. It is imperative that steps are taken to identify the potential symptoms of failure and address any issues before corporate collapse occurs.

Corporate failure occurs when a company cannot achieve a satisfactory return on capital over the longer-term. If unchecked, the situation is likely to lead to an inability of the company to pay its obligations as they become due. The company may still have an excess of assets over liabilities, but if it is unable to convert those assets into cash it will be insolvent.

2 Why do companies fail?

Test your understanding 1
Required:
Identify some of the reasons for corporate failure.

There are many reasons why businesses fail. Two key reasons include:

- failing to adapt to changes in the environment

- strategic drift, i.e. a rigid approach to strategic planning. Strategy is developed in accordance with unchanged assumptions (which may have proved successful in the past) and may drift away from environmental fit.

Failing to adapt and strategic drift

Reasons include:

(1) **Failing to adapt to changes in the environment**

Reasons for failing to adapt include:

- complacency
- risk-averse decision making
- economies of production and administration
- limited opportunities for innovation and diversification
- limited mental models.

Complacency is a charge frequently levelled at managers, and there are, no doubt, occasions when senior managers convince themselves that everything is fine, when it is not. However, the charge is frequently made with the benefit of hindsight, rather than observation of the efforts made by those managers at the time. There are several entirely sensible reasons why managers are reluctant to make large strategic changes.

First, it is not possible to quantify the risks of making a major change. Several studies have shown that predicting changes in the environment and devising appropriate counter-measures is among the most difficult things a manager is required to do. Only in hindsight are the dynamics clear. It is worth remembering that case studies are written backwards, where a known outcome is traced back to its origins.

Faced with such difficulties, managers are reluctant to make large-scale changes that might risk increasing the problems, and might be very difficult to implement adequately. Rather, they select options of relatively limited impact – a process referred to as logical incrementalism.

Secondly, changes to production can reduce the opportunities for economies of scale, and raise the firm's cost base. There is always a temptation to try to retain share, by reducing price, rather than make fundamental changes to a product of its method of production and risk escalating costs.

Thirdly, it may be that management is entirely aware that the strategic situation is worsening, but be unable to see opportunities to innovate or diversify out of trouble. It must be accepted that there are situations where there are no feasible solutions, and there might be better uses of the shareholders' funds than attempts to turn the business round.

Finally, a large part of the problem is caused by the mental models of those who have control of the strategy within an organisation. A mental model is the way that individuals think about problems and issues. We look (below) at Johnson's notion of strategic drift, where the firm's mental models stop the company from changing quickly enough to keep up with environmental change.

(2) Strategic drift

Strategic drift is a term devised by **Johnson** (1988) to describe as a warning to those who champion the idea of strategy emerging as a series of logical, incremental steps. Johnson argues that this limits the rate of change to the speed at which management might feel comfortable, which has many advantages (particularly in implementation), but might be inappropriate in periods when the environment moves very quickly.

As outlined above, the organisation takes a series of logical, incremental steps that enables it to change ahead of the market, developing a competitive advantage. However, the rate of change in the market place speeds up, and the firm's incrementalist approach is not enough to maintain its advantage, and it is left behind. At this point, the firm must abandon the approach, and adopt radical, discontinuous change in order to stay with the market leaders.

Johnson's main argument is that the reasons for failing to increase the tempo of change are largely cultural, rather than technical. He argues that the corporate paradigm, as revealed by its cultural web and described in an earlier chapter, is the biggest constraint on strategic thinking and action. It is important to see that management cannot change a corporate paradigm, partly because they are themselves caught up in it, and partly because some elements of it are not amenable to management techniques. Logical incrementalism is successful because it does not challenge the underlying paradigm, allowing change to take place relatively smoothly. More revolutionary change must damage the paradigm before it can begin.

Illustration 1 – Administration of British Home Stores (BHS)

BHS, the 88 year old UK department store chain, collapsed in 2016 resulting in the loss of 11,000 jobs. So what went wrong? Potential reasons cited for the company's demise include:

- **Product** – a failure to respond to changing tastes and intensification of competition on the high street.

- **Stores** – these were tired looking and compared unfavourably to other department chains.

- **Pension deficit** – the deficit was greater than the schemes assets meaning that the retailer was unable to find buyers for the business as a whole.

- **Rent increases** – the company was locked into long contracts paying considerably above the market rate for rent in many of its 164 stores.

- **Poor decision making?** Questions have been raised over the ability of the owners to breathe new life into the business, for example the brand and product portfolio was repositioned unsuccessfully.

3 Symptoms of failure

The following information can be used when assessing the likelihood of corporate failure:

Quantitative information	Qualitative information

• Analysis of the company accounts to identify problems relating to key ratios such as liquidity, gearing and profitability.
 	
• Other information in the published accounts such as:
 	
  – very large increases in intangible fixed assets
 	
  – a worsening cash position shown by the cash flow statement
 	
  – very large contingent liabilities
 	
  – important post balance sheet events.
	• Information in the chairman's report and the director's report (including warnings, evasions and changes in the composition of the board since last year).
	
	• Information in the press (about the industry and the company or its competitors).
	
	• Information about environmental or external matters such as changes in the market for the company's products or services.

Test your understanding 2

Required:

You have been asked to investigate a chain of convenience stores and assess the likelihood of corporate failure. What would you include in your analysis?

Additional example on symptoms of failure

Insureme was the market leader in home and motor vehicle insurance with a 28% market share. The company has lost its market share over the last two years and this may lead to the demise of the company.

Required:

Discuss five performance indicators, other than decreasing market share, which might indicate Insureme might fail as a corporate entity.

Solution:

Poor cash flow

Poor cash flow might render an organisation unable to pay its debts as and when they fall due for payment. This might mean, for example, that providers of finance might be able to invoke the terms of a loan covenant and commence legal action against an organisation which might eventually lead to its winding-up.

Lack of new production/service introduction

Innovation can often be seen to be the difference between 'life and death' as new products and services provide continuity of income streams in an ever-changing business environment. A lack of new product/service introduction may arise from a shortage of funds available for re-investment. This can lead to organisations attempting to compete with their competitors with an out of date range of products and services, the consequences of which will invariably turn out to be disastrous.

General economic conditions

Falling demand and increasing interest rates can precipitate the demise of organisations. Highly geared organisations will suffer as demand falls and the weight of the interest burden increases. Organisations can find themselves in a vicious circle as increasing amounts of interest payable are paid from diminishing gross margins leading to falling profits/increasing losses and negative cash flows. This leads to the need for further loan finance and even higher interest burden, further diminution in margins and so on.

Lack of financial controls

The absence of sound financial controls has proven costly to many organisations. In extreme circumstances it can lead to outright fraud (e.g. Enron and WorldCom).

Internal rivalry

The extent of internal rivalry that exists within an organisation can prove to be of critical significance to an organisation as managerial effort is effectively channelled into increasing the amount of internal conflict that exists to the detriment of the organisation as a whole. Unfortunately the adverse consequences of internal rivalry remain latent until it is too late to redress them.

Loss of key personnel

In certain types of organisation the loss of key personnel can 'spell the beginning of the end' for an organisation. This is particularly the case when individuals possess knowledge which can be exploited by direct competitors, e.g. sales contacts, product specifications, product recipes, etc.

4 Corporate failure prediction models

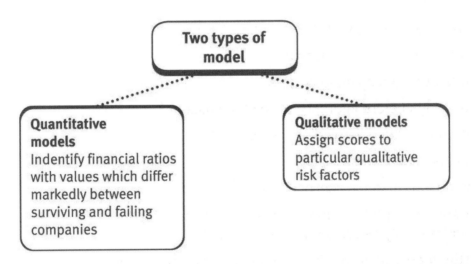

4.1 Quantitative models

Model	Explanation
Beaver's univariate model (1966)	A simple, but flawed, model that assesses the financial status of a company by reviewing one ratio at a time.
The Z score (1968)	A more sophisticated model that combines key ratios into a single discriminate score. This is a key model and will be discussed in more detail below.

Taffler and Tishaw's model (1977)	Developed their own version of the Z score model based on a combination of four ratios.
The ZETA model (1977)	This model addressed some of the problems associated with the Z score model.
Performance analysis score	Ranks all company Z scores in percentile terms, measuring relative performance from 0 to 100. Any downward trend over time should be investigated.
H score model	Similar to the previous model in that it is a ranked percentile score of between 0 and 100. The threshold is 25, below which companies are described as being in the 'Warning Area'. This score means that only 25% of companies have characteristics even more indicative of failed companies and therefore corporate failure is a real concern.

The Z score

The Z score model uses publicly available financial information about an organisation in order to predict whether it is likely to fail within a two year period.

The Z score is generated by calculating five ratios, which are then multiplied by a pre-determined weighting factor and added together to produce the Z score. The formula is:

Z score = $1.2X_1 + 1.4X_2 + 3.3X_3 + 0.6X_4 + 1.0X_5$ Where:

X_1 = working capital/total assets

X_2 = retained earnings/total assets

X_3 = earnings before interest and tax/total assets

X_4 = market value of equity/total liabilities

X_5 = sales/total assets

The score indicates the likelihood of failure:

- **Less than 1.81** – companies with a Z score of below 1.81 are in danger and possibly heading towards bankruptcy.

- **Between 1.81 and 2.99** – companies with scores between 1.81 and 2.99 need further investigation to assess the likelihood of failure.

- **3 or above** – companies with a score of 3 or above are financially sound and are expected to survive.

Test your understanding 3

Required:

Using the data below calculate the Z score for each of the four companies and comment on your findings.

	Company B	Company C	Company D	Company E
X1 = Working Capital/Total assets	0.717	0.06	1.3	0.25
X2 = Retained earnings/Total assets	0.847	0.03	0.8	0.21
X3 = EBIT/Total assets	3.107	0.09	1.1	0.5
X4 = Market value of Equity/Total liabilities	0.42	0.541	–	–
X5 = Sales/Total assets	0.998	–	0.5	0.16

Evaluation of quantitative models

The **advantages** of quantitative methods are:

- Calculations are simple

- An objective measure of failure is provided.

However, **limitations** include:

- The prediction of failure for firms with a score below 1.8 (or indeed success for firms with a score of 3 or above) is highly probable but not guaranteed.

- The model is based on a statistical analysis of historic patterns of trading by a group of US companies and may not be relevant unless the company under examination falls within the same economic circumstances and industry sector as those used to set the coefficients in the model.

- Further analysis is needed to fully understand the situation, e.g. cash flow projections, detailed cost information, environmental review.

- Scores are only good predictors in the short-term.

- The world economy has changed significantly since the development of this model (the data is now 50 years old).

- Figures are open to manipulation through creative accounting which can be a feature of companies in trouble.

- The Z score model only gives guidance below the danger level of 1.81. Further investigation is needed for those organisations with scores between 1.81 and 2.99.

4.2 Qualitative models

Qualitative models are based on the realisation that financial measures are limited in describing the circumstances of a company.

The models use a variety of qualitative and some non-accounting factors to predict corporate failure.

The types of factors included are management experience, dependence on one or few customers or suppliers, a history of qualified audit opinions or an uncertain business environment in terms of the industry sector and/or the general economic situation.

Argenti's A Score

The most notable qualitative model is Argenti's A score model.

The model suggests that there are three connected areas that indicate likely failure; defects, mistakes made and symptoms of failure. Each of these areas is divided into further headings and scores are given under each of these headings.

Argenti suggested that the failure process follows a predictable sequence:

(1) **Defects** – include management weaknesses (such as an autocratic chief executive, the failure to separate the role of the chairman and chief executive, a passive board of directors, a poor record of responding to change in the business environment or poor skills and experience of the management team) and accounting deficiencies (such as no budgetary control or lack of cash flow planning and/or costing systems). Each defect is given a score. A mark of 10 or more out of a possible 45 is considered unsatisfactory.

(2) **Mistakes** – will occur over time as a result of the defects above. Mistakes are scored under three headings; high gearing, overtrading or failure of a big project. A score of more than 15 out of a possible 45 is considered unsatisfactory.

(3) **Symptoms of failure** – mistakes will eventually lead to visible symptoms of failure, e.g. deteriorating ratios, creative accounting or non-financial signs such as delayed investment, frozen salaries, falling market share or high staff turnover.

If the overall score is more than 25, the company has many of the signs preceding failure and is therefore a cause for concern.

The scores in the three areas themselves are also of interest. For example, a high score in mistakes may indicate poor management.

Failing companies often score highly, around 60.

Evaluation of qualitative models

The key **advantages** of these models are:

- the ability to use non-financial as well as financial measures
- the ability to use the judgement of the investigator.

However, these strengths can also be seen as **weaknesses** since the models:

- are based on the subjective judgement of the expert
- require a large amount of financial and non-financial information.

5 Performance improvement strategies

The key to preventing corporate failure is to spot the warning signs early, and take corrective action quickly.

The actions needed depend on the particular situation. Once the signs of impending failure are seen, it is important to investigate and identify the causes.

These may be related to a range of different functions within the business, such as financial management, marketing or production.

It may sometimes be necessary to seek external advice to help to identify the problem.

It is important that the managers of the business accept that there is a problem and that mistakes have been made and to move on to a solution, rather than apportioning blame.

Many actions are available. Examples include:

- Major strategic change, such as getting out of a loss-making business, or making changes to the way operations are managed, such as changes to production management.
- Implementing controls to prevent further loss.
- Acquiring or developing new business (if resources allow) so as to spread the risk.
- Ensuring that the different parts of the business are in different stages of the life cycle or that there is a balanced portfolio (as per the BCG matrix) in order to ensure that cash flow is managed effectively and that the business survives.
- Learning from mistakes (either their own or their competitors), such as over-priced acquisitions or large project failures, by performing due diligence and risk assessment in advance of the investment.
- Managing major risks, such as fluctuations in commodity prices or foreign exchange rates, by using hedging techniques.

The best strategy to prevent failure is to have effective management systems in place to begin with.

6 The performance management system

The performance management system will need to reflect the performance improvement strategies:

- a link should be established between the new strategic goals and CSFs and KPIs

- performance targets should be set at all levels and these should relate to the achievement of strategic objectives

- continuous review of actual performance against targets will be required

- additional training and development needs must be met.

Test your understanding 4

You have been asked to recommend actions which need to be taken to prevent failure of an electronics manufacturer which is in financial difficulties. On investigation, you ascertain that the company has been making losses for the last two years. Although the product is well thought of in the market, sales are decreasing slightly. Returns and customer complaints are high. The manufacturing time for the products is 30 days and raw materials inventories are generally held for two weeks. There are also high levels of finished goods inventories. Receivables days are 100.

Required:

What actions do you suggest should be taken?

7 Long-term survival and the product life cycle

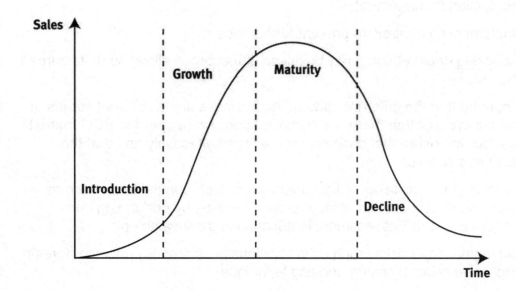

Classic life cycle

The 'classic' life cycle for a product has four phases, with different CSFs.

- An **introduction phase**, when the product or service is first developed and introduced to the market. Sales demand is low whilst potential customers learn about the item. There is a learning process for both customers and the producer, and the producer might have to vary the features of the product or service, in order to meet customer requirements more successfully.

- A **growth phase**, when the product or service becomes established and there is a large growth in sales demand. The number of competitors in the market also increases, but customers are willing to pay reasonably high prices. The product becomes profitable. Variety in the product or service increases, and customers are much more conscious of quality issues.

- A **maturity phase**, which might be the longest stage in the product life cycle. Demand stabilises, and producers compete on price.

- A **decline phase**, during which sales demand falls. Prices are reduced to sustain demand and to slow the decline in sales volume. Eventually the product becomes unprofitable, and producers stop making it.

Long-term survival necessitates consideration of **life-cycle issues**:

Issue 1: There will be different CSFs at different stages of the life cycle. In order to ensure that performance is managed effectively KPIs will need to vary over different stages of the life cycle.

Issue 2: The stages of the life cycle have different intrinsic levels of risk:

- The development and introduction periods are clearly a time of high business risk as it is quite possible that the product will fail. Revenues will be low and expenditure high.

- The risk is still quite high during the growth phase because the ultimate size of the industry is still unknown and the level of market share that can be gained and retained is also uncertain.

- During the maturity phase the risk decreases. Revenues will be high and total assets will be static or decreasing.

- The final phase should be regarded as low risk because the organisation knows that the product is in decline and its strategy should be tailored accordingly. However, costs such as decommissioning costs may be incurred during this stage.

Understanding and responding to these risks is vital for the future success of the organisation.

If there is an analysis of the developing risk profile it should be compared with the financial risk profiles of various strategic options, making it much easier to select appropriate combinations and to highlight unacceptably high or low total risk combinations. Thus for an organisation to decide to finance itself with debt during the development stage would represent a high total risk combination.

It will be the scale of financial resources which the organisation calls on over the life of its products which will dictate its survival.

Student accountant articles: visit the ACCA website, www.accaglobal.com, to review the article on 'business failure'.

8 Exam focus

Exam sitting	Area examined	Question number	Number of marks
December 2014	Quantitative models, life-cycle issues, reducing probability of failure	4	20
December 2012	Qualitative models	4	11
December 2010	Corporate failure	5	15
December 2007	Indicators of corporate failure	5(b)	10

Chapter summary

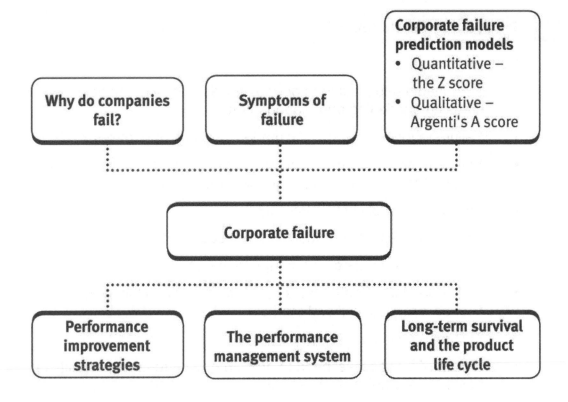

Test your understanding answers

Test your understanding 1

Reasons include:

- Poor leadership leading to poor business planning, financial planning, marketing and management.

- Failure to focus on a specific market because of poor research.

- Failure to control cash by carrying too much stock, paying suppliers too promptly, and allowing customers too long to pay.

- Failure to control costs ruthlessly.

- Failure to adapt your product to meet customer needs.

- Failure to carry out decent market research.

- Failure to build a team that is compatible and has the skills to finance, produce, sell and market.

- Failure to pay taxes.

- Failure of businesses' need to grow, merely attempting stability or having less ambitious objectives.

- Failure to gain new markets.

- Under-capitalisation.

- Cash flow problems.

- Tougher market conditions.

- Poor management.

- Companies diversifying into new, unknown areas without a clue about the costs.

- Company directors spending too much money on frivolous purposes thus using all available capital.

Test your understanding 2

Examples of issues to include:

- an analysis of key ratios, such as liquidity, gearing, cash flow and activity ratios, including trends
- changes in the cash flow of the business
- any history of significant losses
- liability position
- ability to pay creditors on time
- human resources, for example level of dependence on key staff, labour difficulties
- skills and abilities of senior management and an assessment of the strengths and weaknesses of the company
- developments in the market, such as the likelihood of new supermarkets being built near stores
- any regulatory changes which are likely to affect the company
- an analysis of the company report to identify any significant changes over the year.

Test your understanding 3

	Company B	Company C	Company D	Company E
1.2X1	0.86	0.07	1.56	0.3
1.4X2	1.19	0.04	1.12	0.29
3.3X3	10.25	0.3	3.63	1.65
0.6X4	0.25	0 .32	0	0
1.0X5	1	0	0.5	0.16
Z score	13.55	0.74	6.81	2.4

Companies with a Z score of below 1.81 are in danger and possibly heading towards bankruptcy, i.e. company C.

A score between 1.81 and 2.99 means that they need further investigation, i.e. company E.

A score of 3 or above companies are financially sound, i.e. companies B and D.

Test your understanding 4

The evidence suggests that the company has problems in financial management, production, purchasing and marketing.

Actions required:

- Improve credit control to reduce the debtor days.

- Address the production process to:

    - reduce manufacturing time and stock levels to reduce the requirement for working capital and save costs. This should also improve the ability to respond to customer demands and reduce the need to hold stocks of finished goods

    - improve final product quality to reduce returns and improve customer satisfaction.

- Improve marketing activity to address customer satisfaction issues and increase sales.

The role of quality in performance measurement

Chapter learning objectives

Upon completion of this chapter you will be able to:

- discuss and evaluate the application of Japanese business practices and management accounting techniques, including:
    - Kaizen costing
    - Target costing
    - Just-in-time, and
    - Total Quality Management
- assess the relationship of quality management to the performance management strategy of an organisation including the costs of quality
- justify the need and assess the characteristics of quality in management information systems
- discuss and apply Six Sigma as a quality improvement method using tools such as DMAIC for implementation
- evaluate whether the management information systems are lean and the value of the information that they provide (e.g. using the 5 S's).

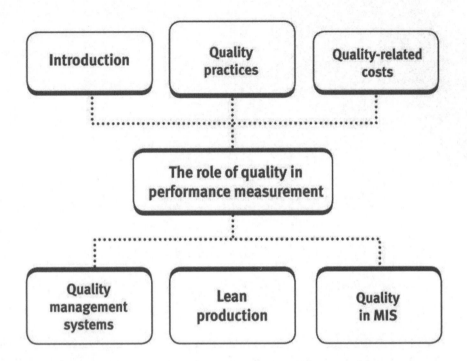

1 Assumed knowledge

Quality was covered briefly in PM. Chapter 13 builds on this knowledge and adds to it.

2 Introduction

In today's competitive global business environment, quality is one of the key ways in which a business can differentiate its product or service, improve performance and gain competitive advantage. Quality can form a key part of a strategy.

Quality can be defined in a number of ways:

- Is the product/service free from errors and does it adhere to design specifications?

- Is the product/service fit for use?

- Does the product/service meet customers' needs?

Test your understanding 1
Required:
Explain the reasons why quality may be important to an organisation?

Other important definitions

Quality management involves planning and controlling activities to ensure the product or service is fit for purpose, meets design specifications and meets the needs of customers. Quality management should lead to improvements in performance.

Quality control involves a number of routine steps which measure and control the quality of the product/service as it is developed.

Quality assurance involves a review of the quality control procedures, usually by an independent third party, such as ISO. It aims to verify that the desired level of quality has been met.

Quality certification

The International Organisation for Standardisation **(ISO)** is one of the major bodies responsible for producing quality standards that can be applied to a variety of organisations.

The ISO 9000 quality standards have been adopted by many organisations. An ISO 9000 registered company must:

- submit its quality procedures for external inspection
- keep adequate records
- check outputs for differences
- facilitate continuous improvement.

A certified company will be subject to continuous audit.

There are a number of advantages and disadvantages for a company of becoming ISO certified:

Advantages

- Recognised standard – the company's reputation for quality will be enhanced since ISO is a recognised international standard of quality.
- Marketing – ISO certification will act as an excellent marketing tool. It will help to differentiate the company, on the grounds of quality, in the customers' eyes.
- Improved profitability – fulfilment of the ISO criteria should help the company to improve quality. This, in turn, should reduce costs and improve quality.
- International competitiveness – ISO certification is becoming increasingly useful in international markets and may help the company to compete on a world stage.

> **Disadvantages**
>
> - Cost – fees are upward of $1,500 depending on the size of the company.
>
> - Time – documentation can be time consuming to produce.
>
> - Bureaucracy – the scheme encourages bureaucracy with lots of form filling and filing rather than positive actions.
>
> - Rigid policies – these might discourage initiative and innovation and may therefore hinder the quality process.
>
> - Not all embracing – ISO certification will form a small part of a quality practice such as TQM.

3 Quality-related costs

- Monitoring the costs of quality is central to the operation of any quality improvement programme.

- KPIs should be developed based on the costs of quality and these can be used as a basis for staff rewards.

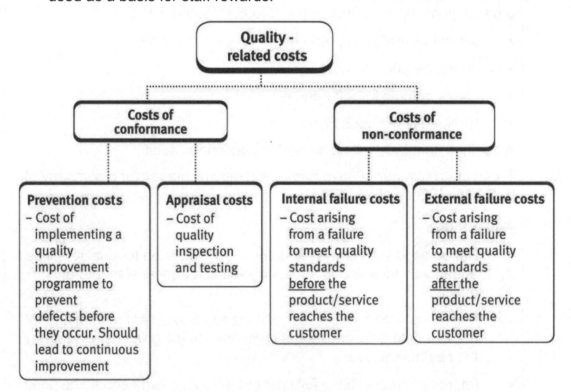

- The organisation's costing system should be capable of identifying and collecting these costs. This will lead to a greater management focus on quality since 'what gets measured gets done'.

Test your understanding 2

Required:

Provide an example for each of the four sub-categories of quality cost.

Test your understanding 3

The following information has been supplied for Company X.

	$000
Revenue	320,000
Costs:	
Design engineering	5,000
Warranty	8,950
Estimated lost contribution from public knowledge of poor quality	9,561
Training	560
Process engineering	3,450
Rework	7,545
Customer support per repaired unit	645
Product testing	65
Transportation costs per repaired unit	546
Inspection	13,800

Required:

Prepare a cost analysis that shows the prevention, appraisal, internal failure and external failure costs for Company X. Your statement should show each cost heading as a % of turnover and clearly show the total cost of quality (including any opportunity costs).

4 Quality management systems

4.1 What is a quality management system?

A **quality management system** (QMS) is a set of co-ordinated activities to direct and control an organisation in order to continually improve its performance.

The total cost of conformance is the cost of operating a QMS. The more rigorous the QMS, the lower the costs of non-conformance will be.

4.2 Implementing a QMS

Delivering products which meet the desired level of quality will only occur if all the factors that have an impact on quality are managed effectively.

A QMS should pervade the whole organisation recognising the quality impact of all areas of the organisation. There are a number of ways of implementing a QMS. For example, ISO 9001:2005 recommends that the design should be based on 8 principles:

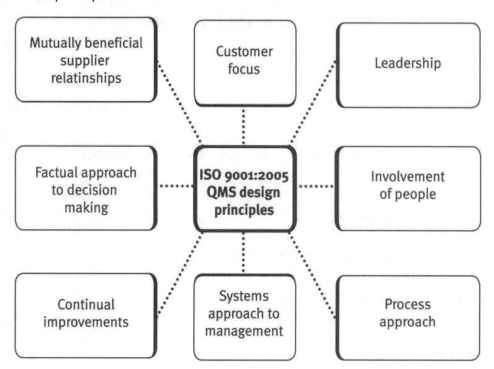

 Test your understanding 4

Required:

Explain how the 8 principles of ISO 9001:2005 should result in quality improvements.

4.3 Impact of a QMS on performance management

The adoption of a QMS should complement an organisation's strategy and help it in achieving its quality objectives. An effective QMS should:

- minimise the overall costs of quality

- improve customer satisfaction due to higher levels of quality

- improve staff morale and productivity due to the involvement and pride taken in the work done.

5   Quality practices

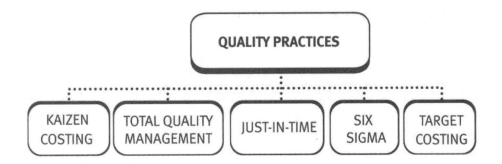

5.1 Kaizen Costing

What is Kaizen?

Kaizen is a Japanese term for the philosophy of continuous improvement in performance via small, incremental steps.

Characteristics:

*   Kaizen involves setting standards and then continually improving these standards to achieve long-term sustainable improvements.

*   The focus is on eliminating waste, improving processes and systems and improving productivity.

*   Involves all areas of the business.

*   Employees often work in teams and are empowered to make changes. Rather than viewing employees as the source of high costs, Kaizen views the employees as a source of ideas on how to reduce costs. A change of culture will be required, encouraging employees to suggest ideas (perhaps using quality circles) to reduce costs.

*   Allows the organisation to respond quickly to changes in the competitive environment.

 Illustration 1 – Kaizen

Many Japanese companies have introduced a Kaizen approach:

*   In companies such as Toyota and Canon, a total of 60–70 suggestions per employee are written down and shared every year.

*   It is not unusual for over 90% of those suggestions to be implemented.

Illustration 2 – British cycling

British cycling's revolution through small, incremental improvements

When Sir David Brailsford became performance director of British cycling, he believed that if it were possible to make a 1 % improvement in a whole host of areas, the cumulative gains would end up being hugely significant. He was on the look-out for all the weaknesses in the team's assumptions and saw these as opportunities to adapt and make marginal gains. For example:

- By experimenting in a wind tunnel he noted that the bike was not sufficiently aerodynamic. Then by analysing the mechanics area in the team truck, he discovered that dust was accumulating on the floor, undermining bike maintenance. So he had the floor painted pristine white, in order to spot any impurities.

- The team started using antibacterial hand gel to cut down on any infections.

- The team bus was redesigned to improve comfort and recuperation.

Many critiqued the approach and saw David Brailsford as laughing stock. However, the last two Olympics have seen the team win an unprecedented host of gold medals and, never having previously secured a win in over 100 years, British riders have won the Tour de France a number of times since 2012.

Continuous improvement explained

Continuous improvement is the continual examination and improvement of existing processes and is very different from approaches such as business process re-engineering (BPR), which seeks to make radical one-off changes to improve an organisation's operations and processes. The concepts underlying continuous improvement are:

- The organisation should always seek perfection. Since perfection is never achieved, there must always be scope for improving on the current methods.

- The search for perfection should be ingrained into the culture and mind-set of all employees. Improvements should be sought all the time.

- Individual improvements identified by the work force will be small rather than far-reaching.

What is Kaizen costing?

Kaizen costing focuses on producing small, incremental cost reductions throughout the production process through the product's life.

The steps in Kaizen costing are as follows:

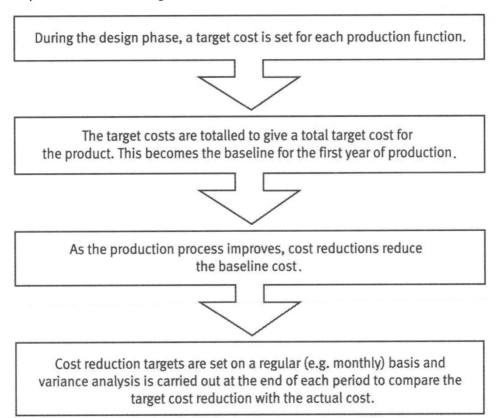

During the design phase, a target cost is set for each production function.

The target costs are totalled to give a total target cost for the product. This becomes the baseline for the first year of production.

As the production process improves, cost reductions reduce the baseline cost.

Cost reduction targets are set on a regular (e.g. monthly) basis and variance analysis is carried out at the end of each period to compare the target cost reduction with the actual cost.

One of the main ways to reduce costs is through the **elimination of waste**.

Impact of Kaizen on traditional management accounting techniques

There is a marked distinction between a traditional standard costing system and a modern Kaizen costing approach.

- A traditional standard costing system would not be suitable in a Kaizen environment. Workers who are used to a command and control structure will have to change their behaviour and speak out about possible improvements.

- Standard costs will have much less value as they are fixed over a relevant period where as Kaizen costing can respond more easily in a dynamic environment.

- Standard costing is used to control costs whereas Kaizen costing has the advantage of focusing on cost reductions.

- In a standard costing system, employees are often seen as the source of problems where as in a Kaizen system, employees often work in teams and are empowered to make changes.

Target costing

 Target costing involves setting a target cost by subtracting a desired profit from a competitive market price.

It is the opposite of conventional **cost-plus pricing** which arrives at a selling price by adding the standard cost to the desired profit.

> ### Test your understanding 5
>
> **Required:**
>
> What are the disadvantages of cost-plus pricing for an organisation?

The **steps** in target costing are as follows:

(1) A competitive market price is set based on what customers are willing to pay and how much competitors are charging for similar products.

(2) The desired profit margin is deducted from this price to arrive at a target cost.

(3) The difference between the estimated cost for the product and the target cost is the cost gap.

(4) Techniques are used to close the gap, for example:

- Can any materials be eliminated or can a cheaper material be substituted without affecting quality?

- Can productivity be improved, for example by providing additional training?

- Can a cheaper source of labour be used, for example lower skilled labour, without compromising quality?

- Can the layout of the factory be redesigned, for example by reorganising production into teams and ensuring all production is done at a single site?

- Can a move to a just-in-time production system be considered?

- Can the incidence of cost drivers be reduced?

- Can production volumes be increased to improve economies of scale?

Many of these techniques will be employed at the **design** stage.

Attention should be focused on reducing the cost of features perceived by the customer not to add value; this is called **value analysis**.

Note: Target costing can also be applied to the **service sector**.

Key features of target costing

- **Target costing forces a focus on the customer:** Product decisions and cost analysis have to take account of customer requirements such as quality, features and price. This is not always the case with other cost management methods.

- **Successful target costing considers all costs** related to production and distribution of the products and involves the whole supply chain. This may even include joint working between suppliers and manufacturers to share information and enable cost reductions, particularly for products for which raw materials contribute a high proportion of the manufactured cost.

- **Target costing considers the entire life-cycle** of the product, so that total costs to the manufacturer are minimised.

- **Target costing begins very early in the development** phase of new products, so that changes are made before production begins. Decisions made at this stage generally determine a high proportion of the costs of any product.

- **Target costing is a multi-disciplinary approach** which involves staff from all functions in the analysis and decision making.

- **Target costing is an iterative process** in which teams are making judgements and trade-offs between product features, price, sales volumes, costs and investment requirements.

- **Target costing provides cost targets** for individual inputs and processes which can be used for performance monitoring.

Target costing question

Question

Edward Electronics assembles and sells many types of radio. It is considering extending its product range to include digital radios. These radios produce a better sound quality than traditional radios and have a large number of potential additional features not possible with the previous technologies (station scanning, more choice, one touch tuning, station identification text and song identification text etc).

A radio is produced by assembly workers assembling a variety of components. Production overheads are currently absorbed into product costs on an assembly labour hour basis.

Edward Electronics is considering a target costing approach for its new digital radio product.

Required:

(a) Briefly describe the target costing process that Edward Electronics should undertake.

(3 marks)

(b) Explain the benefits to Edward Electronics of adopting a target costing approach at such an early stage in the product development process.

(4 marks)

A selling price of $44 has been set in order to compete with a similar radio on the market that has comparable features to Edward Electronics' intended product. The board have agreed that the acceptable margin (after allowing for all production costs) should be 20%.

Cost information for the new radio is as follows:

Component 1 (Circuit board) – these are bought in and cost $4.10 each. They are bought in batches of 4,000 and additional delivery costs are $2,400 per batch.

Component 2 (Wiring) – in an ideal situation 25 cm of wiring is needed for each completed radio. However, there is some waste involved in the process as wire is occasionally cut to the wrong length or is damaged in the assembly process. Edward Electronics estimates that 2% of the purchased wire is lost in the assembly process. Wire costs $0.50 per metre to buy.

Other material – other materials cost $8.10 per radio.

Assembly labour – these are skilled people who are difficult to recruit and retain. Edward Electronics has more staff of this type than needed but is prepared to carry this extra cost in return for the security it gives the business. It takes 30 minutes to assemble a radio and the assembly workers are paid $12.60 per hour. It is estimated that 10% of hours paid to the assembly workers is for idle time.

Production Overheads – recent historic cost analysis has revealed the following production overhead data:

	Total production overhead ($)	Total assembly labour hours
Month 1	620,000	19,000
Month 2	700,000	23,000

Fixed production overheads are absorbed on an assembly hour basis based on normal annual activity levels. In a typical year 240,000 assembly hours will be worked by Edward Electronics.

Required:

(c) Calculate the expected cost per unit for the radio and identify any cost gap that might exist.

(13 marks)

(Total: 20 marks)

Answer

(a) The target costing process should be undertaken as follows:

Step 1: Establish the selling price by considering how much customers will be willing to pay and how much competitors charge for similar products.

Step 2: Deduct the required profit from the selling price.

Step 3: Calculate the target cost, i.e. selling price minus profit.

Step 4: Find ways to reduce the cost gap, e.g. cheaper materials, cheaper labour, increased productivity or reduced waste.

(b) The benefits are as follows:

– Target costing has an external focus, i.e. it considers how much customers will pay/ competitors will charge.

– Cost control can occur earlier in the design process and the required steps can be taken to reduce the cost gap.

– The performance of the business should be enhanced due to better management of costs.

– The focus will be on getting things right first time which should reduce the development time.

(c) (W1) **Production overhead** (using high low method)

	Production overhead $	Labour hours
High	700,000	23,000
Low	620,000	19,000
Difference	80,000	4,000

- Variable overhead = $80,000 ÷ 4,000 = $20 per hour

- Total cost $700,000 = fixed cost + variable cost ($20/hour × 23,000). This gives a monthly fixed cost of $240,000. (Note: the total cost at the low level of production could also be used to find the fixed cost).

- Annual fixed cost = $240,000 × 12 = $2,880,000

- Overhead absorption rate (OAR) = $2,880,000 ÷ 240,000 hours = $12 per hour

---

Cost card and cost gap calculation

	$ per radio
Component 1	4.10
Component 1 delivery = $2,400 ÷ 4,000	0.60
Component 2 wiring = $0.50 × 0.25 metres × 100/98	0.128
Other material	8.10
Assembly labour = $12.60 × 0.5 hours × 100/90	7.00
Variable production overhead = $20/hour (W1) × 0.5 hours	10.00
Fixed production overhead = $12/hour (W1) × 0.5 hours	6.00
Total cost	**35.928**
Desired cost	35.20
Cost gap	**0.728**

Target costing and Kaizen costing

- Target costing usually occurs at the beginning of a product's life.

- Kaizen costing uses the principles of target costing but it is the process of long-term continuous improvements by small, incremental cost reductions throughout the product's life.

- With Kaizen costing, any target cost that is established will be revised on a regular basis.

5.2 Total Quality Management

What is total quality management?

Total Quality Management (TQM) is a philosophy of quality management that originated in Japan in the 1950s.

Fundamental features of TQM:

- **Prevention of errors before they occur:** The aim of TQM is to get thing's right first time. This contrasts with the traditional approach that less than 100% quality is acceptable. TQM will result in an increase in prevention costs, e.g. quality design of systems and products, but internal and external failure costs will fall to a greater extent.

- **Continual improvement:** Quality management is not a one-off process, but is the continuous examination and improvement of processes.

- **Real participation by all:** The 'total' in TQM means that everyone in the value chain is involved in the process, including:

    - Employees – they are expected to seek out, identify and correct quality problems. Teamwork will be vital.

    - Suppliers – quality and reliability of suppliers will play a vital role.

    - Customers – the goal is to identify and meet the needs of customers.

- **Management commitment:** Managers must be committed and encourage everyone else to be quality conscious.

Illustration 3 – TQM success/failure

A TQM success story

Corning in one of the world's leading innovators in materials science. This is partly due to the implementation of a TQM approach, the leadership stamp of the, then, CEO James Houghton. Houghton announced a $1.6 billion investment in TQM. After several years of intensive training and a decade of applying the TQM approach, all of Corning's employees had bought into the quality concept. They knew the lingo – continuous improvement, empowerment, customer focus, management by prevention and they witnessed the impact of the firm's techniques as profits soared.

An example of TQM failure

The communication and services company BT launched a total quality program in the late 1980s. This resulted in the company getting bogged down by quality processes and bureaucracy. The company failed to focus on its customers and later decided to dismantle its TQM programme. This was at great cost to the company and they have failed to make a full recovery.

Performance measures in a TQM environment

Measuring performance is a key part of a TQM programme. The cost of implementing TQM and measuring performance can often be offset by the costs saved through increased efficiency, improved product quality and higher levels of customer service.

Performance measures must be linked to the TQM programme's CSFs, be widely understood, be based on correct data and data should be easy to collect.

Each organisation will develop its own way of measuring TQM performance but key areas to investigate may be:

- **Effectiveness**, i.e. the extent to which goals are achieved. Examples include comparing actual and expected figures for:
  - quality of product or service (may be gauged through customer feedback)
  - quantity of units sold
  - number of on time deliveries
  - speed of response, and
  - unit cost.

- **Efficiency** will compare actual with planned use of resources such as labour, staff, equipment and materials.

- **Economy** will compare the actual costs of TQM with the planned cost, i.e. cost of prevention, detection, internal failure and external failure.

5.3 Just-in-time

What is just-in-time?

Just-in-time (JIT) is a demand-pull system of ordering from suppliers which aims to reduce inventory levels to zero.

JIT applies to both production within an organisation and to purchasing from external suppliers.

JIT purchasing is a method of purchasing that involves ordering materials only when customers place an order. When the goods are received they go straight into production.

JIT production is a production system that is driven by demand for the finished products (a 'pull' system), whereby each component on a production line is produced only when needed for the next stage.

JIT is often used in conjunction with other continuous improvement methods.

Illustration 4 – Toyota

Toyota pioneered the JIT manufacturing system, in which suppliers send parts daily – or several times a day – and are notified electronically when the production line is running out.

More than 400 trucks a day come in and out of Toyota's Georgetown plant in the USA, with a separate logistics company organising shipment from Toyota's 300 suppliers – most located in neighbouring state within half a day's drive of the plant.

Toyota aims to build long-term relationships with suppliers, many of whom it has a stake in, and says it now produces 80% of its parts within North America.

Requirements for successful operation of a JIT system

Requirements include:

- **High quality and reliability** – disruptions cause hold ups in the entire system and must be avoided. The emphasis is on getting the work right first time:

  - Highly skilled and well trained staff should be used. – Machinery must be fully maintained.

  - Long-term links should be established with suppliers in order to ensure a reliable and high quality service and to minimise any stoppages in production.

- **Elimination of non-value added activities** – for example, value is not added whilst storing the products and therefore inventory levels should be minimised.

- **Speed of throughput** – the speed of production should match the rate at which customers demand the product. Production runs should be shorter with smaller stocks of finished goods.

- **Flexibility** – a flexible production system and workforce is needed in order to be able to respond immediately to customers' orders.

- **Lower costs** – another objective of JIT is to reduce costs by: – Raising quality and eliminating waste.

  - Achieving faster throughput.

  - Minimising inventory levels.

Test your understanding 6

Required:

Explain the advantages and disadvantages to an organisation of operating a JIT system.

JIT and supplier relationships

A company is a long way towards JIT if its suppliers will guarantee the quality of the material they deliver and will give it shorter lead-times, deliver smaller quantities more often, guarantee a low reject rate and perform quality-assurance inspection at source. Frequent deliveries of small quantities of material to the company can ensure that each delivery is just enough to meet its immediate production schedule. This will keep its inventory as low as possible. Materials handling time will be saved because as there is no need to move the stock into a store, the goods can be delivered directly to a workstation on the shop floor. Inspection time and costs can be eliminated and the labour required for reworking defective material or returning goods to the supplier can be saved.

The successful JIT manufacturer deliberately sets out to cultivate good relationships with a small number of suppliers and these suppliers will often be situated close to the manufacturing plant. It is usual for a large manufacturer that does not use the JIT approach to have multiple suppliers. When a new part is to be produced, various suppliers will bid for the contract and the business will be given to the two or three most attractive bids.

A JIT manufacturer is looking for a single supplier that can provide high quality and reliable deliveries, rather than the lowest price. This supplier will often be located in close proximity to the manufacturing plant.

There is much to be gained by both the company and its suppliers from this mutual dependence. The supplier is guaranteed a demand for the products as the sole supplier and is able to plan to meet the customer's production schedules. If an organisation has confidence that suppliers will deliver material of 100% quality, on time, so that there will be no rejects, returns and hence no consequent production delays, usage of materials can be matched with delivery of materials and stocks can be kept at near zero levels.

Jaguar, when it analysed the causes of customer complaints, compiled a list of 150 areas of faults. Some 60% of them turned out to be faulty components from suppliers. One month the company returned 22,000 components to different suppliers. Suppliers were brought on to the multi-disciplinary task forces the company established to tackle each of the common faults. The task force had the simple objective of finding the fault, establishing and testing a cure, and implementing it as fast as possible. Jaguar directors chaired the task forces of the 12 most serious faults, but in one case the task force was chaired by the supplier's representative.

JIT and service operations

Although it originated with manufacturing systems, the JIT philosophy can also be applied to some service operations.

- Whereas JIT in manufacturing seeks to eliminate inventories, JIT in service operations will seek to eliminate internal or external queues of customers.

- Other concepts of JIT, such as eliminating wasteful motion and seeking ways of achieving continuous improvement are also applicable to services as much as to manufacturing activities.

The impact on management accounting

The introduction of a JIT system will have a number of effects on the costing system and performance management.

- Allowances for waste, scrap and rework are moved to the ideal standard, rather than an achievable standard.

- Costs are only allowed to accumulate when the product is finished.

- The inevitable reduction in inventory levels will reduce the time taken to count inventory and the clerical cost.

- Minimal inventory makes it easier for a firm to switch to backflush accounting (a simplified method of cost bookkeeping).

- Traditional performance measures such as inventory turnover and individual incentives are replaced by more appropriate performance measures, such as:

  - total head count productivity

  - inventory days

  - ideas generated and implemented

  - customer complaints

  - bottlenecks in production

  - the amount and effectiveness of staff training.

Illustration 5 – JIT and management accounting control systems

Management accounting systems within a JIT environment must be capable of producing performance and control information consistent with a JIT philosophy. Information must therefore be produced that directs management attention to the following issues:

- elimination of waste

- reduction in set-up time

- continuous improvement.

5.4 Six Sigma

- Six Sigma is a quality management programme that was pioneered by Motorola in the 1980s.

- The aim of the approach is to achieve a reduction in the number of faults that go beyond an accepted tolerance level. It tends to be used for individual processes.

- The sigma stands for the standard deviation. For reasons that need not be explained here, it can be demonstrated that, if the error rate lies beyond the sixth sigma of probability there will be fewer than 3.4 defects in every one million units produced.

- This is the tolerance level set. It is almost perfection since customers will have room to complain fewer than four times in a million.

Illustration 6 – The Six Sigma approach

A hospital is using the Six Sigma process to improve patient waiting times. An investigation of the views of patients has revealed that:

- patients do not want to be called before their appointment time as they do not want to feel that they have to be at the hospital early to avoid missing an appointment

- the maximum length of time they are prepared to wait after the appointment time is 30 minutes.

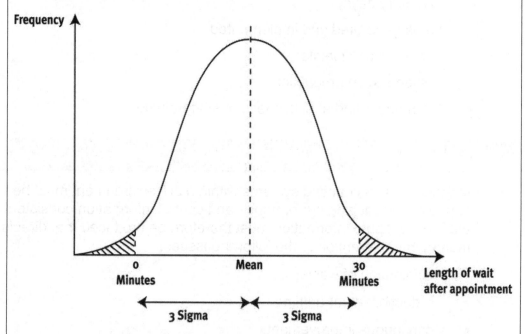

The aim of the Six Sigma programme will be to ensure that no more than 3.4 waits in every million occurrences exceed 30 minutes or are less than 0 minutes.

Key requirements and criticisms

There are a number of **key requirements** for the implementation of Six Sigma.

- Six Sigma should be focused on the customer and based on the level of performance acceptable to the customer.

- Six Sigma targets for a process should be related to the main drivers of performance.

- To maximise savings Six Sigma needs to be part of a wider performance management programme which is linked to the strategy of the organisation. It should not be just about doing things better but about doing things differently.

- Senior managers within the organisation have a key role in driving the process.

- Training and education about the process throughout the organisation are essential for success.

- Six Sigma sets a tight target, but accepts some failure – the target is not zero defects.

Literature on Six Sigma contains some **criticisms** of the process and identifies a number of limitations as follows.

- Six Sigma has been criticised for its focus on current processes and reliance on data. It is suggested that this could become too rigid and limit process innovation.

- Six Sigma is based on the use of models which are by their nature simplifications of real life. Judgement needs to be used in applying the models in the context of business objectives.

- The approach can be very time consuming and expensive. Organisations need to be prepared to put time and effort into its implementation.

- The culture of the organisation must be supportive – not all organisations are ready for such a scientific process.

- The process is heavily data-driven. This can be a strength, but can become over-bureaucratic.

- Six Sigma can give all parts of the organisation a common language for process improvement, but it is important to ensure that this does not become jargon but is expressed in terms specific to the organisation and its business.

- There is an underlying assumption in Six Sigma that the existing business processes meet customers' expectations. It does not ask whether it is the right process.

The five steps of the Six Sigma process (DMAIC)

Step 1: Define customer requirements/problem
- customer requirements can be divided into those that are the minimum that is acceptable, those that improve the customer's experience and those that go beyond the customer's expectations
- quality problem defined in specific, quantifiable terms
- a mission statement is prepared explaining what will be done about the problem. This should also be in specific, quantifiable terms
- a project team is set up from across the organisation and is given the resources to address the problem.

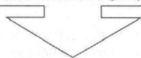

Step 2: Measure existing performance
- the project team does some preliminary work to measure how the current process is working and identifies what is causing the quality problem
- measures should focus on areas where customers will value improvement
- the performance measurement system must be reliable (redesign may be required).

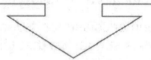

Step 3: Analysis of the existing process
- the project team investigates their preliminary concerns and test different theories to get to the root cause of the problem
- techniques such as Pareto analysis will improve the focus of action on the issues that give rise to the majority of quality problems (i.e. 20% of the causes will give rise to 80% of the problems).

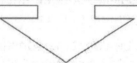

Step 4: Improve the process
- Potential solutions are developed for process re-design. The most appropriate solution will be one that achieves the mission statement within the cost and resource constraints of the organisation.

Step 5: Control the process
New controls are designed to compare actual performance with targeted performance to make sure the improvements to the process are being sustained

How does Six Sigma improve the quality of performance?

Six Sigma improves quality in a number of ways:

- An increased focus on the customer.

- The identification of business process improvements as key to success.

- Management decision making is driven by data and facts, for example the number of customer complaints as a key performance measure.

- The proactive involvement of management and effective leadership to co-ordinate the different Six Sigma projects.

- It involves collaboration across functional and divisional boundaries focusing the whole organisation on quality issues.

- The increased profile of quality issues and the increased knowledge of quality management that comes from the use of different layers of trained experts.

Test your understanding 7

Required:

How can management accountants contribute to the Six Sigma process?

Additional question on quality

Required:

Explain how management accounting/management techniques such as total quality management, just in time, value analysis, activity based costing and the balanced scorecard could contribute towards the analysis of the relationship between costs and quality.

Answer:

Total Quality Management (TQM)

TQM is an approach that seeks to ensure that all aspects of providing goods and services are delivered at the highest possible standard, and that standards keep improving. The underlying principle is that the cost of preventing deficient quality is less than the costs of correcting poor quality. This denies the idea that improved quality can only be secured with greater expenditure, but adopts the approach that improved quality will reduce costs.

Quality related costs are concerned with both achieving quality and failure to achieve quality.

Quality costs can categorised as:

- **Prevention costs** – communicating the concept, training, establishing systems to deliver quality services

- **Appraisal costs** – e.g. inspection and testing

- **Internal failure costs** – wasted materials used in rejects, down time resulting from internal service quality failures, resources devoted to dealing with complaints

- **External failure costs** – loss of goodwill and future business, compensation paid to customers and rectification costs.

The TQM view is that by getting it right first time and every time, the prevention and appraisal costs will be outweighed by the savings in failure costs, hence lower costs and improved quality are congruent goals. TQM requires everyone in the organisation to have identified customers, whether external or internal, so that a continuous service quality chain is maintained all the way through the organisation to the final customer.

Just In Time (JIT)

JIT is a manufacturing and supply chain process that is intended to reduce inventory levels and improve customer service by ensuring that customers receive their orders at the right time and in the right quantity. The system should facilitate a smooth workflow throughout the business and reduce waste. Goods are produced to meet customer needs directly, not for inventory.

Cost reductions should arise from:

- Lower raw material and finished goods inventory levels, therefore reduced holding costs.

- Reduced material handling.

- Often a reduction in the number of suppliers and lower administration and communication costs.

- Guaranteed quality of supplies reduces inspection and rectification costs.

Quality improvements should arise from:

- Fewer or even single sourcing of supplies strengthens the buyer–supplier relationship and is likely to improve the quality.

- The absence of customer stockholding compels the supplier (if they want continued business) to guarantee the quality of the material that they deliver.

- The necessity to work regularly and closer with hauliers strengthens the relationship with them. The deliveries become high priority and more reliable.

- Customers are not faced with the traditional problems of having to wait until their supplier's inventories are replenished. The system is designed to respond to customers' needs rapidly.

- Direct focus on meeting an identified customer's need, production is merely to add to an anonymous pile of inventory.

Value analysis

Value analysis is concerned with concentrating on activities that add value to the product/service as perceived by the customer. It examines business activities and questions why they are being undertaken and what contribution do they make to customer satisfaction. Value added activities include designing products, producing output and developing customer relationships. Non-value added activities include returning goods, inventory holding, and checking on the quality of supplies received. Wherever possible eliminate the non-value added activities.

Value analysis commences with a focus on customers. What do they want? What do they regard as significant in the buying decision: function, appearance, longevity or disposal value? This is concerned with identifying what customers regard as quality and then providing it: do not expend effort on what they regard as unimportant. It is about clarifying what the constituents of quality are on the Costs and Quality diagram. Having decided this there is a need to develop alternative designs, estimate costs and evaluate alternatives.

Activity Based Costing (ABC)

ABC is concerned with attributing/assigning costs to cost units on the basis of the service received from indirect activities e.g. public relations, recruitment, quality assurance general meetings. The organisation needs to identify cost drivers – the specific activities that cause costs to arise e.g. number of orders taken, telephone calls made, number of breakdowns or the number of visitors to an attraction.

ABC intends to avoid the arbitrary allocation of overheads to products/services by identifying a causal link between costs, activities and outputs. Because of higher degrees of automation, the increasing significance of overheads in the cost make up of output intensifies the need to improve the apportionment of them. Accountants can contribute towards providing better cost information to the value analysis referred to above. Product managers need to know what they are getting for their money – what is the real cost of quality? What are the cost driving activities that do not impact on quality? What activities that generate minimal costs have a significantly favourable impact on quality?

The Balanced Scorecard (Kaplan and Norton)

The Balanced Scorecard provides a framework for a business to achieve its strategic objectives include both financial and non-financial objectives. The approach claims that performance has four dimensions: financial, customer, internal business, and innovation and learning. The customer perspective asks: How does the business appear to the customers? The internal business perspective asks: What do we need to do to satisfy shareholders and customers, including the monitoring of unit costs? The innovation and learning perspective looks at how products and processes should be changed and improved.

The scorecard is concerned with monitoring and measuring the critical variables that comprise the customer and internal perspective. The choice of variables for inclusion in the scorecard is significant because the scorecard report is a design for action. Inappropriate indicators will trigger damaging responses. For example, the organisation needs to monitor what factors customers regard as contributing to improved quality, not what the business thinks it should provide. Therefore the scorecards would be suitable for inclusion as quantifiable indicators on the axis on the Costs and Quality diagram. The Balanced Scorecard attempts to improve the range and relationship between alternative performance measures, in the case under discussion, costs and quality.

6 Lean production

6.1 What is lean production?

Lean production is a philosophy of management based on **cutting out waste** and unnecessary activities including:

- **Over-production** – produce more than customers have ordered.

- **Inventory** – holding or purchasing unnecessary inventory.

- **Waiting** – production delays/idle time when value is not added to the product.

- **Defective units** – production of a part that is scrapped or requires rework.

- **Motion** – actions of people/equipment that do not add value.

- **Transportation** – poor planning or factory layout results in unnecessary transportation of materials/work-in-progress.

- **Over-processing** – unnecessary steps that do not add value.

Lean production is closely related to quality practices such as Kaizen, JIT and TQM.

Comparison of Toyota (a lean pioneer) to a non-lean car manufacturer

	Non-Lean manufacturer	Lean pioneer – Toyota
Production	Mass production requiring: - time to set up machinery and - skilled engineers.	Production smaller batches leading to: - quick set up - flexibility - production line staff trained to do set ups - job for life - defined career path - empowered staff.

 KAPLAN PUBLISHING

Human resources	Cyclical nature of industry resulting in: • staff layoffs • unmotivated staff.	• Job for life • Defined career path • Empowered staff
Employee roles	• Assembly worker • Foreman • Housekeeper • Engineer	Eliminates non-value adding activities so all workers trained on all aspects hence no indirect wages.
Production problems	• Couldn't stop the production line • 20–25% defects	• Stops the production line and then the team works to solve issues quickly • Zero defects
Suppliers	Chosen on cost	• Use supplier expertise • Fair price • JIT
Sales	• Sell through dealers • Narrow product range	• Sell direct to customers • Customer feedback valued • Flexibility resulting in wide product range

Test your understanding 8

Although the lean approach was developed in the manufacturing industry it can also be applied in the service sector.

Required:

Identify some possible sources of waste in a restaurant business and categorise them according to the seven main types of waste described above.

6.2 Application of lean to management information systems

A lean approach would aim to identify and eliminate waste in the MIS and improve the efficiency of the flow of information to users. The system should be simplified but also improved as a result.

A lean system aims to get the right thing to the right place at the right time, first time.

The MIS should:

- only produce a report if it **adds value**

- only produce a report for the **people who need them**

- should produce information that is **accurate, presented clearly** and can be **retrieved easily**

- be capable of **real time** information processing

- **eliminate waste**, such as data duplication

- be **flexible** enough to adapt to the changing needs of the organisation or to ad hoc requirements

- be **continually improved**, for example regular user meetings should be held to discuss requirements.

The 5 S's concept

The 5 S's concept is often associated with lean principles and has the aim of creating a workplace which is in order. The 5 S's are:

- **Structurise** – introduce order where possible, for example by ensuring that items are arranged so that they are easy to find.

- **Systemise** – arrange and identify items for ease of use and approach tasks systematically. For example, by arranging items so that they can be accurately picked in the shortest time.

- **Sanitise** – be tidy, avoid clutter. This makes things easier to find, makes access more efficient and may improve safety.

- **Standardise** – this involves finding the best way of undertaking a process or task and applying it consistently.

- **Self-discipline** – this relates to sustaining the other S's by motivating employees to do the above daily.

Student accountant article: visit the ACCA website, www.accaglobal.com, to review the article on 'Lean enterprises and lean information systems'.

7 Quality in management information systems

7.1 Features of a quality system

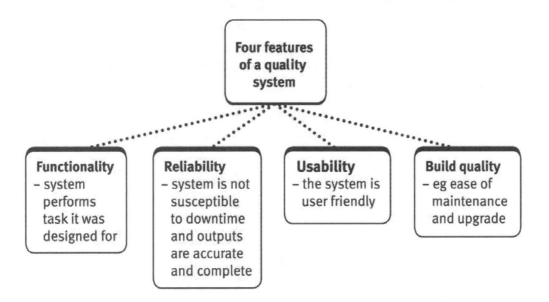

Test your understanding 9

Required:

Explain the consequences of failing to include these four features in a management information system.

7.2 Designing a quality system

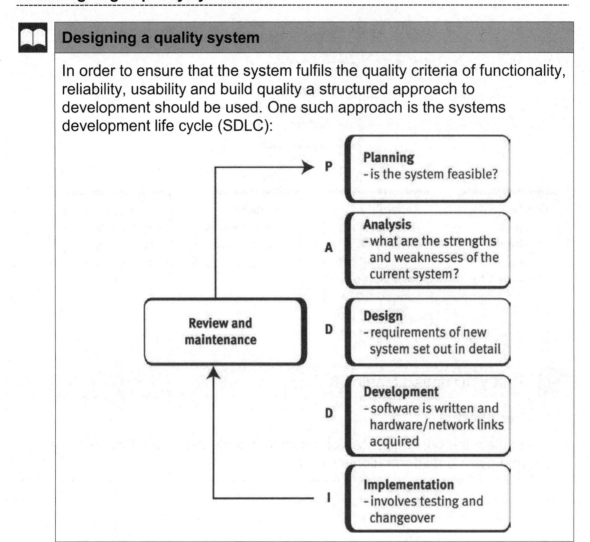

Designing a quality system

In order to ensure that the system fulfils the quality criteria of functionality, reliability, usability and build quality a structured approach to development should be used. One such approach is the systems development life cycle (SDLC):

P — Planning
- is the system feasible?

A — Analysis
- what are the strengths and weaknesses of the current system?

D — Design
- requirements of new system set out in detail

D — Development
- software is written and hardware/network links acquired

I — Implementation
- involves testing and changeover

Review and maintenance

8 Exam focus

Exam sitting	Area examined	Question number	Number of marks
Sept/Dec 2017	Target costing, TQM, quality costs	1(iii)(iv)	25
Mar/Jun 2017	Target costing, Kaizen costing	2	25
Mar/Jun 2017	Lean including lean MIS and 5 S's	3	
Sept/Dec 2016	Quality costs, TQM, lean systems	1(iv)(v)	15
Sept/Dec 2015	Lean, JIT, Kaizen, quality costs	1(iii)(iv)	25
Sept/Dec 2015	Six Sigma – DMAIC	3(a)	15
December 2014	JIT	1(iv)	7
December 2013	Lean management and accountability	3(b)(c)	13
June 2012	Six Sigma	3	17
December 2011	Quality costs, Kaizen and JIT	5	20

KAPLAN PUBLISHING

Chapter summary

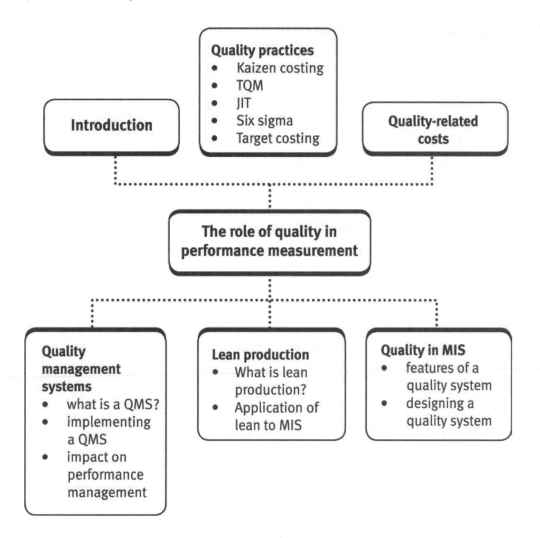

Test your understanding answers

Test your understanding 1

Higher quality can help to increase revenue and reduce costs:

- Higher quality improves the perceived image of a product or service. As a result, more customers will be willing to purchase the product/service and may also be willing to pay a higher price.

- A higher volume of sales may result in lower unit costs due to economies of scale.

- Higher quality in manufacturing should result in lower waste and defective rates, which will reduce production costs.

- The need for inspection and testing should be reduced, also reducing costs.

- The level of customer complaints should fall and warranty claims should be lower. This will reduce costs.

- Better quality in production should lead to shorter processing times. This will reduce costs.

Test your understanding 2

Prevention costs

- Cost of designing products and services with built in quality.

- Cost of training employees in the best way to do their job.

- Cost of equipment testing to ensure it conforms to quality standards required.

Appraisal costs

- Inspection and testing, for example of a purchased material or service.

Internal failure costs

- Cost of scrapped material due to poor quality.

- Cost of re-working parts.

- Re-inspection costs.

- Lower selling prices for sub-quality products.

External failure costs

- Cost of recalling and correcting products.

- Cost of lost goodwill.

Test your understanding 3

	$000	% of revenue
Prevention costs:		
Design engineering	5,000	1.56
Process engineering	3,450	1.08
Training	560	0.18
Total	**9,010**	**2.82**
Appraisal costs:		
Inspection	13,800	4.31
Product testing	65	0.02
Total	**13,865**	**4.33**
Internal failure costs	7,545	2.36
Total	**7,545**	**2.36**
External failure costs:		
Warranty	8,950	2.80
Customer support	645	0.20
Transportation	546	0.17
Total	**10,141**	**3.17**
Sub-total	**40,561**	**12.68**
Opportunity costs	9,561	2.99
Total quality costs	**50,112**	**15.66**

Test your understanding 4

The 8 principles of ISO 9001:2005 should result in quality improvements as follows:

- **Customer focus** – quality may be defined as 'the product/service meeting the customer's needs' and therefore a customer focus should improve quality.

- **Leadership** – leaders should communicate the importance of quality and drive a culture of quality.

- **Involvement of people** – everyone in the organisation should have a quality focus.

- **Process approach** – related activities and resources should be managed in an integrated quality process.

- **Systems approach to management** – groups of related processes should be managed in an integrated quality system.

- **Continual improvement** – quality management is not a one off process, but is the continuous examination and improvement of processes.

- **Factual approach to decision making** – quality procedures should be documented and applied consistently.

- **Mutually beneficial supplier relationships** – long-term links should be established with suppliers in order to ensure a reliable and high quality service.

Test your understanding 5

Cost-plus pricing ignores:

- The price that customers will be willing to pay.

- The price charged by competitors for similar products.

- Cost control – this is not incentivised due to the use of a standard cost.

Test your understanding 6

Advantages of JIT

- Lower stock holding costs means a reduction in storage space which saves rent and insurance costs.

- As stock is only obtained when needed, less working capital is tied up in stock.

- There is less likelihood of stock perishing, becoming obsolete or out of date.

- Avoids the build-up of unsold finished products that occur with sudden changes in demand.

- Less time is spent checking and re-working the products as the emphasis is on getting the work right first time.

- Increased flexibility in meeting the customer's individual needs.

The result is that costs should fall and quality should increase. This should improve the company's competitive advantage.

Disadvantages of JIT

- There is little room for mistakes as little stock is kept for re-working a faulty product.

- Production is very reliant on suppliers and if stock is not delivered on time or is not of a high enough quality, the whole production schedule can be delayed.

- There is no spare finished product available to meet unexpected orders, because all products are made to meet actual orders.

- It may be difficult for managers to empower employees to embrace the concept and culture.

- It won't be suitable for all companies. For example, supermarkets must have a supply of inventory.

- It can be difficult to apply to the service industry. However, in the service industry a JIT approach may focus on eliminating queues, which are wasteful of customers' time.

Test your understanding 7

- The provision of data at all stages in the process.

- Providing expertise in the identification of appropriate output, input and process measures (financial and non-financial) and ways to collect the data.

- Analysis of data.

- Evaluation of possible solutions.

- Identification of performance measures for the control process and monitoring after changes have been implemented.

- Taking part in multi-disciplinary Six Sigma teams.

Test your understanding 8

Suggestions could include:

- Pre-preparing plated servings of perishable desserts which are not ordered and need to be thrown away – over-production.

- Poor kitchen layout which could lead to unnecessary movement of staff and result in waste from motion and from transportation of material or lead to accidents and spillages and waste in processes and methods.

- Poorly trained cooking staff who produce sub-standard meals which cannot be served – product defects.

- Producing too many pre-prepared components such as sauces to be incorporated in dishes which are then not needed – waste from inventory.

- Poor scheduling in the kitchen leading to serving staff waiting for meals to be ready – waste from waiting time.

Test your understanding 9

- **Poor functionality and reliability** may result in:

  - user dissatisfaction, e.g. because the system does not perform the desired task

  - additional costs, e.g. to correct inaccurate reports.

- **Poor usability** may result in:

  - staff dissatisfaction

  - excessive staff training

  - excessive time spent by staff trying to operate the system.

- **Poor build quality** will result in difficulties maintaining and upgrading the system which will impact long-term profit.

Environmental management accounting

Chapter learning objectives

Upon completion of this chapter you will be able to:

- discuss, evaluate and apply environmental management accounting using for example lifecycle costing and activity-based costing.

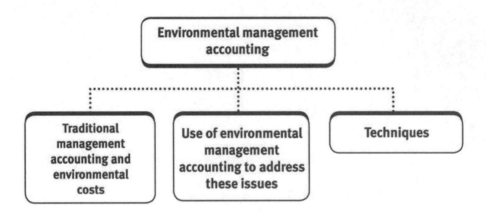

1 Assumed knowledge

Chapter 14 builds on your knowledge of environmental management accounting (EMA) from PM.

2 Introduction

Organisations are becoming increasingly aware of the environmental implications of their actions.

Test your understanding 1

Required:

Discuss the potential benefits to a company of reducing the negative environmental impact of its operations, products or services.

Illustration 1 – Environmental management at BP

BP, one of the world's leading oil and gas companies, describe a number of activities aimed at reducing the environmental impact of the company's operations in its annual review. These include:

- improving the integrity of its equipment and pipelines to reduce the spillage of oil

- reducing the emissions of greenhouse gases, which is measured and reported within the Annual Review

- introducing environmental requirements for new projects

- supporting the use of market mechanisms to bring about emission reductions across the industry

- launching a new business providing energy from alternative sources

- investing in research into biofuels

- developing and marketing fuel which produces lower emissions compared with standard fuels.

3 Traditional management accounting and environmental costs

Managers need to be able to identify the environmental costs that exist in order to be able to measure existing performance and to monitor the effectiveness of any environmental-related activities undertaken. However, traditional accounting systems are unable to identify or to deal adequately with environmental costs.

As a result, managers are unaware of these costs and have no information with which to manage or reduce them.

There are four categories of environmental costs:

Environmental cost category	Description	Problem
Conventional costs	Costs such as raw material and energy costs	These are often 'hidden' within overheads making it difficult for managers to identify and control them
Contingent costs	Costs such as future compliance costs or remediation costs when a site is decommissioned	Often incurred towards the end of a project so are ignored by managers who focus on short-term performance
Relationship costs	Image costs such as the cost of producing environmental information for public reporting	Ignored by managers who are unaware of their existence
Reputational costs	Costs associated with failing to address environmental issues, e.g. lost sales	Ignored by managers who are unaware of the risk of incurring them

Illustration 2 – Reputational costs

In 2010 a blast at the Deepwater Horizon rig in the Gulf of Mexico killed eleven people and caused one of the worst oil spills in history. The environmental impact of the oil spill is ongoing. For example, in 2016 traces of oil from the spill were found in the feathers of birds eaten by land animals. The US presidential commission concluded that the oil spill was an avoidable disaster caused by a series of failures and blunders made by BP, its partners and the government departments assigned to regulate them. It also warned that such a disaster was likely to recur because of complacency in the industry.

> For BP, the company at the heart of the disaster, the effects have had a deep and widespread impact. The company has become synonymous with everything that is dangerous about oil exploration causing massive reputational damage.
>
> BP is working to restore their reputation. For example, in 2016 they joined forces with two other oil and gas companies to create a $1 billion climate change fund focused on researching renewable energy, sharing techniques and reducing the leakage of methane (a big contributor towards global warming).

4 What is EMA?

EMA is concerned with the accounting information needs of managers in relation to the organisation's activities that affect the environment as well as environment-related impacts of the organisation. It involves the production of financial and non-financial information to support the internal environmental management process.

EMA:

- identifies and estimates the costs of environment-related activities (covered in Section 3) and seeks to control these costs. For example:

    - identifies and separately monitors the usage and cost of resources such as water, electricity and fuel and enables these costs to be reduced, for example through redesigning the product or the production process

    - estimates future contingent costs ensuring they form part of any investment decision and giving scope upfront to reduce these costs through product or process redesign

- assesses the likelihood and impact of environmental risks

- includes environment-related indicators as part of routine performance monitoring

- makes managers aware of reputational costs in order to focus their attention on managing the risk of them occurring

- benchmarks activities against environmental best practice.

Importantly, the focus of EMA is not all on financial costs but it also considers the non-financial environmental cost or benefit of any decisions made.

5 EMA techniques

Three key techniques exist. The techniques can assist an organisation in achieving the aims of EMA covered in Section 4. They are not mutually exclusive.

5.1 Activity- based costing (ABC)

Environment-related costs can be analysed into:

- Costs which can be attributed directly to a cost centre, for example a waste filtration plant. It should be relatively straightforward to identify and, to some extent, control these costs.

- Environment-driven costs which are generally hidden in overheads. ABC will aim to separately identify and control these costs:

  - The costs are removed from general overheads and traced to products or services.

  - This means that cost drivers are determined for these costs and products are charged for the use of these environmental costs based on the amount of cost drivers that they contribute to the activity.

  - This should result in a more realistic product cost.

  - It should also result in better control of environment-related costs by reducing the incidental cost drivers or eliminating certain activities.

Advantages and disadvantages of ABC

Advantages	Disadvantages
<ul><li>Better/fairer product costs.</li><li>Improved pricing – so that the products which have the biggest environmental impact reflect this by having higher selling prices.</li><li>Better environmental control.</li><li>Facilitates the quantification of cost savings from 'environmentally-friendly' measures.</li><li>Should integrate environmental costing into the strategic management process.</li></ul>	<ul><li>Time consuming. Expensive to implement.</li><li>Determining accurate costs and appropriate cost drivers is difficult.</li><li>External costs, i.e. not experienced by the company (e.g. carbon footprint) may still be ignored/unmeasured.</li><li>A company that integrates external costs voluntarily may be at a competitive disadvantage to rivals who do not do this.</li><li>Some internal environmental costs are intangible (e.g. impact on employee health) and these are still ignored.</li></ul>

5.2 Lifecycle costing

Traditional costing techniques based around annual periods may give a misleading impression of the costs and profitability of a product. Lifecycle costing considers the costs and revenues of a product over its whole life rather than one accounting period. Therefore, the full cost of producing a product over its whole life will be taken into account. These costs include costs incurred **prior to, during** and **after** production and will therefore include the **full environmental cost** of producing a product over its whole life.

It is important that all of the environmental costs are identified and included in the initial project appraisal. For example:

* Managers should design products carefully to reduce waste over the manufacturing life of the product.

* Managers must pay attention to decommissioning costs that will be incurred after the end of the project and should plan for these costs.

For an organisation to be able to claim to be financially and environmentally responsible, it must have plans in place to cover these costs.

> **EMA and TQM**
>
> In order to reduce lifecycle costs an organisation may adopt a TQM approach. It is arguable that TQM and environmental management are inextricably linked insofar as good environmental management is increasingly recognised as an essential component of TQM. Such organisations pursue objectives that may include zero complaints, zero spills, zero pollution, zero waste and zero accidents. Information systems need to be able to support such environmental objectives via the provision of feedback – on the success or otherwise – of the organisational efforts in achieving such objectives.

Test your understanding 2

The following details relate to a new product that has finished development and is about to be launched.

	Development	Launch	Growth	Maturity	Decline
Time period	Finished	1 year	1 year	1 year	1 year
R & D costs ($m)	20				
Marketing costs ($m)		5	4	3	0.9
Production cost per unit ($) (see note)		1.00	0.90	0.80	0.50
Production volume		1m	5m	10m	4m
Other costs ($m) (see note)					1m

Note: The production cost per unit includes environmental-related production costs. The 'other costs' relate to decommissioning costs that will be incurred at the end of the decline stage.

The launch price is proving a contentious issue between managers. The marketing manager is keen to start with a low price of around $8 to gain new buyers and achieve target market share. The accountant is concerned that this does not cover costs during the launch phase and has produced the following schedule to support this:

Launch phase:		$ million
Amortised R&D costs	(20 ÷ 4)	5.0
Marketing costs		5.0
Production costs	(1 million × $1 per unit)	1.0
		─────
Total		11.0
		─────
Total production (units)		1 million
Cost per unit		$11.00

Required:

Prepare a revised cost per unit schedule looking at the whole lifecycle and comment on the implications of this cost with regards to the pricing of the product during the launch phase.

5.3 Flow cost accounting

This technique looks at material flows and material losses incurred at various stages of production. It makes the flow of materials much more transparent and by doing so it aims to reduce the quantities of materials leading to increased ecological efficiency.

Illustration 3 – Cost reduction at McCain Foods

One example of energy saving is McCain Foods, which buys an eighth of the UK's potatoes to make chips. It has cut its Peterborough plant's CO_2 footprint by two-thirds, says corporate affairs director Bill Bartlett. It invested £10m (approximately $15m) in three 3MW turbines to meet 60 per cent of its annual electricity demand. McCain spent another £4.5m (approximately $6.75m) on a lagoon to catch the methane from fermenting waste water and particulates, which generates another 10 per cent of the site's electricity usage. It also wants to refine its used cooking oil, either for its own vehicles fleet or for selling on.

McCain want to become more competitive and more efficient.

Question practice

The question below is taken from a past exam. It is an excellent question on EMA. Make sure that you take the time to attempt the question and review/learn from the answer.

Test your understanding 3

FGH Telecom (FGH) is one of the largest providers of mobile and fixed line telecommunications in Ostland. The company has recently been reviewing its corporate objectives in the light of its changed business environment. The major new addition to the strategic objectives is under the heading: 'Building a more environmentally friendly business for the future'. It has been recognised that the company needs to make a contribution to ensuring sustainable development in Ostland and reducing its environmental footprint. Consequently, it adopted a goal that, by year 17, it would have reduced its environmental impact by 60% compared to year 1. It is currently year 11.

The reasons for the board's concern are that the telecommunications sector is competitive and the economic environment is increasingly harsh with the markets for debt and equities being particularly poor. On environmental issues, the government and public are calling for change from the business community. It appears that increased regulation and legislation will appear to encourage business towards better performance. The board have recognised that there are threats and opportunities from these trends. It wants to ensure that it is monitoring these factors and so it has asked for an analysis of the business environment with suggestions for performance measurement.

Additionally, the company has a large number of employees working across its network. Therefore, there are large demands for business travel. FGH runs a large fleet of commercial vehicles in order to service its network along with a company car scheme for its managers. The manager in charge of the company's travel budget is reviewing data on carbon dioxide emissions to assess FGH's recent performance.

Recent initiatives within the company to reduce emissions have included:

(a)   the introduction in year 10 of a homeworking scheme for employees in order to reduce the amount of commuting to and from their offices and

(b)   a drive to increase the use of teleconferencing facilities by employees.

Data on FGH Telecom:

Carbon Dioxide emissions

Measured in millions of kgs	Year 1 Base year	Year 9	Year 10
Commercial Fleet Diesel	105.4	77.7	70.1
Commercial Fleet Petrol	11.6	0.4	0.0
Company Car Diesel	15.1	14.5	12.0
Company Car Petrol	10.3	3.8	2.2
Other Road Travel (Diesel)	0.5	1.6	1.1
Other Road Travel (Petrol)	3.1	0.5	0.3
Rail Travel	9.2	9.6	3.4
Air Travel (short haul)	5.0	4.4	3.1
Air Travel (long haul)	5.1	7.1	5.4
Hire Cars (Diesel)	0.6	1.8	2.9
Hire Cars (Petrol)	6.7	6.1	6.1
Total	172.6	127.5	106.6

Required:

(a) Perform an analysis of FGH's business environment to identify factors which will affect its environmental strategy. For each of these factors, suggest performance indicators which will allow FGH to monitor its progress.

(8 marks)

(b) Evaluate the data given on carbon dioxide emissions using suitable indicators. Identify trends from within the data and comment on whether the company's behaviour is consistent with meeting its targets.

(9 marks)

(c) Suggest further data that the company could collect in order to improve its analysis and explain how this data could be used to measure the effectiveness of the reduction initiatives mentioned.

(3 marks)

(Total: 20 marks)

Student accountant article: visit the ACCA website, www.accaglobal.com, to review the article on 'environmental management accounting'.

6 Exam focus

Exam sitting	Area examined	Question number	Number of marks
Sept/Dec 2016	EMA and lifecycle	3(b)(c)	17
December 2014	EMA	3	25
June 2011	EMA	5	20
December 2010	Environmental performance	4	20

Chapter summary

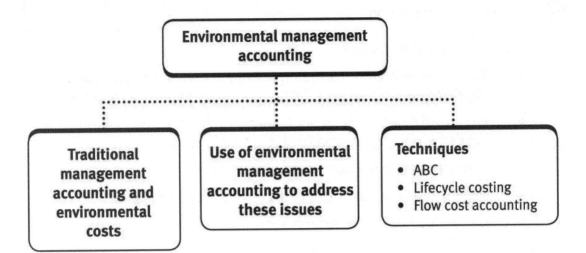

Test your understanding answers

Test your understanding 1

The benefits are as follows:

- This approach ensures the organisation meets with legal and regulatory requirements relating to environmental management.

- Increased sales as a result of meeting with customers' needs and concerns relating environmental management.

- Helps to maintain a positive public image.

- Manages risk, for example of an environmental disaster.

- Can reduce costs, for example through improved use of fuel and water.

- Should contribute to sustainable development, i.e. the meeting of current needs without compromising the ability of future generations to meet their own needs.

Test your understanding 2

Lifecycle costs		$ million
Total R&D costs		20.0
Total Marketing costs	(5 + 4 + 3 + 0.9)	12.9
Total Production costs	(1 × 1 + 5 × 0.9 + 10 × 0.8 + 4 × 0.9)	17.1
Decommissioning cost		1.0
		———
		51.0
		———
Total production (units)	(1 + 5 + 10 + 4)	20 million
Cost per unit	(51 ÷ 20)	$2.55

Comment

- The cost was calculated at $11 per unit during the launch phase. Based on this cost, the accountant was right to be concerned about the launch price being set at $8 per unit.

- However, looking at the whole life-cycle the marketing manager's proposal seems more reasonable.

- The average cost per unit over the entire life of the product is only $2.55 per unit. Therefore, a starting price of $8 per unit would seem reasonable and would result in a profit of $5.45 per unit.

Test your understanding 3

(a) Government regulations relevant to FGH's environmental strategy include requirements to recycle materials, limits on pollution and waste levels along with new taxes such as carbon levies to add additional costs. Performance indicators would be additional costs resulting from failure to recycle waste, fines paid for breaches and the level of environmental tax burdens.

The general economic climate is relevant to the strategy including factors such as interest, inflation and exchange rates. For FGH, the general economic environment is not good and cost savings from reductions in energy use would help to offset falling profits. Also, the difficulties indicated in raising capital could be monitored through the firm's cost of capital. This would be especially relevant if the environmental initiatives lead to significant capital expenditure for FGH.

Trends and fashions among the general public appear to be relevant for FGH as the public will be end-users of its services and environmental action could improve the brand image of FGH. Suitable performance indicator would be based around a score in a customer attitude survey.

Technological changes in the capabilities available to FGH and its competitors will affect its environmental strategy. New environmentally efficient technologies such as hybrid cars and solar recharging cells would be relevant to the cost and product sides of FGH. Performance indicators would involve measuring the impact of the use of new technology on existing emission data.

(b) The company has a target of cutting emissions by 60% of their year 1 values by the year 17. Overall, it has cut emissions by 38% in the first nine years of the 16-year programme. There was a reduction of 16% in the last year of measurement. If this rate of improvement is maintained then the company will reduce its emissions by 82% (62% × (84% ^ 7)) by year 17. However, it should be noted that it is unlikely that there will be a constant rate of reduction as it normally becomes more difficult to improve as the easy actions are taken in the early years of the programme.

The initial data are rather complex and so to summarise, three categories for the three types of transport were considered (Road, Rail and Air). The largest cut has been in rail related emissions (63%) while the contribution from road transport has only fallen by 38%. The road emissions are the dominant category overall and they are still falling within the programmed timetable to reach the target. However, it is clear that air travel is not falling at the same pace but this may be driven by factors such as increasing globalisation of the telecommunication industry which necessitates travel by managers abroad to visit multinational clients and suppliers.

One unusual feature noted is that the mix of transport methods appears to be changing. Rail travel appears to be declining. This is surprising as rail is widely believed to be the lowest emitting method from these forms of travel. However, caution must be exercised on this conclusion which may be due to a change in the emissions technology relating to each category of travel rather than the distance travelled using each method.

The major change that is apparent from the basic data is the move from petrol to diesel-powered motor vehicles which in the commercial fleet appears nearly complete. It will be more difficult to move company and private cars to diesel-power as there will be an element of choice on the part of the car user in the type of car driven.

Working

Measured in millions of kgs	Year 1	Year 9	Year 10	Change on base year
Commercial Fleet Diesel	105.4	77.7	70.1	−33%
Commercial Fleet Petrol	11.6	0.4	0.0	−100%
Company Car Diesel	15.1	14.5	12.0	−21%
Company Car Petrol	10.3	3.8	2.2	−79%
Other Road Travel (Diesel)	0.5	1.6	1.1	120%
Other Road Travel (Petrol)	3.1	0.5	0.3	−90%
Rail Travel	9.2	9.6	3.4	−63%
Air Travel (short haul)	5.0	4.4	3.1	−38%
Air Travel (long haul)	5.1	7.1	5.4	6%
Hire Cars (Diesel)	0.6	1.8	2.9	383%
Hire Cars (Petrol)	6.7	6.1	6.1	−9%
Total	172.6	127.5	106.6	
Index	100%	74%	62%	
YoY change		−16%		

Simplifying categories

Road travel	153.3	106.4	94.7	–38%
Air travel	10.1	11.5	8.5	–16%
Rail travel	9.2	9.6	3.4	–63%
Total	172.6	127.5	106.6	–38%

Mix of travel method in each year

Road travel	89%	83%	89%
Air travel	6%	9%	8%
Rail travel	5%	8%	3%

(c)   The analysis could be improved by collecting data on the total distances travelled so that employee behaviour can be tracked. This would allow measurement of the effect of switching away from physical meetings and using teleconferencing facilities. This may be particularly effective in cutting air travel which has been noted as a problem area.

It would also allow assessment of the homeworking scheme which should reduce total distance travelled. Although, the full environmental benefit will not be apparent as much of the travel would have been a regular commute to work which an employee will not be able to claim and so is unlikely to record.

Finally, the collection of distance travelled data will allow a measure of the effect of changing modes of transport by calculating an average emission per km travelled.